from The Correctional Education Company ...

● *the highest quality correctional education materials, training, and services* ●

BOOKS

THE EX-INMATE'S COMPLETE GUIDE TO SUCCESSFUL EMPLOYMENT
(revised, expanded 3rd edition)
-- by Errol Craig Sull

The first and only book that covers ALL aspects of the job search for the inmate soon-to-be-released or newly released ex-inmate. 460+ pages , this book is the standard guide throughout the United States ... because it works. Written by correctional educator, ex-inmate, trainer, and career counselor Errol Craig Sull.

BARS & BOOKS: HOW TO SUCCESSFULLY REACH & TEACH INMATES
(revised, expanded 2nd edition)
-- by Errol Craig Sull

The only truly comprehensive book that offers the insights, suggestions, experiences, and ideas to help new and "seasoned" correctional educators become the best they can be. In 468 pages, virtually all facets of correctional education and teaching are explored, including: understanding the inmate ... teaching strategies ... handling stress and burnout ... setting and achieving goals ... developing and implementing classroom activities and projects ... creating a successful transition program ... teaching inmate students how to study ... peer tutoring ... and much more!

MAKIN' IT: A PAROLE & PROBATION SURVIVAL GUIDE
-- by Errol Craig Sull

This 128-page book will help to motivate, guide, instruct, and remind ... a book EVERYONE on parole or probation should have. Topics include: more than 300 "Quickie Contact" #s, support services, quick tips to landing and keeping employment, confronting attitude and stress "bumps, rebuilding relationships, handling problems on the outside .. and much, much more!

VIDEOS

1) "FROM PRISON TO PAYCHECK: THE GREAT ESCAPE": This 8-tape video program [five+ hours total running time] is extremely effective in introducing and thoroughly explaining to students all aspects of the job search, both while incarcerated and after release. The eight volumes -- [1] Introduction & Mental Preparation ; [2] Planning Your Job Search [3] Resumes & Cover Letters; [4] Getting Ready for Release; [5] Your First Weeks Out; [6] Dealing with THE Question of Incarceration; [7] The Job Interview; [8] Staying Out – for Good!! -- come with a detailed Instructor's Guide, as well as copy-ready handouts for Volume 3.

2) "OKAY, EX-INMATE: NOW THAT YOU HAVE A JOB, KEEP IT!": More than 60% of all newly-released ex-inmates lose their jobs within the first month. This 3-tape (nearly five hours) video series covers all aspects of on-the-job information, scenarios, problems, and other items that newly-hired ex-inmates need to know. The three volumes ... [1] On the Job Everyday, Everywhere: a General Survival Guide to Staying Employed; [2] Interpersonal Communications: Write, Speak, Listen, Remember, and Move Your Way to Success at Work; [3] Customers & Colleagues: Effectively Working with Each. Comes with Instructor's Guide.

3) "IN THEIR OWN WORDS: TRUE STORIES OF SUCCESSFUL EX-INMATES": Inmates need and thrive on motivation from other ex-inmates who have been released, who have found and kept employment ... and that's just what this one tape program (length: one hour) offers with 10 ex-inmates interviewed. With Instructor's Guide.

from The Correctional Education Company ...

● *the highest quality correctional education materials, training, and services* ●

NEWSLETTER

THE CORRECTIONAL EDUCATOR: a quarterly newsletter (with a fifth, special edition each Fall, *The Correctional Educator's Job Outlook for Inmates and Ex-Inmates*), this publication is for correctional providers and related professionals. It is written to provide you with the best, broadest, up-to-date, and expert practical information, advice, insights, suggestions, and stories to make your teaching, counseling, and advising sessions for inmates and ex-inmates as thorough and productive as possible.

TRAINING SEMINARS

The Correctional Education Company conducts on-site and regional training seminars for both correctional educators / providers and inmates. **Call or write for more details, including the list of dates and locations of regional seminars; references are available from all previous seminars**.

CAREER COUNSELING SERVICES FOR CORRECTIONS PROFESSIONALS

As the only career counseling agency in the United States devoted to the field of corrections, Aardvark Resumes & Career Counseling, in conjunction with The Correctional Education Company, offers complete resume and cover letter development services AND career counseling and career wellness services / consulting for the corrections professional. Whether you be correctional educator, administrator, counselor, officer, or other correctional professional, Aardvark can be of assistance to you. **For more details, contact us for a copy of our brochure.**

FOR OUR COMPLETE CATALOG

The Correctional Education Company,

433 Franklin Street -- Patio Suite, Buffalo NY 14202.

(716) 882-3456.

FAX: (716) 882-7053.

E-MAIL: prisonedu@aol.com

WEB: http://www.prisonedu.com

The Ex-Inmate's Complete Guide to Successful Employment

3rd Edition

Errol Craig Sull

For the inmates and ex-inmates everywhere ...

"Campbell believed the prison system was a complete socialist way of life. No wonder Gilmore had gotten into trouble. For twelve years, a prison had told him when to go to bed and when to eat, what to wear and when to get up. It was absolutely diametrically opposed to the capitalist environment. Then one day they put the convict out the front door, told him today is magic, at two o'clock you are a capitalist. Now, do it on your own. Go out, find a job, get up by yourself, report to work on time, manage your money, do all the things you were taught not to do in prison. Guaranteed to fail. Eighty percent went back to jail."

-- Norman Mailer, *The Executioner's Song*

The Ex-Inmate's Complete Guide to Successful Employment

by Errol Craig Sull

3nd Edition, 2000
copyright, 2000, 1998, 1990

Excerpt from The Executioner's Song by Norman Mailer, copyright 1979. Published by Little, Brown. Reprinted by permission of the author and the author's agents, Scott Meredith Literary Agency, Inc., 845 Third Avenue, New York, NY 10022.

ISBN 0-9627558-0-X
Library of Congress Catalog Number 90-83990

Published in the United States of America by Aardvark Publishing, a division of The Correctional Education Company, 433 Franklin Street -- Patio Suite, Buffalo NY 14202. PHONE: (716) 882-3456. FAX: (716) 882-7053. E-MAIL: prisonedu@aol.com WEB SITE: http://www.prisonedu.com

Acknowledgments

MARVIN JOSEPH SULL, my father, who taught me the love of writing and reading and gentleness, and made me realize just how valuable and positive a prison experience can be through his 63 letters of history lessons, literary tidbits, religious insights, and smiles ...

ESTHER SEENA SULL, my mother, whose patience, understanding, solid business advice, and always being there made me understand her love as both a parent and friend ...

CATHY SKORA, my lady and best friend, who continued to love me and stick by me (through both editions) with her concern, suggestions, warmth, friendship, and pragmatism when I acted like a jerk ...

MICKEY, CHUCKY, & EVONNE, my brothers and sister, who gave me humor, motivational kicks in the derriere, glad news, a helluva' lot of support, and helped remind me there was a beautiful life after prison ...

SCOTTIE CARTER, my counselor in prison, who had the perfect blend of taskmaster, citizen of the world, football coach, and Merlin the Magician to turn my mind and soul 180 degrees to the good ...

ALICIA SAMPSON, the editor for my first edition, who mixed her love and understanding of the written word with late nights full of blueberries and coffee ice cream to argue, debate, and discuss with me the essence of commas, glories of a properly turned phrase, & the ultimate triumph of a well-written chapter ...

PAT CUNNINGHAM, my artist, who has yet to let me down with his whimsy, animated insight, and Irish green shirts ...

RICKY GENTRY, former prison buddy, whose death made me realize just how necessary it was to write this book ...

Table of Contents

"Make it a rule of life never to regret and never to look back. Regret is an appalling waste of energy; you can't build on it; it's only good for wallowing in."

Katherine Mansfield, English short story writer

●●●●●●●●●●●●●●●●●●●●●●●●●●●●●

"When one door of happiness closes, another opens; but often we look so long at the closed door that we do not see the one which has been opened for us."

Helen Keller, American author and lecturer

A SPECIAL NOTE TO YOU, THE INMATE & EX-INMATE ...

8 Important Points

(1) THIS BOOK IS WRITTEN SPECIFICALLY FOR YOU!! *The Ex-Inmate's Complete Guide to Successful Employment* will give you -- whether male or female, adult or juvenile -- the best possible training for your career search and a thorough understanding of what it takes to get and keep a job ... **with the problems, situations, laws, and information that is specific to you as inmate or ex-inmate**. This means reading it thoroughly, using it as a reference source, and following its suggestions and guidelines.

(2) WORK PAGES. There are several pages of work activities; these should be filled in. Work pages on goal setting, time management, resume development, stress management, personal strengths, and several other areas will contribute to your overall personal and professional growth.

(3) IF YOU HAVE BEEN GIVEN THIS BOOK TO KEEP, MAKE NOTES THROUGHOUT IT. I invite you to make notes in the margins and anywhere else in the book you wish to mark down some thoughts, as well as underlining or highlighting passages, suggestions, or items that you think are especially valuable. This will prove extremely helpful when you are reviewing, when you begin interviewing, and even after you land the job. If this book is not yours to keep, please don't write in it so that others may benefit from its use as you will.

(4) GETTING & KEEPING A JOB IS CRUCIAL TO YOU STAYING OUTSIDE! Many ex-inmates try to "beat the system," hustle or do drugs again, and / or have others carry them. Don't let any of these happen to you! You have an opportunity to make it, to "stand on your own two feet." Follow the conditions of your release, don't be afraid to ask your parole officer (if not on parole: a social services counselor) for help when you feel panic setting in ... and work like hell to get and stay employed!

(5) UNDERSTAND & ACCEPT ONE VERY IMPORTANT FACT: THERE ARE JOBS AVAILABLE FOR YOU!   No matter what the employment and economic condition of the country, there are jobs and careers available to you as an ex-inmate!

In the late 1990s and beyond, several items have developed that make this the very best time for ex-inmates to find jobs. These are: [a] more and more workers are needed in the service sector area, an area where many inmates and ex-inmates have skills; [b] more ex-inmates than ever in the work force, with many in positions to hire or influence management's hiring decisions; [c] more employers now have good experiences in working with employees who are former inmates.

(6) YOU MUST TAKE FULL RESPONSIBILITY FOR GETTING THE JOB DONE! Although you receive assistance in the form of information while incarcerated from your teachers, and while you will probably find support groups and programs that will help you after your release, ultimately you must learn to depend on yourself. This means looking to yourself for motivation, taking final responsibility for your actions and decisions, and accepting that it is you who will decide if you fail or succeed in a crime-free life after prison. If you can't accept this responsibility you are doomed to fail -- plain and simple.

(7) OCCASIONALLY, I HAVE REPEATED SOME ITEMS IN THE BOOK. This is not an oversight. Rather, there are certain subjects or pieces of information that fit in several different topics; I felt they were important enough to offer you 2nd, 3rd, and / ormore courses on them. (Check the Index for a complete listing of all items.)

(8) FOR WHOM DO YOU WANT TO SUCCEED? Before you start reading, grab a pen or pencil! Either in the space below (if this book is yours) or on a separate sheet of paper, write some names: yours and the most important people in your life outside of prison. It is for these people that you read this book ... and for whom you will make every effort NOT to come back to prison!!

MY NAME: _____

AN IMPORTANT PERSON IN MY LIFE: _____

AN IMPORTANT PERSON IN MY LIFE: _____

AN IMPORTANT PERSON IN MY LIFE: _____

AN IMPORTANT PERSON IN MY LIFE: _____

AN IMPORTANT PERSON IN MY LIFE: _____

AN IMPORTANT PERSON IN MY LIFE: _____

FOR THOSE OF YOU IN JAIL, NOT PRISON: THIS BOOK IS EQUALLY IMPORTANT FOR YOU!!

Virtually all of what is contained in this book is of equal importance to you, even though you may be doing a sentence of one year or less, if you are awaiting sentencing for a felony conviction or have been convicted and are awaiting transfer to prison, or if you are in a jail due to overcrowded conditions in a state or Federal prison. No matter what your reason for being in jail, employment is just as crucial to you as it is to someone in prison.

ALMOST THE SAME NEGATIVES AS PRISON. Jail can still place a stigma on you (either from others or from yourself) of having been incarcerated or "locked up." And if convicted of a felony, it also makes you have to answer "yes" to THAT question ("Were you ever convicted of a felony?"). Finally, whether in jail for a misdemeanor or felony, it does keep you out of mainstream society, and thus probably out of work.

4 Reasons Why It's Usually More Difficult for an Ex-felon to Land Employment

A man or woman who has a felony conviction and has been in prison usually finds it harder to land a job than someone who has been in jail and does not have a felony conviction, primarily because of the longer time incarcerated.

(1) RE-ADJUSTMENT MORE DIFFICULT. An ex-felon has had a much longer stretch of living by prison rules and inmate codes than someone who has been in jail, and thus quite often finds it more difficult to readjust to life in the free world.

(2) LOST TOUCH WITH CONTACTS. An ex-felon may have lost touch with contacts on the outside (family, friends, employment, etc.) due to the longer length of time away from these contacts.

(3) THE PUBLIC'S IMAGE. Society's image of "being in prison" carries more weight to it, in general, than one being in jail. Movies and TV stories are made about felons sentenced to and doing time in prison, not jail; each day, newspapers and TV & radio news carry the stories of those convicted of murder, rape, arson, robbery, drug dealing, embezzlement, stock fraud, etc., going to prison, NOT to jail.

(4) THE JOB APPLICATION. Many job application forms carry the question, "Were you ever convicted of a felony?" while not asking the question, "Were you ever convicted of a misdemeanor?"

<u>*No Matter if You're in Jail: You'll Have Your Share of Problems, Too!*</u>

Don't think that just because you're not doing "hard time" you won't have any problems in landing and keeping a job, that your time in jail won't present any obstacle. While I sincerely hope that you start working as soon as you are released from jail, I also know that this is not a perfect world, and having been incarcerated can become a problem for ANYONE searching for employment.

THREE NOTES REGARDING WORDS USED IN THIS BOOK

(1) "PRISON" VS. "JAIL." To keep things simple, I have used the word "prison" to refer to all facilities where adults and youth serve their sentences after conviction. Other words -- such as "incarceration" or "bid" -- can obviously refer to time spent in a prison, jail, bootcamp, work camp or detention facility.

(2) NO PRISON LINGO OR SLANG. You need to start getting your mind ready for the outside world, and this includes getting rid of the prison lingo and slang that so often is used on the inside, and beginning to communicate in a fashion that's acceptable to the business world. Thus, you won't find me talking about "the Man," "the squares," "the joint," "square-John," and other such names and descriptions.

(3) "INMATE" & "EX-INMATE" VS. "CON" / "CONVICT" & "EX-CON" / "EX-CONVICT." Anyone who has spent any time behind bars knows there is a definite difference between these two sets of words (although technically they mean the same). "Convict" (and its various forms) indicates one who has an "us vs. them" attitude, that is, buck the system, cause problems, only listen to and trust other convicts; "inmate" (and its various forms) describes one who is open to change and others' assistance, wants to sincerely change his or her attitude, and is eager for a chance to start over after release.

In addition, the media enjoys feeding on such well-worn cliches as "the big house," "the slammer," and "ex-con"; this does a great job of perpetuating the public's stereotype of the prisoner and ex-prisoner as one who is worth little, will always be a danger to society, and can't be trusted.

They may only be words, but words offer specific images, and I don't particularly care for the image that "ex-con," et al., offers. Thus, with few exceptions (quotations), I use "inmate" and "ex-inmate" throughout this book.

REMEMBER: You can easily be led to a book but it's up to you to drink from it: if not, you'll eventually die of a thirsty mind.

WELCOME ... TO THE BEGINNING OF THE REST OF YOUR LIFE!

Fear, uncertainly, anxiety, nervousness: these are not the usual words that one associates with the news that he or she is going to be out of prison soon, in the outside world. Yet beyond the initial rush of knowing that prison life and all that you dislike about it will soon be gone comes the realization that you need to find employment and keep that employment; that you need to secure housing, food, and clothing; that you need to re-adjust to life and people on the outside; that you need to embrace an attitude that is more optimistic and enthusiastic; and that you need to develop a strong sense of self-responsibility and self-motivation. Indeed, fear, uncertainty, anxiety, and nervousness seem like pretty normal reactions when these items are added to what freedom from prison brings.

You're at a crossroads of sorts, now, and -- depending on which way you CHOOSE to go -- your path can be one that is full of optimism and unlimited possibilities or a path that continues one you've already walked: strewn with frustration, disappointment, anger, failure, and prison. Most people, if offered these two choices, would, of course, pick the first path. Yet again and again, ex-inmate after ex-inmate end up on the second path; they had no intention on being there, but they just couldn't continue on the first path because of obstacles, confusion, and unknowns they encountered. Finally, they just gave up and jumped over to the second path -- a path they know too well.

This book is here as your complete guide to show you how to stay on the first path, the path to optimism and unlimited possibilities ... and success.

> "Two roads diverged in a wood, and I --
> I took the one less traveled by,
> And that has made all the difference."
> — Robert Frost, American poet

JOB HUNTING FOR EX-INMATES: IT CAN BE ROUGH

The anchor to keep you on that first path is a job. For once you are employed other items and other responsibilities in your life can come about just a little bit easier: income to pay for the basics of life (such as food, clothing, and shelter); the means to support a family; the means to pay any court-ordered fines, restitution, and fees; a way to be more independent and begin living a crime-free life; an opportunity to meet new people, have some fun, and establish a secure future; and -- perhaps most important -- the opportunity to prove that you can put a history of mistakes and failures aside and substitute it for a life of success.

Of course, we've all heard and read about the job hunting horror stories with language that goes something like this: "Sorry, we don't hire ex-cons" ... "Personally, I'd hire you, but the company has a policy about hiring ex-felons and I'm just going by the rules -- I'm sure you understand, don't you?" ... "Now, what have you been doing for these past few years that aren't accounted for on your resume?"

Almost anyone who has spent time in prison has some story to tell about his or her quest for a job (and a fresh start) ... and how his or her prison record caused some degree of difficulty in landing a position.

OFTEN, IT'S BACK TO PRISON. Unfortunately, too many ex-inmates give up, think they can't work within the system, and go back to that second path I spoke of: making money and surviving the only way they think can work for them -- illegally. The usual result? Back to prison for a longer time ... or worse.

The Story of Ricky

When I was doing my years in prison, I met a fellow inmate named Ricky -- he eventually became my cellmate. A high school dropout, he had spent most of his adult life pushing drugs, forging and selling prescriptions, and doing second story burglaries. Jail and prison had seemed like revolving doors to him, and here he was once again.

HE WANTED "TO GO STRAIGHT."   During the time we knew each other -- about a year -- I was able to convince Ricky to finish his high school education in prison, which he did. Receiving his GED (General Equivalency Diploma) was a big moment for him, and he really believed that he could go straight when he went back to the "free world."

IT DIDN'T HAPPEN.   Ricky tried, on several occasions, to get a job, but each time he was turned down. The reasons? He was an ex-inmate (or "ex-con," as the employers would tell him) ... he didn't know how to dress for the interview ... he didn't seem prepared ... he needed more than a GED. Frustrated and depressed, Ricky went back to his old hustling ways. The end result? While attempting to rob someone, he was shot and killed.

Use This Book So You Won't End Up Another Ricky!

While Ricky's end may be an extreme example, his problems with landing employment and his decision to revert to what he knew best -- his illegal activities -- were very much the norm then and too often still are now.

Although part of the blame certainly lay with Ricky, it can also be said that Ricky didn't know how to get a job, he didn't know how to explain his time in prison, and he didn't know how to sell himself.

Ricky paid the ultimate price for not being able to make it within the guidelines and expectations of the free world. But is going back to prison an alternative to Ricky's end that you can live with?

YOU CAN BEAT THE ODDS – AND STAY OUTSIDE!! Using the suggestions, guidance, exercises, and examples offered in this book, you will gain a positive mental attitude, preparation, assistance, and tools needed to successfully land not only a job, but a job that can lead to a respected, responsible, and high-paying career ... and a life full of that optimism and those unlimited possibilities I spoke of earlier.

A NOTE ABOUT ME

I've Been Where You are and Where You're Going

As I mentioned above, I spent several years in prison -- in a state facility. I thought I knew all the answers and believed I didn't need anyone to tell me what to do or to help me turn my life around. This attitude went on for about a year in which I had more than my share of troubles: fights, "the hole," and other problems. Until I met Scottie Carter.

Scottie was a counselor and she was able to tap into me unlike anyone else. She saw through me and was able to touch certain buttons even I didn't know I had. Scottie got me to start thinking about where my life was heading, about the skills and education I had put in moth balls and was no longer using, and about my attitude. Quite frankly, if it weren't for Scottie and the role of correctional education, I'd probably be dead, doing a longer bid, or still running the streets on a day-to-day basis; as corny as it may sound, I have no problem in saying that Scottie Carter and prison education turned my life around.

Unfortunately, the job preparation and related transition programs at my institution was so minimal one could say it didn't exist. Thus, upon my release, I experienced many of the same problems and frustrations and disappointments that Ricky and others have gone through. Using what I had learned from Scottie, a combination of prior training, my smarts and other resources, making a "ton" of mistakes, and determining that I was going to succeed I finally landed a job on a newspaper as managing editor.

Shortly afterwards, I founded Aardvark Resumes & Career Counseling, and -- a few years later -- The Correctional Education Company. Both companies are primarily involved in correctional education counseling, training, and consulting, with a specific focus on transition and employment assistance for inmates and ex-inmates. I work with correctional educators and administrators, adult inmates and ex-inmates, and youthful offenders in the United States, Canada, and abroad. My overall goal in all of this? To make your transition from inside to outside as easy as possible, and to help you with all aspects -- directly and indirectly -- that relate to finding employment, keeping employment, and ultimately making a success of your life beyond prison.

DON'T EVER GIVE UP – YOU WILL BE THE ULTIMATE LOSER! There may be times when you get depressed, when you think things won't work out, when you believe that no-one will hire you because of your past prison record. However, life does go on and falling back on your past life and your life as an inmate as excuses will only go so far. Take a winning attitude, take a motivating attitude -- **you CAN succeed after prison!**

SOME GENERAL GUIDELINES
FOR YOUR CAREER SEARCH ... AND BEYOND

While each chapter and each subject area in this book has specific guidelines and suggestions for you, there are some general points that pertain to all aspects of your career search and just about every area of your life. I call these "Guidelines for a Fresh Start After Prison"; they'll greatly help you lay the foundation you need to find employment, to keep employment ... and to begin and maintain a successful life beyond prison.

Guidelines for a Fresh Start After Prison

(1) HAVE PATIENCE. Makin' it takes time, it takes patience; success is not going to come overnight. The prison doors opening only mean that one obstacle is down; you still have many more to overcome.

(2) UNDERSTAND YOUR LIMITATIONS. While you should always strive to improve, improve, improve, when you're released you may find that your reading level is at a basic level; that your math or English or some other academic subject is still not up to par; that your vocational training has left you at entry level. Accept this and apply for jobs and job levels where your limitations will not automatically prevent you from being interviewed or hired.

(3) DON'T BE AN IDIOT! All you need is one stupid move, and it's back to prison. Don't break any conditions of your parole, don't opt for "just one more shot" at some crime, don't give in to the needle or the bottle, don't let others talk you into ridiculous decisions. Do any of these and you've started to tumble, my friend, and you just blew the best chance you ever had at staying out and staying straight.

(4) NEVER BE AFRAID TO ASK QUESTIONS. The only way you're going to learn what to do, what not to do is by asking questions ... tons of them. "The only stupid question is the one not asked": you may have heard this before and it's true. It's much better to ask and find out you already knew the answer than not to ask and find out later you were wrong or needed the information.

(5) COUNSELORS CAN BE VERY COOL. Too many people think talking to professional counselors is a waste of time, is uncool, is a sign of weakness. Just the opposite. Sometimes, counselors are the only people who can help you over difficult times, who can put your direction and emotions back on track, who can give you advice not available from anyone else, who can let you know that your decisions are good ones. So don't be afraid to seek one out -- at times, in our strive for independence and self-reliance, input from trained professionals can help make our efforts a bit smoother, a tad more on target.

(6) DEVELOP A SENSE OF HUMOR. Lighten up, smile upon occasion, don't be afraid to laugh at yourself. Any aspect of life seems easier with a sense of humor, and people feel friendlier to others who have a sense of humor. And best of all, you'll feel better about yourself.

(7) HIRE YOURSELF. If you treat your employment search like a hobby or something to do in your spare time you'll seldom be successful. Yet if you go about it as if it's a full-time job, you'll be much better at it, for you'll put in a focused and enthusiastic effort. And this same approach holds true for any goal, assignment, or task you want or need to accomplish.

(8) EXPLORE THE POSSIBILITY OF HALFWAY HOUSES. If your institution has ties to halfway houses in your community, check out the possibility of being eligible for one. Not only do they offer shelter, food, a counselor, and a "family" of others who are getting out of prison, but it's a good transition jump-off start to help out while you look for and get used to employment and your first weeks and months on the outside. But remember: you need go beyond just a strong effort at staying clean, straight, and motivated -- you need to do it!

(9) DON'T PROCRASTINATE. Sometimes, it's easy -- too easy -- to put off doing something until tomorrow or the next day ... or whenever. And when we need to do something that we're perhaps a bit afraid of or don't wish to face -- like asking about a job, doing research at the library, going to an interview, or meeting with a parole officer -- procrastination seems like a safe alternative. Well, life after prison means growing up and facing your responsibilities and appointments. So don't put off but rather do it -- when it's supposed to be done!

(10) DEVELOP AN ACTION PLAN. <u>No sense going ahead if you don't have some idea as to where you're going, how you're going to get there, what you're going to do once you get there, and where you're going next.</u> Begin developing a plan to survive and thrive after prison that incorporates the basics (finding shelter, food, clothing), your job hunt, family and other support resources, a budget, and any other areas that you think important. And once you have a plan, stick to it -- it's your road map to the straight and narrow.

(11) DON'T LET YOURSELF GO. Once you're out of prison and there are no correctional officers telling you what to do and no gates or bars restricting your freedom, there may be a tendency on your part to run away from civilization, to take on traits that are just the opposite of what you need to succeed. In a word, this is stupid. So ... don't get fat, don't get sloppy, don't sleep the day away, don't forget about showers, and all those other items that separate you from the animals. The better you look out for yourself, the better impression you'll make on others.

(12) NEVER FORGET YOUR TIME IN PRISON. As much as you want to put it behind you, it's good to think about it now-and-then, especially if you start contemplating doing something illegal. Look around you, smell around you, touch around you; don't ever forget it: no matter what obstacles or problems you run into on the outside, it'll never be as bad as being back on the inside. And if you hanker for the "good ol' days" of prison, perhaps you just don't have what it takes to succeed on the outside in the first place. For anyone who wants to stay inside doesn't want self-responsibility, can't find self-motivation, and ultimately doesn't think much of self -- and without these three, you'll never be a success in the free world.

(13) DON'T USE RACISM, BIGOTRY, & PREJUDICE AS EXCUSES. It's a real world, not an ideal world, and some people don't like other people because of skin color, ethnicity, religion, or nationality. Sure, these sometimes do keep people from getting hired, from promotions, from being treated fairly in many other areas of life. You can protest and file suit and write angry letters, but meanwhile other opportunities and many minutes of life are passing you by. Become better than others through your education, your skills, your abilities, your attitude. While this won't eliminate all the problems you'll have in life because other people are jerks, it sure beats any alternative you come up with.

(14) EMBRACE LEARNING AS A WAY OF LIFE. Never do you want to let your mind level off; if you do, it'll eventually whither away. Always strive to improve your mind, both formally (community courses, college, seminars, workshops) and informally (reading magazines and books, CD-ROM and Internet programs, educational TV, visiting museums and libraries, sitting in on free lectures, etc.) The more you know the better prepared you'll be for all areas of life.

(15) GET INVOLVED IN YOUR COMMUNITY. There are so many activities taking place in your community: citizens groups, hobby clubs, church and temple committees, volunteer agencies, sports leagues, and many others. While always keeping your time and efforts primarily focused on employment and your family, community involvement can help you through meeting new people, getting job contacts, developing new interests, and building a more positive image. Of course, there's also the fun, the excitement, the learning, and the overall good feeling that result from community involvement. So ... reach out!

REMEMBER: Guidelines are not written in stone, are not legally binding, and are not dictated by God; only you can give them life.

FOR SPECIAL POPULATIONS

Although the information in this book is addressed to ALL inmates and ex-inmates, there are barriers, special situations, targeted assistance, and focused suggestions that can impact certain, specific populations. For you who may fall into one or more of these categories, read the information in this section.

Minorities

Native American Indians, African-Americans, Hispanics, Polynesians, and several other ethnic and national minorities comprise a major portion of our prison system. If you fall into this minority category, you may feel that the odds of you making it after release are especially overwhelming. Statistics, of course, all too often bear this out. However, in addition to putting forth the same effort and work plan that all inmates and ex-inmates should, there are additional opportunities and assistance available to you IF you take the time to do some research.

Don't forget the following:

● <u>Employment assistance and many scholarships are available</u> (and sometimes specifically set aside) for various minorities. (Both the Internet and local libraries are a good source to find these.)

● <u>Contact local and national minority associations</u> (many are listed in the Yellow Pages, under "Associations," as well as on the Internet). Not only do these often have job postings and provide some type of job assistance, but they can be invaluable in questions and problems relating specifically to culture, family, and legal issues.

● <u>Don't forget your neighborhood</u>. As much as we would like to think of the United States as offering equal opportunity to all, we know that, in reality, this does not always happen. When coming out of prison, you may well find that a neighborhood comprised primarily of your minority will be more accepting of you coming back to society, including various forms of assistance, educational programs, and employment opportunities. One word of caution, though: if you first got into trouble in your old neighborhood, steer clear of those you once hung with -- you are trying to get straight, not get broken.

Older Inmates

● As the country gets older, so do attitudes about older workers (40+) change for the better.
● Older workers are often seen as more reliable; can be counted on for long-term employment; work well under stress; don't panic in crisis situations; have knowledge and skills to offer others.
● Alert: companies may not offer older workers salaries as large as younger counterparts.
● Your key to interview success: look, act, and think young, not like "an old man" (or "old woman").
● If you have a physical problem brought on by older age, don't use this as an excuse for yourself or others. Rather, concentrate on your strengths; if asked, assure an interviewer that your "problem" won't get in the way of your work.
● Contact organizations (such as "40+") that specialize in employment assistance for the older worker.

Women

● Your keys to interview success: good ability to present, never dress / act sexy, show self-confidence.
● Never use children as an excuse for needing special hours or time off.
● There are organizations specific to helping women seeking employment -- contact them.

Youthful Offenders

● Your keys to interview success: professional & "clean-cut" image, speak well, be attentive and serious.
● Map out your professional skills and personal strengths: this will impress the interviewer.
● There are many organizations and assistance available to help youth get jobs -- check them out.

THE NATIONAL ASSOCIATION OF EX-INMATES

A new and very exciting non-profit organization is forming that can be of assistance to all ex-inmates: The National Association of Ex-Inmates. It has several purposes: to serve as an information and referral support organization for inmates and ex-inmates; to disseminate information and serve as a unified voice to the public, employers, and politicians so these groups may better understand the ex-inmate and his/her value to society; to develop programs of support to assist ex-inmates in their effort to successfully transition to a life permanently free of crime and as contributing members of society.

For further information, write or contact NAEI at the address or numbers listed below, on this page.

FINALLY: I'M AVAILABLE IF YOU'D LIKE TO CONTACT ME

This book has been written for you by an ex-inmate who is fully involved in the professions of correctional education and career counseling. Please: don't hesitate to write me with your questions, comments, or suggestions. You are assured that each item will receive a reply. I may be reached at:

The Correctional Education Company
433 Franklin Street -- Patio Suite, Buffalo NY 14202
PHONE: 716-882-3456 / FAX: 716-882-7053 / E-MAIL: CorrectionalEd@juno.com

> **REMEMBER: Accept the fact that you will experience disappointments, frustrations, dead-ends, rejections, and nos ... then swallow them like cornflakes for breakfast and go on with your job search -- and life.**

Chapter 1

"What Do I Have to Show for My Time in Prison?"

"Fall seven times, stand up eight."

Japanese Proverb

My first six months in prison were pretty rotten. I felt as if life were passing me by, that I was accomplishing nothing, and that my career training -- as a teacher, professional career counselor, writer, and speaker -- would be wasted for as long as I was in prison. Rather than think about what I could do to better myself on the inside to help me when I was released, all I could think about, cry about, and complain about was that I wanted to be free and that it certainly wasn't going to do me any good to stay locked up.

WISDOM OF THE LIFER

During this down time, I became friendly with a lifer who had been in for 12 years. It was impossible for me to understand how this man had kept his sanity, especially knowing that he was, in all probability, never going to be released.

THE MOST IMPORTANT ELEMENT IN GETTING A JOB WHILE INCARCERATED. The more we talked over several weeks, the more I came to realize the single most important element in getting one's self ready for a new start and a job on the outside was to make full use of everything prison could offer!

You see, my lifer friend told me that the only way he was able to do more than just survive was to take advantage of the educational opportunities, work assignments, and general day-to-day living experiences that were a part of his prison stay. Do this, he said, and implement it so you can continually improve your attitude, your outlook, your approach to life.

Even if he was never released, he had promised himself that he would use his time wisely, improve his mind, and make this prison sentence -- no matter how long -- a valuable learning experience.

My reaction, at first, was still one of skepticism, of non-belief. However, since I wasn't going anywhere soon and certainly had time on my hands, I figured that if I began to get busy it might make my sentence go by faster.

REMEMBER: Prison's going to be your entire world for **X** amount of years -- accept this and use everything around as a self-improvement course in preparation for the day you **DO** return to the outside world.

DISCOVERING YOUR STRENGTHS

I did a quick assessment of my strengths: I was a good writer and speaker, had been a college teacher, had been active in a variety of professional and social organizations, and had experience in career counseling and resume writing. Slowly, I began using these skills to help others while I was in prison:

- **teaching reading and public speaking**
- **writing and/or editing letters**
- **organizing a Jaycee chapter**
- **assisting others about to be released in writing resume and cover letters, interviewing techniques, and job search strategies**
- **starting a prison newspaper**
- **serving as a volunteer prison tour guide**
- **helping guards and other inmates write or edit college essays, job applications, and book reports**
- **teaching others how to study**
- **co-organizing a Sesame Street Goes To Prison program**

What Your Activities in Prison Can Do For You

THREE ACCOMPLISHMENTS. These involvements earned me no money but I was accomplishing three things: (1) I was keeping my mind active; (2) I was preparing myself for the task of looking for employment once I was released; (3) it made my sentence much easier to handle, and seemed to make the time go by much faster.

> **REMEMBER: While in prison, never worship the evil gods Laziness, Sloppiness, and Wastefulness. No matter what your skills, no matter what your educational background, and no matter how long or short your prison sentence, you can use the time inside to your advantage.**

What Are YOUR Strengths?

<u>*EXAMPLES OF STRENGTHS (also known as positives or assets)*</u>*:* There are hundreds of various strengths people can possess; examples of some include: good ability to communicate; handle stress well; outgoing personality; can work independently of supervision; a team worker; get along well with others; dedicated; will put in whatever work is necessary to get the job done; speak a second language; enjoy volunteering; cheerful; always put in a second effort; punctual and dependable; have a positive attitude; enjoy learning and self-improvement.

<u>*LISTING YOUR STRENGTHS*</u>. In the spaces provided on the next page, list YOUR strengths. Again: **no matter what you did on the outside, no matter what your education, you do have POSITIVE strengths that can be used to better others** ... and thus ultimately better yourself.

● **REGARDING ACTIVITIES INSIDE PRISON:** Remember that there are many activities in prison. There are those that the institution provides, such as Arts & Crafts, Basketball, Library, Educational programs, Discussion Groups, Newspaper, and various clubs. There are also activities that inmates involve themselves in to survive, to have acceptance in an inmate group or gang, to make some money. Examples are drugs, counterfeiting, stealing, etc. No matter what your activities, look at those POSITIVE skills you need to make what you do successful. See pages 58-64 for detailed information.

● **REGARDING ACTIVITIES PRIOR TO PRISON:** Sometimes, we forget about those activities we did on the outside, sometimes minor ones, that can offer strengths of ours. So go through your memory bank of past jobs, hobbies, community and volunteer work, military duty, help you gave to family or friends, schooling, professional associations -- anything that required you to use various strengths of yours.

Worksheet: List Your Strengths

Be honest when listing these; no one needs to see what you've written. (If you need additional room, use a separate sheet of paper.)

1) _____

2) _____

3) _____

4) _____

5) _____

6) _____

7) _____

8) _____

9) _____

10) _____

11) _____

12) _____

13) _____

14) _____

DISCOVERING YOUR WEAKNESSES

Now that you have some of your strengths listed, it's time to take a look at the other side. (By the way: I say "some" because as you go along in this book and as you look back at your prison experience / continue in your prison experience, you will undoubtedly discover additional strengths -- as well as additional weaknesses -- that you forgot about or did not know you had!)

Here I speak of your weaknesses, your negatives, those parts of your self that need to be changed so that you can STAY on the outside, so that you can KEEP a job, so that you can MAINTAIN a close relationship with family and friends ... and so you WON'T end up with more time added to your sentence while doing your time!

<u>MY WEAKNESSES</u>. Well, I made a list of my weaknesses, too, and I was much more honest than I would have been if I knew someone else was going to read them:

- **I couldn't bring myself to open up to anyone about faults, problems, worries, or mistakes I had or had made**
- **I was too quick to jump into a project; I sometimes did not think things through**
- **I was not in the greatest physical condition**
- **I found it very difficult to accept compliments**
- **I had a very big ego problem**
- **I was mainly interested in sexual relationships with women, even though I led them to think that I wanted much more than that**
- **I had a tendency not to think about budgets when spending money**
- **I was not a good delegator**
- **I would seldom listen to others' advice; I often had a "know-it-all" attitude**

By listing these weaknesses, these negatives of mine, it gave me a clearer idea of what I had to work on while locked up so, once released, I could be a better person and more personally and professionally successful.

What Are YOUR Weaknesses?

WRITING DOWN YOUR WEAKNESSES (also called negatives). It's usually easier for us to list our weaknesses on paper (but harder to do so by mouth; see Chapter 7 for details), not only because we tend to know what we could do to be more successful, but also because inmates are so often told about their negatives by prison officials, the judge, counselors, family, friends, non-friends (!), clergy, prison buddies, and others.

Often, they are right, although it seems like we don't want to admit it. Take into account what you think or know are your weaknesses, along with what others have pointed out to you that could be corrected. In the spaces on the next page, HONESTLY list ALL those weaknesses, negatives, and faults you feel you need to correct.

By the way: when I say "honestly list all those weaknesses," I mean just that -- honestly. For many inmates, one of the most difficult things to do is to say, in essence, "I'm not perfect" or "I have certain faults." The only perfect people are those found in cemeteries or fantasies, and the mark of a truly whole person, a person who is at ease with him or herself is one who cannot only admit to being weak in certain attitudinal, emotional, informational, and / or physical areas BUT has the courage and determination to improve upon those areas. I want this person to be you!

EXAMPLES OF WEAKNESSES: As with strengths, there are also hundreds of weaknesses floating around. Some of these are: don't listen well to directions, don't care for authority; have a big ego; think others are always in the wrong, that it's seldom my fault; do not work well in a group; am a racist or bigot; poor ability to communicate; get angry very quickly; have an overall negative attitude; carry a "chip on my shoulder"; not willing to put in extra effort; more concerned with my own interests than helping others; not willing to put in the extra effort; use foul language; not willing to take responsibility for my own actions; do not enjoy reading or learning; not a good listener; very short attention span.

[NOTE ABOUT WEAKNESSES FROM ACTIVITIES IN PRISON AND BEFORE PRISON: As with strengths, there are many instances when we have displayed our weaknesses, to both others and ourselves. The more of these you remember, the more weaknesses you'll come upon ... and the better the opportunity to work on doing away with them!]

REMEMBER: When you can openly and honestly admit your weaknesses, negatives, and faults, you have started the process of setting goals for yourself -- a most important step involved with getting and keeping a job.

Worksheet: List Your Weaknesses, Faults, and Negatives

As with listing your strengths, be honest when listing these; again, no one needs to see what you've written. (If you need additional room, use a separate sheet of paper.)

1) _____

2) _____

3) _____

4) _____

5) _____

6) _____

7) _____

8) _____

9) _____

10) _____

11) _____

12) _____

13) _____

"THIS IS MY VACATION" MENTALITY

TIME FOR SUMMER VACATION. Many were the fellow inmates I encountered who had the attitude that their stint in prison was going to be their vacation from life before they returned to the everyday, "nine-to-five" treadmill.

After all, they reasoned, they didn't have to buy food or clothing, a place to sleep was provided, medication and health care were free, there was no need to work for a living, and they were told when to get up and when to go to sleep. It seemed easy, it seemed carefree.

WHEN "SUMMER VACATION" IS OVER. Yet while all these freebies and easy living routines were fun and relaxing for many of my inmate colleagues, they did nothing to prepare them for job searching. It can be compared to the two students on summer vacation break from school: one lounges at the beach all day and parties all night, while the other takes an additional course, holds down a job, and parties once in a while. Whom do you think the employer will more seriously consider for a job?

Don't let the "vacation mentality" trap you: it will only be harder for you once on the outside, looking for employment. The fact that you were in prison is an additional hurdle you have to get over that most other job searchers don't have. Why make the process even more difficult by having to tell someone, in essence: "I didn't do anything to improve myself and I didn't gain anything that could be of use to you while I was incarcerated, Mr. or Ms. Employer."

TAKE A GOOD LOOK AROUND YOU.   Notice the number of fellow inmates who do little to improve themselves? You'll find some addicted ... to TV (usually cartoons, martial arts movies, and sitcoms), to sleep, to cards and the like, to reading of only "junky" magazines and books, to exercise and sports. The key word here is "addicted": any of these in moderation and combined with efforts at learning and improving ourselves is great. Don't leave prison with nothing to show for it but good times, much sleep, and gobs of bitterness: if you do, you've wasted what could have been a very productive time for you. Prison represents a wonderful opportunity to better yourself -- do it!

BETTERING YOURSELF IN PRISON

There are four areas in which you can improve, and thus definitely increase your edge in landing the job you want:

(1) <u>VOCATIONALLY</u> (what trades or skills have you learned or improved upon?)

(2) <u>EDUCATIONALLY</u> (have you improved your ability to write, to read, to speak, to spell, to study, and other areas?)

(3) <u>PHYSICALLY</u> (have you put / kept yourself in good physical condition? do you have good hygiene and grooming habits?)

(4) <u>MENTALLY / EMOTIONALLY</u> (have you acquired a positive mental attitude? have you learned how to handle being incarcerated? are you through feeling sorry for yourself?)

Let's take a closer look at each one of these:

#1
<u>VOCATIONALLY</u>

There are thousands of prisons, jails, detention centers, work camps, and prison farms in the United States, each with its own job assignments, life experiences, and activities in which you can become involved.

YOUR JOB ASSIGNMENT IN PRISON

In many of these institutions, each inmate has an initial interview (and perhaps a series of tests) to help determine what type of job or assignment he/she is best suited for while doing time. Sometimes you will end up with a job you like, other times you'll be assigned a job you don't like. No matter which, however, take advantage of learning any skills you can. In addition, you can learn how to handle situations that may also come up in the real world of work, after release.

If You Don't Like Your Job Assignment

GIVE IT A CHANCE. If you do draw a prison job or assignment you wish you didn't have, at first give it a chance -- it is possible that trained counselors, professional staff, and/or tests have found some talents in you that you did not know you had or never thought much about. Many are the inmates who were given a prison assignment they didn't care for, couldn't imagine how they were selected for such a job in the first place ... and wound up not only liking it but pursuing it as a career on the outside!

IF IT DOESN'T WORK OUT. There are those instances, of course, when a job and you won't become acquaintances, let alone fast friends. **When this happens, there are THREE ways to handle it: two that can benefit you and one that will do you no good:**

(1) YES!! Set up an appointment (if one is necessary) with the guard or staff member in charge of assignments. Very calmly and clearly explain why you don't like the work. Offer an alternative that you think you'd like and where you feel you can make a better and more positive contribution.

(2) YES!! If, after presenting your case for a different job, you are turned down, keep your cool and don't get angry! Rather, go back to the job, make the best of it by seeing what skills you might be able to learn or improve upon, and then -- if you still want out -- try again to get transferred after a month or so of continually working to the best of your ability.

IF YOU CAN'T GET TRANSFERRED OUT. If it appears that you can't get a transfer out of this work assignment as long as you are in your particular prison, either try to transfer out to another prison (keeping in mind that it could be worse) or do the best job possible until your time is up. Meanwhile, continue learning skills!

(3) NO!! Be a fool and get angry, cause trouble, make it difficult for others to do their work. This can take you many routes: a harsher attitude toward you by the guards, certainly no chance of changing jobs (except, perhaps, to a more difficult or unpleasant one!), possible transfer to another prison that you would not want to be in, perhaps some time in solitary, and maybe an extension of your sentence.

Any of these could also carry a negative remark or recommendation about you that might follow you outside the prison walls to any prospective employer. And, perhaps most important, you have taken an opportunity away from yourself to learn skills and experience situations that can help you after prison.

Using Prison Work Experience in Your Job Search

In Chapter 2 of this book, the specifics are discussed of how you can use your prison work experience to your best advantage in looking for a job, and show you examples of how specific prison work assignments can be translated into job experience on the outside.

> **REMEMBER: To find that one job, that one career that can make you sing, do cartwheels, and enjoy every day you wake up might at first mean a path of off-key, "gotta' make the doughnuts," "here we go again" jobs ... but these are the jobs that'll keep you alive and surviving until you reach #1 on the employment hit parade.**

#2
EDUCATIONALLY

Most prisons offer the opportunity for you t o improve your mind, whether it be through use of structured classes, the library, or discussion groups. What's important here is not so much the method you choose, but that you DO choose at least one of these opportunities ... and continually use it to improve your mind and your abilities while in prison. DO choose at least one of these opportunities ... and continually use it to upgrade your mind and your abilities while in prison.

THE STORY OF CARTOON

My prison buddy Cartoon is a good example of how this education of self can be of help on the outside, not only in landing a job but just in coping with life in the free world on a daily basis.

HE WASN'T ACCOMPLISHING MUCH. In and out of reform school and prison since he was 12, Cartoon could barely read or write, and the only jobs he ever held were as a floor sweeper and migrant farm work during the summers. It was much easier for Cartoon to use his fists, a switchblade, and some loud language to get his money than it was for him to use his mind.

This time he was serving the tail end of a four-year stretch, and really had not accomplished too much this time around, with the exception of winning some card games and getting thrown in "the hole" a few times for fighting. Obviously, what faced Cartoon when he got out was more of the same, and an eventual return to what was becoming his home away from home.

Education Made a Positive Difference in Cartoon's Life

What changed Cartoon? There was no miracle, no divine revelation, no forced assignment to a school class. Rather, just by luck he was assigned a new cellmate who enjoyed reading, liked to talk, and had graduated high school. Conversations with his roommate led to questions, and these questions led to the source of the answers: books.

EVENTUAL SUCCESS ON THE OUTSIDE. For the first time in his life, Cartoon felt like he was missing something by not knowing how to read very well. Although there were only six months left on his sentence, he enrolled in a Basic Reading Class, continued his lessons on the outside, eventually received his GED, and -- after three years -- became a Foreman of a Night Cleaning Crew.

---

4 Things You Can Learn from Cartoon's Experience

No matter how little or how much education you have, you can always improve:

(1) TAKE ADVANTAGE OF THE EDUCATIONAL OPPORTUNITIES AROUND YOU. Don't be a fool and pass on the many opportunities you have to improve your mind while doing time.

Some institutions offer schooling all the way up to a college degree (although the number that do have greatly decreased since the elimination of Pell grants for prison inmates); most have libraries (if not, you can always find a way of getting hold of magazines and/or books); and virtually every prison has some type of discussion group you can join that will help you improve your mind, your ability to communicate with others, and a chance at better understanding yourself.

Get involved in one, some, or all of these -- if you don't, the only one losing out is you!

(2) PREPARE YOURSELF FOR EMPLOYMENT ON THE OUTSIDE. Use the learning resources available at your institution to help you prepare for life on the outside and, specifically, your job search.

(3) DON'T WAIT. DON'T wait for something to happen before you decide to further educate yourself: don't wait until you have only a few months on your sentence ... don't wait until you have a definite date for your parole hearing ... don't wait until you're told that it's education or a longer sentence. (However, certainly better late than never: if you are a short short-timer, you can still benefit greatly by improving your education.)

(4) IF YOU DECIDE TO WAIT, YOU'LL LOSE OUT. Others are going to pass you by with job offers, new friends, and other opportunities. There's not much you can do about the amount of time you've been sentenced to (no matter if you get out early on parole or good behavior: there is still time you have to complete), so why not go out and use it to your advantage?

REMEMBER: There are two ways to approach life: wait for life to come and grab you, or for you to go out and grab life.

IF YOU'RE STILL NOT CONVINCED THAT EDUCATION CAN DO YOU SOME GOOD

There are always going to be some hard-nosed and skeptical inmates who think education and learning are "sissy stuff," that it's better to be shooting craps, doing drugs, playing cards, roughing somebody up, reliving memories of life before prison, or bragging about your plans for life after prison. When all this quiets down, is ANY of this going to help you get a job on the outside and stay out of prison? The answer is a definite NO!

> **REMEMBER: Society owes you zip, zilch, zero, and zingo, and if you intend on keeping yourself out of prison and want to get serious about some solid employment, use the time you now have to LEARN, to IMPROVE, and to BETTER yourself.**

#3
PHYSICALLY

Before you have a chance to sell your mind during a job interview, you sell the way you look, the way you are seen by others. This includes clothing (discussed in Chapter 2 and Chapter 6), hygiene, grooming, and overall physical appearance. Many has been the job lost because someone looked out of shape, had poor grooming, or had unpleasant hygiene.

SIMPLY BECAUSE YOU ARE IN PRISON IS NO EXCUSE FOR "LETTING YOURSELF GO." Just the opposite: if you are sincere about wanting to make a clean start once on the outside, and landing a good job, than you ought to consider your prison time as training time for development of good habits you will maintain for a lifetime.

THE PUBLIC'S IMAGE OF THE EX-INMATE. This has been fueled and exaggerated by TV, movies, magazines and newspapers, comedians, books, plays, and cartoons. Consider that although there are more than 1 million men and women behind prison bars (and approximately 2 million behind jail and prison bars on any given day), this is still a very small percentage of the nearly 300 million of us who live in the United States.

Thus, many who have never been in prison believe what they have read, seen, or been told about an inmate, because that is the only contact that most Americans have with prison inmates.

IN GENERAL, WHAT IS THE PUBLIC'S PERCEPTION? Any ex-inmate, so most of the public believe, is somebody: mean-looking, with a swagger that says "don't mess with me" ... disheveled, who looks very much like a street person or bag lady ... who has bad breath and other odors ... who is either an overweight slob or a muscle-bound jock.

Knowing that many ex-felons have this image problem, you want to be certain that you go out of your way to LOOK and APPEAR every bit the professional who is serious about employment. There are too many people who have never spent a day incarcerated looking for employment: you need every edge you can get to help you land the job, and looking the role of someone who is serious about employment will greatly help.

> **REMEMBER: Start this physical, hygienic, and grooming preparation while in prison, doing time (no matter how much time is left on your sentence), not waiting until you are released. Poor habits acquired while in prison will take much longer to break once on the outside, and a job interview is not the place to start practicing.**

Each area that constitutes physical fitness requires a closer look:

PHYSICAL FITNESS: ITS IMPORTANCE

Employers have become increasingly aware of the importance of excellent physical fitness in their employees due to the many studies proving a physically fit employee has a more positive attitude, misses fewer work days (due to illness or fatigue), and is more productive, as well as the heightened emphasis placed on it by the media for more than a decade now.

This means you no longer can take for granted being hired merely on your skills, education, and/or experience -- physical conditioning counts for much in today's job hiring process ... whether you think it fair or not.

THE BENEFITS OF BEING PHYSICALLY FIT. When you look good, you appear more confident to others, and self-confidence increases. Your clothes fit better, thus making you look neater and better organized; your stamina will increase, making it easier for you to put in the time and effort necessary to be a success at your job; and since you are a representative of the company you work for, you will be doing a solid job promoting the professional image of your company.

Exercising in Prison

You do have the opportunity to exercise in any prison, whether it be with weights and / or an exercise machine, outdoor and / or indoor games and exercise, simple exercises you can do in a cell, or a combination thereof. (The first prison I was in kept me in my 8 x 10 cell most of the time, but that did not keep me from doing sit-ups and push-ups, running in place, stretching, and doing isometrics using the bars and the wall.) Yet exercise by itself is NOT enough to give you the proper conditioning you need to "stay in shape" -- food plays an equally important role.

Eating Smart / Good Nutrition

Institutional food tends to be very heavy in starches, and thus calories. Many of these foods are also fried or use food additives that make the foods fatty as well. In addition, your choice in foods is very limited, as you must eat what is provided -- you can't run down to the local supermarket! Set a menu plan for yourself that will keep you from gorging on the pastas, breads, and fried foods; watch the Little Debbies and other snack foods; and no matter how overcooked, eat the vegetables offered. As much as possible, you want to establish a balanced, healthy combination of foods.

> **REMEMBER: You are training your mind and your body to help you stay on the outside and make your life a success, and good eating and exercise habits will do much to help you make these goals a reality.**

HYGIENE

The Effects of Prison On Your Hygiene

It is easier to let your hygiene (the way in which we keep all parts of our bodies clean) fall by the wayside in prison. Why? You do not have access to as many clean clothes as you would on the outside. You cannot shower or wash your clothes whenever you'd like. And often, you can only brush your teeth and wash up at pre-set times.

Also, incarceration usually means more frequent exposure to germs, to the outside elements, and (with most inmates) to physical labor. Too, you may not be able to purchase and/or have sent to you all the toiletries and cleaners you'd like (examples: mouthwash, special soaps, a water pic, items in glass and/or non-see-through containers, nail or toenail clippers).

In addition, because it is sadly true that many inmates come from poor economic and educational backgrounds where they may not have been exposed to proper hygienic habits, very often there is an overall lack of regular hygiene awareness in prison.

Poor Hygienic Habits Spread

The result of this poor hygiene? It tends to spread to those other inmates who, while initially coming to prison with good hygienic habits, fall prey to what others are hygienically NOT doing around them. Some inmates even believe that there really is no reason to practice good hygiene, now that outside society has been yanked away. Nothing could be further from the truth!

18

3 Reasons to Maintain Good Hygiene

(1) YOU MUST DO IT FOR YOURSELF. First of all, if for no one else, you must do your utmost to maintain excellent hygiene habits for yourself. Do you want to stink? Do you want your teeth falling out in later years? Do you want head lice and such? Do you want to eat with dirty hands?

(2) YOU COME INTO DAILY CONTACT WITH OTHERS. Too, you will be mingling with others -- other inmates, staff, counselors, guards, perhaps friends and/or family during visitation -- and you want to make every effort to show them that you still have your self-esteem and pride.

(3) EMPLOYERS DEMAND GOOD HYGIENE. Beyond the immediate, you must also look to the time when you will be free and looking for a job. What employer wants to hire someone with rotting or no teeth, who has offensive odor (whether it be breath, body odor, or soiled clothes), who has dirty fingernails, who has dandruff (or worse, lice!), who picks his or her nose, whose skin is not clean, or who constantly scratches? NONE!

Improving Your Hygiene While Inside

What can you do while in prison to make certain you don't carry any poor hygiene habits with you, while at the same time maintaining a daily pattern of good hygiene? Establish a routine of practicing good hygiene on a daily basis while inside prison ... the more you stick with it, the better you'll feel and the more natural these positive habits will seem to you once on the outside. [See Chapter 6, pages 241-242, for hygiene tips as they relate to the job interview.]

Good Hygiene Suggestions

More specifically, try the following examples of good hygiene (not all may be allowed or feasible in your institution, but do the best you can):

- **Brush your teeth in the morning, after each meal, and before you go to bed; floss your teeth at night.**
- **Wash your hands and face at least in the morning and evening; take a shower at least once a week, ideally once a day; use soap to wash yourself.**
- **Use a good shampoo and conditioner on your hair; brush or comb your hair every day.**

- Change your underwear and socks each day (if necessary, wash them out in your sink and let them dry overnight); if possible, have your clothes laundered once per week.
- Keep your fingernails and toenails clipped.
- If mouthwash is not allowed, at least chew on a stick of gum or breath mint.
- Use underarm deodorant.
- If possible, use a body powder or talc after you shower.
- Visit the dentist or physician when a problem occurs with your teeth or other areas of your body.
- If you have a special skin or other medical problem that requires a certain cream, ointment, or other medication, make certain you let the prison doctor or nurse know about it.
- Don't pass gas or belch unless it cannot be helped; when you must do it, try to do it away from others.
- Always keep a handkerchief or tissue on you in case you have to sneeze, spit, or cough; if you do not have a handkerchief, cover your mouth if you need to sneeze, spit, or cough.
- For women: make sure you take care of feminine hygiene needs (i.e., adequate care / supply of feminine products).
- Take any prescribed medication on a regular basis.

GROOMING

Grooming differs from hygiene in that it focuses more on the way you look, that is, your overall visual appearance to others. The most obvious aspect of good grooming is the clothes you wear, yet very often inmates let this fall by the way. Why? Because many inmates believe there is no one to impress and/or since they have a uniform that's not owned by them, why bother to look at the uniform as anything other than something to cover their body?

You Must First Impress Yourself

The better you look, the better you are going to feel. In addition, anyone else with whom you come into contact will show you a bit more respect -- respect that is earned by taking pride in one's appearance.

REMEMBER: The habit of good grooming certainly extends beyond prison walls to your day of release and your efforts in landing a job and keeping the job once hired. If you don't care about the way you look on the inside, chances are pretty good that you're not going to care very much about how you look on the outside.

Employers Demand Good Grooming

How many employers do you know who would hire a sloppy dresser with uncombed hair, scuffed shoes, unpressed and dirty clothes, and in need of a shave (or, in the case of women, with unshaved legs)? They are far and few between.

Good Grooming Suggestions While Inside

Maintain good grooming habits you brought with you; if you haven't previously had good grooming habits, or have let them slip while inside, capture (or re-capture) them now:

● **Keep your clothes looking as neat and clean as possible; in some institutions, it is possible to get your shirts and pants pressed -- do it!**
● **Keep your shoes and belt shined.**
● **Brush or comb your hair so it is neat looking.**
● **Clip or cut any hairs that protrude from your nose or ears; if you are allowed a beard and/or mustache, keep it/them neat.**
● **If you shave, shave every day or as often as necessary to maintain a clean, fresh look; if possible, use an aftershave lotion or light cologne (it'll make you feel more civilized!).**
● **For women: if wearing makeup or nail polish, keep it light, fresh, and tasteful.**
● **Concerning tattoos: it's common to find ex-inmates with tattoos ("tats"); many of these are often acquired in prison. But remember: these can get in the way of an employer's positive impression of you, especially if the graphic and/or the message are not in the best of (mainstream society's) taste. While they may seem "cool" now, they do last forever ... and you need be concerned with your overall appearance beyond the walls. (2 Suggestions: if you insist on getting a tattoo or adding one to your collection, at least: [1] do so where an employer won't see it! [2] be certain the artwork looks professional and that you keep the size discreet and the message / graphic tasteful.)**

#4
MENTALLY / EMOTIONALLY

> **REMEMBER:** The experiences of being incarcerated, of having much of your self-esteem stripped away, and of being deprived of regular contact with the outside world play major havoc with your mental and emotional selves.

THE NEW EXPERIENCE OF PRISON

We cry when we thought we never would; we are afraid when we really never knew fear; we reach out to family and friends for support in a manner we never thought necessary; we become painfully aware of many items we so often took for granted when free; and we experience a new set of rules and social order far different from those we lived by on the outside.

Prison Changes You Emotionally & Mentally

Ask anyone who has been inside for a while and he'll/she'll tell you -- no matter how adjusted and easy-going he or she now seems -- those first few months of prison were very difficult times. Gradually, you begin to cope with your new environment, and you often find that your personality has greatly changed in allowing you to survive and make the best of prison surroundings.

INSIDE VS. OUTSIDE. With this personality change, there also comes about a change in virtually all inmates in their emotional and mental outlook on life and, specifically, the way they react to others, to events, to crises, and to needs. While this change is more often than not a must if you want to make it through your prison sentence, it can also be your biggest undoing when looking for a job, when trying to keep a job (and, in general, in making an effort at fitting back into society).

Mental & Emotional Changes are Hardest to Shake

If you take a look at the three prior areas previously discussed -- vocational, educational, and physical -- each are skills or habits that are acquired, somewhat like slipping on a new coat. There are many ex-inmates who have learned a trade, improved their education, and have worked themselves into great physical shape while inside, but could not let go of the negative mental and emotional effect prison had on them.

Some Examples of Negative Mental and Emotional Attitudes That Carry Over Once You are Released

- **feeling sorry for yourself**
- **feeling that society owes you a living**
- **holding a very low self-image and low self-esteem**
- **thinking that everyone who asks something of you or compliments you is not sincere, but instead is trying to use you**
- **carrying a chip on your shoulder**
- **believing that everyone will be looking at you, first and foremost, as an ex-inmate**
- **walking into a job interview with the thought, "I'm not going to get this job"**
- **feeling lost because now you are on your own and must earn whatever you need to survive and live**

[NOTE: There are, of course, many, many other negative mental and emotional attitudes that can attach themselves to you. In addition to those listed above that might fit you, also add others that you feel describe you.]

I Did It and You Can Do It!

I went through most of these when I was on the inside, and certainly carried some of these with me once I was released. Yet I learned how to turn my negative mental and emotional attitudes back to totally positive ... and how to deal with the negative ones whenever they showed up for unexpected visits. This helped me immensely in adjusting to my freedom, in making new friends, in landing a job, and in eventually starting the companies I mentioned in the Introduction.

5 Suggestions for Maintaining a Positive Mental & Emotional Attitude

(1) **LIGHTEN UP YOUR OUTLOOK**. If you only look at prison as a giant cell that keeps you away from the free world, you're going to be constantly depressed, angry, on edge, and bitter. You might as well accept the fact that you're in for awhile, and that your REAL free world is the one in which you now exist.

Play Mental Games

When I was doing time, I played mental games that made it easier for me to accept where I was: I would tell myself that I was on the Island of Captiva for an extended rest and relaxation period; that I was a writer doing several years location research for some book; that I was one of the few who had applied for and been admitted to Ucon University for studies (of the thousands of applicants waiting to get in!). These may seem crazy but they did help me take a negative situation and environment, and turn them into more positive ones. Give it a try -- it'll work!

FUN & SILLINESS HELP. As well as helping me with a more positive outlook, these different scenarios did much to make my situation seem lighter, and thus allowed me to more easily deal with my incarceration. As best as possible, try to inject a little fun and silliness into your prison stay -- it will keep you from getting hard on life, on others, and on yourself.

(2) **MAKE YOUR PRISON EXPERIENCE WORK FOR YOU**. If you let prison hurt you, it will hurt you; if you let prison help you, it will help you. Sound crazy? Let me put it in context of my own time spent in prison.

The Two Choices

When the Court was deciding what to do with me, if they said, "Now Errol, you have a choice: you can either go free or spend some years in prison," which do you think I would have chosen?

24

Certainly, very few of us want to go to prison; it's much more enjoyable to be able to open a refrigerator at 2:30 a.m. and find some leftover chicken to munch on; to pick up a phone and chat for an hour or so; to jump into a car and go to a movie ... I think you catch my drift. But neither I nor you had that second choice, and so off to prison we went.

What I did with my experiences -- experiences to a great part forced on me because I had to be in prison until my sentence was completed -- resulted in many positive involvements and accomplishments (listed earlier) that I was able to use to my and others' benefit on the outside.

> **REMEMBER: If you really do want to start fresh, stay clean, and enjoy all aspects of life once you are free, then you will accept this isolated time as an opportunity ... an opportunity to improve what you have and an opportunity to prepare yourself for life on the outside.**

> **REMEMBER: If you look at prison as a major black mark on your existence that will always be there to hurt you and prevent you from being successful, it will do just that. But if you step back for a moment and grab hold of your prison experience for the good it can do you and the improvement it can do to you, it can become a very positive life experience.**

(3) THE FELLOW INMATES YOU GET TO KNOW ON THE INSIDE ARE IN NO WAY A REFLECTION OF ALL THE PEOPLE ON THE OUTSIDE.

Let's face it: prison has more than its share of fights, killings, rapes, bad feelings between inmates and between inmates and guards/staff, stealing from one another, poor hygiene, illness, racial and religious prejudice, and those who want to continue breaking the law once on the outside. It shouldn't come as a surprise.

25

Prison, by the very reason for its existence, has a fraternity of those individuals who have been judged guilty of a crime or crimes.

The Two Types of Inmates

Certainly, many inmates are imprisoned who are really innocent or made "one mistake" and don't have any intention of coming back. However, there are many others in prison who not only are guilty of what they have been accused, but also have committed other crimes; ran with a crowd that was rough and perhaps also broke the law; never had proper medical care and health training; and often have little more than a high school education, whether completed or not ... and don't really care to improve upon these conditions.

With all these people poured into one confined area, there is going to be more tension, more negatives, and more unpleasantness than one might experience in a lifetime on the outside.

The Candy Store & The City Dump

To bring this down to basics, if you step inside a candy store, there's a much higher concentration of sweetness; if you step into a city dump, there's a much greater concentration of filth, of disease, of bad smells.

Yet neither the candy store nor the city dump are where we spend our daily lives in the free world -- they are concentrated corners of goodness and badness. Prison is the same, with an extremely high concentration of negatives. It is by no means a proper representation of the people you will be meeting on a regular basis in the free world.

> **REMEMBER: While it often seems as if prison is a barrel of sludge into which you were tossed, you do have the option of sinking into it or floating above it.**

Don't Pick Up a Negative Attitude About Other People

This point is extremely important, because I have seen many first time inmates leave with a hatred for blacks, whites, Jews, Catholics, Southerners, Northerners, auto mechanics, runners, weightlifters, gays, straights ... the list is almost endless, and I'm sure you can add your own.

IT CAN REALLY COST YOU... The result is a negative attitude about people that can keep you from landing a job, get you fired from a job, cause you to lose friends and lovers, and perhaps put you back in prison.

Again, keep in mind that your prison world is a concentrated world of people with many more negative ideas, attitudes, and actions than you would normally run into on the outside.

...*OR IT CAN REALLY HELP YOU*. Accept the concept of prison housing concentrations of negative attitudes, and your emotional reaction to the many individual backgrounds you encounter on the outside will be much more positive, and certainly more enjoyable for you and others.

About Prejudice, Hatred, Macho, & Crude

A final note to those of you who entered prison with prejudices, hates, and a disdain for education; who believe that breaking the law on the outside is the only way for you to "attend to business"; or who believe that macho and tough is the only way to survive: any of these negatives will only work AGAINST you, not for you.

ON THE OUTSIDE, YOU NEED TO CO-EXIST WITH THE SYSTEM. While prison allows (and often fosters) prejudice and hatred, accepts those who care little for educational enlightenment, and thrives on a society of macho and crude, employers abhor these qualities in their employees. You would do well to use your prison time to understand the dislikes, hatreds, prejudices, and other negatives that do not sit well with mainstream society (or sometimes the law).

> **REMEMBER: Make a conscious effort to rid yourself of those negatives you have and / or don't adopt those you don't yet have, upgrade your education, and learn to exist on your wits, not fists. The ultimate benefactor of these efforts will be you.**

(4) COMMUNICATE WITH THE OUTSIDE WORLD. One of the best ways to keep a balanced, positive mental and emotional outlook is by keeping in contact with people on the outside.

You most likely have friends and family to whom you can write, with whom you can visit, and, when allowed, call. I strongly recommend that you continue your exchange, for it not only lets you know that you are loved and supported -- so very important when one is incarcerated -- but also gives you the opportunity to stay current on events and conditions in the free world.

Personal Correspondence

I also realize that you, like some fellow inmates I knew, might have no one on the outside to whom you can write. Do not despair: there are organizations that exist to help you find a pen pal; sometimes newspapers or magazines allow free listings from inmates looking for someone who would like to correspond. (CAUTION: Be careful of any ads or letters that request money. There are people and organizations that prey on inmates. See Chapter 11, pages 413-415, for details on this.)

Ask your prison buddies, notice the classifieds in your newspapers. When you get an address of an organization, magazine, or newspaper that you can write, take the time to do so. Outside contact will improve your mental and emotional response to doing time.

Prison Organizations, Clubs, & Activities

Also, many prisons have various organizations in which inmates can involve themselves. Groups such as the Jaycees, Lifers Club, Toastmasters, sports teams, and others often invite outside groups or individuals to participate, be a guest, give a speech, or present a program. This is another opportunity for you to make contact with one or more persons from the other side of the walls.

Making Contacts for Your Job Search

It is especially important that you use pen and ink to begin exploring resources that can possibly benefit you once free.

Examples: schools to continue the education you began in prison; job possibilities; various contacts to assist you in a job search, finding room and board, etc.; and a variety of information to help you make a smoother transition back into society. The specifics of whom to contact and why are covered in detail in Chapter 2.

(5) **SETTING GOALS**. When you exist within a prison environment, it is very easy to forget about goals and objectives, and just do things and live life on a day-to-day basis.

<u>*PRISON TIME MAKES IT DIFFICULT TO SET GOALS*</u>. No matter if your sentence is one year, five years, or 15 years, you have an idea of what each of your days will be like, day after day, week after week, month after month. And too often, the daily regimen of prison can make it seem as if nothing really gets accomplished, save for one more day less of the time you have to serve. All the more reason to set goals. (The longer your sentence, of course, the less you feel like setting goals: the light at the end of the tunnel seems much farther away. Your approach? This only gives you more time to set -- and accomplish -- more goals, whether small or large.)

REMEMBER: By establishing certain objectives you wish to accomplish, and a time frame in which these accomplishments will take place, you not only keep your mind busy and emotionally feel better about yourself, but you are developing the type of strengths and skills that are admired by employers and looked for in their employees.

Setting Goals Can Help You in Many Ways

Time management, organization, project coordination, research ability, adeptness at finishing a task, and determination are some of the areas in which setting goals can help you.

MAKING YOUR TIME GO FASTER. In addition, when you set goals you start making the time you have to do actually seem less because you are dividing it up into smaller, manageable segments. If, for example, you are serving a five year sentence with no goals, those five years appear very long, indeed.

However, if those five years are divided into goals of reading 100 books, completing your GED in two years, beginning work on a college degree (whether formally or informally), getting your waist down to a size 34, learning to play chess, acquiring a vocational skill, and becoming a starting member of the prison basketball team, your time spent in prison will seem very full, with the time going by much faster than you would have thought.

Achieving Your Goals Takes Continued Effort

It will never be easy to reach all your goals; they will take much effort on your part. There will be times when achieving some of your goals may seem impossible; often, you'll feel that you just don't have the time to reach your goals; and sometimes, your self-motivation will get stuck. But setting and achieving goals are an everyday part of life for successful people, and if you want to succeed after prison -- if you TRULY want to succeed -- then now is the time to not only start goal setting but to make certain that you continually strive to achieve those goals. To help you get started, there is a detailed discussion on Goal Setting in Chapter 11, pages 394-397. Read these pages carefully, read them thoroughly: the better you understand how to set and achieve goals, the easier it will be for you to do so.

Keeping a Record of Your Goals

Keep an accurate record of your goals, the time you have allotted to meet each one, and any problems or complications you have in meeting them (or, for that matter, any positive insights you learn along the way). Fill out the Goal Planning Worklist (Chapter 11, page 396) with your goals on them. This way, you can always see the progress you've made and perhaps better understand any difficulties you have in reaching your goals.

If You're Not Sure About Your Goals

If you are not sure as to what are realistically obtainable goals, don't hesitate to talk with a counselor or staff member in whom you feel you can confide. To set unrealistic, unobtainable goals is very frustrating, and will only bring your mental and emotional attitudes down into the negative side.

REMEMBER: Setting goals is like collecting books: acquiring them is easy; opening each one and sticking with it until it's completed is the hard part.

☺☺☺☺☺☺☺

Put these suggestions into action!

If you fully put into practice the suggestions and ideas outlined in this chapter, the time you spend in prison will be positive and go a long way in preparing you to find a job once you are released. But it's not going to happen until you decide that you want it to happen -- it takes work, dedication, and tossing away any "vacation mentality" you might have.

As I've said, I've been where you now are, so I know that you can do it ... if you really want to!

REMEMBER: There's only one way to look at a prison sentence, and that's positively. You've been given an opportunity to change your life; to begin the vocational, educational, physical, and mental / emotional changes necessary for a successful (and legal) life on the outside -- do it!

Chapter 2

What To Do When There are Six Months or Less Left

"You may be disappointed if you fail, but you are doomed if you don't try."

Beverly Sills, American opera singer

● INTRODUCTION ●

WHEN SHOULD YOU BEGIN YOUR JOB SEARCH?

One of the questions I'm asked quite frequently by inmates is, "When should I start getting ready for my job search?" In truth, your job search should begin as soon as your sentence begins ... no matter if that sentence is many years or a few years. Certainly, if you have to serve more than five years, getting ready for the job search may not only seem quite a ways off but perhaps a bit crazy at this point! Yet, as was mentioned in Chapter 1, if you begin to set and strive to reach various goals, begin to work on bettering yourself, as your sentence grows shorter you'll not only be better prepared when you finally leave but these efforts will help the time go by much quicker and easier.

In the last year of your sentence, of course, is when the real job search preparation activity should begin. Time is growing very short at this point, and you need to begin seriously doing those things that are crucial in anyone's job search. And in the last six months (or less) of your sentence, your job search activity must reach its peak, for you'll be out of prison before you know it ... and you want to be as fully prepared as possible for that day.

SO ... WHAT <u>DO</u> YOU DO IF YOU HAVE LESS THAN SIX MONTHS TO GO OR ARE NEWLY RELEASED?

If you've done 12 years, six months left on your sentence seems like nothing; but if you've served two or three years, six months could seem like an eternity. Yet with only six months (or less) before you again face the real world of needing to earn a living, many inmates begin to panic: they haven't done anything yet in terms of their job search; they've taken a transition or employability class in prison but haven't yet acted on it; or while they have been working on their job search, they're still quite frustrated at the time it seems to take to do everything and with the lack of solid feedback they're receiving.

And if you're newly released and reading this book, you're probably in somewhat of a panic state, too, because you didn't put in as much effort as you should have in your job search while incarcerated. This has happened to MANY ex-inmates; don't feel that you're alone.

PUT EVERYTHING INTO GEAR ... NOW!

The past, of course, cannot be undone, so whether you're newly released or have six months or less to go on your sentence, NOW Is the time to get serious about your career search ... and approaching your life with the attitude that you ARE going to stay out, you ARE going to be successful, and you ARE going to live a life free of crime and any addictions.

The first thing: don't worry, but rather make a decision that you are going to put into play the suggestions, information, resources, programs, and ideas contained in this book. Whether you have six months or one month left, or are on the outside, the only difference between you and others who have been working on their job search for some time is that you've got some catching up to do ... and you CAN do it!

You should, of course, have been taking care of or need to take care of everything discussed in Chapter 1. This means establishing some solid goals and getting rid of some negatives, as well as developing very positive habits ... habits that now must be used to start focusing on your job and career choices.

It's Time to Hire Yourself!

Preparing for your career search means concentration, time, and effort. Too often, job searchers take an approach of, "oh yeah, I'll do that in my spare time," or, if they have decided to pursue the preparation and search with vigor, little attention is given to structured, definite goals. The result is often disappointment, frustration, and a very low percentage of success.

While winding down the time until you are released, there are two areas that you need to work on:

(1) Personal skills and strengths

(2) Various aspects of the job search

These must be started on NOW if you want your first few days and weeks of job searching to go as smooth and as problem-free as possible

#1
PERSONAL SKILLS & STRENGTHS

YOUR JOB DESCRIPTION. During these six months (or less), you must take the attitude that you are hiring yourself as an employee in your one-person firm, and your only job description for the position is:

Thoroughly prepare and research within defined goals and timetables so that employment may be gained in the shortest time possible with the least amount of problems and the greatest amount of satisfaction.

A DETAILED LOOK AT DEVELOPING THESE STRENGTHS. No, this job description does not read very easy because it's a big assignment. Yet knowing that you have to "go to work" each day and put in a specific number of hours or complete a certain number of objectives will do several things for you, EACH related to the interpersonal skills that are so important when looking for and successfully landing employment:

SELF-MOTIVATION

Self-motivation is a key to success on the outside. While prison life, by its very nature, means structure beyond that which you (probably) ever imagined, it also means (very often) more emphasis on a structure of when to eat, sleep, play, go to work assignments, and the like. The system is TELLING you what and where to go.

Even if you have enrolled in an educational program, there are instructors giving you assignments that you know must be completed within a certain time frame.

REMEMBER: In deciding to thoroughly prepare yourself for the task of landing a job once released, YOU AND ONLY YOU are the SOLE motivator and taskmaster deciding how much effort will be put into the career preparation, when you will do your research and planning, and how consistent you will be.

<u>*Why Inmates Have a Problem with Self-Motivation*</u>

Unfortunately, it is true that most incarcerated individuals -- when on the outside, prior to their arrest -- have had a problem with imposing structure on their lives and managing their time efficiently.

To the contrary of what many people think, prison only strengthens this disorganization and haphazard daily approach to living.

<u>LAZINESS OF THE MIND</u>. Why? By giving you little opportunity to practice or train in self-motivation, time management, setting goals, and organization, a laziness of the mind sets in where we get used to having others determine our life for us. You may not like it, but nonetheless this IS prison and our choice in this matter is very limited.

REMEMBER: The more you motivate yourself within prison walls to accomplish your goal of landing a job outside those walls, the more you will gain one of the most important qualities that employers look for in an employee: self-motivation.

Self-Motivation Equals Success

The employees who come in early and leave late because they WANT to complete the job; the employees who learn more and study harder because they WANT to get ahead; the employees who WANT to be a success based on their best quality of work, not quantity of months or years with a company -- these are the persons who know how to spell P-R-O-F-E-S-S-I-O-N-A-L S-U-C-C-E-S-S.

REMEMBER: Professional success goes a long way in giving us personal success as well.

ACCEPTING STRUCTURE / DEVELOPING TIME MANAGEMENT

Somewhat of an extension of Self-Motivation is getting yourself used to the work time structure you will encounter (and need to embrace) in looking for a job and once you are working on the outside. Certainly, your job search should be structured so that you put in X amount of hours each day, and every day make it a point to follow up on item a, item b, etc. Also, depending on the type of employment field you are seeking or enter, the specified hours of that job will vary, as will other structures imposed on you. For each employer has specific guidelines, rules, and a "game plan" (just as each prison, jail, halfway house, and other penal institutions have theirs).

As an example: a computer programmer usually has a more definite and regular time schedule each day, while a salesperson or copywriter has hours that often vary day-to-day. Each, however, will have additional structures imposed on his or her duties and employment by a supervisor, department head, president, etc.

You Can Always Benefit From Time Management

In EACH instance, however, the need to EFFECTIVELY plan time is IMPERATIVE, and you will find that the most successful of all employees -- no matter what the profession -- are also successful in their management of time. (In Chapter 11, pages 406-409, Time Management is discussed in detail.) And this time plan is a plan that THEY have devised, not one that their company put together for them.

Learn How to Manage Your Time from the Experiences of Prison Life

It's already been mentioned that prison life, to a great degree, imposes time management on you. Yet there are still a number of activities and situations that do allow for you to manage time, a great start for that time management you'll need in your job search, on the job, and in life.

Some of these prison activities and situations that offer you opportunities to better manage your time include:

- studying for classes
- exercise and workout sessions
- writing letters, keeping a journal
- personal reading (novels, magazines, etc.)
- fun or game activities
- self-study (in the library / your cell, room, or dorm)
- coordinating audio / visual materials for the institution
- correspondence courses
- volunteer maintenance activities (e.g., taking care of flower beds, coordinating clubs)
- serving as a tutor or aide to another inmate on your own

How Do You React to Structured Time?

Observe YOUR daily life inside, and then circle ONE of the following statements that best describes your reaction to structure inside prison (or outside, if you have recently been released):

(1) I use only the structure that is given me by the institution I am in to guide my daily life patterns

(2) I use the structure that is given me by the institution I am in, as well as some of my own self-imposed structure, to guide my daily life patterns

(3) I use the structure that is given me by the institution I am in, equally combined with my own self-imposed structure, to guide my daily life patterns

(4) I fight the structure of the institution whenever I can, and only use my own self-imposed structure

THE ANSWER. Here, the ideal approach to doing time would be 3, with 2 in second place. In these last six months, you must begin to start preparing your mind and habits to an employment environment on the outside that functions on a balance between company regulations and structure and YOUR guidelines and structure.

The Jump From Prison Structure to Free World Structure

Unfortunately, the jump for most newly-released ex-felons from being in an institution to working in the free world is a shock, and one of the major shocks is in trying to adjust to an environment where you must set your own time schedules, as well as work within those awaiting you. Yet it is something that must be done if you want to succeed on the outside, so start managing your time now -- it'll serve you very well on the job and in life!

> **REMEMBER: If you are not used to setting structure and working within structure, and if you have not started to prepare yourself for it while doing time, it is much more difficult to adjust to when outside.**

PROCRASTINATION

Procrastination is a fancy, one word way of saying putting something off until another time. It's important that you cast off the attitude of, "Well, I can always do it tomorrow."

Why Prison Increases Procrastination

In prison, each day seems to go on forever, because the next day and next day and on and on all seem to be pretty much the same. If you are reading a book and decide not to finish a chapter, you can always do it ... tomorrow; if you are running the track and have promised yourself to jog five miles but you've only done four, you can always run five ... tomorrow; if you don't like a course you're taking and drop out, you can always take it again ... next semester (or next time it's offered); if you start writing a letter or a story or a poem and are just not in the mood to complete it, you can always finish it ... tomorrow.

Two Interesting Facts Concerning Procrastination

(1) "PRE-INMATES" TEND TO BE PROCRASTINATORS. Not surprisingly, you'll find that most inmates were procrastinators before their conviction. Whether looking for a job, paying some bills, getting additional education, resolving family or business problems, breaking ties with bad habits / illegal activities, or planning for the future, there was a tendency to put these off until that safe haven of "I'll do it tomorrow."

(2) SUCCESSFUL PEOPLE DON'T PROCRASTINATE. Successful people -- in job, in family, in career, in education -- share one common trait: they are NOT procrastinators. While it may take them a few extra minutes or hours and some extra effort, their "take-care-of-it-now" attitude results in improved efficiency and productivity.

Employers Do Not Like Procrastinators

Procrastination is a trait that employers are definitely not looking for in their applicants or employees; employers do not have much patience to put up with it. No matter the job, procrastination is a definite negative and a guarantee that very soon you will be out of a job.

REMEMBER: If you combine Self-Motivation with Structure and Time Management, you will find that it will be very difficult for you to put things off "just because" !

CONTROLLING YOUR TEMPER / HANDLING STRESS

Doing time means many stress factors coming down on you that, for the most part, you didn't have to deal with on a regular basis when in the free world.

6 Common Factors in Prison That Increase Stress

(1) Being locked up and not able to go or do when you want
(2) Being told what, when, where, and how to do and not to do
(3) Having to fight, avoid a fight, get even, protect what's yours
(4) Lack of sex / being forced to have sex
(5) Learning of bad news that came about as a direct result of you being locked up. (Examples: a lover, husband/wife, friends, parent, or child leaving you, splitting up with you, or telling you they "want nothing more to do with you"; finding out that the job you had before being locked up is no longer available to you; learning that someone close is very ill and you could not be near them; or learning of the death of someone dear to you and not being able to attend his/her funeral)
(6) Being separated from someone very close to you: son / daughter, husband / wife, lover, mother / father, best friend, etc.

4 Stress Factors That Would Be Minor Outside But Sometimes Become Very Big Inside Prison

There are other stress factors, of course, and many of them would be minor if they occurred in the free world. However, they often become major and result in harm to us or others when they happen in prison. These four are the most common:

(1) **THE TV.** Someone changes the TV channel while another is watching it (usual result: a fight or someone getting shanked).

(2) **LOSING OUT.** Someone is snitched out; you lose a work detail you liked (usual result: many angry words, possibly a fight or stabbing, perhaps revenge).

(3) **LACK OF FUNDS.** Don't have enough money to buy a snack (Little Debby, a Coke, etc.) or a smoke (usual result: many angry words, a surly mood, perhaps stealing, maybe breaking something).

(4) **NO MAIL.** Not receiving any mail (usual result: depression, sullen mood, sarcastic attitude towards those who do receive mail).

REMEMBER: You must learn to adapt, to improvise, to overcome on the outside, so you'd better start now.

Keeping a Record of Those Items That Stress You Out

It's important that you keep a record of all the items that stress you out while in prison (and those that come to mind that give you stress on the outside, too). To do this accurately, use the worksheet that appears on the next page ... but give yourself several days or weeks to jot these stress factors down. Why? Some of the situations, people, or thoughts that give you stress may not pop up in the course of a few days; the more time you give yourself, the more accurate your record will be.

Improving Your Ability to Deal with Stress

The large or the small stress items that set us off and are listed on the previous two pages are only some. List below ALL the stress factors that you feel act negatively on you while doing time. (Choose from the ones I've listed, as well as others you may feel affect you but I have not listed.) Use this list as a goal of what to try and overcome and what to step back from, asking yourself the question: "Just how important is this in my life and is it really worth getting bent out of shape over?"

ITEM THAT STRESSES YOU OUT [e.g.: *being locked up in prison*	NOTES ON OVERCOMING IT *take classes, read more, join clubs, exercise more]*
1)	
2)	
3)	
4)	
5)	
6)	
7)	
8)	
9)	
10)	
11)	
12)	
13)	
14)	

IMPROVE YOUR "PEOPLE STRENGTHS"

During these last six months, you have the opportunity to practice and perfect your manners, your interpersonal skills, your speech, your listening ability -- all CRUCIAL in your job search and in keeping and progressing on the job.

THE "SAMENESS SYNDROME." Prison is not a place where the "odd man (or woman) out" has it easy. There is a conformity that is, at first, imposed upon you through the "Sameness Syndrome": same uniform, same haircut, same food, same schedule, same people, and / or same activities (each depending on the individual institution's approach to sameness). These you have little control over, and so make the best of it.

TAKING THE EASY WAY OUT. Yet this Sameness Syndrome spills over into the way you conduct yourself, and usually you begin to go the path of least resistance. This means that it is much easier to flow and exist with the way the bulk of your fellow inmates do and say things, rather than go your own way. This often leads to a breakdown and disappearing of the "who" of you, the individuality of you as you existed on the outside, prior to prison.

> **REMEMBER: Now, with six months or less left on your sentence, it's time to do some serious sculpturing and re-sculpturing of your dimensions, profile, structure, and foundations so they fit nicely into what most of mainstream society appreciates and accepts.**

The 3 Basic People Skills

#1
MANNERS

Most prisons are not satellite offices for Mr. and Ms. Manners. There is a limited amount of time to eat, a limited amount of time to play, and a limited amount of leisure activities. Combine this with the increased stress and tension I mentioned earlier, and you'll find that manners have a tendency of going downhill in prison.

Examples of Bad Prison Manners

This prison environment translates into more demands for something, rather than polite asking; eating fast with large bites; talking with mouths full of food; sometimes not knowing that what you are doing is not considered acceptable manners in the outside business world; making sexual jokes or comments about someone or just openly staring at some part of someone's body. There are others, of course, and you can add them to this list.

Examples of Good Manners / Being Polite

Good manners can be found anywhere ... including prison. Some examples: words and phrases such as "Thank you," "Please," and "You're Welcome" when appropriate; not talking with food in your mouth; opening / holding doors for others; not cutting in line; not using crude language; sending a "thank you" note when someone has done you a favor or given you a gift; showing respect for all; never picking your teeth in public. There are many, many other examples, certainly, that you can tack on to these.

It's Time To Improve Your Manners

What to do? Begin by making a list of those manners or traits you have that you know could use improvement and those that you don't have but need. (Use the "Manners Worksheets," pp. 48-49). After this is done, go to a teacher or counselor (or someone whom you feel you can be open with and also trust) and ask for his / her input. If this person gives you additional items, add these to your list.

> **REMEMBER: You want to blend into society as a positive member of the community, not stand out by being one who doesn't belong in the community.**

Observe Others With Good and Bad Manners

There are counselors, officers, staff, administrators, and visitors from whom you can learn something about manners merely by observing the way they act. And not only can you pick up positive traits, but perhaps observe negative manners that make you feel uncomfortable, and thus give you an additional lesson in what NOT to do.

Read About Manners

Read books, magazine articles, and newspaper stories that may focus on manners in the outside world. Since there is so much written about manners for people who already live outside of prison, it obviously is very important. It becomes especially important to anyone on the inside.

Prison Codes and Manners

There is, of course, an interesting side note to this. Prison has its own (sometimes) strange and unusual codes (manners), very often just the opposite of what those in the free world perceive as typical behavior behind bars.

The unwritten rule of "Please." The prison in which I was in had an unwritten rule amongst the inmates that anything asked for ALWAYS had to have the word "please" in the asking sentence.

How it got started or why, I don't know and no one else knew, but it was there. And it was a help: this constant emphasis on using "please" had a positive effect on many inmates who were not used to using "please" or "thank you."

Each institution is different, and you need to look and pick up what you can use as a POSITIVE from the unwritten manners code in your institution ... and definitely leave behind those that are unacceptable on the outside.

The Manners Worksheets

Remember the list of manners I suggested you make (page 46)? Now it's time to improve upon those manners ... and acquire those you don't have. List and rate your manners on this page (if you need more space, use separate sheet of paper); grade yourself according to the points listed. On the facing page, list those manners you don't have. You now have an overview as to your manners pluses and manners minuses.

Refer to these worksheets every so often and regrade yourself -- with each improvement, you are taking another step closer towards having the manners that are acceptable in the outside business world.

I -- Manners You Now Have

MANNER	RATING	ACTION TO IMPROVE
	(1-10; 1 is worst, 10 is best)	
[example: Courtesy	*4*	*Use "please," etc. more often]*
1) _____		
2) _____		
3) _____		
4) _____		
5) _____		
6) _____		
7) _____		
8) _____		
9) _____		
10) _____		

2 -- Manners You Don't Have

You'll note that there are more spaces for manners you don't have than on the previous worksheet, "Manners You Now Have." The reason for this, unfortunately, is that too often inmates are long on poor manners and short on positive ones. Be honest in listing these that you need to acquire (or have temporarily abandoned): the more you face this gap head on, the quicker you'll be prepared with those manners employers and others in the free world appreciate.

MANNER	WHY YOU DON'T HAVE IT	ACTION TO GET IT
[e.g.: don't talk with mouth full	*In a rush to speak; never thought much about it*	*Make conscious effort to not do it]*
1) _____		_____
2) _____		_____
3) _____		_____
4) _____		_____
5) _____		_____
6) _____		_____
7) _____		_____
8) _____		_____
9) _____		_____
10) _____		_____
11) _____		_____
12) _____		_____
13) _____		_____
14) _____		_____

#2
INTERPERSONAL SKILLS

This is a rather broad category taking into account so many aspects of your living and working with others. Examples would include:

● following directions
● your sense of humor
● type of personality (outgoing or withdrawn)
● selling an idea to another
● confidence level
● handling rejection or defeat
● working as a team member
● leadership ability
● establishing a quick rapport
● developing a feeling of trust

Interpersonal Skills Worksheet

There are many others, of course. On the Interpersonal Skills Worksheet on the next page, list those skills you have and give yourself a grade (as indicated). This will give you a good overall look at where you need to improve the most.

Next, list those interpersonal skills that you don't yet have but would like to have. As you put more effort into developing these and improving on those you have, go back to the worksheet periodically and give yourself an upgraded examination, in the space provided. This will allow you to map your progress.

REMEMBER: The more you develop your interpersonal skills, the more you will come across to an employer, employment agency, personnel representative, or networking contact as an individual who would work well in an employment situation.

Interpersonal Skills Worksheet

Interpersonal Skils You Now Have

NAME OF INTERPERSONAL SKILL [e.g.: *following directions*	RATING (1-10; 1 is worst, 10 is best) *5*	ACTION TO IMPROVE IT *listen better; don't rush]*
1)		
2)		
3)		
4)		
5)		
6)		
7)		
8)		
9)		
10)		

Interpersonal Skills You Don't Have

NAME OF INTERPERSONAL SKILL [e.g.: *sense of humor*	WHY YOU DON'T HAVE IT *prison too depressing*	ACTION TO GET IT *accept time; lighten up]*
1)		
2)		
3)		
4)		
5)		
6)		

#3
COMMUNICATIONS

Although communications primarily consists of speaking, writing, and listening, I've placed primary emphasis here on speaking. This is done for a practical reason: while you will, of course, always need to write and always need to listen, people define themselves more through their ability to speak than other area of communications (unless you happen to be a professional writer or a professional musician!). Additionally, while you are presented with sample resumes and cover letters in chapters 4 and 5, you'll have to speak for yourself during the interview; I want you to do an outstanding job of presenting yourself!

In Chapter 11, pages 397-400, I cover additional aspects of improving public speaking. (Also see Chapter 11, pages 396-397, for writing, and 401-402, for listening. For additional communications listings, see "Communications" in the index.)

I've broken speech down into two areas: the use of foul language and the improper or poor use of language. (Use a grammar guide to review the basics of your language.)

Don't Use Foul Language

There are two types of languages spoken in prison: traditional English (or Spanish or other primary languages) and a second language I call Mo'fo -- foul language. You are familiar with English, Spanish, etc., but many inmates also speak Mo'fo.

Some examples of Mo'fo:

- "I don't want any of that mo'fo food!"
- "Get out of my mo'fo face, man!"
- "You nothin' but a mo'fo fool!"
- "That's a mo'fo great program!"
- "My mo'fo parole came through!"

MO'FO IS NOT ACCEPTABLE IN THE BUSINESS WORLD. This is no big deal in prison; we speak the language of the country we're in, and Mo'fo is spoken a great deal in the country called Prison. But once outside, the ONLY language you'll be expected to speak is English (and/or Spanish or other primary language, depending on the community in which you'll be living).

The use of Mo'fo is especially strong amongst ex-inmates during their first month out of prison. Why? Well, the body may be outside but for many the mind is still inside. Thus you need be especially careful and mindful of what comes out of your mouth, for once the words leave, you can't call them back. And isn't it much better to say what you mean and what most people in the free world find acceptable, rather than saying something that could embarrass you or cause others to form a negative opinion of you?

Mo'fo (and slang), while certainly never the best language to use, is more acceptable when you're with friends in a casual, social situation (if everyone else speaks Mo'fo!), but when spoken in business, Mo'fo' IMMEDIATELY takes away from your professionalism, education, and intelligence -- and certainly turns many people off.

> **REMEMBER: The use of foul language in any phase of the job search and on the job is not acceptable. Use standard English (or the standard form of your native language, if different from English) to explain, to complain, to present, to argue, to sell, to discuss, to teach, and to order: when you do, you will always be accepted as a professional.**

Don't Use Language Considered Improper for Business

In addition, those parts of the English language that are considered non-standard or slang or too casual should NOT be used.

Examples:

- "ain't" (is a non-standard, non-acceptable word)
- "irregardless" (is not a word)
- "gonna" ("going"; do not drop the "ing" on words that end with "ing")
- "They is going" (should be: "They are going")
- "I is playing basketball" (should be: "I am playing basketball")
- "Is you going to Visitors' Day?" (should be: "Are you going to Visitors' Day?")
- "Don't you know nothing? (should be: "Don't you know anything?")
- "Is you goin' home?" (Should be: "Are you going home?")

REMEMBER: If you like cutting, slicing, dicing, and butchering your image, use cheap, second-rate English -- it'll do the trick every time.

If Learning English as a Second Language

When English is not your primary (native) language, mistakes will naturally occur when you speak in English until your command of English is solid. Not to worry. You are making an honest attempt to learn the language that most businesses in the USA are conducted in -- English. What is important, however, is that you take the time to learn English correctly -- the better you master your ability to speak in English, the easier you will be understood by others.

● VARIOUS ASPECTS OF THE JOB SEARCH ●

While prison certainly presents you with more complicated obstacles while looking for a job than those seeking employment in the free world, there is one item that -- unfortunately -- holds true for the vast majority of people looking for a job, whether behind bars or not:

YOU'VE GOT TIME. Again, you have a negative situation -- being in prison -- that you can turn into a very positive experience those outside seeking employment would love to have: plenty of time to fully prepare for the career search.

> **REMEMBER: Most job searchers start their job search too late, rather than giving themselves ample time to prepare -- and time can't be bought, made up, borrowed, stolen, or created.**

DISCOVERING & DEVELOPING YOUR JOB STRENGTHS: AVOIDING PAST JOB MISTAKES

For many inmates, this is the first concrete step toward the job search, as it will help you decide what type of work or position you'd like.

How Do You View Your Life?

Depending on what your life was like prior to prison, or how it's taken shape since being in prison, you will have learned to look at every experience as one of the following:

(1) a positive experience
(2) think that there are negative and positive experiences
(3) believe that most of everything that's happened to you or that you've been involved in is negative

Which one is correct? It's simple:

> **REMEMBER: Every life experience must be looked upon as a positive experience that offers you experience, wisdom, insight, and a better understanding of yourself.**

This relates directly to you being in prison. In Chapter 1, I spoke of accepting the time you are in prison as an OPPORTUNITY. To give you an idea as to what I mean, I'd like to tell you about one of my prison buddies.

THE STORY OF CHICKEN MAN

Chicken Man was 53 years old, had little hair and even less teeth, and had spent most of his adult life in and out of prison. His attitude was one of, "Hell, it's nice in here; I get three squares, don't need no clothes, and can sleep a bunch. And when I get out, I've always got my profession."

His "profession," as he called it, was shoplifting on a grand scale: TVS, jewelry, VCRs, radios, computer software, etc. This time he had two months left on a six-year sentence, and all Chicken Man talked about was the new equipment that had been created and manufactured while he was on the inside, and thus more goods (so he reasoned) for him to pick from once he was released.

His formal education? Not much: two years of high school, and then he dropped out. His employment history -- that which was legal -- consisted of gigs as a gas station attendant, janitor, deliveryman, pharmacy clerk, cashier, and general laborer. He also had held a job for two years many years ago -- as a parts assistant in a plant -- but that ended when the company went out of business.

In prison, Chicken Man hustled to make a few bucks or to get favors: stealing, being a sex toy for whomever was interested, shining shoes, hiring out to do favors for others, selling his medication. (He was an epileptic, and pretended to take his medication, then would build up a stash for other inmates to purchase. He didn't care if he had a seizure, only that he made it through another day).

The "Iceberg Syndrome"

On the surface, it seemed like Chicken Man had little to offer an employer: not much education, no solid experience in any one field, a prison record, and the mind of someone always looking to con, to "pull a fast one." And, unfortunately, this is how not only Chicken Man would depict himself, but also how he came across to just about every employer with whom Chicken Man might come in contact.

Why? The answer is obvious. People are guilty of what I call "The Iceberg Syndrome," that is, only seeing what is immediately visible to them, and not taking the time to look below the surface.

Would You Hire Chicken Man?

Ask yourself the following question, and then answer it: Would you hire someone for a responsible job when all he/she presented you in the way of qualifications was a group of negatives? Of course not!

But if that same person presented positives as well, would you be more inclined to look at the person as a possible employee? The answer here is a definite ... MAYBE, which is not a "yes," but certainly is better than "no."

HOW TO TURN NEGATIVES INTO POSITIVES

Where do we get the positives from Chicken Man's life? After all, I told you he didn't graduate from high school, never held any job of substance or for any length of time, and had a long prison record. The answer is very important:

> **REMEMBER: No matter what you did before prison or in prison that society would consider a negative, you must look beneath the surface to find the positives that you can use in a legal employment situation on the outside.**

It's Time To Take Advantage of What Prison Can Offer

Why are you in prison? Because a judge or a jury found you guilty of committing some crime (at this point, it makes little difference if you were innocent or guilty; the notch of being an ex-inmate is yours), and now you are being punished by society. Since being in prison is part of who you are and what you are, use the time and experiences to your advantage.

EVERYTHING YOU DO IN PRISON HAS POSITIVES

Let's be honest: being in prison does not always produce Sunday school picnics, long walks in the park, or strolls along the beach. You do whatever you need to do to survive, to make the time go by.

This not only means activities that are offered by the prison -- basketball, arts & crafts, library, clubs, counseling and bible study sessions, etc. -- but possibly hustling, hurting, doing drugs and sex, and sometimes killing.

Obviously, the last few items mentioned are not exactly what a potential employer wants to hear about you, but we both know that prison is NOT the real world of business or life on the outside, that there are different rules of survival, and that we sometimes do things in prison that we would not think of doing when on the outside.

> **REMEMBER: All positives -- whether from acceptable or unacceptable prison activities -- can help you better determine the type of job for which you are suited and will enjoy ... and can certainly help you land and keep that job!**

> **REMEMBER: In preparing yourself for employment on the outside, you must consider <u>everything</u> you did on the inside, and pull out from each as many strengths as possible.**

ACCEPTABLE PRISON ACTIVITIES & THEIR POSITIVES

Let's look at some examples of prison activities that are taken for granted as acceptable and see what strengths (positives; assets) you can pull from these:

Involvement in an Athletic Event or Sport

Team player; competitive spirit; quick to handle unexpected situations; can make snap decisions; display confidence; self-motivation; quick learner; outgoing personality; display much concentration; handle stress well; a leader; good physical condition; adapt easily to new situations; can turn a negative situation around.

Arts & Crafts

Work well in team or individual situation; handle responsibility; need little or no supervision; very good with hands; detail-oriented; a fast learner; will put in whatever time is needed to get the job done; emphasis on quality; can handle several tasks at the same time; not easily distracted by outside noises or activities; open to other ideas.

Library

Enjoy learning; excel at research; work extremely well on own and with little or no supervision; open to a variety of ideas and suggestions; detail-oriented; neat and orderly; do not mind clerical responsibilities; proficient at helping others; good problem solver; know when to talk & when to listen; familiar with personal computer; can work well in an unexciting or isolated work environment.

Clubs

Speak well before large or small audiences; a leader; can follow directions; know how to delegate responsibilities; can be counted on for completing assigned tasks; work well under deadlines; interact with all ages, backgrounds, and educational levels; know how to construct and balance a budget; skilled at sales and presentations; make others feel comfortable in new situations; handle several tasks at the same time; organized; self-motivated and know how to motivate others; can efficiently run a meeting; good sense of humor with an outgoing personality.

Counseling & Bible Study Sessions

Not afraid to ask questions; interact with a variety of ages, backgrounds, and educational levels; a leader; a good listener; can explain information and thoughts clearly; follow directions; open to new ideas; organized; know how to lead meetings; solid writing skills; enjoy making others feel welcome; can admit to and learn from making mistakes; enjoy discussions with others.

Educational Courses / Peer Counseling / Tutor / Educational Aide

Good ability to teach / train others; work well with all ages and backgrounds; a team worker; handle responsibilities well in supervised or unsupervised situation; a leader; handle stressful situations well; know how to develop and implement various programs; computer hardware / software experience; Internet / Web Site abilities; experienced in videography, video editing; handle a variety of office support tasks; good listener, speaker, writer; demonstrate much patience; enjoy learning; good at research and resourcing; follow directions well; can be depended on to get the job done; punctual.

Work Assignments

This category offers so many possibilities that any list I give you would go on for an entire page ... and then some! Look over all the possibilities offered on these pages, then begin listing them from your assignment.

NOT ALL STRENGTHS APPLY TO YOU

There are many other strengths, of course, that I'm sure you can think of for each of the above activities. Also, not all positives will apply to you; these are merely possibilities.

DON'T FORGET POSITIVES FROM NON-ORGANIZED ACTIVITIES!

Other activities that are not so much organized but rather just a routine part of the day can also offer positives that you can use when looking for a job. Cleaning your room, going to mess (dinner, lunch, etc.), following the rules of your institution all present you with additional opportunities for gaining positives.

Examples of Strengths From Non-Organized Activities

Following directions, being organized and structured, having manners, handling stress and time management, a team worker, setting goals, and self motivation. Again, all of these may not fit. Think of additional everyday, non-formal or organized activities in which you are involved and the positives (assets or strengths) you gain from them.

REMEMBER: Look at all positive activities as an opportunity to improve vocationally, educationally, physically, and mentally / emotionally .

UNACCEPTABLE ACTIVITIES AND THEIR POSITIVES

Again: You Must Take a Positive from Everything!

NONE of the following activities are acceptable to an employer, nor would you find them acceptable in others. HOWEVER: if you can help your future by dipping into your past, then you've got another resource to mine. But remember: you will NOT be doing these activities outside IF you intend on landing / keeping a job AND staying out of prison. Also: these criminal activities are those that were planned or thought out, NOT from so-called "crimes of passion" where emotion simply took over.

NOTE: None of the unacceptable activities that follow should be engaged in. They are listed ONLY to help you better understand how negatives can also offer positives. Certainly, if any of these ALREADY fit you, fine; use them.

REMEMBER: Before you toss any of your past, illegal activities into a memory wastebasket, always first look for and squeeze out the positives they offer.

These Are For You to Learn From, Not to Share!

While employers are very happy to hear about positive activities in which you were involved, they seldom wish to hear about those that are negative or unacceptable (except for their own fascination, which you never want to appease) ... no matter how many positives you may have learned or gained from them.

So don't forget: **unless specifically asked about an unacceptable activity of yours, keep these activities and the positives you gained from them to yourself!**

Unacceptable Negatives and Their Possible Positives

Hustling (drugs, services, goods, etc.)

Good ability to sell; creative; can meet a need; keen marketing sense; do not get easily disappointed; effective verbal communicator; can talk with a wide variety of ages, backgrounds, and educational levels; know how to close a sale; a quick wit; can make decisions when needed; good at recordkeeping / bookkeeping; a leader; can handle a variety of tasks or lines at the same time; strong self-motivation; high degree of confidence; adept at scrounging and resourcing; skilled at customer service; work well independently; enjoy high risk ventures; adept at computer use; purchasing and/or inventory control experience.

Robbery / Burglary / Con Games

Creative; strong self-confidence; work well independently and / or in a team; follow directions; excellent ability to sell and make a presentation; effective communicator; not easily intimidated; a believable and trusting personality; establish a quick rapport with others; adapt well to new situations or environments; excel at delegating authority and tasks; a leader; can make the hard decisions; good sense of time management; very organized; set goals; good at coordinating one or more projects; resourceful; skilled at marketing / researching; clever and creative

Prostitution

Work well independently or in a team situation; follow directions; not afraid of hard work; creative; will put in whatever time is needed; good at finding a solution to seemingly impossible problems; proven sales ability; recordkeeping / bookkeeping skills; strong in customer service and public relations; outgoing personality with good sense of humor; can delegate tasks; good speaking ability.

Assault / Murder / Manslaughter

Strong confidence level; good communicator; not afraid to speak up or ask questions; self-motivated; not easily intimidated; follow directions; clever and creative; work well independently; task-oriented; not bothered by stress; good sense of time management; excellent physical condition; mechanically inclined; good use of hands; can be counted on to get the job done.

Other Unacceptable Activities

There are other negative activities floating around that you are in or have been involved in. Look at these and come up with some examples of positives you can bring to the outside from these negative experiences.

Counting What You Did Prior to Prison

What you did before you went to prison counts very much toward helping you build an assets list. Start thinking of the various clubs, hobbies, jobs, educational involvements, accomplishments, memberships, certifications, etc., that you experienced when NOT in prison. These are much easier to list, and will be covered in greater detail when we discuss writing your resume in Chapter 4.

> **REMEMBER: Because you did spend time in prison, it is even more important for you to have as many positives as possible to present to a potential employer, so use those you have from acceptable activities on the OUTSIDE and the INSIDE!**

JOB & LIFE WEAKNESSES TO BUILD UPON

It is doubtful that any individual can offer ALL the positives I have listed on the previous five pages. And it is not necessary that you have all of these strengths, or that you want all of them.

In addition, there are weaknesses that every person has and would like to improve upon. If you concentrate on doing this, it will give you a stronger edge in looking for a job, and more skills to present to a potential employer.

These career weaknesses are usually those same interpersonal skills I discussed earlier in this chapter. Once you improve on your personal strengths, you will improve your career strengths. **Likewise, when you improve upon a personal weakness of yours, you have improved upon a career weakness.**

<u>*Now is the Time to Turn Your Weaknesses Around*</u>

For example, you may wish to improve your writing and/or speaking skills; become a good listener; learn how to better follow directions or handle stress; control your temper; get in better physical shape; or gain more confidence and self-motivation. These last six months (or less) are an excellent time for you to begin turning these weaknesses around.

How to Improve Yourself

Courses

There are courses, programs, and activities -- sponsored by the prison -- that are set up to help you improve. School courses, study groups, counseling sessions, and club programs offer STRUCTURED opportunities for you to improve on many areas.

Self-Study

A major key to strengthening what are now career weaknesses is what you do ON YOUR OWN, in addition to the structured learning opportunities.

By observing, by listening, by reading you have countless opportunities to improve. Radio programs. TV shows. Audio tape and video programs. Discussion groups with fellow inmates, friends, and family. Reading. Computer programs. Each of these can bring you information and guidance on how to strengthen your weak areas.

IT'S ESPECIALLY IMPORTANT TO READ. Read, read, read -- as much as you can. But DON'T stick with Westerns, Science Fiction, Romance, Sex, Action, and Mysteries. Reach out for those self-improvement articles, books, and magazines that will help you improve your job strengths, personal strengths, knowledge strengths, and body strengths.

(By the way: biographies and autobiographies about successful men and women are especially helpful because they offer insight to the qualities people need to achieve success.)

> **REMEMBER: While the prison officials babysit and control and guide and mandate your stay, if you want to succeed on the outside you must make efforts on your own to improve -- if not, you will fail once released.**

Put Into Practice What You Learn

And while you are reading, looking, and listening, begin to put into practice what you are learning. If your writing skills have been weak, write more; if your grammar or speech has been poor, talk more; if you have not been much of a leader, take charge a bit more; if you haven't been a good manager of time, plan your days and nights better.

These and many other areas need be improved upon NOW, so when you do get out, it will be as if you had spent X number of years in a business school, and graduated with many of the skills necessary to be a success in today's business world.

REMEMBER: There is the story of the worm, who waits to be eaten, and the story of the bird, who searches out the worm. If you live your life as the worm, you are an excellent candidate for unemployment, low self-esteem, and more time in prison.

AVOIDING PREVIOUS JOB MISTAKES

What Are Job Mistakes?

Job mistakes fall into two categories:

(1) **ACCEPTABLE / LEGAL.** Examples include making a wrong decision; interviewing poorly; not having enough self-motivation; doing poorly in sales; not listening carefully; not working well in a team situation; being a "know-it-all"; having poor interpersonal skills.

(2) **UNACCEPTABLE / ILLEGAL.** Examples include stealing or embezzling; industrial espionage; sexual harassment; coming into work drunk or stoned; juggling the books; not paying taxes; lying about past job experience or education.

Both of these are <u>past</u> mistakes, and DO NOT have to be repeated.

REMEMBER: Use past career mistakes as guides to what you should avoid in the future and what the consequences will be if you don't.

> ## *4 Key Points You Can Do Now to Make Certain*
> ## *Past Job Mistakes Don't Happen Again*
>
> (1) Look over the job mistakes you've made
> (2) Get to understand why you made your job mistakes
> (3) Map out controls and plans to make sure you avoid them
> (4) Develop those strengths necessary to guarantee these mistakes will never recur

A Closer Look: 4 Ways to Prevent a Repeat of Past Job Mistakes

#1
LOOK OVER THE JOB MISTAKES YOU'VE MADE

First, this is a time for honesty, no matter how much it means admitting that YOU'VE screwed up, that YOU are to blame for your career plans / job position not working out. **If you can't be honest with yourself, then you will never be able to be honest with an employer.**

An Example

I'll give you a good example, an example with which you might be able to identify. My career counseling firm has been in business for many years, and during this time I have had hundreds of clients who lost their jobs because they were fired.

How many of these do you think have admitted to me that it was their fault, and not the company's or someone else's? NONE!

Somehow, EACH person fired from a job always found a way to justify it to me ... and to him or herself:

● "The company didn't understand me"
● "I was just borrowing the typewriter, not stealing it"
● "I was going to pay the money back"
● "They just didn't like blacks (or women or older people or Italians or the handicapped, etc.)"
● "I had this medical condition ..."

It's "The Boss vs. Me." For many in this situation, they have always looked upon the employer / employee relationship as "the Boss vs. Me." Setting up this type of scenario in one's mind often leads to a person getting fired; he or she is under the impression that the employer (or supervisor or manager) is out to get him or her, and so stupidity sets in. The employee steals, reacts to a directive with a chip on his or her shoulder, or just goofs off. 99% of the time "The Boss vs. Me" is imagined, and in the 1% where it really does exist, the employee seldom talks with the employer to find out why the employer has such a negative attitude. Does this fit you?

"It's Me ... and Me ... and Me." Another major reason why people get fired is that they forget about the other people around them and rather only think of themselves. Thus, they don't listen well, work poorly in team situations, complete a task on the employee's own agenda, don't take into consideration the good of all, are not punctual, and seldom have any real loyalty to the organization. With these types of problems resulting from an employee who focuses too much on himself / herself, that employee is quickly gone with the wind.

> **REMEMBER: For the lazy worker, getting fired has the benefit of long days on a comfortable couch in front of a TV; for the motivated worker, getting fired makes that couch feel like a straw mattress, something that person never wants to experience again.**

YOUR HONESTY. The list of reasons for getting fired goes on. How honest can you be? If you were ever fired from a job, go to the facing page.

"I WAS FIRED FROM A JOB"

Being fired for something YOU did is obviously a career mistake, but if you cannot HONESTLY admit that it was your fault, then you will be going back to the free world ready to blame your mistakes on someone or something else all over again.

If you have been fired from a job — ANY job at ANY time — completely fill out this worksheet. "Talking" about it on paper will go a long way in making certain that it doesn't happen again.

(1) Describe the job(s) from which you were fired: _____

_____

_____

_____

(2) What was/were the REAL, HONEST reason/reasons you were fired: _____

_____

_____

_____

_____

_____

(3) If you were responsible for you being fired, but at the time blamed it on someone or something else,

explain why you couldn't admit the truth: _____

__ _____

_____

_____

_____

_____

_____

Other Career Mistakes

There are, of course, other career mistakes made besides being fired. Some examples are listed at the beginning of this section under Acceptable / Legal and Unacceptable / Illegal. As I mentioned earlier, however, it is not important at this point if it was a legal mistake or illegal mistake; you now have the opportunity to start over and never again make the same mistake(s).

YOUR JOB & CAREER MISTAKES

In the spaces below, list ALL the career mistakes that you can think of that YOU have made:

1 _____

2 _____

3 _____

4 _____

3 _____

5 _____

6 _____

7 _____

8 _____

9 _____

10 _____

11) _____

12) _____

13) _____

14) _____

REMEMBER: Make the same mistake twice and you're a fool, plain and simple, for it tells others that you haven't cared enough to learn from the first time you made the mistake ... and chances are very strong that you won't be given a third time to make the same mistake.

#2
UNDERSTANDING WHY YOU MADE YOUR JOB MISTAKES

Once you've listed the mistakes you've made, it's time to FULLY understand why you made these mistakes. If you don't know the reason behind YOUR mistakes, then the chances of you making these mistakes again are very high.

Examples of Why You Made Job Mistakes

You'll find that many of these examples of career mistakes are the same ones listed under Acceptable / Legal and Unacceptable / Illegal, earlier in this chapter.

Made a Wrong Decision

Did not have enough knowledge of the subject; made the decision too quickly; did not include all possibilities; did not do enough research or research materials were outdated; was pressured / rushed by an employer, a deadline, a colleague, and/or another appointment; received wrong information from someone; did not double check information given you by someone else or information you gathered.

Interviewed Poorly

Was nervous; did not verbally communicate; clothes / shoes were not at their best; lied about something; used hands too much; displayed lack of confidence; was physically out of shape; did not know enough about the company; was late for the interview; was too concerned about salary; hair was messy / hands were dirty; weak personality; listened poorly; asked questions only about pay and benefits.

Not Enough Self-Motivation

Never concerned with self-motivation; have a personality that waits until told by others to do something; no goals; very depressed; felt that you were in a dead-end job or position; didn't know how to motivate yourself; had trouble accepting responsibility.

Did Poorly in Sales

Not a good communicator; intimidated by others; did not thoroughly learn the product; not good at making a presentation; prefer work where you don't have much contact with others; can't handle rejection; poor management of time; don't deal well with stress; not good at returning phone calls or correspondence; not a goal setter; poorly organized; not willing to settle for an average or small income; didn't follow up on prospect interest.

Stealing / Embezzling

Had no other way to get money needed for necessities; had a drug / liquor habit; wanted to please someone else beyond your regular income; wanted revenge against your employer or former employer; seemed very easy and no one would catch you; felt that the company owed it to you, and you were going to take it, even if they didn't give it to you; pressured into it by someone else because you were not strong enough to resist.

Industrial Espionage

Wanted to stay ahead of the competition; was paid a bonus by your employer; wanted to get even with a former employer or a firm that would not hire you; saw a chance to boost your firm's stock value; had a weak personality and was talked or pressured into doing it; needed extra money and this was the only way you felt you could get it.

Computer Hacking

Enjoy beating the system; felt that I wasn't getting fairly paid; wanted to find a shortcut to get as much information as possible to beat the competition, (etc.); wanted to show off my abilities so I could get a promotion or bonus; felt that another company had wronged me and I wanted to get even; was a good way to use my technical knowledge to make some additional money; was bored; don't believe in privacy laws.

Sexual Harassment

Felt it was okay to come on to a woman or man at work; wanted to pressure her into accepting a raise, promotion, or other responsibilities; did not know how to keep business and personal lives separate; believe that women are less than equal to men; cannot control your sexual urges; don't have the manners or class that is mandatory in a work environment; enjoy making women or men feel embarrassed.

Not Paying Taxes

Used the money for something else; not organized; not a good recordkeeper; don't believe in it, and thus believe that you are not breaking the law; try to find the shortcut, the scheme, or the easy way to do things, no matter if it's legal or not; not a long term planner.

Coming Into Work Drunk or Stoned

Can't face the reality of life; cannot face failure, disappointments, or mistakes; addicted; have little self-control; weak-minded with littler confidence; have little interest in or concern for responsibilities; cannot open up to others; can't handle stress; cannot follow through.

Juggling the Books

Not a good business manager; needed money for something beyond the means of salary; addicted to drugs, alcohol, gambling; thought it would be easy and no one would know; gave in to pressure / demands from someone else; made poor decisions; not a goal setter; poor salesperson or other type of businessperson; always look for the easy way out or a scheme to get money quickly.

Lying About Past Job Experience or Education

Didn't think anyone would check; believe that everybody does it, so it's okay; not enough self-confidence; don't know how to verbally sell yourself; not a good writer; little self-motivation; can't accept who or what you are; always compare yourself to someone else; will do whatever it takes to get the job, even if it's illegal or immoral.

REMEMBER: The more you understand why you made past career mistakes, the greater your chances of never repeating them.

REMEMBER: To ask others to help you better understand why you made a particular mistake on the job and how you can best make certain you don't repeat it again is a sign of strength, not weakness.

Your Employment Mistakes: The Reasons

In the spaces provided below, take the various employment mistakes that you have listed above, in section I, page 74, "Your Career Mistakes," and list the REAL reason(s) as to why you made each career mistake: (Use a separate sheet of paper if you need additional space.)

(1) mistake: _____

reason: _____

(2) mistake:_____

reason: _____

(3) mistake: _____

reason: _____

(4) mistake : _____

reason: _____

(5) mistake:_____

reason: _____

(6) mistake: _____

reason_____

(7) mistake: _____

reason: _____

#3
MAPPING OUT CONTROLS & PLANS TO MAKE SURE YOU AVOID REPEATING YOUR PAST EMPLOYMENT MISTAKES

This is much easier than you might think at this point, because you've already accomplished two major items: listing your career mistakes and understanding why they occurred.

The 5 Steps to Keep You From Repeating Your Employment Mistakes

Preventing your employment mistakes from repeating themselves requires solid planning. These five steps should ALWAYS be followed to prevent your past employment mistakes from popping up again. They will also decrease the possibility of new employment mistakes, and downplay the impact of any employment mistakes you may make:

(1) DEVELOP MORE SELF-CONFIDENCE & SELF-CONTROL. The better you feel about yourself, the more you are able to "put the brakes on" when you want, and the less easily influenced you are by other people or events, the smaller the chances are of you repeating your past employment mistakes.

(2) TRY TO AVOID THE SITUATIONS THAT CONTRIBUTED TO YOUR JOB MISTAKE(S). This is sometimes easier said than done, but try it. The old saying that "everybody has his price" is too often true, and sometimes, no matter how much self-confidence or self-control you have, the EMOTIONAL temptation to do something that is wrong will take over your INTELLECTUAL knowledge that tells you it is wrong and what the consequences will be.

(3) THINK THROUGH & CHECK FULLY YOUR DECISIONS, INFORMATION, OPINIONS, AND INPUT. Far better to be the one who takes a bit longer to do something but is usually right than the one who rushes to judgment but is usually wrong.

(4) PLAN, ORGANIZE, & SET GOALS. "An ounce of prevention is worth a pound of cure," so goes the saying. The more you plan, the better you organize, and the more you set goals, the greater your preparation will be for avoiding or handling possible career mistakes.

(5) WHEN YOU MAKE A JOB-RELATED MISTAKE, DON'T BE AFRAID TO OWN UP TO IT, & IMMEDIATELY BEGIN TO REPAIR ANY DAMAGE. Think of the number of times you made a legitimate, legal, on-the-job mistake, but did not admit it to others OR to yourself. The consequences may be mistrust, losing your job or being demoted, ruining your chances for promotion, or giving the impression that you are careless.

(<u>NOTE</u>: It goes without saying: don't even consider making a job or career decision that is ILLEGAL; the consequences may again be prison, a ban from working in a certain profession or industry, and / or a stiff fine.)

Repair the damage: After you've owned up to the career mistake (again, to BOTH others involved and yourself), begin to minimize the effects of the mistake to your company and colleagues. By facing the problem head-on and working to get rid of it or lessen its impact, you will gain far greater respect from those working with you than if you ran from the problem.

#4
DEVELOP NECESSARY STRENGTHS TO GUARANTEE
THESE MISTAKES WILL NEVER RECUR

In this chapter and Chapter 1, I have given you suggestions and exercises to improve your strengths in mind and body. Like bodybuilders who exercise their muscles on a regular basis, you will find that the stronger your mind and body, the better you will be able to ward off a repetition of past mistakes.

REMEMBER: Because you have worked hard to prevent a past mistake from recurring does not mean that other mistakes won't happen. When they do, understand why they happened, learn from them, and work to make certain these mistakes also become one-time only errors.

● RESEARCHING COMPANIES, CAREERS, OPPORTUNITIES ●

It happens all the time: job hunters wait until the last moment to read up on a company's history, learn about various careers, and research the employment opportunities that exist. The results are often disastrous: poor interviews, limited knowledge of careers available, and little understanding of the career opportunities that await you.

TAKE ADVANTAGE OF YOUR PRISON TIME

Just about anyone on the outside would love to have the time available that you now have to do this researching. As I said earlier, don't waste this time by doing nothing more than reading science fiction, westerns, romances, etc.; by working out and playing various sports; by doing arts and crafts; by being involved in various organizations; and / or by merely goofing off. Yes, there certainly is a time -- and, in a fact, a need -- for these to help you relax the mind and body, but you MUST also make time to do your career researching.

THE MORE PEOPLE YOU KNOW AND THE MORE YOU READ, THE MORE YOU WILL LEARN

Learning how to properly research companies covers a combination of several other chapters and chapter sections you have read and will read in this book. And opportunities to learn about companies, careers, and job possibilities can be found EVERY day!

THE MORE YOU DO, THE MORE EXCITED YOU WILL GET. As you begin to focus in on what you want to do, you will find it very exciting to have a better understanding of what awaits you, what can be offered to you, and how you can best contribute to an employer.

REMEMBER: The time you spend researching companies, careers, and opportunities on the INSIDE will save you valuable time and better prepare you for your career search on the OUTSIDE.

READ NEWSPAPERS, MAGAZINES, & OTHER RESOURCES FOR JOB OPENINGS / CAREER OPPORTUNITIES

Approximately 95% of all people on the outside looking for a job must do so while one or more of the following exist:

- they have a job
- they have recently been fired, laid off, or resigned
- they have a family
- they have another job
- they are attending school

This means there is little time to really scan the papers, magazines, Internet, and trade journals, listen to the radio, or watch TV for job ads and career opportunities. However, in prison YOU do have more time!

3 WAYS TO MAKE THE BEST USE OF YOUR RESOURCES

(1) GET TO KNOW THE AVAILABLE RESOURCES IN YOUR INSTITUTION. Most prisons have **libraries**. Get to know what newspapers, magazines, and journals the library subscribe to, as well as what publications they have but do not receive on a regular basis. Ask the librarians if they can special order newspapers, magazines, or journals.

Also: more prison libraries have computers, some with access to the **Internet**. (In case you don't know: the Internet is a vast web of various computer programs and computer addresses that exist around the world, offering the opportunity to gather information from all points; once you have access to the Internet, you have access to many of these programs. Each Internet address is called a Web Site.) There are many opportunities to gather job-related in formation on the Internet -- don't forget about it!

Additionally: Find out if there are radio **talk shows** you can tune in; these often have regular features on employment tips and/or job listings. **TV shows** also feature specials on employment, give important career information, and have talk shows where guests may offer you insight on a career field; check your TV listings on a regular basis to find out what may be of help to you in this phase of your career preparation.

Finally, don't forget to check in with your **Education Department**. They usually have specific career-related magazines and job search materials that are available to you. Often, there also are specific transition and employability programs: these, too, will usually have materials that you can use.

REMEMBER: Many inmates do not take full advantage of the available resources in their institution. The more you become aware of what you have, the easier and faster your job search homework will be.

A Comprehensive Listing of Resources for the Inmate

In the first edition of this book, I included a comprehensive resource listing; this does not appear in this edition. Why? Unfortunately, many of the resources available to inmates and ex-inmates are usually through the form of local and regional organizations, many of which operate on shoestring budgets. I found that while all my resources were current and operating when this book first went to press in 1990, fully 25% were out of business less than a year later. Others had taken their place, additional ones were no longer operational, more became available ... this cycle continued then and continues now.

I have two suggestions for you regarding outside resources related to the job search:

(1) BEGIN DEVELOPING A LIST THAT IS SPECIFIC TO YOUR NEEDS. Through the suggestions given in this section and those that follow, develop and stay in constant contact with the various organizations, individuals, companies, etc. that can provide resources to you. This is the best way to not only gather as much outside help as possible SPECIFIC to your situation but to also stay on top on who is and who is not still functioning.

(2) CONTACT ME. I have what is probably the most thorough and up-to-date listing of various resources available for inmates and ex-inmates in the United States and abroad. If you have trouble finding certain resources, contact our office; we'll try to help you out.

> **REMEMBER: Resources are like nuggets of gold -- until someone discovers them, they're worth nothing.**

(2) KEEP JOURNALS, PORTFOLIOS. During your time incarcerated, you will find numerous items that can help you once on the outside, not only in your job search but in virtually all other areas. From educational courses and achievements to involvements in clubs and organizations, from information learned through self study to leadership roles taken -- these and other "personal builders" should not be forgotten. To assure this doesn't happen, there are two excellent "recordkeepers" to keep track of all your positives gained while incarcerated: Journals and Portfolios.

Journal

A journal is a continuing record where you jot down accomplishments and disappointments, thoughts on just about anything, quotes from others that you like, comments on a favorite TV episode you saw -- the anything and everything that happens to you and about you. (However, it does differ from a diary in that a journal does not usually have entries that are as personal or intimate as a diary.) Some people keep a journal daily, others weekly, some whenever they feel like it. But if a journal is going to be effective, it does need be kept on a regular basis.

Keeping a journal can do several things for you:

● Remind you of various educational, vocational, and other achievements and involvements that should be included on your resume and brought up in a job interview.
● Help give you a morale and motivation boost through a reminder of your achievements while inside when you're hitting a rough or frustrating spot on the outside.
● Remind you of negative behaviors, involvements, and situations from which you want to stay away and/or to remind you how much you've changed -- for the better.
● Provide you with information (such as resources and contacts) that can be of help on the outside.
● Give you a picture of what life was like in prison, including some of the good times (we all know that there are, indeed, some of these!).

80

A few words of caution about keeping a journal. Before you decide to start keeping a journal, there are a few items to keep in mind:

● Check on any regulations that may exist in your institution against an inmate keeping a journal. Some institutions forbid it and if an inmate is caught, he or she can get into trouble, including additional time added to a sentence.
● Since journals do contain your thoughts, and some that you may not wish others to read, it may prove a problem for you if other inmates get a hold of it. (In some institutions keeping journals are a regular part of the Education Department's program, and to prevent the problem of other inmates reading it, some of these departments keep the journals under lock in their department.)
● If you can keep a journal, once on the outside don't forget about it! There is a tendency for ex-inmates to try and put behind anything that has to do with their prison experience. But your journal can be a big help; use it!

Portfolio

A portfolio differs from a journal in that it primarily focuses on your positives in prison, i.e., degrees or certificates received, papers or tests with good grades, awards or achievements (for example, a certificate of achievement in a club or for winning a sporting event). Portfolios are also more structured than journals; in fact, many correctional institutions provide their students with portfolio outlines, portfolio folders, and examples of portfolios.

As with a journal, keeping a portfolio can do several things for you:

● It can remind you of achievements and accomplishments from your time in prison.
● It can serve as a "one stop shop" for employers that includes, in addition to degrees, certificates, and the like from prison, your resume and cover letters, information on past employers, and letters of reference.
● When you reach a task that seems too difficult to accomplish or an obstacle that appears impossible to overcome, and you really need a morale and motivation boost, a portfolio can remind you of other, similar situations in prison that you eventually did accomplish or overcome.

A few words of caution about keeping a portfolio. Before you start keeping a portfolio, keep in mind:

● As with a journal, be careful as to who gets hold of your portfolio (if you take it out of your classroom)
● Prior to leaving the institution with your portfolio, make certain that you have copies or originals (preferred) of all important papers (including degrees, certifications; birth certificates, social security card), and that all information is up to date
● If you keep a portfolio, once on the outside don't forget about it! There is a tendency for ex-inmates to try and put behind anything that has to do with their prison experience. But your portfolio can be a big help; use it!
● DON'T EVER USE A PORTFOLIO TO SELL YOU DURING AN INTERVIEW! Foremost, the interviewers will rely on your skills and presentation abilities, not "a bunch of papers," in deciding whether to hire you. A portfolio, shoved in front of an interviewer, can be looked on as a crutch ... and you always want to rely, first, on yourself to sell you as a prospective employee.

Portfolio or Journal: Is Either Better?

After reading the above descriptions for each, you can see that a Portfolio and a Journal are different, but they both can be of help to you. If you can keep both, remember that to do so requires time; while your intentions may be good you want to make certain you keep a Portfolio and/or Journal on a regular basis. A suggestion in case you can do both: perhaps you might wish to try a combination, where all important papers, etc., would be held in the back of your journal, in a pocket (so they won't fall out).

REMEMBER: A memory is a wonderful thing but when it comes time to needing a reminder of past accomplishments and achievements there's nothing quite so good as a real, hold-in-your-hand, let-me-look-at-it-again-and-again piece of paper that says, "Yes -- I did it!"

REMEMBER: Employers will trust your memory as far as they can see it, thus it's always better to present them another's memory of you in the form of black letters on white paper -- this they will always trust.

(3) BEGIN READING & COLLECTING JOB ADS, ARTICLES ON CAREER DEVELOPMENT, AND OTHER RELATED ITEMS. First, you need to get a notebook of some kind or index card files that you can paste or tape your ads, articles, etc. into. This way you will have, whenever you need them, such items as jobs you intend on applying for (and a variety of aspects of this), informative articles to help you, letters of reference you receive, and other tidbits.

(Later in this chapter, you will find a more thorough discussion on how to set up your notebook or index card files.)

In addition, not everyone knows what job or career he or she would like when released. I am hopeful, however, that after following and putting into practice these guidelines, you will have a more focused idea as to what type of work you wish to pursue on the outside.

START WRITING COMPANIES FOR INFORMATION

These last six months or so of your sentence is the time to start writing to companies and organizations. You can express your interest in a specific job, obtain information about the firm, attempt to set up an interview (for the job or for further information), and / or add to your job search information.

In later chapters, you will learn how and what to write companies, how to have a successful interview, and what you should do to follow up on what companies send you.

Responding to ads. Depending on how much time you have left before your release date, you will seriously plan to answer an ad for a position that you want, or you will clip the ad to give you an idea of: [1] who is hiring; [2] the type of jobs in which you are interested; [3] addresses to send for information about a potential employer.

> **REMEMBER: By reading ads now, you'll have a much clearer idea as to what job you wish to seek and what's available, what industries are strong & which are weak, and what skills you may need to improve upon.**

PURSUE YOUR INTERESTS, PAST & PRESENT

It makes no difference if this is a job you held or a field you were involved in before prison; a trade or craft you learned while in prison; or an interest you developed from reading this book, talking with friends, or through something you read, saw, or heard.

DON'T FORGET TO RESEARCH!

In addition to sending to companies you have seen listed in an ad for X position, it is also important to locate available printed material to learn as much as possible about your intended job or career. Do this through journals, newspapers, magazines, and newsletters.

BE OPEN TO INFO YOU HEAR IN CLASS & ON TV / RADIO

Your Education Department may have guest speakers, may sponsor a Job Fair, or be involved in other such programs that bring others in to speak with you; your teacher or counselor may mention a name in class or in a conversation; and you may learn of companies and job possibilities on TV or the radio: don't forget about these! They can offer you additional sources for researching and resourcing.

Examples of What You Can Learn By Researching

● a particular job, profession, or industry really isn't what you thought and it's not for you
● a company you had been excited about is now in financial trouble or out of business
● a profession or industry that had interested you is now experiencing a slump
● you need more specific education or experience
● additional information that you will give you a better understanding of a company, a specific job, a profession, or an industry
● company addresses (street, E-mail, Web Site), numbers (phone, fax), and contact names
● articles that profile a company, an industry, a product, or a person in a company
● statistics that can be used during an interview, in developing a presentation, or to help you decide which industries or companies you'd like to seek out or stay away from

REMEMBER: Once you **DO** know what you want to do, now is the time to learn all you can about that certain career, job, industry, or profession; if you **DON'T** yet know what you want to do, exploring various careers, jobs, industries, and professions can help you decide.

Using Research Materials That Must Be Returned

Try to make photocopies of any research materials that must be returned. If this cannot be done, take notes on the material, writing down the MOST IMPORTANT POINTS that you want to keep.

A Reminder: Keep All Your Materials Organized

The more organized you are now, the more efficient your job search will be ... and the better organized you will be on the outside.

REMEMBER: It is much better to have too much information and be overprepared than not have enough information and find that you are ill-prepared.

● NETWORKING ●

NETWORKING DEFINED

Networking is simply you contacting those people who will be your link -- and thus a very big help -- to various companies, organizations, and employers you may wish to work for. (And by the way: why you certainly can do networking on the Internet, networking is not an aspect of or another name for the Internet!)

NOW IS THE TIME TO NETWORK

You may have heard the expression, "it's not what you know but who you know." For an inmate, this is especially true, because you have limited access to phone, travel, and personal visits, and there is also the possibility that your prison record may get in the way of people initially greeting you with open arms.   Developing outside contacts can minimize the drawbacks of these situations.

IF YOU'VE BEEN RESEARCHING,
YOU'VE STARTED NETWORKING

When you started researching various companies, professions, jobs, etc., you also found names of people with each organization you contacted. These could have come in the form of a personal or form letter, a business card, a name in a brochure, or a name that you came across in an article or on the TV / radio.

As you begin to better understand what you want to do when released, keep those names that are associated with your career or job direction.   These can prove to be very helpful.

WHERE ELSE SHOULD YOU NETWORK?

Just about anywhere:

- friends, family, former employers and teachers, and other people you knew before prison
- professionals who work at employment agencies, for companies and public employers, and career counseling firms
- city, county, state, and federal agencies that exist to help in various aspects of the job search
- non-profit organizations (not government) that directly or indirectly assist inmates/ex-inmates
- lawyers, probation and parole officers, your counselor(s) in prison, librarians, pre-release administrators
- Chamber of Commerce, Better Business Bureau, newspapers, radio & TV stations
- members of professional organizations, clubs, societies, and associations
- members of the clergy

YOU DON'T NEED TO WRITE OR CALL EVERYBODY!

This will waste your time, and you are getting to the point in your sentence where you no longer can afford to waste time. But you do want to contact those people whom you think will be of some help, whether that help comes in the form of a name to contact; some information about a company; tips on available jobs; some additional, general job search information; or information on various educational, employment, housing, or funding programs for which you may qualify.

> **REMEMBER: Make no mistake about it: networking provides more job interviews and new jobs than any other way of looking for a job, but it is also the least used.**

WHY MORE PEOPLE DON'T USE NETWORKING

At first, it seems odd that this aspect of the job search that could prove so helpful to the job applicant is not used more. In fact, only 20% - 30% of all job seekers use networking.

To better understand why so many people don't use it, you must keep in mind the following: **There are only two ways to look for a job -- actively and passively.**

THE METHOD MOST JOB SEARCHERS USE. Most people, unfortunately, take a passive approach when job hunting. This means that they will put in the least amount of time and effort -- and then complain that no one wants them or that there are no jobs available!

Two Examples of Passive Job Searching

The two best examples of this passive approach would be: [1] those individuals who send in their resumes and cover letters to ads they have seen in newspapers, magazines, etc.; [2] those who send them to employment agencies.

While you should certainly use these two sources of possible jobs, they should NOT be used exclusively. Just because they are easy to acquire, that is, the newspapers, et al., "bring" you the job ads, and the employment agencies "offer" you jobs and careers, that does not mean they are the BEST sources for jobs ... and, in fact, they are not.

The Effectiveness of Newspaper Ads and Employment Agencies

Newspaper ads account for 15% - 20% of all available jobs, and employment agencies offer another 10% - 15%. That means, at best, you will be covering 35% (out of 100%) of possible job openings. Those are odds I certainly wouldn't want, and I'm sure you don't want either.

HOW EFFECTIVE IS NETWORKING?

Many surveys and polls have been taken, and the numbers are very impressive: 40% - 70% of available jobs are found through networking. So you can see that an ACTIVE job search -- even though it takes more effort -- is definitely worth it.

A DETAILED LOOK AT NETWORKING SOURCES

Finding the people to contact so you can begin developing your network is sometimes very easy, sometimes more difficult. Here are some suggestions:

(1) FAMILY, FRIENDS, FORMER EMPLOYERS, ETC. These are the simplest to contact and get responses from because you already know them.

(2) EMPLOYMENT AGENCIES, COMPANIES, PUBLIC EMPLOYERS, CAREER COUNSELING FIRMS. While you may not know these individuals, they, too, are fairly easy to find. They include: ads in newspapers, magazines, newsletters, and journals; listings in phone books, newspapers (look in the classifieds under "Employment Agencies" and "Resume Services"), and membership rosters; articles on companies and / or their employers found in newspapers; "People on the Move" and "Spotlight on Promotions" sections in newspapers; corporate annual reports; the Internet: these all offer names, addresses, and / or titles (as well as information about the company, profession, and/or industry).

(3) GOVERNMENT AGENCIES, LAWYERS, PROBATION & PAROLE OFFICERS, CLERGY, CHAMBER OF COMMERCES, RADIO & TV STATIONS, PROFESSIONAL ORGANIZATIONS, SOCIETIES, CLUBS, ETC. In addition to everything listed under (2), above, there may be people you know from clubs; attorneys involved in your case; radio stations you listen to or TV stations you watch; probation and parole officers assigned to you; blind mailings you receive. Caution: contact ONLY those individuals whom you think will be most helpful so you don't waste your time and effort.

(4) SPECIAL PUBLICATIONS, LIBRARY CAREER CENTERS, WALK-IN CONTACTS, JOB FAIRS, PLACING WANT ADS FOR YOURSELF. Each one of these is specialized, and all may not be for you. Special publications would include chamber of commerce directories and other such listings of organizations.

● **Library career centers** are more helpful in person, but they still can assist you if you write (or contact them via E-mail or the Internet, if you have access). Once you are released, walk-in contacts can result in on-the-spot interviews, networking contacts, or job applications.

● **Job fairs** are held in cities throughout the country, often specialize in a particular industry, and should be visited when you are out. Also: more and more prisons are also holding job fairs and introducing programs such as "Adopt An Inmate" that brings together outside employers and those incarcerated. To learn more about these programs, talk with a correctional educator in your institution.

● **Placing want ads** describing what you have to offer, while usually not meeting with a very high number of responses, is still another option available to you -- and one that can easily be done during your last six months.

(5) ADDITIONAL NETWORKING RESOURCES. While these may not all apply to you, each offers the potential of supplying you with additional employment contacts:

● **Rejection letters**: If you are very short (on time before your release), you should start to send resumes / cover letters out (the specifics on this in later chapters). Since we don't live in an ideal world, chances are high that you will receive at least one letter of rejection. Don't toss it away. That name on the bottom of the rejection letter is a potential networking contact. (In Chapter 5, you will learn how to properly write this person).

● **Economic / political changes**: Be on the lookout for elections, new industries or companies moving in, economic grants, increased construction, new malls and office buildings -- all in the city where you wish to work. These are good sources for networking names.

● **Obituary notices**: Don't laugh -- people do die unexpectedly, and very often that means a job opening that the firm or organization had not counted on. This may not lead to a job, but it can lead to a contact for further correspondence.

● **job clubs**: Many people are not familiar with job clubs. These are organizations that exist for the sole purpose of helping others (not limited to ex-inmates) find employment and improve their job search skills. These can prove to be a big networking plus. (A weekly listing of job clubs in the United States can be found in a publication called *The National Business Employment Weekly*; contact them at 800-JOB HUNT or their E-mail address of nbew@wsj.dowjones.com for a sample copy.)

● **Hobbies / sports**: In addition to clubs, there may be people you know from past athletic involvements, hobby get-togethers or meetings (tropical fish, railroading, stamps, computers, dogs, etc.), card groups, and other such activities.

● **Your children**: If you have children, have you met their teachers, parents of their playmates, coaches, or principal(s)? Have you been involved in PTA or other school functions? Each of these offer potential networking leads.

● **Others**: This is really a grab bag: past customers or clients; colleagues from the military; co-workers or contacts from public service / charitable interests; doctors, dentist, accountant, banker, insurance agent, car salesman, and other professionals who serviced you prior to prison. Also: ask new inmates about job possibilities they may be familiar with on the outside.

REMEMBER: Virtually every person you ever came into contact with is a potential networking lead. If you ask for their assistance, the worst they can say is "no"; if you don't ask for their assistance, the worst they can say is ... nothing.

REMEMBER: The strength of a spiderweb is linked directly to its network of strands that make up its web; if your network is weak and limited, however, unlike the spider you will become the victim, not the victor, in the search for employment.

9 SUGGESTIONS TO MAKE YOUR NETWORKING MOST EFFECTIVE

(1) IF THERE IS NO NAME, NO TITLE, OR NO ADDRESS WHEN YOU COME ACROSS A PARTICULAR NETWORKING LISTING, DON'T DESPAIR. You'll often have to use more than one source to get what you want, but being persistent almost always pays off.

Example #1

You find an ad in a newspaper that lists the title ("Personnel Director"), the company name, and its address. Here you have two options: [a] simply address the envelope "Personnel Director" and then begin the inside of the letter "Dear Sir or Madam:" [b] write or call the company -- looking to contact the Customer Service Representative or Public Relations Director -- and ask for the person's name.

Example #2

You have the name of a person and the company for which he/she works, but no title or company address. Handle this one of three ways:

[1] Look up the company address in a phone book, and then write the person at that address, not using his/her title (if your phone book doesn't have zip codes, don't worry: your letter will still arrive);

[2] If you do have access to a phone, or have someone who can call for you, call the company and ask for the person's title. If you want to do EVERYTHING via the phone, call information / the post office and ask for the phone number, address, and zip code of the company; almost always you will be given the information;

[3] If you have access to the Internet, see if the firm is listed on a Web site (chances are very high that it will be listed on some list somewhere), then contact it via computer, E-mail, fax, postal service, or phone.

(2) BEFORE YOU START YOUR NETWORKING LETTERS (and calls, if you have access to fairly regular phone use), MAKE   A PRIORITY LISTING OF WHOM YOU WANT TO CONTACT. Given the choice between people who work in a company where you would like to be employed or your Aunt Seena's cousin twice removed, who do you think would be more helpful? Don't leave anyone out you think can help you, but take them in the order of those you think will help you most to those who will probably be of least help.

(3) THERE ARE ADDITIONAL NETWORKING CONTACTS YOU CAN MAKE ONCE YOU ARE OUT OF PRISON. Don't think that your networking has been completed once you are released! You will constantly be meeting new people, reading new articles, etc. Also, on the outside you will have the opportunity for the face-to-face meetings, the ability to travel, and unlimited use of the phone. (See Chapter 9 for more information on this.)

(4) DEVELOP A LIST OF QUESTIONS YOU WILL WANT TO ASK & INFORMATION YOU WILL WANT TO GIVE THE CONTACT. Being prepared prior to contacting your network people will not only assure you of gaining the most amount of mileage out of your contact, but guarantee that you come across as a potential employee who shows confidence, who thinks ahead, and who is well-organized.

Examples of Questions to Ask a Networking Contact

● Can you put me in contact with others who might be in need of my expertise?
● Can you suggest a few names where I can send my resume?
● What type of work does your firm do?
● What is the market for new employees in [NAME THE POSITION / FIELD YOU ARE INTERESTED IN]?
● What type of training program does your company offer?
● What experience and education does your firm require for [NAME OF POSITION]?
● What suggestions can you offer me?
● Would you please refer my resume to others you think might be interested in my qualifications?
● Would you please send me a copy of your firm's annual report and any other information you might have available on your organization?
● Would it be possible to meet with you for an informational interview upon my release?
● Does your firm have any special requirements that your employees must meet?
● What level of pay does [NAME OF POSITION] offer with my qualifications?
● What is the opportunity for advancement?
● Is computer knowledge important for the job?

REMEMBER: When you do not or cannot have your first choice [A], you go to your next choice [B] and make it your first choice [A] until you are in a position to obtain your INITIAL first choice.

Examples of Information to Give Networking Contacts About You

- your experience and education
- the type of job in which you are interested
- your personal strengths
- accomplishments that are important to the job you are seeking or industry profession you wish to enter
- leadership experience
- any writing or public speaking you've done
- computer knowledge
- special skills
- what you accomplished / what organizations you were involved in while incarcerated
- date of release (if appropriate; this would be based on how soon it is and whether you want the contact to know about your release date and / or status as an inmate)

REMEMBER: Honesty -- for inmates and ex-inmates it's not only the best policy, it's the only policy.

REMEMBER: Believe it or not, there are those individuals who will want to help you out because you ARE in prison! These individuals realize that you are in a situation that makes it extremely difficult for you to look for a job, believe that by serving your time you have "paid your debt to society," and are sincerely interested in you getting a "second chance."

---

(5) ONCE YOU RECEIVE A RESPONSE FROM A NETWORKING CONTACT, WRITE AN APPROPRIATE LETTER IN RETURN. The more involved you get in searching for a job, the more you will realize that there is no slacking off and it does take time. Responding to a networking contact who has written you is very important, as it helps you to establish that personal rapport you are seeking.

Depending on the type of response you receive, your letter will be:

- a thank you for the information
- a thank you for interest shown in you
- a thank you for referring your resume on to someone else
- a thank you that also supplies additional information asked for by your contact
- a thank you & confirmation of an interview date / time that the contact suggested in his/her letter to you

There are, of course, many other possibilities, as well as variations to the letters listed above. Detailed information on the use of cover letters and related correspondence, as well as a wide variety of sample letters, can be found in Chapter 5.

> **REMEMBER: Writing letters is one of the most time-consuming parts of the job search, but it also can be the most productive. Always follow up any correspondence you receive from a network contact.**

(6) KEEP ALL YOUR NETWORKING CONTACTS IN CARD FILES OR IN A NOTEBOOK, WITH SPACE FOR COMMENTS ON WHAT HAPPENS WITH EACH ONE. The choice is yours; use a system that is easiest for you and best organizes your materials.

Your records should include: the name of the person you wrote, the date you wrote him/her, the type of response you received, and what action you took / will take.

Using Codes

You might wish to put a little code on each card, depending on the response you receive from a networking contact. Example: "H" would mean Hot, a contact that is eager to help you; "L" would mean Lukewarm, for those people who can't promise you anything concrete but may contact you if anything comes up; and "C" is for Cold, those who can't or won't do very much for you.

The Importance of Your Contact List Being Organized & On Paper

By having your contact list on cards or paper, in a priority order, and labeled H, L, or C, you will have an efficient record that you can refer to at anytime. It will also help you organize; may give you an indication as to what type of contact is helping you best; and will give you a well-deserved pat on the back that says, "Yes, I definitely AM working on my future outside of prison!"

> **REMEMBER: Always keep some visible reminder around of your on-going efforts to find employment after release -- it's a great motivator!**

A Network Worksheet and sample index or card file can be found on the next two pages.

Building a Network Worksheet

"Who can help me find employment?"

Name	Relation	Address	Questions	Comments
1				
2				
3				
4				
5				
6				
7				
8				
9				
10				
11				
12				

Sample Index or Card File

Use the outlines below to keep a running record of your networking efforts. (These may also be used for responses to resumes you send out.) If you do not have access to index cards, use any paper you have available.

ORGANIZATION NAME:_____

ADDRESS / PHONE: _____

REFERRAL SOURCE: _____

CONTACT PERSON: _____

DATES OF CONTACT AND TYPE OF CONTACT (LETTERS, PHONE, ETC.):

_____

_____

_____

COMMENTS / EVALUATION: _____

_____

_____

FOLLOW-UP ACTIVITIES

EMPLOYER: _____

ACTIVITY	DATE	NEXT STEP

(7) MAKE A LIST OF RE-DOS: CONTACTS WHO HAVE NOT RESPONDED TO YOUR LETTER(S). Again, more hard work, more effort, more time -- but well worth it all because of the importance of what you are striving to achieve.

(8) NOW IS THE TIME TO START GATHERING REFERENCE LETTERS. References are especially important to the ex-inmate seeking employment, as the individual will be speaking favorably about you the person and you the professional.

(For detailed information on what references to obtain, how to obtain them, how reference letters should be written, and a sample letter requesting a reference, refer to Chapter 4, pages 137-140.)

> **REMEMBER:** A few good words about you in a Reference Letter go a long way in getting you noticed as a competent job applicant, not as an ex-inmate.

(9) IT ALWAYS HELPS TO SEND ALONG A COPY OF YOUR RESUME WITH YOUR NETWORKING LETTER. While you may not need to send a copy of your resume to your mother or father, boyfriend or girlfriend, rabbi or priest, it won't hurt, either. And it certainly would be to your advantage to send a resume to an employer, employment agency, or any other non-family, non-friend networking contact.

See Chapter 4 for details on writing and using resumes.

> **REMEMBER:** The more preparation now, the fewer tears and less frustration later.

● WRITE & MAIL OUT RESUMES & COVER LETTERS ●

You will find that people seeking jobs too often waste time in doing this crucial portion of the job search, and the usual result is missed opportunities and lost employment. Again, you have these six months or less available to you when it's time to start sending out your resumes and cover letters -- DO IT!

The following items need be done during your last six months. (Chapter 4 covers thoroughly the writing and sending of resumes and Chapter 5 details cover letters and related correspondence.)

DECIDE TO WHOM YOUR RESUMES & COVER LETTERS WILL BE SENT

Just like you did with networking contacts, you need to organize a list of who, what, when, where, and why you are sending your resumes / cover letters. You will certainly need to be organized in your new job, and being organized now will help you feel that you have your life under control -- not out of control, as it may have been.

USE YOUR NETWORKING LIST FOR YOUR RESUMES & COVER LETTERS

You will have received some very positive letters, asking you to send a copy (or a second copy, if you sent one in your networking letter) of your resume for employment consideration -- do it!

Out-of-Date Job Ads

Some of the ads that you may have saved for networking purposes are probably out-of-date if you clipped them early on in your last six months. Toss those no longer applicable.

WHEN TO START MAILING YOUR RESUMES & COVER LETTERS

During your last six months, just about any time is right for mailing resumes and cover letters, based on the circumstances. Some employers will ask for a resume to keep on file, suggesting you contact them again a short while before your release. Others will need a resume immediately, because they are looking to hire right away. Use your own judgment in combination with what is said in the ad or the letter you received.

Applying For a Position Six Months Before Your Release

Under some circumstances, it is NOT too early to actually apply for a specific position or industry four - six months before your release. These would include:

- government jobs (city, county, state, federal) where there are positions with on-going openings
- employers with whom you've established a good relationship and are eager to have you back or as a new employee upon your release
- seasonal positions, such as retail help during Christmas season or lifeguard positions in the summer
- senior management positions where you have extensive and near-perfect qualifications, and the firm would probably spend six months or more looking for the right candidate
- companies that have announced plans to expand, to open a new plant or office

LOOK FOR COMPANIES THAT ARE GROWING

When reading the newspaper(s), note -- as you did when networking -- companies that are expanding or experiencing solid business health. These are organizations where they may not have advertised for workers, but are certainly ripe to receive resumes. In addition to articles about the company or a product / service of the company, also be on the lookout for ads touting the company or its products/services: this may be an indication of that company's strength in its industry, and thus a possible candidate for new employees.

SEND YOUR RESUMES TO EMPLOYMENT SPECIALISTS

Start sending your resumes and cover letters to those employment agencies, search firms, and other organizations whose primary purpose is to help find jobs for others. Just be as certain as you can that you send your materials to those who can help you in your field.

If, for example, you are seeking a position as a secretary, you would not want to send your resume to an employment agency that specializes in placing computer professionals. You should have this information from the work you did in networking.

See Chapter 9 for detailed information on these firms.

DON'T FORGET ABOUT P.O. BOX NUMBER ADS

Job applicants are often skeptical of responding to ads that have a P.O. box address. They feel that the company may not be legitimate ("If they are on the up-and-up, why don't they list their name and / or address?") or the job may not be as good as some of the larger ones. Neither one of these is seldom true.

7 Reasons P.O. Box Addresses Are Used

(1) THE COMPANY DOES NOT WANT AN APPLICANT APPLYING BECAUSE OF THE COMPANY'S NAME OR REPUTATION. They want to know that you are primarily interested in the position, not the prestige, salary, or benefits that come with the company. The P.O. box also acts as a screen to (somewhat) limit the responses to those applicants who are qualified, thus saving the company time.

(2) TO KEEP A COMPANY'S HIRING ACTIVITY SECRET FROM ITS COMPETITORS.

(3) MANAGERS HAVE TIME TO SCREEN REPLACEMENTS FOR A WORKER WHOSE JOB IS ON THE LINE.

(4) A SENSITIVE POSITION IS BEING ADVERTISED.

(5) P.O. BOX ADS PERMIT COMPANIES TO TEST THE MARKETPLACE. This gives them an idea as to the depth and quality of personnel for anticipated or future openings.

(6) EMPLOYERS WANT TO LEARN IF THEIR EMPLOYEES ARE LOOKING FOR OTHER EMPLOYMENT.

(7) THE COMPANY DOES NOT HAVE TO ANSWER RESUMES, THUS SAVING CLERICAL WORK.

> **REMEMBER:** The vast majority of companies placing **P.O.** box ads are solid, legitimate organizations.

2 Suggestions For Using P.O. Boxes

(1) READ THE ADS CAREFULLY. Be wary of ads that use glittering generalities to describe the company and the position available. The more detailed an ad is, probably the more likely it is to represent a valid job opening.

(2) MAKE SURE THE AD FITS YOU. Scrutinize each notice before replying. The position should fit your area of interest and match your background experience as closely as possible. (Example: If an ad calls for a manager of shipping, parrot that title in your cover letter and/or on your resume if you held a similar position.)

● GET TO KNOW ALL ASPECTS OF THE JOB SEARCH! ●

Beyond networking and researching, there are many other parts to the job search. Read, learn, and practice those that you will need to know once on the outside. It's now time to get serious about landing employment ... and starting your new life on the outside.

EXAMPLES OF WHAT YOUR JOB SEARCH INCLUDES

● writing resumes and cover letters
● interviewing techniques and questions
● dressing correctly for the interview and the job
● negotiating salary and benefits
● learning more about pay scales for your employment area
● knowledge of professional affiliations & organizations in your field
● taking care of the day-to-day items that will allow you to more smoothly and efficiently slide back into mainstream society (such things as: opening a checking account, obtaining a credit card, getting a library card, making certain you have transportation)

These -- and much more -- will be covered in more detail in later chapters.

REMEMBER: The last six months of your sentence: playtime's over, and it's time to fully prepare yourself for finding and keeping a job. If you **DON'T** take this time to improve, to perfect, and to better, chances are very high that your life in the free world will be not too sweet and but a memory once again.

Chapter 3

What You Shouldn't Do

"Men trip not on mountains, they stumble on stones."

Hindustani proverb

● PRISON MAKES IT MORE DIFFICULT TO STAY FOCUSED ON YOUR JOB SEARCH ●

You've read about the many things to do while preparing for your career search. There are, however, various items that you need to avoid as well. Some of these can intrude on the good habits you are trying to establish, others can simply destroy any real chances you have of succeeding (and staying) on the outside.

For the most part, these "nos" are common sense, and in some cases, you've been told not to do them by your counselor or parole officer, or they are against the terms of your parole agreement.

PRISON REALITY. But when in prison, it's much easier to steer away from the work that's involved in looking for a job than playing a game of pool; it's more fun to hang out with a gang inside or your old gang outside than stick to doing research and practice; and it probably pays more money dealing drugs than taking legal employment.

To make matters worse, the final and continual effort has to come from YOU -- not a teacher, counselor, parole officer, family member, friend, etc. Yes, they can remind you of rules and remind you of what is probably in your best interests, but you must ultimately make the right (or wrong) decision.

REMEMBER: The key to making the right choice and the best decision is to think each situation through, examine the possible consequences, and then act on what your head tells you.

REMEMBER: Me, myself, and I: the three people you must always be able to depend upon when it comes time to motivating yourself.

---

10 THINGS YOU SHOULDN'T DO
DURING YOUR LAST SIX MONTHS IN PRISON

(1) YOU SHOULDN'T KEEP YOURSELF IN A NEGATIVE MENTAL ATTITUDE. There are many inmates who harbor grudges -- against individuals, society, law enforcement officials, and others. Some even go to the point of "swearing revenge" once they're released. This anger, this hostility, and this (perhaps) one act of revenge might make you feel good in the short run -- for an instant or so, but aside from perhaps doing something that is illegal, you are only hurting yourself.

A Negative Attitude Will Have You Blaming Others

It's time to start forgetting about who or what put you in prison, and start being positive about the opportunities that await you. If not, this negative mental attitude often carries over into your job search.

Examples of How a Negative Attitude Can Affect You

If you get a rejection letter, you blame it on the employers not liking you because of the color of your skin, because you were in prison, or because they just "didn't want to give you a break" -- you can't consider that it might be your fault. In the interview, a negative mental attitude can come across very quickly, and you are labeled hostile, arrogant, with a "chip on your shoulder" -- and certainly won't get the job.

REMEMBER: A negative mental attitude keeps positive experiences and thoughts locked out of your life.

(2) YOU SHOULDN'T HANG AROUND WITH INDIVIDUALS WHO ARE GOING TO BE NEGATIVE INFLUENCES ON YOU. Yes, I know -- much easier said than done.

Before Prison

When many inmates were on the outside (prior to prison), they ran with a group or gang that was into a host of illegal activities. In addition, and sometimes worse, the attitude of these gang members is usually very anti-social, anti-authority, and anti-respect.

The problem for these inmates is twofold: not only have they been instilled with this negative approach to life, but very often they stay in contact with the gang while in prison, and the gang members expect the inmates to rejoin the gang when they get out.

> **REMEMBER: Life is full of hard choices, and breaking with long-time friends who are negative influences on your life is one of those hard choices you need to make.**

Inside Prison

Inside prison, there are also gangs that are negative in their beliefs, goals, and deeds: racists; drug pushers; anti-authority in general; con game specialists; and others. Each prison has its gangs or groups of inmates with whom you "don't mess around"; there are also many inmates who continue to be associated with their gangs from the outside.

You may now be in with one of these groups, or you may have been until you left prison. Now, however, is the time to not only start taking care of what I talked about in #1 (above), but also to slip out of the negative group you hung with. Yes, this can be very hard, but it also is necessary.

REMEMBER: Gangs may seem like family but their influence keeps you from making the positive inroads necessary for a successful, crime-free life on the outside ... if that's what you truly want.

REMEMBER: Bottom line -- you've GOT to think of yourself first, because no one else is going to get you a job and keep you from going back to prison except yourself.

(3) YOU SHOULDN'T CONTINUE USING PRISON LANGUAGE. This is the language I spoke of in Chapter 2 and call "Mo'fo." I used it, you use it, just about anyone who has done time has used it. "Mo'fo" is the language we're usually surrounded with at prison; it's a sign of being tough ("get away from that darn blanket" somehow just doesn't cut it!); and it's often the language that must be used if we don't want to be labeled a snitch, a wimp, or the like.

Use the Language of the Business Community

Even though a more civilized form of "mo'fo" is spoken in the free world, it is NOT used in ANY aspect of the job search: letters, phone calls, interviews, networking, and follow up. You want to impress as any well-spoken applicant wants to impress, and use of "mo'fo" will not do you any good.

If the Employer Knows You Served Time

If the employer / job search contact knows you served time, then you really have to impress. Keep in mind that stereotype image of the inmate that many business people have: amongst other things -- the bulging biceps, only two teeth in your mouth, and a skull-and-crossbones tattoo on your arms that says "Death Before Dishonor"! -- they think that ex-inmates have something called "foul mouths." Show them otherwise!

> **REMEMBER: One foul word from you during a job interview can destroy your several months of preparation to get the interview.**

(4) DON'T DO DRUGS, DON'T PROSTITUTE, DON'T GAMBLE, DON'T BOOZE IT UP.

You do things to survive in prison, as well as to make the time go by faster. I saw more drugs with easier access to them in prison than I ever came into contact with on the outside; liquor and a variety of things that will substitute for liquor (mouthwash, spray deodorant, liqueur candies, hair spray are some; there are many others, some of which you are probably familiar with) are not difficult to come by; gambling in many forms goes on day and night; and prostitution -- male and female -- goes on as well.

How These Can Affect You in the Free World

Okay, playtime is coming close to being over, and this means getting away from the drugs, prostitution, gambling, and liquor; if not, they can bite you in ... well, you know where:

● **DRUGS**: These, of course, are illegal and most companies now have drug testing programs for job applicants. In addition, they will definitely dull your ability to perform high quality and productive work.

● **PROSTITUTION**: Sex certainly has its place, but prostitution is virtually illegal in the United States. You can have your parole revoked if caught, a reputation of being a prostitute does not help you get hired or promoted, and there is always the threat of AIDS and other sexually transmitted diseases.

●&● **LIQUOR & GAMBLING**: These, done in what is referred to as "socially acceptable" amounts (meaning just a little bit), is not necessarily going to hurt you, but can do tremendous damage if done at the wrong times (anything related to your job search), and especially if you are addicted.

And a P.S. to all four. As an ex-inmate, it may seem that you are always having to prove yourself ... and you do, unfortunately. You are fighting a many years-old image of the ex-inmate that continues through an occasional ex-inmate who commits a terrible crime, and thus is spotlighted in the media; and continued stereotypes and caricatures of ex-inmates that have been constantly fed to the public. Thus an ex-inmate who is caught drugging it, prostituting, or drinking and gambling excessively (or at all, if he / she is addicted) has a much harder time being "forgiven" -- you can't undo it once it's done!

If You Are Addicted

If you are addicted (to whatever!), seek out and get help. There are clinics in virtually every city in every country. However, as you well know, you've got to truly WANT to stop and have the draw of a successful life outside of prison with respect from friends, family, and employer be strong enough for you.

REMEMBER: Drop excess down to moderation and illegal to legal: both are necessary if you want to land employment, keep employment, and not return to prison.

(5) DON'T CONTINUE RUNNING SCAMS AND CON GAMES. Again, this is something that is done by many inmates involving a wide variety of products, services, and money. While illegal, it's done on the inside for a variety of reasons: to make some spending money, to get free items, to "put one over" on others, and to fight the rules and regulations of the prison.

How This Can Hurt You On The Outside

The major problem here is that the mentality of thinking you can con just about anyone carries over in the free world, and can get you in a lot of trouble ... not to mention keeping you from getting a job or holding onto one. What comes across to others: someone who is insincere, who is dishonest, and who always tries to take shortcuts (around the system).

REMEMBER: What you and other inmates think is "smooth" and "cool" on the inside is very often not welcome on the outside. If you've been involved in scams and con games in prison, it's time to let them go.

109

(6) DON'T PLAY THE TOUGH, THE ENFORCER, THE BULLY. Sometimes, prison means you must survive by might -- but that does not work too well in the free world if you want to get and keep a job. No, I don't think you're going to tell employers they have to hire you or you'll beat them up; you're not going to flex your muscles and demand someone give you a job. But there are two problems that could occur if you've lived by your fist, nails, and feet:

Two Possible Problems On the Outside

(1) FIGHTING. There is more of a tendency for you to want to get into a fight. While this may not show up in your job search and interview, it could happen on the job or at a company event (such as a picnic). Not only do you need to understand that the physical might and brute force that may have worked -- and, in fact, may have been necessary -- in prison will work against you in the free world, but if you have a problem with controlling your anger you must work on this as well. (For more specific information on anger management, see Chapter 1, pages 42-44, and Chapter 11, pages 387-388.)

(2) EMOTIONAL, NEGATIVE REACTION: Sometimes, this "fight mentality" carries over into your job search, on-the-job interaction with fellow employees and clients, and with friends and family members [see item #1, above]. This emotional reaction to something can get in the way of you thinking clearly and calmly ... and may result in you losing an opportunity for employment, or worse.

> **REMEMBER: Save your fists and hot temper for a boxing ring, a punching bag, or a real need to defend yourself or someone else.**

(7) DON'T FALL BACK ON THE "OH WOE IS ME, I AM / WAS IN PRISON" ROUTINE. If you are going to be successful in finding and keeping a job once you are released, you've got to do it ON YOUR OWN, rather than use your prison experience as a crutch.

Employees Who Make No Excuses Are Respected

Employers respect applicants more if the applicants make no excuses, do not expect special treatment, and DO sell themselves on their experience, skills, education, enthusiasm, and willingness to work.

Ex-Inmates Aren't the Only Ones With Problems

Everyone has problems, and many people have suffered through situations that, to them, are just as negative as you having been in prison. While falling back on having been in prison as a crutch may cut you some slack initially, it will quickly wear thin; people will respect you ONLY when you take full responsibility for your actions.

Whatever Effort Is Necessary, Do It

While it's true that certain habits from prison die hard or continue to haunt for a while after your release (you may have heard of soldiers suffering "flashback" from their war experiences), it is in your best interest to try and get these under control as soon as possible. This might mean professional counseling or talks with friends or family, and certainly includes a determined effort on your part.

> **REMEMBER:** Certainly, there is a time and a place to work on any problems or negatives that remain from your prison experience ... but your job search and employment do not offer that time nor the place.

> **REMEMBER:** Grab tightly to this positive thought: "Prison was an opportunity for me to improve, to grow, and to better understand myself."

(8) DON'T TRY TO PRETEND THAT YOUR PRISON EXPERIENCE NEVER HAPPENED. Yes, I said to put it behind you, but your time in prison is something that cannot be erased. It existed, and "sweeping it under the carpet" only means that you are tossing away X amount of years of your life.

In addition, there may be times when you need to just "let it out," i.e., cry or just talk to someone about what you went through on the inside. There's nothing wrong with this and it is, in fact, quite healthy -- to keep these feelings bottled up inside you can be very traumatic and emotionally frustrating.

Again: Use Your Prison Time As a Positive Experience!

As you read in the first two chapters of this book, there is much that you can gain from your prison experience. And if you handle questions about your prison time correctly (see Chapter 8), you will find that, in many cases, having been in prison can actually help you in your job search, as well as in everyday living.

> **REMEMBER:** Every facet of your life must be looked over for the positive it can contribute to you -- each good, bad, and ugly moment.

(9) DON'T CONTINUE "JAIL HOUSE RELIGION" OR EX-INMATE "LOVE AFFAIRS" UNLESS THEY ARE REAL. Jail House Religion: you may be guilty of it or know of others who have adopted it. It's the grasping of religion while you're in prison to help you make it through the years, perhaps get special privileges, and maybe lend a hand in helping you get released. Whatever the reason, Jail House Religion shows through very quickly for its insincerity, especially once you are on the outside (when it is quickly abandoned when no longer useful).

Employers Don't Like Contradictions

In addition, you may have been talking about your religious beliefs in the researching, networking, and other job search efforts you've done during your last six months in prison. Then you start interviewing with and receiving job offers from some of those people you contacted, some of those people who are glad to hear from someone who seems so solid in his / her religious beliefs. What will these employers think if this strong religious belief you claimed to have while inside prison suddenly disappears? Employers do not like things that don't jive, that seem to contradict one another -- and it gives them good cause not to hire.

REMEMBER: If you sincerely believe in your religion, wear it like a pair of private underwear, not a public suit.

Ex-Inmate Love Affairs

Ex-inmate love affairs very often end in couples breaking up or getting divorced / separated. What is an ex-inmate love affair? First, if you have a true love waiting for you on the outside, than this won't concern you. If not, however, this could be a problem.

"FALLING IN LOVE" AFTER PRISON. When a man or a woman has been in prison for a long time, and there has been little or no contact with the opposite sex during this time, often that man or woman will "fall in love" with the first member of the opposite sex that he or she spends time with.

This is very similar to what happens when water has been penned up behind a dam, and the dam is suddenly thrown open. A wall of water gushes forth for a short while, before leveling off with little force. The end result of a relationship can be the same: a fiery passion that was first experienced in that initial burst of romance quickly fades into a ho-hum nothingness ... but perhaps with children, bills, and other results of the former relationship around.

"FALLING IN LOVE" ON THE INSIDE.. There are also inmates who start corresponding with another on the outside, is convinced that he or she is "in love," and makes financial and other life decisions (including marriage) based on this belief. This type of relationship also often ends in relationships that go nowhere ... quickly.

A Word of Advice: Take Your Time!

In either situation -- a prison romance that blossoms through the mail (or any other form of contact with someone from the outside) or an ex-inmate love affair -- be careful! Spend time getting to know the person; ask yourself if it seems like a real love or merely an infatuation. And remember: just because you have sex with someone does not mean that you're suddenly in love! If your love relationship with another is real, it will certainly live through some extra months of growth -- on both sides!

How Relationship Problems Can Hurt Your Job Search

Infatuation relationships can be a real problem. If a relationship is not going well, it can negatively affect our moods, including our motivation and enthusiasm for other items ... such as a job search. Problems with relationships can also often spill over into our attitude on the job and how we act with other people. The more you can be certain the relationship is real, the less problems it will cause you.

REMEMBER: Before you make a final commitment in a love affair, take time to touch the thorns as well as smell the roses.

(10) **DON'T BE STUPID!** You now have an chance to use your prison experience as a plus in your job search, and you have the opportunity of a fresh start on the outside. Don't ruin either of these by doing something that is ... stupid.

Some Examples of Stupidity!

● Doing something in prison that will get you thrown in the hole, have more time added on to your sentence, hurt your chances for parole and/or early release, or get in the way of a prison official or counselor giving you a good recommendation.

● Doing something on the outside that will result in breaking your parole terms, going back to prison, having those who helped you and love you turn against you, or making a bad reputation for yourself.

● Disregarding any of the nine "DON'TS" that are listed in this chapter! (Once out of prison, there are usually several more obstacles you have to hurdle to land and keep a job, above those obstacles that most people who have not spent time in prison have to deal with. More on this in Chapter 9.)

REMEMBER: Dictionaries do a very good job in defining the word "stupid" ... there's no need for you to breathe life into it.

● ABOUT COMMON SENSE ●

I said at the start of this chapter that these 10 DON'TS are mostly common sense. However, prison sometimes does strange things to common sense, and often gets in the way of thinking clearly and positively. **To do your job search right and keep the job you land, you must be better than the average good citizen ... and this means using common sense!**

3 Tips to Keep Your Common Sense ... Common Sense

(1) MAKE IT A POINT TO THINK WITH YOUR HEAD FIRST. I've said "don't be stupid" and other such things in this book, all to impress upon you the importance of thinking first, THEN acting, not the other way around. Yet inmates have a bad habit of acting first, then reassessing afterwards, when it's too late. Common sense has one core, this one; start putting the thought process first and you'll up your common sense inventory by at least 100%!

(2) DON'T BE SO QUICK TO DISMISS YOUR "GUT FEELING." "I can't put my finger on it but it just doesn't seem right" ... "I've got this funny feeling that it should be the other one" ... "My gut feeling is telling me that I'd better not do it": we've all experienced feelings like this at one time or another, and many times they're right. Are they psychic? magic? Hardly. So-called gut feelings are really our brain pulling out memories of long-ago past experiences, information, and emotions that serve as warnings that something just doesn't seem right (or something DOES seem right). Before you dismiss these feelings, "listen" to them, think about them; they may be an additional, internal guideline to better common sense that you have.

(3) STAND ON YOUR OWN TWO FEET. This means to not be so easily led by others, to be enough of a person to make your own decisions. True, it's always important to get input and suggestions from others, but YOU be the one to make the final decision (when you have authority to do so!), not someone else. The more you're willing to take responsibility for your actions, the more you'll be seen as a person who has common sense .... not one who merely accepts another's decision, then suffers the result of that person's bad decision by being told, "Well, why'd you do that? Don't you have any common sense?" (Inmates hear this all the time!)

Use common sense to keep the don'ts away!

REMEMBER: Common sense is often most uncommon for inmates -- you'll need tons of the stuff to do well on the outside, so start loading up with it now.

Chapter 4

Writing and Using Resumes

"The secret of success in life
 is for a man to be ready for
his opportunity when it
comes."

Benjamin Disraeli, British statesman and novelist

It's time ... time to start reaching beyond your institution in a very real, very formal way to find employment: your resume and cover letter. Unlike letters you sent out for networking purposes, your resume and cover letter are aimed at doing the best possible effort in selling yourself in terms of your qualifications as a job candidate. This could be for a job interview, it may be to learn more about a company, perhaps it's to obtain an application for employment -- the reasons are many (and are covered in more detail in this chapter and the next through specific resume and cover letter examples).

The resume is about you about you about you about you!

SELF-EVALUATION PROFILE

As you start developing your resumes and cover letters, it's crucial to have a clear picture of yourself. To better do this -- and the progress you've made and still need to make -- fill out the Self-Evaluation Profile on the facing page. Refer to it and re-evaluate it often: it will not only serve as a good base of information for your resumes and cover letters but can be a constant indicator of your overall growth.

Self-Evaluation Profile

One important aspect of choosing a job objective and work environment is understanding yourself. Self-evaluation can help you analyze what's important to you in the kind of work you will do and the kind of organization in which you will work.

Your answers in this self-evaluation should be honest. They are meant to help you and should not represent a "good" or "bad" value judgement.

1) What are the things you do best? Are they related to people, data, things?

_____ related to _____
_____ related to _____
_____ related to _____

2) Do you express yourself well and easily?
Verbally: Yes _____ No _____   In Writing: Yes _____ No _____

3) Do you see yourself as a leader of a group or team? Yes _____ No _____
Do you see yourself as an active participant of a group or team? Yes _____ No _____
Do you prefer to work on your own? Yes _____ No _____
Do you like supervision? Yes _____ No _____

4) Do you work well under pressure? Yes _____ No _____
Does pressure cause you anxiety; in fact, is it difficult for you to work under pressure?
Yes _____ No _____

5) Do you seek responsibility? Yes _____ No _____
Do you prefer to follow directions? Yes _____ No _____

6) Do you enjoy new ideas and situations? Yes _____ No _____
Are you more comfortable with known routines? Yes _____ No _____

7) In your future, which of the following things are most important to you:
a. Working for a regular salary _____   b. Working for commission _____
c. Working for a combination of both _____

8) Can you be on call or available beyond normally scheduled working hours? Yes _____ No _____

9) Are you willing to travel more than 50 percent of your working time? Yes _____ No _____

10) What kind of environment is important to you?
a. Do you prefer to work indoors? Yes _____ No _____
b. Do you prefer to work outdoors? Yes _____ No _____
c. Do you prefer an urban environment (population over a million)? Yes _____ No _____
Population between 100,000 to 900,000? Yes _____ No _____
d) Do you prefer a rural setting? Yes _____ No _____

11) Do you prefer to work for a large organization? Yes _____ No _____

12) Are you free to move? Yes _____ No _____
Are there important "others" to be considered? Yes _____ No _____

13) Do you have disabilities (e.g., physical, mental, emotional) that need to be considered? Yes _____ No _____

● THE BASICS OF A RESUME ●

WHAT'S A RESUME?

When just about anyone goes looking for a job, the first thing that is required by prospective employers and employment agencies is a resume. This is a short advertisement for yourself, and primarily lists those FACTUAL items of your life that sell you as THE employee for a particular job opportunity or career.

Since the resume is almost always read before an employer or career counselor speaks with you, it is your first opportunity to make an impression on the reader. This means that much thought must go into the writing of your resume, because once it leaves your hands, you can't get it back.

> **REMEMBER: You only have one chance to make a first impression with your resume, so it must be your best effort at presenting your qualifications and strengths.**

THE ADDED IMPORTANCE TO INMATES & EX-INMATES

SELLING YOU. As an inmate, you do not have the freedom to visit or phone an employer, employment agency, or career counselor (as often as you'd like) on the outside, so a resume becomes especially important to you. There is little (or regulated) opportunity for follow-up phone questions, clarifications, or additional information input, and prison mail can often be too time consuming. So you must be especially careful that your resume is your best written effort at selling you as a good candidate for a particular job or career. For you, as an inmate, a resume must shout louder about your assets than someone else who has the freedom to drop resumes off in person, to call employers with clarifications and updates whenever he/she would like, and to do "cold call" drop-ins to companies whenever that prospective employee would like.

<u>CHANGING THE INMATE IMAGE</u>. Whether inmate or ex-inmate, just the mere fact that you have a resume goes against the image that many people on the outside carry about inmates and ex-inmates. I talked in earlier chapters about the importance of you playing according to the rules of the business world you will be entering and beginning to leave your "I am an inmate" mind set behind you. A good resume will go a long way in establishing you as a highly capable, mature adult who just happens to be an inmate or ex-inmate.

WHAT'S INCLUDED ON A RESUME?

First, keep in mind that a resume contains information about your PAST and your PRESENT. Things you are going to do in the future -- a degree you plan on pursuing, a club you plan on joining, a hobby you intend to take up, skills you want to develop, etc. -- do NOT belong in your resume, unless you are in the process of working toward it now with the final degree or certification awarded at its completion. (If applicable, these future items can be listed / mentioned in your cover letter.)

Employers are looking at your resume with two thoughts: "what have you done, and what can you do for me?" You can talk about what you will do in the future, but employers need an overview of WHAT you are (versus the "who," that comes out during the interview and partially in the cover   letter): your experience past and present will reveal this information.

<u>Major areas covered in your resume</u>:

- contact information (your name, address, phone number, etc.)
- objective
- employment history
- education
- awards / honors
- career-related accomplishments
- professional affiliations
- activities (school, community, company, etc.)
- references (imperative for inmates and ex-inmates)

Other topics that may be included in your resume: These should be or could be included, depending on your background and / or their importance to the job for which you are applying. Examples:

- ● sports, educational, other achievements
- ● leadership positions held / ability to work in team
- ● computer skills
- ● personal characteristics
- ● hobbies, interests
- ● military history
- ● travel
- ● technical knowledge

REMEMBER: Include on your resume any topics or subjects that you believe contribute to selling you as a qualified candidate. Do not include items that merely take up space and have little to do with your ability to be successful on a job or in a career, or are so old as to carry little weight by their inclusion.

HOW EFFECTIVE ARE RESUMES?

You can probably ask 100 different people this question and come up with 100 varying answers, about half telling you resumes are a great way to get an interview, the other half saying they were ineffective. For inmates and newly-released ex-inmates, the resume can be a very successful marketing tool in the job market, especially when you either do not have the option of or are limited in stopping by a company to ask about employment.

In addition, the resume is an excellent opportunity for you to make a positive presentation of yourself. (For many people -- not just inmates and newly-released ex-inmates -- the resume is the first opportunity in a long time that an individual has had to actually think about his or her positives and all the assets that person has to offer an employer.) Obviously, the more positive information out there about you, the better!

Yes, resumes are but one item in several you have available in reaching out to employers. But you do not want to let one tool pass you by, for if you do -- resumes included -- you are limiting your opportunities for success in the job market.

REMEMBER: If but one employer out of 798 to whom you've sent resumes asks you to come in for an interview and eventually offers you a job, your resume effectiveness is 100%!

WHAT'S THE PURPOSE OF A RESUME?

<u>A resume can serve several purposes</u>:

- ● initiate or reinforce an employer's decision to interview you
- ● assist you in determining your strengths and weaknesses, career direction, and primary objective
- ● supplement any application you may be required to fill out
- ● help your contacts and contacts you are trying to establish understand your qualifications
- ● allow you to immediately apply for a job you learn about or a promotion that becomes available
- ● offer the reader an initial look at your writing and proofreading abilities (attention to detail)

REMEMBER: The primary purpose of your resume is always to ultimately gain an interview for a position.

LENGTH OF A RESUME

At one time, the standard length of a resume was one page, but no more. As jobs and lifestyles have become more complex, individuals have become involved in more activities, been given greater responsibilities, and completed more education.

In addition, increased career opportunities have meant that few employees no longer stay with one organization or at one job for their entire working life, but rather have several employers and hold a variety of positions.

These changes equal more information that most job applicants have to list on their resume. Thus, while many resumes remain at one page, other resumes are now two pages.

For those individuals with an extensive amount of related information, they will often have a two page resume plus one or more additional sheets, called "Addendum." (More about Addendums later in this chapter.)

REMEMBER: No matter how many pages a resume might be, it is not very helpful if it is not written correctly, not proofread thoroughly, and does not present you in the best way possible.

STYLE OF YOUR RESUME

You may have heard resume styles put into categories such as chronological, functional, biographical, and other such names. Resume guide books, courses that teach resume writing, and many career counselors / resume writers will offer certain resume formats (such as the few I've just listed) and tell you to fit your information into a particular format style.

Hogwash!

THE "FORM" RESUME... Remember that a resume is a brief description of you, and there is no one else like you in the world. If you have but a few resume styles or formats from which to choose, it's the same as asking you to pour yourself into a pre-made mold: you have to adjust to fit the dimensions of the mold.

There is a major problem in doing this. While there will always be some aspects of the resume form that will work for you, there are also some that will not, as the resume form was not designed with YOU specifically in mind! And isn't it best to have a resume that can work 100% for you, rather than less than full power?

DEVELOPING YOUR OWN RESUME. While you do not want to throw facts on a piece of paper in any helter-skelter manner, you do need to have the flexibility to develop a resume that can showcase your qualifications as best as possible. The answer to this is developing a resume to match YOUR dimensions; to develop a resume that is specific for your skills, interests, and history. This means not only borrowing from other resume styles, but also adding some of YOUR style, YOUR thoughts, YOUR creativity.

REMEMBER: **Develop your resume around what you know about yourself, rather than pouring yourself into an already existing resume form that doesn't know you from Adam.**

● DEVELOPING YOUR RESUME ●

SPEND THE TIME NECESSARY FOR YOU TO DO THIS RIGHT!

It should be obvious from what you've thus far read how important a properly developed resume can be for you. Yet far too often inmates take an approach of, "I'll get to it when I can" or "I have loads of time to do this, so why should I put in the time now?" Yet it is precisely because a resume is so important to you and because you do have the time -- far more time, in fact, than most people on the outside -- that you should put whatever effort is necessary into developing your resume. *If you think that a resume can be dashed off in 90 minutes or so, forget it! It's going to take you several hours of thinking and writing and re-writing to get it done right.*

You and I both know that quiet time can always be found in a prison -- in a classroom, library, or cell, for example -- so make use of this. There will always be time for comic books and TV and the like after you have a job; right now, the overwhelming amount of all your efforts has to go into your exit from prison and making it on the outside ... and your resume is one of the first keys to helping you get started.

A WORKSHEET FOR YOU TO FILL OUT

<u>THE RESUME DEVELOPMENT GUIDE</u>. On the next three pages, you will find The Resume Development Guide. This will help you to construct the parts and framework of what will become your resume. Think about each section carefully before filling it in. While developing your resume, keep handy and refer to: Self-Evaluation Profile (page 125). This can bring added insight to your resume (and, later, to your cover letters).

Don't forget to check this form over every now-and-then: you want to be certain that your resume is always up-to-date; the best way to do this is immediately adding new information to The Resume Development Guide, then updating your resume as necessary.

Finally: don't hesitate to let someone else look over your filled-in answers. You may have forgotten some information or you may have worded some information in a manner that may sound right to you but is actually a bit off course. You always want to have ALL your background to work with, and a background that ACCURATELY reflects you!

Resume Development Guide

The questions asked on this page and the next two are to give you a start in developing your resume. You will probably find that some of your answers will need more space. That's fine; write those answers out on a separate sheet of paper, and you'll begin to see the various pieces of your resume taking shape, ready to be fit together.

Answer everything, even though you think it may not be used in your resume. It will give you a broader understanding of your qualifications, and may lead you to think of items you had forgotten.

SECTION I: BEGINNING

1) Name / Address / Phone # (if available) to be used to contact you:_____
_____

2) Objective: _____

SECTION II: EMPLOYMENT (begin with most recent):

1) Name of Employer: _____ Location: _____
  Your Title: _____ Dates Employed: _____
  Responsibilities: _____
  _____
  _____
  _____
  _____

2) Name of Employer: _____ Location: _____
  Your Title _____ Dates Employed: _____
  Responsibilities: _____
  _____
  _____
  _____

3) Name of Employer: _____ Location: _____
  Your Title: _____ Dates Employed: _____
  Responsibilities: _____
  _____
  _____
  _____

4) Name of Employer: _____ Location: _____
  Your Title: _____ Dates Employed: _____
  Responsibilities: _____
  _____
  _____
  _____

Resume Development Guide

(page 2)

SECTION III: EDUCATION (most recent to earliest):

A) College / University: _____ Location: _____

  Degree received: _____ Years: _____

  Major field of study: _____ Minor: _____

  Grade Point Average (GPA or QPA): _____ Dean's List: _____

  Most important courses: _____

  _____

  Honors / Achievements / Awards: _____

  _____

  Worked while attending school / # of hours worked: _____

  Percentage of education you paid for (including any loans): _____

  School organizations, clubs, sports, etc. (include offices held): _____

  _____

  College / University: _____ Location: _____

  Degree received: _____ Years: _____

   Major field of study: _____ Minor: _____

  Grade Point Average (GPA or QPA): _____ Dean's List: _____

  Most important courses: _____

  _____

  Honors / Achievements / Awards: _____

  _____

  Worked while attending school / # of hours worked: _____

  Percentage of education you paid for (including any loans): _____

  School organizations, clubs, sports, etc. (include offices held): _____

  _____

B) High School: _____ Location: _____

  Degree: _____ Year received: _____ Average: _____

  Honors, Awards, etc.: _____

  Activities: _____

C) Additional education (certificate courses, seminars, workshops, vocational training, internships, etc.) :

  _____

  _____

  _____

  _____

  _____

  _____

  _____

Resume Development Guide

(page 3)

SECTION IV: COMMUNITY / VOLUNTEER WORK (include offices held):

1) Name / Responsibilities:_____
_____

2) Name / Responsibilities:_____
_____

SECTION V: PROFESSIONAL MEMBERSHIPS / AFFILIATIONS (include offices held):

1) Name / Responsibilities:_____
_____

2) Name / Responsibilities:_____
_____

SECTION VI: COMPUTER / TECHNICAL SKILLS:

_____
_____
_____

SECTION VII: EMPLOYMENT ACCOMPLISHMENTS / HONORS / ACHIEVEMENTS (include employer name):

1) _____
2) _____
3) _____
4) _____
5) _____

SECTION VII: ADDITIONAL INFORMATION:

1) Hobbies / interests: _____
2) Foreign languages: _____
3) Licenses / certifications: _____
4) Military service: _____
5) Willingness to travel : _____ Date of Birth: _____
6) Health: _____ Married / Single / # of children: _____
7) Strongest personal traits: _____
8) References: _____
9) Permanent resident, green card, visa, etc.: _____
10) Other: _____
11) Other: _____
12) Other: _____
13) Other: _____

THE KEY TO WRITING AN EFFECTIVE RESUME

The reader has a very short time to scan your resume -- really, just seconds. Yours is one of many, and so it must make its mark quickly, to the point, and stand out from the others. Often, a resume reader will put it down because the writer has rambled or not clearly thought out how he/she best should sell himself/herself.

THE "52 PICK-UP STICK" RESUME. The bulk of resumes that are written today are in a format that I call "52 Pick-Up Stick": there are facts scattered throughout the page(s), but in no particular order. You cannot ASSUME that the reader will look between the lines or completely understand what you are talking about.

UPSIDE DOWN PYRAMID. To make your resume as effective as possible, construct it in the form of an upside down pyramid, with the most important facts at the top, and the rest of the material continuing in a DESCENDING order of importance:

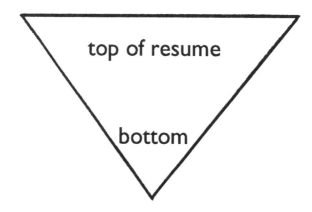

top of resume

bottom

As you will learn later in this chapter -- and will see in the resume samples -- by developing your resume in this inverted pyramid shape you will have an outline that allows you to most effectively show off your strengths AND reach the employer's eyes in a quick manner.

REMEMBER: You want your resume to deliver as if you are being served on a silver platter.

25 TIPS
TO HELP MAKE YOUR RESUME MOST EFFECTIVE

Before you begin developing your resume, there are certain points that are important for you to know.   Resumes have changed in their look and contents over the years, and you want to be certain that yours reflects these so they are most effective for you. In addition, because of your "status" as inmate or ex-inmate, there are some aspects of your resume that may differ -- this section addresses these as well. Finally, it's often the small things that count, and since -- as an inmate or ex-inmate -- you need to be better than others applying for a job, it's very important you pay attention to these "fine tuning" tips in this section.

#1
KNOW WHAT TO LEAVE OUT

<u>DON'T INCLUDE EVERYTHING</u>. Some people think that everything you've ever done belongs in your resume. This is not true.

An Example

It's possible that the person reading your resume may not like your religion, political beliefs, etc. This can result in you not getting called in for an interview ... not fair, but that is part of life's reality.

<u>YOU DON'T WANT ANYTHING THAT CAN BE INTERPRETED AS A NEGATIVE</u>.   While your resume should be a portrait of you, it should not be one that can be left open to controversy or too much of a personal statement.   What you do on YOUR time or once you HAVE the job is different, but at this stage, while you are selling yourself, you want all positives and neutrals, nothing (as much as possible) that can be interpreted as a negative.

Don't Include These in Your Resume!!

● **political affiliations, union memberships, religion** [exceptions: applying for a job with a political party or to a religious organization; company that prefers union people]

● **academic standing / grade point averages that are below the upper 25% or at least a "B" in college**

● **high school career if you have college coursework** [exception: exceptional grades or accomplishments]

● **summer jobs** [exceptions: you are a recent high school or college graduate with little other employment; jobs that relate to your career choice; you accomplished something outstanding]

● **previous salaries, names of supervisors, reasons for leaving a job, street address of employer**

● **birth date, marital status, name of spouse, childrens' names, social security #, weight & height, health**: [exceptions: in some professions, like sales, being single could be a plus; your weight and height if the job is manual labor]

● **skills that most people in business assume you have** [being able to read and write, for example]

#2
DON'T BE AFRAID TO USE THE DICTIONARY, ETC.

Use a dictionary for spelling and a grammar guide for punctuation, capitalization, etc. If unsure how to use these or these are not available, show your resume to a counselor, friend, etc., and ask him or her to check it over. Mistakes reflect on your education, your inattention to detail, your lack of patience ... and therefore your qualifications.

3
BE CAREFUL OF SPACING

Skip a line or double space when changing to a new subject in order to emphasize data.

#4
IF YOU USE A COMPUTER OR TYPEWRITER

Beyond taking less time and giving your resume a neater look, using a computer offers two other solid advantages: it shows you're up-to-date on technology and can do word processing. But whether computer or typewriter, don't forget about upper and lower-case letters, underlining, and tabulator keys for consistent indentation. And if you do need to hand write your resume because you have no access to a typewriter or computer, and can't find anyone to type your resume for you, be certain that your printing is neat!

#5
UNDERSTAND THE POSSIBLE IMPORTANCE OF "INTERESTS"

While you may think listing interests or hobbies on a resume is a waste of time, it isn't. Employers: [a] may find something you and he/she have in common; [b] they can show you are a well-rounded person; [c] they can be good "icebreakers" in an interview.

#6
THE LAYOUT OF YOUR RESUME IS IMPORTANT

Balance the material on the page so that the total effect is pleasing to the eye. Leave sufficient margins so that each page does not look too crowded. Fill the page, so as not to leave excessive space at the bottom; don't crowd so much copy on one page -- in an attempt to have a one page-only resume -- that the overall result is hard to read and uninviting to look at.

> **REMEMBER: Does your resume look like someone's you'd like to read if you were the employer? If not, you need go back to the drawing board.**

133

#7
ALWAYS EDIT

As you edit your material, keep in mind your intended purpose. Eliminate unimportant details. Write and rewrite until you are satisfied that your descriptions are factual, positive statements of your experience, showing promise of potential (and continued) growth. And if you have a second page of your resume that only has one or a few lines on it, re-edit your resume again so this "spillover" is gone -- with it, your resume looks unprofessional.

#8
BE CAREFUL IN YOUR USE OF ABBREVIATIONS

Do not use abbreviations except for titles, degrees, commonly accepted computer and business terms, names of states, or companies known by their abbreviations (examples: IBM and AT&T). (This also holds true for cover letters, as you will learn in Chapter 5.)

#9
AVOID CLICHES & TRITE PHRASES, WORDINESS, AND SLANG

TRITE EXPRESSIONS / CLICHES. These are phrases that are so old and often repeated they have become stale. Unfortunately, they slide almost automatically into your writing unless you are alert to them. When these appear on your resume (and letters), they not only weaken your writing, but the reader may see you as a person who has not thought about what you are saying and that you don't show much individuality in your writing or thinking. This could result in you NOT getting the interview.

If you have sent a resume written with these type of phrases to individuals for networking / information assistance, they may be less than enthusiastic about helping you. After all, the quality of who you are can also reflect onto others whom you ask for assistance!

Examples of Cliches and Trite Phrases

- beyond the shadow of a doubt
- dyed in the wool
- tired but happy

- cool, calm, and collected
- on the fast track
- point with pride

- diabolical skill
- sadder but wiser
- easier said than done

<u>WORDINESS (Vagueness)</u>. Also poor is using "puffy" or inflated language -- a problem that inmates often have in an attempt to impress others (and to make up for an incomplete education). Believe me, this does not impress and it often gets in the way of your message. What's more effective is to write your resume (and cover letters) using phrases that are to the point and "lean," i.e., they don't contain any unnecessary words.

2 Examples of Wordy (Vague) Writing in a Sentence

(1) VAGUE SENTENCE: "The solution impacted directly on the firm's relations with the union, in a positive manner." <u>TRANSLATION</u>: "Solution improved relations with the union"

(2) VAGUE SENTENCE: "My background has afforded me the opportunity to assume diversified responsibilities in a multiplicity of areas in the field of publishing." <u>TRANSLATION</u>: "Experience in both copy editing and design"

Examples of Wordy Expressions to Avoid and Their Acceptable Substitutions

<u>AVOID</u>	<u>USE INSTEAD</u>
as per your request	as requested
as soon as	when
at the present time / at this point in time	now
at your earliest convenience	soon OR promptly
enclosed herewith please find	enclosed is OR I enclose
due (OR owing) to the fact that	because
first of all	first
for the reason that	because
in accordance with your request	as requested
in view of these facts	therefore
it is probable that	probably
please accept my thanks	thank you

SLANG. This is simple: don't use it -- ever! You are trying to give a good image of yourself, and slang will do just the opposite.

#10
YOU MUST COMMUNICATE CLEARLY

You may write incomplete sentences or splinters of sentences as long as your meaning is clear and the style is consistent throughout. The test is whether your text is readable and understandable. Use punctuation marks intelligently and simple words that convey exactly the meaning you intend. (See pages 180-182 and 397-405 for more on communications.)

Two Grammar Distinctions for Resumes

PRESENT TENSE / PAST TENSE. Use present tense in referring to activities in which you are currently engaged ("WORK in the library"), past tense for any previous activity ("WORKED as a carpenter").

And when writing in the present tense, do so in what is called first person ("**work** in a team environment") rather than third person ("**works** in a team environment"). Use of this third person in referring to yourself (example: writing "she oversees six staff" when the "she" refers to you) is NOT acceptable UNLESS it is contained in a quotation by another person (example: "Manager's compliments included: 'She certainly was one of the best drivers we had' ").

USING "I." It is not necessary to start a sentence or phrase with a first person pronoun, that is, "I" (exception: unless the text does not make sense without it). Since you are writing about yourself, verbs (the action words, such as: "go," "making," "enjoy," etc.) will imply the "I" as the subject of your sentences.

As an example: "I assisted customers" and "Assisted customers" mean the same thing, because you are the person (subject) who did the assisting. Since a resume should be kept as brief as possible, unnecessary words -- such as the "I" in this example -- can be left out.

#11
KNOW WHEN TO INCLUDE REFERENCES

There is debate over whether references should be included in your resume. Those who say "no" argue that the employer knows you can provide references, so why put something in your resume that is taken for granted.

The "yes" side counters with the argument that mentioning references on your resume shows that you are fully prepared and are quite ready to back up your qualifications with others' recommendations.

For Inmates / Newly-Released Ex-Inmates:
Include Reference Information With Your Resume

I strongly suggest including information about references. Being in prison for any length of time usually cuts off many references / contacts you might have had if you were still on the outside. Also, your short time out has usually not yet allowed you to establish a track record of employment and erase any "bad person" image that someone may hold because you were in prison. References that attest to your abilities and to you as a "good person" will help counter this negative image.

For Ex-Inmates Who Have Been Out For Some Time:
There Is No Need to Include Your References

In normal situations (if you have not recently spent time in prison, and thus have some kind of a positive track record established), I recommend that you leave mention of references off your resume / do not include reference letters or sheets.

(Exception: if you have an exceptional reference letter from someone in the same field, industry, profession, etc. to which you are applying.)

> **REMEMBER: Good references can give you some fine tasting frosting when your cake is not at its best.**

WHO MAKE GOOD REFERENCES?   Any legitimate praise you can get from someone who has known you in a professional or educational role -- counselor, pre-release director, teacher, librarian, administrator, former employer (or present employer, if you are in a work release or halfway house-type of situation), etc. -- would make an excellent reference. Potential employers are interested in how other professional or educational people regard your performance and capabilities. Employers to whom you send resumes will assume that these individuals will judge you more objectively than someone with whom you have a personal relationship.

WHO MAKE POOR REFERENCES?   Friends, family, and others one knows on a personal basis (clergy, physician, defense attorney, etc.) are usually not considered good references for those who have NOT been incarcerated because it is assumed these references will always "sing praises." After all, would someone list a personal reference who would not give a good reference? However, for an inmate or newly-released ex-inmate, there really is no poor reference (unless you are foolish enough to include someone who has a questionable or criminal past!), for the reason given on the previous page: any help you can get in selling your positive side and solid assets is great!

HOW TO INCLUDE REFERENCES IN YOUR RESUME (in order of preference):

(1) LETTER: Ideally, a letter from your reference (attached to your resume)
(2) SEPARATE SHEET: If a letter is not possible, have a separate sheet (on the same paper and type style, if possible, as your resume) with names, titles, work addresses / phone numbers
(3) STATEMENT: If neither 1 or 2 is available, the very last item on your resume should say "References furnished upon request." [Exception: if your references are being maintained for you through your school, say: "References available through {give name, address, phone # of school}"]

DEVELOPING A REFERENCE LETTER / LETTER OF RECOMMENDATION: There may be times when the individual you ask for a reference agrees, but does not know how a reference letter should be written. Also, sometimes references will ask the applicant to write the letter, and then the reference will sign it.

If your reference needs help in developing the letter for you, make a copy of the Guide for Developing Reference Letter / Letter of Recommendation (on the next page) and send it to your reference. (You can also use this as a guide if you need to write the letter.) It will assure your Letter of Reference contains the points an employer looks for.

5 Important Points in Writing a Reference Letter

(1) ON BUSINESS STATIONERY. The reference letter should be on your reference's business stationery.

(2) IF YOU HAVE AN OLD REFERENCE LETTER. If you can get it updated, that's fine. If not, you can use the old reference letter as long as it contains information that relates to certain qualities / qualifications of yours that your chosen career / job calls for.

(3) NEVER SEND YOUR ORIGINAL REFERENCE LETTER(S). They are tough to get, and even tougher to replace. ALWAYS send copies.

(4) THE USUAL NUMBER OF REFERENCES IS THREE. Two is acceptable. If you can get four or five, fine: you can pick those most suited to your career choice.

(5) ALWAYS BE COURTEOUS & CONSIDERATE. This will provide your references with the favorable impression you wish them to have of you. A copy of your resume and a brief letter (Chapter 5, page 214) recalling courses or employment will jog their memories and give them additional information about you. (Exception: If any of your references work in your prison, ask, then follow with a letter.)

REMEMBER: It's imperative, crucial, critical, important, and necessary that you are always, without question, polite, polite, and polite in any requests for references.

Guide for Developing
Reference Letter / Letter of Recommendation

First, keep in mind that the prospective employer looks to your reference for OBJECTIVE information about you. No matter how personal or friendly your reference may have been / is toward you, he/she must regard you as an employee, student, or client first. Thus, such statements as "My friend Sue was a good worker" or "Miguel proved so efficient that we developed a close friendship" distract from your reference's professionalism and credibility.

1 Your reference's letter should begin with a paragraph that explains in what capacity you worked / are working with the organization (or were a student or client) and for how long. If a past employer and there is a "positive" reason for you being out of work (that is, the company shutting down versus you having been fired), also have it stated in this paragraph. If the reference is a former teacher or professional other than an employer, have him/her mention that you successfully completed the course, program, etc. (if this is true).

2 Next (or included in the first paragraph, depending on how involved your duties / assignments were / are), have a description of your responsibilities' extent , # of people supervised, difficulty of the subject matter, complexity of counseling sessions, etc.

3 & 3A In the next paragraph (or two paragraphs, if there is enough valid material), have him/her state the POSITIVE personal traits he/she found especially valuable in you, some contributions / achievements made that benefited the organization or program, and the overall positive impact you had on the company, department, class, program, customers, and / or other individuals.

Examples of items to be included:

● "improved work atmosphere markedly"
● "efficient and proved to be example for others"
● "increased sales by 38% and overall bottom line profits"
● "a hard worker who could always be depended upon"
● "displayed constant enthusiasm for improving and learning"
● "took a leadership role; always assisted in training"
● "excellent communicator; commands the respect of others"

4 The second-to-last paragraph should have the reference end the letter by saying something like, "I very highly recommend [YOUR NAME] to any company looking for a quality employee who has what is so necessary for an employer to succeed: outstanding knowledge, people skills, management ability, common sense, and loyalty."

5 The last paragraph is one sentence and should read very similar to: "If you have any questions or need additional information, please don't hesitate to contact me."

#12
DON'T SEND A PICTURE WITH YOUR RESUME!

If you send your picture, it can lead to discrimination against you. A person may not like the color of your skin, style or color of your hair, a mustache or beard, the shape of your face, etc. When you develop your resume and cover letter, you want the person reading your resume to judge you -- as much as possible -- on your QUALIFICATIONS, not on personal makeup.

Prejudice, Discrimination, and Bigotry Do Exist. There is nothing to prevent an interviewer from personally feeling negative toward you because of your skin color, sex, hair style, etc. However, once you are in the room with that person, you have one sales tool to use that was not available prior to the interview: your mouth. If you include your picture with your resume, you may never get the chance to use your mouth!

If You Send a Picture and Do Get an Interview. A picture also leads to preconceived notions and expectations. The first impression the interviewer will make will be to mentally compare your real appearance with the picture.

There are a Few Exceptions. Some jobs, such as modeling or TV broadcasting, are visually oriented and depend (to some extent) on the way a person looks. In situations like this, they may require you to send a photo with your resume / application. This is fine, as long as they require a picture from EVERY applicant applying for the same position.

> **REMEMBER: Often, employers have a pre-conceived image of an individual's effectiveness as a worker based on the way that person looks. There are no "perfect" people images around, except in the fantasy mind of each person -- why allow someone to possibly attach any negative qualities to you based solely on the way you look and before the employer has had a chance to speak with your mind?**

#13
BECOME AWARE OF THE COMPUTER'S IMPACT ON RESUMES

THE SCANNABLE RESUME

One of the major changes that the computer industry has brought about is the increasing use by companies of "electronic applicant tracking," the use of digital imaging technology that can keep a resume alive in a computer database for years, while saving the employer time, money, and personnel efforts in the process.

When an employer needs an applicant with certain qualifications, appropriate "keywords" can be programmed into the computer software, and the computer will then search out those resumes that contain these keywords. This is great news for you, but only if you know how to develop a scannable resume. If your resume is not written with scanning in mind there's a good chance that the computer will pass your resume over, no matter how well qualified you may be; an interview opportunity may be lost forever.

To make certain your resume is scannable, keep in mind the following:

- Exotic typefaces, underlining, and decorative graphics don't scan well.
- It's best to send originals, not copies, and not to use a dot-matrix printer.
- Too-small print may confuse the scanner; don't go below 12-point type.
- Use standard 8 & 1/2" x 11" paper and do not fold. Words in a crease can't be read easily.
- Use white or light beige paper. Blues and grays minimize the contrast between the letters and background.
- Avoid double columns, as the scanner reads from left to right.
- The scanner likes nouns; it's not too keen on so-called "action word/phrases" (made up of verbs). Examples: "manufacturer" rather than "manufactured"; "sales penetration" rather than "sales penetrated"; "construction analysis" rather than "analyzed." Technical jargon is a good idea. Examples of other noun-type information: job titles, location, languages spoken, level of education (by name of degree or certification), special programs.
- Provide a laser printer original, if possible. A typewritten or a high-quality photocopy is also acceptable. If you must print, do so neatly, in block letters, and in dark ink.
- Describe your experience with concrete words rather than vague descriptions

Suggestion: Send "Person Friendly" & "Scanner Friendly" Versions of the Same Resume

Although I have included a sample of a resume that is written for both scanning and a person read, you may wish to develop two versions of the same resume for optimal results. The first resume would be a "normal" one, i.e., it would have bold print, italics, indentation, etc. To this add a second, Scanner-Friendly version of it, in 12-point font with no bolding, italicizing, indents, columns, or anything that a scanning program would have a problem with. You might want to attach a note explaining that the second copy is included only for scanning purposes; it can be discarded if they don't do scanning.

Use of Fax, E-mail, Internet

If you have access to any of these (and don't forget to ask someone else with access to one of these who is willing to help in your job search), your resume can be helped in several ways:

● Resumes can be transmitted via fax, E-mail, and the Internet to many more companies at a faster pace and for less money than the postal service.
● The use of these -- called "electronic employment automation" -- can show employers that you are up-to-date on the use of 21st century office support technology.
● To many inmates, having an institution indicate on envelopes from inmates that the enclosed mail is from an inmate can be a drag ... and perhaps hurt employment opportunities. The use of an E-mail address (or World Wide Web site address or fax) can eliminate this. Again, this would probably have to be done through a friend. (If you are using an outside mailing / remailing address, fine; but do refer to point #1, above.)

> **REMEMBER: You may be locked away from the outside world, but the outside world still continues. Your knowledge and / or use of computer technology will go a long way in extending your reach from stagnant to progressive.**

#14
KNOW HOW TO USE "ACTION WORDS" AND SELF-DESCRIPTIVE WORDS

"ACTION WORDS"

If you've previously written a resume, you are probably familiar with so-called "action words" (and "action phrases"), words -- verbs or adverbs -- that demonstrate power, force, initiative ... in a word, action. (These were also discussed in the previous section, under scannable resumes.) These are words or phrases that you would use in your resume to describe your responsibilities, accomplishments, involvements, etc. They describe something you did, an action you took, but are NOT used for descriptions of you (see next section, below, "Self-Descriptive Words").

Examples of Action Words

- actively, accelerated, adapted, administer, analyze, approve
- coordinate, conceived, conduct, completed, control, created
- delegate, develop, demonstrate, direct, distributed, designed
- effect, eliminated, established, evaluate, expanded, expedite
- founded, furnished, fielded, fill, formatted, fulfill
- generate, governed, guided, gather, gave, graded, greeted
- harmonized, helped, handled, haul, hit
- influence, implemented, interpret, improve, initiated
- launched, lead, lecture, lifted, learn, landed, labeled
- maintain, manage, motivated, moderated, moved
- participated, performed, plan, pinpointed, program, proposed
- recommend, reduced, reinforced, reorganized, responsible
- schedule, significantly, set up, solve, streamline, successfully
- teach, train, taught, took, turned, topped

SELF-DESCRIPTIVE WORDS

In your resume and letters, you will need these words to describe your qualities and your personality. They are NOT used to describe an action you undertook or the results of that action.

Examples of Self-Descriptive Words

- active, adaptable, aggressive, alert, ambitious, analytical, attentive
- broad-minded, conscientious, consistent, constructive, creative
- dependable, determined, diplomatic, disciplined, discrete
- economical, efficient, energetic, enterprising, enthusiastic, eager
- forceful, imaginative, independent, logical, loyal, mature, methodical
- objective, optimistic, perceptive, personable, pleasant, positive
- realistic, reliable, resourceful, respective, self-reliant, sincere
- sophisticated, systematic, tactful, talented

A Word of Caution on the Use of Self-Descriptive Words

Although trite phrases and cliches were described in Hint #9 (page 140), an extra word of caution should be made here about the use of "tired" self-descriptive words, words to describe one's self that sound too much like they were taken off a word rack at J.C. Penney's rather than individually tailored by you. The two worst culprits in this category are "hard-working" and "responsible for" -- come up with more creative ways to demonstrate these descriptions (including examples). Your resume will be better off for it and, ultimately, so will you!

#15
THE DIFFERENCE BETWEEN A CURRICULM VITAE & A RESUME

From the Latin, its exact translation is "the course of one's life or career." For many employers, the curriculum vitae (sometimes called vitae or C.V.) is the same as a resume, and you may find these terms used interchangeably, so don't panic when you hear it.

(For the record, they are not the same. A curriculum vitae is used primarily by applicants seeking academic or administrative positions in institutions of higher learning, and calls for extensive detail of one's educational, professional membership, publications, and presentations background.)

#16
KNOW WHEN AND HOW TO USE ADDENDUMS

On page 130, I discussed the length of a resume and indicated that resumes may need be longer than two pages because a person may have so much information important to his/her qualifications that the resume could easily become three, four, or more pages.

This presents a major problem for employers. Receiving so many resumes on a daily basis, they spend 8 - 30 seconds INITIALLY scanning through a resume. If a resume appears to be a small book, often the resume is passed over. The use of an Addendum can solve this.

HOW AN ADDENDUM WORKS

(1) GENERAL & SPECIFIC. Once your resume is developed, look it over to see what items might be mentioned in general, with specifics included in the Addendum. These would include such subject areas as "Professional Affiliations," "Courses," "Community Involvement," "Computer Knowledge," and others where there may be several items to list.

(2) THE WORDING. On your resume, when it's time to mention a subject that would also spill onto an Addendum sheet, type in "See Addendum for complete listing." under the subject title. On the Addendum page, type the subject heading, such as "Details of Professional Affiliations" or "Complete Listing of Computer Knowledge." Then list the details.

(3) SAVES TIME. This way, if employers don't have the time to read the entire resume, they at least have a full sketch of your background in the first two pages. If they are interested in what your resume says, they can then go on to the Addendum for those details that could not fit on your resume.

(4) VERY FEW INMATE RESUMES NEED AN ADDENDUM. Only if you have an unusually long listing of items, or if you are writing a Curriculum Vitae (discussed under Hint #15) would you need an Addendum.

#17
ALWAYS SUMMARIZE YOUR RESUME AT ITS TOP

As has already been said, employers initially scan a resume in 8 - 30 seconds ... and the key word here is "scan." Yours is one of many and you can't expect an employer to thoroughly read your resume the first time she/he gets it, so you want to write your resume in a manner that not only best presents you but does so in a style that is quick and easy: summarizing your strengths at the top will do this.

Here's how it works: simply take those assets of yours that you feel are the Big Guns (such as a G.E.D. certification or college degree, solid experience in a particular field, an achievement related to your work interest, or exceptional communicative skills) and put them under a section called "Overview" or "Summary" at the top of your resume, right under your objective. This makes it much easier and quicker for an employer to learn about you! (Examples of this section can be found in the resume samples later in this chapter.)

#18
A NEW KID ON THE BLOCK: THE PORTFOLIO RESUME

In Chp. 2 (pp. 80-82), the use of portfolios was discussed. What's kinda' neat is that there may be potential job situations when you can take the portfolio you've created in prison and turn it into what is a relatively new tool in the job search, the portfolio resume.

A portfolio resume is really a marriage between the traditional resume (that we've been discussing) and a portfolio; it offers potential employers a written history of the candidate while also showing specific examples of his / her work. This could be a good option for you if you've accumulated some pieces of work inside (say, for example, in carpentry, horticulture, barbering, or automotive repair) that you can't bring with you but would sell you much better if pictures (or samples, if appropriate) of them were included with your resume. If this does fit you, then talk to your correctional educator or counselor to work out the logistics.

#19
IF APPLICABLE, SHOW TEAM-BUILDING & LEADERSHIP

It makes no difference if you're applying for an entry-level position, a "blue collar" or "white collar" job, or a management position: any employer who sees words such as "team member," "team builder," "leadership role," "leader," or "directed leadership" on your resume will give you extra points! Search your background for anything that shows you can work effectively in a team and / or that you've taken a leadership role. And don't forget to look at any activities or assignments from prison -- these count just as well.

#20
DON'T TALK ABOUT YOUR WEAKNESSES;
DON'T HIGHLIGHT ANY MINOR LEAGUE MATERIAL

These are two areas that resume writers often forget about, and it can hurt them. Let's look at each:

1) **FORGET YOUR WEAKNESSES**: You're selling your strong points, not your weak ones, so forget about them ... for now! Remember that employers are seeking out the BEST candidates for a job, and it's bad enough when he/she puts up roadblocks to a person's efforts at landing an interview. Don't you make the job easier by pointing out your own faults! Wait until the interview, then -- and only if you feel a weakness of yours could present a problem -- bring it up. In the interview you have the strength of your voice and in-person presence to minimize any weaknesses, two selling points that are not available on your resume.

2) DRAW ATTENTION TO YOUR MAJOR LEAGUE STUFF: As you'll see from the resume examples that follow, the spotlight goes on that material that is the best; you want the reader to first be impressed by your most important items. Read over your resume carefully and be certain that you haven't accidentally drawn attention to material that is minor league quality at best (but still important enough to make the cut to the resume).

#21
DON'T EXPLAIN THE NEGATIVE EXPERIENCES OF YOUR LIFE

Okay you've been to prison for a while ... and maybe you one time declared bankruptcy ... and perhaps you were once fired from a job ... and possibly you lost $1269 worth of company tools: none of these belongs on your resume. For inmates, of course, the biggest "resume problems" are usually explaining time in prison and explaining a spotty job history. As you'll see from the resume samples in this chapter, there are some clever, honest ways to handle this. But writing down, "I was in prison during this time" or "I haven't really worked very much" is not the way to sell you! Let's get you into the interview first, okay?

#22
DON'T BOAST OR BRAG

Yes, a resume is where you sell yourself, and it's certainly important that you offer up your best assets. However, there's also a line you don't want to cross -- the Bragging Line! When an employer reads, for example, "First employee in firm's history to assemble 150 doohickeys in an hour," that's okay -- it's a fact, pure and simple. But if you were to write, "Considered the best employee firm has ever hired due to first-ever assembly of 150 doohickeys in one hour," that's bragging, pure and simple. Sure, because you've been in prison and perhaps had a poor job history you may want to overcompensate for it on your resume -- but don't. Let the facts on the resume speak for themselves; as for the boasting or bragging, let the employer reading your resume do that to someone else in his or her company because the facts on your resume indicate that you look like a winner!

#23
DON'T EVER, EVER, EVER LIE!

With rare exceptions, resumes (and cover letters) will NOT get you a job, merely an interview. Yet the information contained on your resume will be considered by the employer as the foundation upon which the rest of you is built ... so don't lie!

Any lie, any misstatement, anything that looks as if it might have been stretched or inflated will certainly result in your resume being tossed into the circular file: the wastebasket. Honesty is a BASIC quality that each employer expects from an applicant and demands from an employee.

During the early 1980s, when so many people were out of work in the U.S., many applicants wrote "creative" resumes: they lied to give themselves a better edge in the competitive job market. Companies hired firms (and still do) to check out these resumes, as well as many of their employees. The results? As you probably guessed, a large number of applicants were weeded out because they had lied at various points on their resumes. However, employees who had been with organizations for several years were also let go because it was found they, too, had lied on the resume they initially submitted.

As you will see from the resume samples in this chapter, a well thought out and properly constructed resume does not have a need to lie -- no matter what level your skills, education, and other qualifications.

#24
GET SOMEONE ELSE'S INPUT

Before you type or write your "ready to mail" copy, let someone else take a look at your resume. Get his or her reaction to it. It's always possible that he or she will remind you of something you had forgotten or give you a suggestion that could improve some aspect of your resume.

Also, consider your own reaction after setting it aside for a day or two: would you hire the person described in this resume? If you're not quite sure, you may want to re-write it so it does a better job in selling you.

> **REMEMBER:** Your resume is a walking billboard advertising you -- you want others to regard you as a quality product with good potential, not a sugar-coated cardboard cutout that will crumble in the rain.

#25
LEARN HOW TO HANDLE RESUME REJECTION

Hey, it goes with the territory: resumes that get no responses or resumes that get a "thanks but no thanks" response in the mail. And let's face it: as an inmate, what you don't want is someone else telling you -- so it seems -- that you're not good enough. Well, hold your horses, Fred! Before you get into a major depression funk, drop your self-esteem even lower, and hit a point of emotional fright, first understand a few things:

(1) NO COMPANY IS OUT TO GET YOU PERSONALLY. The company has certain requirements for each job, and no doubt has many applicants for any job available. While your resume will certainly sell you into interviews, your background is not going to be perfect for every employer.

(2) SOMETIMES, COMPANIES JUST DON'T HAVE THE TIME OR PERSONNEL TO ANSWER EACH RESUME. It may not be nice, and you certainly may think all your work in developing your resume at least deserves some response, but it just isn't going to happen every time.

(3) DON'T FORGET TO USE ANY REJECTION LETTERS AS NETWORKING RESOURCES. Talk about turning lemons into lemonade, this is a great example! Just about every rejection letter has a company name on it. Use the "rejection letter" (found in Chapter. 5, page 219) to follow up on the rejection letter the company sent you: often, this second effort on your part can lead to an interview because it shows you're not easily discouraged, it shows initiative on your part, and it gets your name in front of an employer again -- all nice little pluses!

Continue going forward -- that's the way to handle resume rejection!

● HANDLING PRISON TIME ON YOUR RESUME ●

Employers get a bit nervous when they see time gaps in a resume. If, for example, you've had a good work record from 1977-1991, but have been in prison from 1991-1997, it would look rather strange if your resume had six years left out.

TRYING TO HIDE SOMETHING. Many employers will not call you in for an interview, based on this one item. They assume (in this case, rightly so) that you are trying to hide something. This gives the readers an immediate negative feeling ... and they'll probably move on to the next resume.

There is an old expression that you may have heard: "The best defense is a good offense." This means that before you are placed in a position where you have to defend or explain yourself, you come out with the information first.

DIFFERENT WAYS. However, this does not mean that you account for your prison time on your resume by stating these X number of years were spent in prison (see Hint #21, page 155). Depending on the length of your prison time, the number of times you've been in prison, and the relationship you've established with the recipients of your resume, this section can be written in several ways.

> **REMEMBER:** You always look at your prison time as years spent improving your education, your mind, and your skills; it must be accepted as a plus, not a negative in your life.

Examples of how you can handle your prison time appear on the next page.

Explaining Prison Time on Your Resume: Examples

Depending on how you spent your time in prison, what you gained during this time could be listed under "Experience, " "Education," "Leadership Skills," "Interests," others, and combinations of these. Also, the style in which your resume is written will determine if you need to include dates. As with all other facts on your resume, be certain that your prison information is correct, thorough, and remains consistent with other sections of your resume. Some examples of how different sections of your resume might read follow (these do NOT represent one person, but rather various individuals and backgrounds):

(UNDER "EMPLOYMENT")

BRICKLAYER, State of Texas (Midland, TX), 1986-1997. Began in apprenticeship program; worked up to Certified Bricklayer. Mixed mortar; cleared and laid out site; assisted in the building and repairing of a variety of structures, including: floors, walls, fireplaces, curbs, and curing bins. **Complimented by supervisor for quality of work.**

(UNDER "TECHNICAL SKILLS" OR "MECHANICAL SKILLS")

MECHANICAL SKILLS: Use of lathe to make a variety of wooden and metal structures ... knowledgeable in auto, truck, and heavy duty equipment repairs ... know set up ... specific machines include: Lancer 1040 Series, Micron Electronic Grinder, XR7 Metal Lathe, various manual machines ... **use of computer (IBM compatible) with Snifter software; input all jobs; checked daily for inventory replacement.**

(UNDER "EMPLOYMENT")

LABORER, New York State Department of Corrections (Wende, NY), 1989-May 1990. Worked in several capacities, including wheelman, driver, digger, loader, and in maintenance. Extensive knowledge of road repaving, edging, and striping. Extremely strong; don't easily tire. Member of eight-man crew. **Punctual with no sick days.**

(UNDER "EMPLOYMENT")

ADMINISTRATIVE AIDE / TYPIST (Chula Vista, CA), 1985-1995. Duties: Word processing (46 wpm); answered phones; used Microsoft WORD .. **devised method of filing that saved time and increased accuracy; offered position of Senior Administrative Aide but left for better position (more responsibilities).**

(UNDER "EDUCATION")

UNIVERSITY OF TENNESSEE: completed three semester courses in English, Introduction to Computers, and Business Management ... (1987-1988).

(UNDER "LEADERSHIP ACTIVITIES" OR "MEMBERSHIPS")

PRESIDENT, Jaycee Chapter, 1991-1992. Overall responsibility for programming, membership recruitment, and special events for 85-member chapter. **Initiated newsletter; increased membership by 25%; successfully implemented three fund-raising events.**

(UNDER "ADDITIONAL INFORMATION," "PERSONAL," OR "INTERESTS")

INTERESTS: Reading (Westerns), sewing, movies.

3 POINTS ABOUT SENDING / RECEIVING MAIL

Depending on your institution's regulations, whether you want others receiving your resumes (and cover letters) to know about your current address (prison!), and your institution's address, how you send mail and receive mail can get complicated. The following will help:

(1) ADDRESS: Many prisons have a P.O. Box for a mailing address; this is excellent, as it does not indicate you are writing from prison. Others, however, tell you that your return address should be, for example, "Cell Block 4, East Wing"; if you can change this to "#4-E" (and the post office will accept it), fine. If you are going to put a friend's or relative's address (and phone #) on your resume, be certain that your mail / messages will be forwarded to you within a day or so of their receipt (you don't want any job-related mail to sit around for awhile!). Of course, if you are writing to individuals who know you are in prison or you are informing them that you are in prison, then your normal prison address is acceptable.

Some prisons do present an added problem by having an address such as "171 Prison Way"; or by having the full prison name printed on the envelopes given to inmates (when these are the envelopes you must use, for whatever reason) OR stamping the prison name / address on all outgoing inmate mail. Any of these will certainly let whoever receives the envelope immediately know that you are in prison. What to do? Well, there are two options: [a] Find a friend, relative, or someone on the outside who will let you use his or her address. This way, you can send your resumes and cover letters in an envelope (non-prison return address on it) within an envelope OR have the person with the outside address take your resume, etc and put it in a clean envelope that he/she then will address. [b] See about the possibility of having your mail "institution free" when it is job-related. Keep in mind this would only be considered by an institution for an inmate who has an exemplary record!

(2) CHECKING / CENSORING MAIL: Most prisons have a policy of checking or censoring incoming mail, and some extend this to outgoing mail. Check on the policy of your institution so that you can know what limitations, if any, are on career search information you receive from the outside. Also, be certain that those writing you who KNOW you are in prison do not write or enclose anything that could get you into trouble. Follow these same guidelines for yourself if outgoing mail is checked.

(3) FORWARDING ADDRESS: It may happen that you are released before all your mail reaches you ... and this could include some important information about your job search. Find out what your prison's policy is on forwarding mail to you after you leave. You may want to put two addresses on your resume (allow at least one week prior to your release as the last day you should be sent mail in prison). An example:

> 1321 Cathy Road, Tampa, FL 83145 [before 10/10/98]
> 16 Seena Street, Lower, Bay City, FL / (421) 622-9860 [after 10/10/98]

ABOUT THE RESUME SAMPLES THAT FOLLOW

Earlier in this chapter I mentioned that there is not one set style of a resume, but rather many. The resume examples in this chapter can be used in their exact formats or can be mixed up, switched around, and modified to best mirror your qualifications.

USE THESE OR CREATE YOUR OWN. Each sample was developed to best showcase your positives and minimize the possibility of negatives cropping up. Naturally, you will be shown, have seen, or have heard about other resume styles. Many of these will work fine, as long as they follow certain guidelines (see the 25 Hints, pp. 131-151). Don't be afraid to experiment, to create a few different kinds of resumes. After you've done this, you'll have a better "feel" as to which resume style is best for you.

ABOUT THE PRINT SIZE & PAGE SIZE OF THE SAMPLES. In most cases, the print on the sample resumes is smaller than you should use. Also, in order to fit a full resume page on each of this book's pages, the resume page sizes were reduced.

You Will Find Three Sets of Resume Samples

SET #1: This is actually a combination exercise and example, showing how a poorly constructed resume can be rewritten to account for prison time. The finished resume is written in THREE forms: as a traditional resume, as a resume that can be read by a person or scanned into a computer, and to be used only as a scannable resume.

SET #2: These resumes are samples that specifically incorporate prison time.

SET #3: Here you'll find resumes that may or may not incorporate prison time; they can be used either way.

> **REMEMBER:** Whether you want to be a laborer or librarian, an electrician or entomologist, a counselor or cashier, teacher or truck driver: all jobs initially or eventually need your resume.

Set #1
EXAMPLE OF A BAD RESUME
(What can you find that's wrong with it?)

SAMUEL TAKASOKO	Married
3015 Jennifer Street	Height: 5' 11"
Okolona, MS 45681	Weight: 175 lbs.
(515) 896-9421	Health: Excellent
CAREER OBJECTIVE:	Desire an entry-level position where my skills and education can be used to their fullest by a dynamic and fast-growing company.
EMPLOYMENT HISTORY:	
Sepetember 1982 - October 1988:	Mississippi State Depart. of Roads
	1530 Jefferson Davis Boulevard
	Tupolo, MS 45684
	Immediate Supervisor: Bubba Hall
	Position: Engineering Technician
	As an employee of this department I was responsible for preliminary and final surveing, inspection of highway and waterway construction, and initial highway design.
November 1991 - December 1997:	Mississippi State Department of Roads
	D.J. McCamey State Office Building
	Meridian, MS 45032
	Immediate Supervisor: Miriam Cassidy
	Position: Engineering Technician
	As an employee of this department I was responsibile for preliminery highway survey.
EDUCATION:	
February 1995 - September 1997:	Advanced Training Center
	189 Mercer Street
	Tupolo, MS 45684
	I completed a two-part program of 910 hours.
September 1983 - June 1987:	Okolona Senior High School
	Simon & Garfunkel Street
	Okolona, MS 45681
SALARY OBJECTIVE:	$18,000 -- $21,000

Set #1
(continued)
EXAMPLE OF A BAD RESUME: WHAT'S WRONG WITH IT

(1) <u>NOTHING STANDS OUT</u>: With the exception of the applicant's name, everything is written in light print. Also, information in the job descriptions is too long; one paragraph should be broken into two or three. And where the applicant actually worked for only one firm (Mississippi State Department of Roads), it reads as if he worked for two. Also, the two positions he held are in a reversed order. The overall result: missed facts and confusion.

(2) <u>THE RESUME MERELY LISTS FACTS</u>: There is nothing about accomplishments, achievements, highlights, computer experience, etc. Descriptions are ho-hum and therefore don't do a good job of selling the applicant.

(3) <u>NEEDLESS INFORMATION INCLUDED</u>: Height, Weight, Marital Status, and Health definitely have no place on this resume. And if any or all of them did belong on this resume, they should never be listed at the top: an employer is more concerned about your skills, education, and experience than he/she is in your personal statistics.

(4) <u>DATES STAND OUT BY THEMSELVES</u>: Headings and section names in resumes, just like in a newspaper or magazine, are separated from the rest of the text by blank space (called "white space"). The purpose is so that the reader's eye will be attracted to these first, before reading the main text. With dates, however, there is a problem. If you have held a series of jobs, and especially for a short period of time, the dates sticking out (as these do on the "Bad Resume" example) draw attention to your short terms of employment; the reader may think you are a "job jumper." Finally, this applicant has a gap of three years (perhaps he was in prison?); he draws attention to it.

(5) <u>CAREER OBJECTIVE IS UNCLEAR AND IS "PUFFY"</u>: An objective is just what it says: what position / what area are you focusing on? Employers want you to get right to the point. Also, doesn't it stand to reason that you would be looking to work with a company that is "dynamic" and "fast-growing"? The opposites are "so-so" and "slow-growing": when was the last time you knew of anyone looking to work for a company like that? Don't put such puffery and fat in your resume -- it detracts from your professionalism.

(6) <u>COMPLETE STREET ADDRESSES</u>: Quite simply, they're not needed and take up space.

(7) <u>SPELLING ERRORS / REPETITION OF SAME WORDS</u>: "September," "responsible," "surveying," and "preliminary" (the last one) are misspelled. "Preliminary" is used twice; a word like "beginning" could be used to eliminate the sameness. Also: no mention of "team" or "leadership" in any form.

(8) <u>LISTING OF HIGH SCHOOL</u>: Since the applicant completed an advanced education program and nothing extraordinary in high school, there is no need to include it. Also: what certification did he receive at ATC?

(9) <u>USE OF THE FIRST PERSON PRONOUN "I"</u>: Resumes need get information across fast; employers scan them over very quickly. Since it is understood that it is your resume, there is no reason to write "I" (or "my," "me," etc.)

(10) <u>SALARY / REFERENCES</u>: Salary should not be included on a resume; references should be, if inmate or newly-released ex-inmate.

(11) <u>NOT SCANNABLE</u>: The resume is written in a two-column format, one that scanners can't read.

Set #1
(continued)
THE BAD RESUME REWRITTEN: NOW IT DOES A GOOD JOB!

SAMUEL TAKASOKO

3015 Jennifer Street, Okolona MS 45681

(515) 896-9421

CAREER OBJECTIVE:
ENGINEERING TECHNICIAN

SUMMARY:

- 15+ years solid experience as Engineering Technician
- Credited for developing time-saving method of surveying
- Special expertise in highway design / highway curves
- Called upon by State of Mississippi to solve emergency engineering problem
- Certificate of Completion: Engineering Technician Master
- Computer knowledge: Microsoft WORD, Excel, RoadEze Technical Software

---

RELATED EXPERIENCE:

Mississippi State Department of Roads, 1982-1997:

ENGINEERING TECHNICIAN (Meridian MS / 1991-1997): Worked with team responsible for central Mississippi electronic highway system and software, including state-of-the-art design of highway curves. As Team Leader, had major involvement with initial highway survey.

- selected by State of Mississippi as member of emergency highway engineering crew
- credited by supervisor for developing time-saving method of surveying
- assisted in the training of less-experienced Engineering Technicians
- supervised team crews of up to eight

ENGINEERING TECHNICIAN (Tupolo MS / 1982-1988): Duties included initial and final surveying, inspection of highway and waterway construction, and first stages of highway design and drafting.

- promoted from Engineering Technician Trainee after only four months
- developed improved surface table for drafting / drawing blueprints

EDUCATION:

ADVANCED TRAINING CENTER (Tupolo MS): *Certificate of Completion, Engineering Technician Master.* Completed 910-hour program, 1997. Computer training: Microsoft WORD, Excel, RoadEze Technical Software.

REFERENCES:

FURNISHED UPON REQUEST

Set #1
(continued)
THE BAD RESUME REWRITTEN: FOR HUMAN OR SCANNER
(NOTE: The scannable nouns that have either been added or had been in previous example appear in *italics*.)

SAMUEL TAKASOKO
3015 Jennifer Street, Okolona MS 45681
(515) 896-9421

CAREER OBJECTIVE:
ENGINEERING TECHNICIAN

SUMMARY:
- *15+ years* solid experience as *Engineering Technician*
- Credited by *supervisor* for developing time-saving method *(TimeRelay)* of surveying
- Special expertise in *North American highway design / highway curves*
- Called upon by *State of Mississippi* to solve emergency *road sinkhole* problem
- *Certificate of Completion: Engineering Technician Master*
- Computer knowledge: *Microsoft WORD, Excel, RoadEze Technical Software*

RELATED EXPERIENCE:
Mississippi State Department of Roads, 1982-1997:

ENGINEERING TECHNICIAN (Meridian MS / 1991-1997): Member of *team* responsible for central Mississippi *electronic highway system* and *software (Excel)*, including state-of-the-art *design of highway curves*. As *Team Leader*, had major involvement with initial *highway survey*.

- selected by State of Mississippi as *member of emergency highway engineering crew*
- credited by supervisor for developing *TimeRelay* method of surveying (saves time)
- *Co-Trainer* of less-experienced Engineering Technicians ... *team supervisor* (up to eight crew members)

ENGINEERING TECHNICIAN (Tupolo MS / 1982-1988): Duties included initial and final surveying, inspection of highway and waterway construction, and first stages of highway design and drafting.

- *promotion: from engineering Technician Trainee* to *Engineering Technician* after only four months
- developed improved surface table *(TableEase)* for drafting / drawing blueprints

EDUCATION:
ADVANCED TRAINING CENTER (Tupolo MS): *Certificate of Completion, Engineering Technician Master*. Completed 910-hour program, 1997. *Computer training: Microsoft WORD, Excel, RoadEze Technical Software*.

REFERENCES:
FURNISHED UPON REQUEST

Set #1

(continued)

THE BAD RESUME REWRITTEN: FOR SCANNER ONLY

SAMUEL TAKASOKO
3015 Jennifer Street, Okolona MS 45681
(515) 896-9421

CAREER OBJECTIVE:
ENGINEERING TECHNICIAN

SUMMARY:
- 15+ years solid experience as Engineering Technician
- Credited by supervisor for developing time-saving method (TimeRelay) of surveying
- Special expertise in north American highway design / highway curves
- Called upon by State of Mississippi to solve emergency road sinkhole problem
- Certificate of Completion: Engineering Technician Master
- Computer knowledge: Microsoft WORD, Excel, RoadEze Technical Software

---

RELATED EXPERIENCE:
Mississippi State Department of Roads, 1982-1997:

ENGINEERING TECHNICIAN (Meridian MS / 1991-1997): Member of team responsible for central Mississippi electronic highway system and software (Excel), including state-of-the-art design of highway curves. As Team Leader, had major involvement with initial highway survey.

- selected by State of Mississippi as member of emergency highway engineering crew
- credited by supervisor for developing TimeRelay method of surveying (saves time)
- Co-Trainer of less-experienced Engineering Technicians ... team supervisor
  (up to eight crew members)

ENGINEERING TECHNICIAN (Tupolo MS / 1982-1988): Duties included initial and final surveying, inspection of highway and waterway construction, and first stages of highway design and drafting.

- promotion: from Engineering Technician Trainee to Engineering Technician after only four months
- developed improved surface table (TableEase) for drafting / drawing blueprints

EDUCATION:
ADVANCED TRAINING CENTER (Tupolo MS): Certificate of Completion, Engineering Technician Master. Completed 910-hour program, 1997.Computer training: Microsoft WORD, Excel, RoadEze Technical Software.

REFERENCES:
FURNISHED UPON REQUEST

Set #2
EXAMPLES OF RESUMES THAT INCORPORATE PRISON TIME

About the Sample Prison Resumes: On this page and the next three, there are three sample resumes that incorporate various activities accomplished / involved in while incarcerated. As you read them, note how the information that comes from prison (highlighted in *italics*) blends in with the other information on the resume. In some instances, you would not have known that the items came from prison if they were not highlighted in *italics*.

SAMPLE #1 -- GOOD PRISON RESUME

ROBERT P. JONES
146 Sanders Road - #5-E, Joliet, IL 60432 [until 5/3/98]
1175 Oak Street, Chicago, IL 60432 / (815) 664-9865 [after 5/3/98]

MAJOR AREAS OF INTEREST:
CUSTOMER SERVICE and ADMINISTRATION

PROFILE:
- **Solid background in Customer Service and Administration**
- **Specialized skill in turning negative situations around**
- **Computer literate (IBM; WordPerfect software);** *college courses in Business*

STRENGTHS:
CUSTOMER SERVICE: *Work extremely well in developing trusting and lasting rapport with clients ... know when to talk, know when to listen ... follow-through with all customer concerns and paperwork ... take the initiative; do not wait for a client to ask a question ... enjoy working with others ... present professional image.*

ADMINISTRATION: Experienced with: courier deliveries, *operation of IBM PC and use of WordPerfect software,* developing reports, phone work, payroll ... some involvement with sales telemarketing in a team environment ... *good at organizing office for best use of time and space efficiency ... can handle several projects at once ... not a "clock watcher"; will put in whatever hours needed ...* assisted customers with hands-on training ... **complimented by many clients for training ability and by management for improving office efficiency.**

EMPLOYMENT:
- ***ADMINISTRATIVE ASSISTANT,** Dr. Suzanne Charles (Joliet, IL), March 1994-present.*
- **CUSTOMER SERVICE REPRESENTATIVE,** Computers Unlimited (Chicago, IL), 1985-1994.

EDUCATION:
- ***UNIVERSITY OF CHICAGO:** Completed course in Office Administration.*
- ***SPECIAL TRAINING:** Eight-week course (16 hours), "Principles of Business"; received Certificate of Completion, 1997.*

ADDITIONAL INFORMATION:
- **INTERESTS:** *Exercise, reading, arts & crafts, and volleyball*
- **REFERENCES:** *Furnished upon request*

Set #2
(continued)
EXAMPLES OF RESUMES THAT INCORPORATE PRISON TIME

SAMPLE #2 -- GOOD PRISON RESUME

ELIZABETH STONE
P.O. Box 456, Hartwell, GA 30643

** DENTAL ASSISTANT **

PROFESSIONAL STATEMENT:

"A successful Dental Assistant depends not only on one's experience and education, but also a combination of people skills, attention to detail, ability to communicate, self-motivation, knowledge of product, and dedication to employer.

"I not only offer this mixture, but know that any dental practice I become associated with will find a continuation of their integrity and commitment to quality, technical excellence, and dedication to client service."

PERSONAL & PROFESSIONAL STRENGTHS:
... take and develop x-rays
... outgoing, friendly personality
... good sense of humor
... assist with crowns, implants, and bonding
... teach clients total dental care

EDUCATION:
** *SCOTTIE CARTER, D.D.S.:* Trained for six months; promoted to position of Dental Assistant.
** **HARTWELL SENIOR HIGH SCHOOL**: Graduate.

ADDITIONAL INFORMATION:
** **PREVIOUS EMPLOYMENT**: Line Worker, Evonne Jacqueline Caterer, one year. **Team member.**
** **INTERESTS**: Movies, dance, camping, *reading, learning*
** **REFERENCES**: *Attached*

Set #2
(continued)
EXAMPLES OF RESUMES THAT INCORPORATE PRISON TIME

SAMPLE #3 -- GOOD PRISON RESUME

PHILIP ROBERT ARMANIA

168 Mercer Street, P.O. Box 56, Steilacoom, WA 98388-0900 [before July 24, 1997]
1722-E Towns Apartments, Shelton, WA 98584 [after July 24, 1997]

OBJECTIVE

Manager, Retail Clothing Store / Department

SUMMARY OF QUALIFICATIONS

- **Five+ years Management & Sales experience, Men's Clothing**
- **Outgoing personality; enjoy working with clients**
- **Developed / taught staff training programs**
- **Awarded Lifesaving Medal by city mayor**
- **Permanent resident of U.S.**
- *Know custom tailoring*
- **High school graduate**

CURRENT RETAIL CLOTHING EXPERIENCE

CLOTHING CONSULTANT / PERSONAL TAILOR (Steilacoom WA), *1994-present. Advise adult males (all ages) on appropriate attire for interviews and business meetings, as well as the correct care of present wardrobe; tailoring includes custom and repair alterations, construction of accessories.*

- *Leadership role in training new workers on use of machinery*
- *Complimented by supervisor on attention to detail, ability to learn quickly*
- *Improved customer satisfaction by assisting with special services at no cost to them*

[PAGE 1 OF 2]

163

SAMPLE #3 -- GOOD PRISON RESUME
(continued)

PHILIP ROBERT ARMANIA
    Page Two

ADDITIONAL RETAIL CLOTHING EXPERIENCE

ASSISTANT MANAGER / SALES ASSOCIATE (Shelton, WA), 1991-1994. Managed suburban men's clothing store with primary emphasis on high school and college students. Trained staff in customer service, fashion coordination, and sales techniques; opened and closed store; scheduled vacations; balanced registers and made deposits; had hiring and firing input; created and set-up store & window displays.

- **developed Tuxedo Division where none previously existed**
- **aggressively marketed high schools / colleges for prom business**
- **on own time, visited fashion shows, read fashion magazines / reviews**

EDUCATION

GRANVILLE HIGH SCHOOL (Shelton, WA): graduated 1991.

- **graduated #23 of 431 in senior class [top 18% of class)**
- **member: Fashion Club, Drama Club (assisted with costumes)**
- **worked part time (20 hours weekly)**

OF SPECIAL NOTE

Awarded city's Lifesaver Medal for assisting and helping to rescue boy who had fallen in lake.

PERSONAL STRENGTHS

- work well as team member or independently
- *adapt easily to new environments*
- *able to effectively work with negative personalities*

INTERESTS

Enjoy fashion, design, *tailoring*, dancing, visiting with friends, movies, plays, football and baseball
-- REFERENCES AVAILABLE UPON REQUEST --

Set #3
EXAMPLES OF RESUMES WHEN PRISON IS NOT A FACTOR

SAMPLE #1 -- GOOD NON-PRISON RESUME

ELIZABETH MARIE JUAREZ
NATIONAL ROAD MANAGEMENT / PROMOTIONS / ENTERTAINMENT

1921 Fairview Lane, #3, Dallas, TX 90955

(612) 895-9043 [H] ... (612) 913-5421 [Voicemail] ... E-MAIL: emj@aol.com

---

QUALIFICATIONS:
* **Manager, highly successful area concert management firm**
* **10 years experience, road management, promotions, unions**
* **Well-experienced in booking groups throughout the United States**
* **Familiar with payroll, personnel, marketing, purchasing, customer relations, "personality" egos**
* **Successful in assisting annual local fund-raising event**

RELATED EMPLOYMENT:
MANAGER, Shootin-Stars Productions (Dallas, TX), 1994-1997. Began by buying out a band; added a management and booking agency; handled 2-3 bands at a time [extensive travel in the U.S. & Canada]; in 1986, added booking agency called Big D Entertainment; **had the largest roster of entertainment in Dallas with approximately 20 bands.**

MANAGER / MUSIC LOGGER, Self-Employed (Dallas), 1994-1996. Managed two area clubs, including all live acts; continued to work as music logger for Big D Entertainment [live music checks of bars and nite clubs throughout Texas].

BOOKING AGENT / ROAD MANAGER, Big D Entertainment (Dallas), 1993-1994.   Handled approximately 25 acts, including total responsibility for two; extensive travel.

MANAGER / BOOKING AGENT / SOUND MAN, Dallas-area band, 1991-1992. **Originated "Rock Wars" contest at area nite club.**

ADDITIONAL INFORMATION:
* education: graduate, LBJ High School; certified in Computer Operations
* exceptional strengths in promotions
* enjoy travel, music, exercise

Set #3
(continued)

EXAMPLES OF RESUMES WHEN PRISON IS NOT A FACTOR

SAMPLE #2 -- GOOD NON-PRISON RESUME

CHARLES IAN RICHARDS

#9 Melbourne Court, Fargo, ND 31167 / (876) 643-0087

OBJECTIVE

Clerical position

RELATED EMPLOYMENT

CLERK, *Roberts, Azert, Mard & Jones, P.C.* (Fargo, ND), 1994-1999. Usual responsibilities: handled incoming and outgoing mail, photocopying, library, filing, light typing, errands, banking, serving clients' lunches.

OFFICE ASSISTANT, *Plains Petroleum* (Fargo), 1991-1994. Worked with 10 people; duties: computer (Data General); same duties as above on a smaller scale.

LEGAL SECRETARY / SECRETARIAL ASSISTANT (Fargo), 1985-1990. Worked with law firms, hospital, and private firms in developing a solid and efficient office. Usual responsibilities.

EDUCATION

●**GEORGETOWN UNIVERSITY**: Russian studies, three years; have basic understanding of Russian.
●**BRYANT & STRATTON BUSINESS INSTITUTE**: courses: Shorthand (grade: "A"); Business Management ("A"); Data Processing ("B").

PERSONAL

... **work well in team setting**
... **dependable and punctual**
... **neat-appearing; professional**
... **thoroughly dedicated to the employer**
... **can be relied upon for confidential matters**

ADDITIONAL INFORMATION

-- **INTERESTS:** enjoy reading western novels, country dancing, gardening, camping
-- **REFERENCES:** furnished upon request

Chapter 5

Cover Letters and Other Related Correspondence

"I don't like work -- no man does -- but what I like is in the work -- the chance to find yourself."

Joseph Conrad, English novelist and short story writer

● INTRODUCTION ●

MUST REASONS: WHY WRITING LETTERS IS IMPORTANT

During the time you are in prison (especially your last six months) and when you are released, there will be a variety of letters you will need to write that relate to your job search. The letters:

- often serve as your first introduction to a possible employer
- first inform someone of your need for his or her assistance in looking for a job
- are a measure of your writing ability
- are a chance for you to give a quick picture of yourself
- allow you to continually communicate with others so you will not be forgotten
- allow you to show personal qualities such as self-confidence, organization, thoroughness, and self-awareness of your worth

Also, depending on the situation and the type of letter written, it is also possible to:

- present the positives you gained from your prison experience
- change an employer's mind who initially said he did not want to meet with you
- establish some job specifics, such as salary, geographic location, long term interests, and non-employment contributions you can make to the company
- develop solid networking contacts
- win a favorable impression from possible employers that will be long-lasting and help you once you are released / land employment
- learn about assistance & resources available to ex-inmates

Unless you are a writer, not many people truly enjoy writing the different letters that are part of the job hunt. Yet it is something that must be done, and **for an inmate about to be released or an ex-inmate who is newly released, writing these letters is especially important.**

> **REMEMBER:** Because you are in prison, you do not have the luxury of personal meetings and phone calls whenever you'd like (as you would when in the free world). Letters allow you to make up for this.

"COVER LETTERS" VS. "LETTERS OF APPLICATION"

These are two names for the same letter. You will find that some employers and employment agencies will call it a "cover letter," while other will refer to it as "letter of application." For our purposes, I will refer to them as cover letters.

PRINTED, COPIED, AND FORM LETTERS

> **REMEMBER:** A resume and cover letter are somewhat like a blackboard and a pointer. The resume becomes your blackboard, allowing you to describe the various selling points you have to offer the employer. The cover letter highlights, or points out, what you especially want the reader to notice.

Employers expect your resumes to be more general than your letters, and thus you will find most job seekers have their resumes printed or photocopied in bulk quantities. Yet this is NOT what they expect in a cover letter!

(See Chapter 4 for detailed information on writing resumes.)

Form Letters / Letter Copies Do Not Impress Employers

If employers receive a letter that is obviously a form type of letter, they will get the (correct) impression that you are sending out a vast quantity of the same letter and that your interest in their firms is really not that special. The same holds true for letters that are photocopied or printed: it tells the employer that you are lazy, are not willing to put in the dedicated time, and that you are simply taking a "shotgun" approach.

An individually composed letter, however, tells employers that you are interested enough in their organizations to take the time and compose the letter SPECIFICALLY to fit the job advertised / your employment interests.

And if you have access to a printer and a word processor, a computer, or an electronic typewriter, individually composed cover letters can be much easier than you may think: while you can have the form of your letter all set to go, each time you print it out you change the specifics of the letter to match the company or ad to which it's going. (Several samples of these letters may be found later in this chapter.)

(When I receive a pre-printed cover letter from a job applicant, I will put that person's resume on the bottom of the pile ... and very often will not get to it.)

REMEMBER: Each letter you write connected with your job search must always be written individually, not printed or photocopied in bulk with each reading the same.

● COVER LETTERS: THE BASICS ●

3 IMPORTANT ITEMS THAT CAN ALWAYS BE ACCOMPLISHED WITH EACH LETTER YOU WRITE

(1) SHOW THAT YOU ARE INTERESTED. You will show the person to whom you are writing that you are personally interested (remember, this is not a form letter, but a letter you composed on a computer typed, or -- if you don't have access to either of these -- hand wrote). Employers especially appreciate this.

(2) INDIVIDUALIZE EACH LETTER. It allows you to individualize each letter to the specifics of the situation, thereby making the contents of your letter right on target to its need, as well as giving it a very personal touch.

(3) SELL YOURSELF. Since your letter in most instances will be the very first contact someone has with you, it gives you the opportunity to establish yourself as a mature, skilled, and confident person who knows how to communicate and get his or her point across.

HAND WRITTEN VS. COMPUTER GENERATED OR TYPED

Prisons are not always offices at our disposal with typewriters, copiers, word processors, and computers. If you have access to one or more of these, that's great and will make your job search that much easier.

IF YOU DON'T HAVE OFFICE EQUIPMENT. However, if you don't have access to these, then it will require a bit more work on your part. Business writing -- and any type of letter connected with your job search would be a business letter (except, perhaps, those you write to friends or family) -- requires that a letter, ideally, be typed.

If this is not possible, you will have to hand write each letter; there is no way to get around this. (I strongly suggest that you don't have someone else do it for you -- you need the business writing practice!)

REMEMBER: Getting a job should now be your #1 priority, and that means sacrifice and hard work during your last six months in prison, and a continuation of this after your release.

Using Longhand (cursive) versus Hand Printing

If you must write your letters by hand, print them, don't use longhand. You write in longhand when you are writing to friends or family. Any business letter, such as those written when looking for a job, must be printed, for two reasons: [a] Many people simply have sloppy handwriting! Not only does this make for more effort by the reader (something that only puts you in a negative light), but also may not get the right information across. [b] It shows that you know something about business writing etiquette. That is, you know the general rules for writing a business letter. A tiny thing like this counts as a plus with the employer, because it shows that you are thinking as a person who is serious about getting a job and know how to work within its many rules and guidelines.

ABOUT TYPES OF PAPER, SMUDGES, CROSSOUTS, ETC.

Type of Paper

Ideally, all job search letters and your resume should be on a somewhat heavier stock (if someone can get this for you, have them ask for a 22# or 24# weight). Acceptable business paper includes styles known as Laid, Linen, and Rag.

IF YOU CAN'T GET THE BEST. However, if you don't have access to this, then use the type of paper that most companies use for a copier; it's usually a 20# weight.

IF 20# COPIER PAPER NOT AVAILABLE. If this 20# copier paper is not available, then use paper from a pad or paper that is distributed by the prison. You do the best with what you have available. Don't ever use the excuse that you didn't write because you didn't have the right paper!

Preferred Paper Size

For resumes, cover letters, and other related letters, the preferred size is 8&1/2" x 11". However, if this is not available, then use whatever size you have. (Envelopes, by the way, should be what are known as Legal Size, or #10; if this size is not available, again, use whatever size you have.)

Lined Paper vs. Non-Lined Paper

If you can write straight (versus crooked) on paper that is not lined, then do it this way. However, if you feel that lines will make your printing look better, then use the lines. (Obviously, if you have a typewriter, word processor, or computer, you don't need lined paper.)

Smudges

Be careful NOT to smudge your paper with grease, dirt, leaking ink, etc. Find a workplace that is clean and allows you enough space to write, type, etc. If hand printing your letters, do so on a flat table.

Mistakes and Erasures

Ideally, of course, would be to correct mistakes on a computer: it's quick, easy, and your paper will never give away your secret -- that there was an error or two!

But this is prison, and many inmates don't have computers (and may not when they became ex-inmates), so let's consider this. First, for mistakes, don't cross out or write over; rather, use a liquid correcting fluid or an eraser. (If you do not have access to either of these, or if you feel your letter still looks sloppy, then copy it over!)

If using a typewriter, use liquid correcting fluid, liftoff tape, a typewriter eraser, or -- if you are fortunate enough to have one -- the delete key; do NOT x-out or type over a correction!

Ragged Edges

If using paper from a pad, make certain that you tear off the ragged perforation at the top that is sometimes left. This will give your paper a more professional, cleaner look.

COLOR OF PAPER

<u>*THE PLUS AND MINUS OF WHITE*</u>. Until scanning came about (discussed in the previous chapter), white was not the best color to use, as so many people use white that your resume and cover letter would blend in with everyone else's. However, as I mentioned when discussing color of paper to use for resumes, scanners work best when being fed white, an off-white, or a beige (cream-colored) paper. So ... ideally, try to use beige. However, if this is not available to you, use white -- and the best quality you can hold of.

Now, there are four other points to consider:

(1) IF YOU KNOW THAT YOUR RESUME WILL NOT BE SCANNED, OPT FIRST FOR A BEIGE OR LIGHT GREY. These colors are professional yet will help you stand out from the vast number of resumes and cover letters that use white paper.

(2) IF SENDING YOUR COVER LETTER AND RESUME TO A RATHER CONSERVATIVE COMPANY OR PROFESSION, USE WHITE. Banking, law, government (yes, all three fields are open to many inmates!), as well as certain companies, prefer a very traditional approach to a cover letter and resume, and this means white paper.

(3) DON'T LET LACK OF A WHITE, BEIGE, OR GREY PAPER PREVENT YOU FROM SENDING OUT YOUR COVER LETTER & RESUME. Color of paper, of course, is not nearly as important as the contents of the resume or letter. While green, blue, or loud colors are the least favorable to employers (unless applying for a job with a rock band or a very creative advertising firm!) because they are hard on the reader's eyes and not considered professional, ultimately you should use whatever paper you have available so you can get the cover letter / resume process going!

(4) IDEALLY, ENVELOPE COLOR SHOULD MATCH THAT OF YOUR COVER LETTER AND RESUME. While you know that almost every envelope is thrown away within a few seconds of its being opened, in those few seconds you have shown someone that you are professional enough to want to match all colors of your correspondence. This amounts to one more small plus in your favor. But again, prison's not an ideal world -- if they don't match, fine; just get them out!

FOLDING RESUMES & LETTER
(to place in envelopes)

THE FLY IN THE OINTMENT: SCANNERS. Since scanners have a problem reading anything in a crease, your first thought may be to not fold your resume and cover letter. Two problems with this, however: [a] It's somewhat bulky to send all your resumes and cover letters in a large envelope, and sometimes these don't get priority reading (as it may be mistaken for "junk" or other non-important mail; [b] It's much more expensive to send it unfolded! My suggestion: follow the directions below for folding, but lay out your resume so that, when folded, there is either no text in the fold or text that you consider unimportant (next to you Big Guns stuff!). Obviously, if you know that your resume won't be scanned, then you need not be concerned about text in the fold crease.

FOLD LENGTHWISE & IN THIRDS. When folding your letters (and resumes), no matter what the size of the paper, fold them lengthwise and in thirds. Preferred is that the bottom third be folded up, and the top third be folded OVER the bottom third. This way, when the letter or resume is opened, the top -- the beginning -- will be the first part that the reader sees.

INSERTING THE RESUME & LETTER IN THE ENVELOPE. Put the letter on top of the resume BEFORE you fold. Once this is done, fold both items together in the manner described above. Place it in the envelope so if the envelope is opened from the rear (where most envelopes are opened), when your letter / resume is pulled out it will be the front of the letter, not the back of the resume, that greets the reader. (If you are sending a letter with no resume, your letter would be inserted in the same manner.)

Your cover letter is important is important is important!

REMEMBER: One typo, one mistake on your cover letter can make the reader forget about all the other great stuff you've got to offer -- so proofread, proofread, proofread!

10 TIPS
TO HELP MAKE YOUR LETTERS MOST EFFECTIVE

Now that you have the basics about writing your cover letters (and other job-related letters), there are some additional items you need to know to help "tweak" your letters to a fine polish of effectiveness. Read these over, then integrate the suggestions into your letters: the more effort you put into them know, the better your letters will be.

(By the way, there is a bonus to all this writing effort beyond landing a job. As much as you may not like to hear this, you are always going to have to write, no matter what kind of job you have! Obviously, the better your ability to communicate -- including your writing -- the better your opportunities for respect, promotions, and self-confidence. *Always keep this in mind!*)

#1
KNOW HOW TO PROPERLY ADDRESS YOUR ENVELOPES

No matter the size of the envelope, it should be addressed as follows:

```
YOUR NAME
YOUR ADDRESS                                    STAMP
CITY / STATE/ ZIP CODE




                    NAME OF PERSON
                    TITLE
                    NAME OF COMPANY
                    STREET ADDRESS
                    CITY / STATE / ZIP CODE
```

177

10 Tips Concerning Envelopes

(1) SALUTATIONS. It is not necessary to use salutations such as "Mr.," "Ms.," "Mrs.," or "Miss."

(2) USE OF "DR." If the individual you are writing is a medical doctor, use "Dr." before the individual's name; if the person is an academic doctor, put "Ph.D." after the person's last name, with a comma following the last name [example: "Charles Ian, Ph.D."].

(3) ABBREVIATIONS. In the acceptable abbreviations mentioned above, DO NOT spell out the abbreviations [example: do not write "Doctor Doris Anthony"]. However, it is preferred by the U.S. Postal Service that you use their state abbreviations (NY for New York or CA for California, for example). As for abbreviations for words such as "county," "lane," "street," "avenue," "boulevard," etc., this is pretty much up to you -- abbreviate or spell out. However, do keep in mind that this is a piece of business correspondence from you, and thus more formal than casual writing. Also: if you are responding to a company name and address, write out that company's name and address as it originally appeared.

(4) USE OF "ESQUIRE" OR "ESQ." Often, inmates have a habit of writing "Esquire" or "Esq." after their names. Don't do this -- it is very outdated (the last time this was used on a broad scale was during the late 19th / early 20th centuries!). Nowadays, about the only time you see this is after an attorney's name.

(5) DRAWING ON ENVELOPES. Don't draw cute little pictures, caricatures, cartoons, symbols, etc. on your envelope. Likewise, don't use fancy calligraphy. Many inmates do this when writing friends, family, etc. However, you are trying to create an impression of yourself as a professional, someone who knows how to write a business letter and envelope, and an individual who is serious. No doodles and no fancy writing!

(6) QUOTES / RELIGIOUS PHRASES ON ENVELOPES. Don't write any religious phrases or quotes, limericks or poems ("Deliver this letter, the quicker, the better"!), or other such items. Again, this takes away from your professionalism. Exception: it is acceptable to type / print and underline, in the lower left corner of the envelope, "Personal and Confidential." (See pages 182-183 for discussion of religious phrases in cover letters.)

(7) RECYCLING STAMPS. Don't play the recycled stamp game. If you are caught, there are several negative possibilities that could hurt you, including the recipient of your letter having to pay the postage and you losing your mail privileges, not to mention a lost contact on the outside.

(8) WHENEVER POSSIBLE, ADDRESS YOUR LETTER TO AN INDIVIDUAL. The more specific the address, the greater the chance it will reach a decision-maker. And be certain that any titles are correct, that all spelling is correct.

(9) YOUR ADDRESS. This was discussed in the previous chapter but it's important enough to repeat it here. Many times inmates will use something such as "#213-E" or "Suite 213-E" when their actual return address would be "Cell 213, East Block." This is done, of course, so that the person receiving the envelope will not think it came from someone in prison. As long as the post office will accept this (and your institution), then go ahead and do it. It's a nice way to get you thinking outside of the prison walls, as well as the reader seeing one more item that labels you professional, mature, and trying to put prison behind you.

(10) WHEN TO MAIL. You'll find that business mail is lightest toward the end of the week, so pick a day that will give you delivery on a Thursday or Friday. (Local mail takes 1 - 2 days for delivery.)

#2
MAKE COPIES OF YOUR LETTERS

It is IMPERATIVE that you make copies of EACH letter, even if it means writing out a copy!

4 Reasons to Make Letter Copies

(1) TO REFRESH YOUR MEMORY. You never can tell when an interviewer will ask you a question about something you wrote in your cover letter.

(2) FOR FOLLOW-UP CORRESPONDENCE. So you can follow up on your letters -- whether they be cover letters, networking letters, thank you letters, etc. -- you need to have copies for both the dates and information contained in them.

(3) IT SHOWS YOU'RE MAKING AN EFFORT. There is a psychological plus in keeping copies of all your correspondence. It shows YOU that you've done work toward landing employment, and that you are making the transformation from inmate to working person!

(4) THEY CAN BE OF HELP AFTER YOU'VE BEEN HIRED. There are three possible ways your old cover letter / job search letters can be valuable:

        a] There may be something that was stated to you in a letter you received, or something you wrote in one of your letters, that will come in handy.

        b] There is valuable information that can help you continue to improve your career skills, as well as information you might be able to use for the benefit of the company or co-workers.

c] If, for whatever reason, the job does not work out or you decide it's in your best interest to search for another position, you'll have much of the material needed for your new career search, as well as a record of to whom you sent letters and resumes.

REMEMBER: Your memory may be good, but that still leaves "better" and "best" available -- make copies of your letters so your memory of what you wrote will always be sharp.

#3
WORK ON IMPROVING YOUR WRITING SKILLS

One of the biggest problems with many inmates is poor writing skills. While the letter samples in this chapter -- if used as they are written -- present good use of the English language, you must keep in mind what was mentioned earlier: good writing skills eventually are necessary in almost any job. (See pages 136 and 397-405 for more communications information.)

Why eventually? You may begin as a construction worker, hairdresser, cook, cashier, delivery person, or other such job where writing skills are not very important. However, unless you want to stay in jobs such as these, with little or no advancement, you will need to improve your writing. *And the more one advances on a job, the less he or she uses those skills for which that person was initially hired, and the more he or she will need and use communicative skills!*

How You Can Improve Your Writing

If there is an English or writing course offered at your institution, take it, if you can. Certainly there are many books available that can teach you the basics of good writing.

Once you are released, inquire about taking a continuing education course, a workshop, or a seminar on English / basic writing.

Last but perhaps most important: WRITE -- letters to friends, job search letters, a journal. Just like exercising your body, your writing will improve the more you use it. If you don't, all the courses you take and books you read will not help a bit.

What Aspects of Your Writing Need Improvement?

What should you focus your improvement on? The basics never go out of style, and they are the parts of the English language that do in most writers. Included: grammar, spelling, punctuation, rhetoric, structure, and composition. Learn these, and you'll be ahead of most employees in the work force when it comes to writing!

> **REMEMBER:** Begin improving your writing skills **BEFORE** your release. Upon your release, continue to practice. Your opportunity for career success gets brighter as your writing gets better -- don't quit!

> **REMEMBER:** You may moan, complain, and gripe; you may become frustrated, angry, and upset; and you will find a 1001 other things that are probably more fun to do. But having the ability to write well is a skill that will always do you proud -- put in the practice time to learn it now so you won't have to be embarrassed by its absence later on.

#4
DON'T USE BIG WORDS TO IMPRESS OTHERS

This was discussed last chapter, and it holds true for letters as well. While many people have a tendency to use "50 cent" words to impress others, this is especially true of inmates. The reason, as I mentioned: one of the ways to demonstrate that you do not have a "prison mentality" and that you are an intelligent person is to use words that sound impressive.

After all, why use the word "talkative" when you can say the same thing by using "loquacious"? Why not use "copious" instead of the word "large?" How about using the word "predilection" when you have "preference" meaning the same thing? Words such as these do not impress employers and, in fact, will probably turn them off.

REMEMBER: Use words that the greatest number of people will understand -- this is a key point in successful business writing, and it should be one of yours.

#5
DON'T ADVERTISE RELIGION IN YOUR BUSINESS LETTERS

Do not begin, end, or write anywhere else in your letters such religious phrases as "In Jesus' Name We Pray," "God Be With you," or "May You Have a Good Sabbath." (Refer to point #6, page 178.)

Inmates will often put these religious phrases or quotes in their letters because they think it will impress the reader (in this case, a possible employer or someone who might help you in your job search) or because they are trying to "sell" their religious beliefs to others.

This religious writing does not belong in the business world, and is a surefire way NOT to impress someone.

Only Exception for Religious Writing: Must Meet 2 Points

(1) You are applying to an organization or company that has as its PRIMARY function the practice, teaching, and / or worshiping of a religion.

(2) You are TRULY religious!

#6
USE A DICTIONARY!

While I generally mentioned the importance of good writing earlier, make certain that you check each of your letters for spelling errors or typos prior to mailing them (even if you use a computer's SpellCheck feature, as it won't get every typo). Use a dictionary; even though you may be an excellent speller, there is always going to be a word or two that you sometimes are confused by.

Also, be certain that you have the correct spelling of the person to whom you are sending the letter, as well as his or her correct title and address. Errors in any of these areas are interpreted by the reader as sloppiness, carelessness, & lack of thoroughness on your part.

#7
KEEP YOUR LETTERS ORGANIZED

Keep all your cover letter / job-related letter copies together (as well as the rest of your career search materials). Whether this be in a spiral notebook or an old shoebox, a folder or a clipboard, it is important that you keep everything ORGANIZED and easily accessible so that you won't have trouble locating what you need.

REMEMBER IMPORTANT PAPERS. Sometimes, you may be asked for proof of or an I.D. number from a birth certificate, social security card, GED certificate, and other such items. As you do acquire these, keep them together, preferably with your letter copies. This will ensure they will be readily available when you need them.

#8
IF ASKED ABOUT SALARY HISTORY / SALARY REQUIREMENTS

Sometimes, you will be asked to give a history of your past salaries and / or what salary you are seeking. This throws off many job applicants, and could prove especially difficult for inmates or newly-released ex-inmates who may have a spotty job history ... and perhaps not a "normal" paying job in quite some time. Use the following advice and you won't have a problem in responding to any question about your salary history or requirements:

3 Points Concerning Salary History

(1) SHORT OR SPOTTY EMPLOYMENT HISTORY. If you do not have a very lengthy employment record, then your salary history can be added as the LAST paragraph of your cover letter (before "Yours Truly," "Sincerely," etc.). It would read:

"My salary history, as requested, is: [EXAMPLE: "Marv's Pancake House: $7.41 hour ending, $6.21 beginning; Esther's Spaghetti Shack: $5.80 ending, $5.55 beginning; newspaper route: approximately $50.00 weekly."] As for a salary received from the institution while incarcerated (usually ranging from several cents to a little more than a dollar per hour), refer to point #3, below.

(2) LONG SALARY HISTORY. If your salary history is too long for a short paragraph to be inserted in your cover letter, you need to attach an additional sheet (use the same paper that you did for your resume and cover letter). In this case, add the following sentence as the LAST paragraph of your cover letter: "My salary history, as requested, is attached."

On the additional sheet (typed and centered on the top as "Salary History") would be a listing of your positions and salaries, from last (most recent) to first. Include any raises you received while with an employer, as well as your beginning and ending wages.

(3) PAY DISPARITY. A question often raised by a job applicant is how to handle a major difference in monies between the most recent salary and the one you are looking to get. If you last made $18,000 a year, how can you justify a $10,000 jump to $28,000? (And even more of a difference: how does once go from making a dollar or less per hour in a prison to a regular salary on the outside?)

The answer is that you actually are earning TWO wages: one that is being paid to you by your employer, and one that you think you OUGHT to be making (based on your accomplishments, time with the organization, pay in similar companies, etc.). This way, the salary you are asking seems very much in line with your past salary progressions.

Using the salaries I gave in this paragraph, an example would be:

EMPLOYER	ACTUAL SALARY	(COMPARABLE SALARY WORTH)
House of Gemelia (ending)	$18,000/yr.	($22,000/yr.)
House of Gemelia (starting)	16,500/yr.	($20,000/yr.)
The Battered Sole	15,000/yr.	($17,500/yr.)
Gabe's Grooming House	14,500/yr.	($14,500/yr.)

To respond to the question of salary history, your answer might sound something like this:

"My salary history for my most recent position, as requested, would be comparable to the average industry wage of $14,500 per year for a Cashier."

When written in this manner, you are not drawing attention to a large wage difference between what you most recently earned and that salary you'd like or what the potential new job offers. Once in an interview and asked to explain this in more detail, you'll have the advantage of your face-to-face presence and your mouth, two crucial job-selling tools that you don't have in a cover letter!

Salary Requirements

When asked for salary requirements, add the following paragraph as the LAST paragraph of your cover letter [before "Yours Truly," "Sincerely," etc."]:

"My salary requirement, as per your request, is [HERE YOU WOULD CHOOSE ONE OF THE FOLLOWING: (1) A SPECIFIC FIGURE, FOR EXAMPLE, "$28,000"; (2) A RANGE OF SALARIES, WITH AN EXPLANATION ADDED, FOR EXAMPLE: "$15,000 – $18,000 annually, depending on the responsibilities"; (3) "is negotiable."]

[IF YOU ARE ASKED TO SUPPLY BOTH YOUR SALARY REQUIREMENTS AND HISTORY, ADD THIS SENTENCE: "Also, my salary history is {CHOOSE THE SENTENCE THAT WILL FIT A LONG OR SHORT SALARY HISTORY AS DESCRIBED UNDER SALARY HISTORY, ABOVE.}]

For information on negotiating salary during the job interview, see Chapter 10, pages, 376-378.

#9
WHEN THERE IS NO RESPONSE, FIRST WRITE

In Chapter. 4, (Hint 25, page 151), I discussed how a company may initially reject your interest by either sending you a "Thanks But No Thanks" letter or through no response. Too often, job seekers give up on firms who do not respond to their resumes / cover letters, thinking, "Well, if the company was interested in me I would have heard something." Maybe yes, but maybe no.

Remember that there are many possible reasons for a company not to send you a response, and until that company sends you a letter that says outright it is not interested in you as a job candidate (for example: "Leave us alone. We have no interest in you whatsoever. If you write us again, we will call the police."), always take the approach that there is a possibility of employment.

To follow up on this possible job opening even though the company has yet to contact you:

(1) WAIT 7 - 10 DAYS BEFORE RE-CONTACTING THE PROSPECTIVE EMPLOYER.
Companies need be given a fair time period to look over the resumes, then to follow up on those resumes.

(2) FOR YOUR INITIAL FOLLOW-UP, DO NOT CALL. There is a tendency to want to call the employer and say, "Hey -- I sent you my resume a week ago; what's the story?" After all, a call is quick, you can get an immediate response, and you don't have to go through the pain of writing another letter -- right? Perhaps, but this phone follow-up will probably end in a negative reaction from the employer, for several possible reasons: the employer was not prepared for your call, and thus you've perhaps interrupted him / her; the employer would probably not have your resume in front of him / her, thus you present a waste of time; since the employer is listening to you, he / she will not remember all you say on the phone. And all of these, of course, assume that you've actually made it through to the person who will read your resume! (Exceptions to this rule: found in the letter samples, but note none are for this type of specific situation.)

(3) THE ADVANTAGES OF DOING YOUR INITIAL FOLLOW-UP IN A LETTER. By writing, you stand a better chance of the decision maker reading your letter; the employer can read it at his or her convenience, thus you do not interrupt nor waste the individual's time; and the person reading your letter will have your points in front of him or her, thus being able to re-read anything. In addition, writing shows you to be an interested, assertive individual but not in an aggressive, "I'm only thinking of me" manner.

(4) IF YOU RECEIVE NO RESPONSE TO YOUR INITIAL FOLLOW-UP LETTER, CALL.
You've been patient, you've been polite, and you do deserve some kind of answer! But always be polite.

#10
DON'T BE AFRAID TO GIVE YOUR PERSONAL TOUCH

Okay, you've done a great job in developing your resume and cover letter; each sells your assets to their best. Can you do anything else to point out what you think is especially important for the employer to see? Yep, there sure is! Don't be afraid to highlight those points on your cover letter and / or resume that you want to really stand out. Look, no one said that once your cover letter and resume are finished they're holy -- since you can't be in the room when they're read and say, "I'd like you to especially notice point X and X," the next best thing is to highlight these points. It's up to you to sell yourself -- don't be afraid to reach out!

> **REMEMBER:** Job search letters may not be as glamorous or stylish as a resume, but boy can they do a great job at selling!

● TRACKING YOUR JOB SEARCH PROGRESS ●

CAREER SEARCH LOG I -- Resumes & Cover Letters

On page 195 you will find a blank copy of Career Search Log I. (Career Search Log II, to be used to track your job interviews, can be found in Chp. 6, pages 232-234.) This will prove EXTREMELY helpful to you, and should ALWAYS be filled in and kept up to date.

WHEN TO USE. Should be used ONLY for resumes / letters sent and phone calls you make, as well as responses you get to your resumes / letters and phone calls.

Career Search Log I -- How to Use It

(1) **THERE ARE SIX COLUMNS:**

"Prospective Employer / Key Person & Phone #": Write the name of the possible employer or job contact person you are writing / calling, and his / her phone number, if available.

"Date Letter and / or Resume Sent": Date you first sent a letter and/or copy of resume to the person.

"Follow Up (1st)": This would be the date of your next letter / phone call to this person.

"Follow Up (2nd)": Date of your third contact to the same person.

"Response": Write in what the individual says he or she will or will not do for you.

"Remarks": These are YOUR comments. Things to be included would be what your next step will be, your reaction to the person you contacted, if you included a resume with your cover letter, etc.

(2) **KEEP THIS LOG.** As with all other career search materials, don't throw this Log away. There are several ways in which this can be helpful. [Examples: record of dates; an overview of what industries / professions are hiring; helping you to become better organized.]

(3) **NEVER RUN OUT.** If you feel you will need more copies of Career Search Log I, either photocopy it or make a handwritten copy.

(4) **WRITE!** By now, you may feel that you've had it with writing: keeping a journal, perhaps a portfolio; filling out a Self-Evaluation Profile and a Resume Development Guide; writing your resume and then your cover letters; and now keeping a Career Search Log to track your resumes and cover letters [and later another Career Search Log, this one to keep track of your interviews]. But getting a job is NOT easy, and as an inmate you've got some major problems to overcome, some major thinking to do. I suggest you do ALL this writing so you can be a job candidate who is exceptionally well-prepared, because if you are not, someone else will come along who is -- and he or she will get the job, not you!

CAREER SEARCH LOG I					
Prospective Employer / Contact and Phone #	Date Letter/ Resume Sent	Follow Up (1st)	Follow Up (2nd)	Response	Remarks

● COVER AND RELATED LETTERS SAMPLES ●

THE LETTER EXAMPLES: SOME GENERAL INFORMATION

There are 3 Sets of Letters

(1) NON-PRISON EMPLOYMENT. A variety of cover letters to be used in your effort to obtain an interview when the employer does NOT know that you are or have been incarcerated.

(2) PRISON EMPLOYMENT. A variety of cover letters and related job search letters where you are either telling someone that you are / have been in prison, or the person knows this fact prior to you writing him or her.

(3) A MIXTURE. A variety of "non-prison" letters that focus on other aspects of the job hunt.

At the top of each letter is a very clear title / explanation of the letter and when it should be used.

Use Them As They Are or Change Them

Remember that these are SAMPLES; you can either use these letters the way they are presented, or you can change them to more specifically fit your needs. In addition, you will find other cover letter styles (in books, from friends, etc.) that differ from the samples presented here. While many of those letters are acceptable, I designed the letters in this book to meet the unique needs of YOU, the inmate / ex-inmate.

If You Need a Letter Not Included in the Samples

There is always the possibility that you will need a letter that I have not included in these examples. If this happens, USE COMMON SENSE! There are enough different letters with a variety of suggestions that you should be able to compose the letter you need.

The Style of the Sample Letters

Any letter you write should reflect YOUR style and the way you would speak on paper (see point #2, page 171). The letter samples included in this chapter are written in a style that draws middle ground: they do not sound like they came from a Harvard graduate, but neither do they sound like they were written by a high school dropout.

If you do use these letters, but feel that your writing skills are below their level, there is but one thing for you to do: what has been previously suggested -- to practice, PRACTICE!

10 Points About the Directions/Guidelines That Appear on the Letter Examples

(1) YOUR NAME AT THE BOTTOM. At the bottom of each page, you will find the following notation: [YOUR NAME TYPED HERE, SIGNED ABOVE]. If you do not have use of a computer or typewriter and are hand printing your letters, print your name, then sign it above. Also: If available, type your phone number (with area code) below your typed / printed name:

> *John Smith* (signed)
> John Smith (typed)
> (817) 503-4646 (typed)

(2) RAGGED RIGHT. You'll find that all letters are written with the left side justified (even), but the right side ragged (uneven). You do yours this way, as it gives the reader the impression that your letters were done personally and individually; they don't have as slick and polished a look as your resume, which has its paragraphs justified left and right.

(3) THE DIRECTIONS IN THE LETTERS. There are several times in the letters where directions and guidelines are given. Whenever these appear, they are ALWAYS in capital letters contained inside brackets. When you type or write the information requested / suggested, use standard English grammar. [EXCEPTION: In some cases, to make a job title stand out, it will be capitalized in the example.]

(4) NON-TRADITIONAL COMPANIES. At different places, you will see the word "organization" by itself, or you'll have the choice of using "organization" or "company." There are employers that are not necessarily a company in the traditional sense. Examples would include associations, a church or temple, government, unions, and political groups. For employers such as these, use the word "organization" (or, when appropriate, you can substitute the type of employer -- association, union, etc. -- for the word "organization").

(5) PARAGRAPH NUMBERING. For your convenience, each paragraph begins with a large number. (These are NOT to be included in your letters!) This can assist you in three ways:

    a] You can always make certain you include the right number of paragraphs in your letter.

    b] You will always know the correct order of the paragraphs.

    c] Some letters refer you to another paragraph number in a letter different from the one on which you are working. This allows you greater flexibility and individuality in writing your letters.

(6) CENTERING. Always try to center your letter on the page (leaving an approximate equal amount of space on the bottom and the top).

(7) ABBREVIATIONS / SALUTATIONS. As with abbreviations for letters (see this chapter, page 178, #3), do not use abbreviations in your letter, unless the abbreviation is a commonly accepted one. [EXAMPLES: "Dr." for doctor or physician; "i.e." for "that is"; "IBM" for International Business Machines; "MIG" or "TIG" to explain certain types of welding; various computer terms, such as CRT, PC, and WWW.] As for salutations, if you don't the name of the person, NEVER begin a letter with "Dear Sir" unless you know ONLY a male will read it!

(8) THE "X". On each letter example, you will find a large **X** near the upper right corner. This is to remind you to include YOUR name and return address on your cover letter. Some inmates have stationery printed with their name and address across the top; others write it / type it in, either near where I have put the "X" or in the center of the page -- either is acceptable.

If you are unsure as to where or how to place your return address, ask a staff member (librarian, teacher, etc.) or consult a composition / rhetoric guide.

(9) "ADVERTISED COVER LETTER." On several letters, you will find a notation that says, "TAKE ITEM FROM "ADVERTISED COVER LETTER, PAGE 196." This refers to one paragraph in this cover letter -- the 1st one -- that is comprised of three separate lines and should be written as such. This better catches the reader's attention.

(10) BOLD PRINT. Occasionally, you will find certain sections of the letters written in **bold** print. This is done to catch the reader's attention. If you cannot do this, underline these sentences OR use a highlighter -- you want them to stand out!

THE LETTER EXAMPLES: PRISON VS. NON-PRISON

(1) NON-PRISON LETTERS. You will find, perhaps to your surprise, there are a large number of letters that make no mention of you being a convicted felon or having spent time in prison. There are three reasons for this:

3 Reasons Why You Would Use Non-Prison Letters

1] THERE'S NO REASON TO TELL SOMEONE ABOUT YOUR PRISON EXPERIENCE IF IT'S NOT NECESSARY. While a prison experience should be used to better yourself personally, professionally, and educationally, it makes no sense to write someone a letter that says, in essence, "Hello, I'm in prison and looking for a job." As was discussed earlier, many people in the free world who have not spent time in a penitentiary have an immediate dislike and mistrust for any inmate / ex-inmate.

It is much better to first establish your positive points so that the employer has a generally good feeling about you. If the subject of your prison time comes up later, it will not stand out so much because the employer has gotten to know you as a job applicant first, ex-inmate second, NOT the other way around!

2] WILL YOUR CORRESPONDENCE BE KEPT PRIVATE? If the employer or contact person to whom you are writing has no problem about you being in prison, that's fine. But what guarantee do you have that someone else will not see your letter or hear that you spent time in prison? And perhaps that person has the authority or influence to hire or not hire -- and HE / SHE may not like ex-inmates!

Also, correspondence from successful applicants almost always becomes a permanent part of their personnel files. If it's not requested to have something in writing that says you were in prison, the fewer people there are who can possibly use this against you at a later time, the better.

3] START THINKING OF YOURSELF AS A PROFESSIONAL. I've said this before, but it is too important of a point not to repeat: you MUST start thinking as a free world person, you must start acting like a professional -- no matter if you are a cook, manager, banker, electrician, laborer, teacher, stock broker, etc.

REMEMBER: Too many ex-inmates use their prison experience as a crutch to get ahead or an excuse to fail: you must stand and begin to look at yourself as simply a person ... a person whose mind set as an ex-inmate is fading with each passing day.

---

(2) PRISON LETTERS. As mentioned earlier, you will find letters that do mention / explain your prison experience. These are important, and you will find many opportunities to use them.

REMEMBER: You shouldn't try and pretend your prison experience never happened, but rather know when you need to talk about it and know when you don't.

LETTER SET #1

LETTERS SEEKING EMPLOYMENT / EMPLOYMENT ASSISTANCE
(non-prison)

COVER LETTER: ADVERTISED POSITION
(you have firm name and street address)

[DATE]

[NAME OF PERSON]
[TITLE]
[NAME OF COMPANY]
[STREET ADDRESS]
[CITY / STATE / ZIP CODE]

1 [– CHOOSE ONE ITEM AS A PHRASE FROM RESUME & LIST HERE;
   EXAMPLE: "– 20 YEARS SOLID COMPUTER SERVICES EXPERIENCE ..."]

[– CHOOSE ONE ITEM AS A PHRASE FROM RESUME & LIST HERE; EXAMPLE:
"– B.S., BUSINESS STUDIES; ADVANCED STUDIES IN THE SAME AREA ..."]

[– CHOOSE ONE ITEM AS A PHRASE FROM RESUME & LIST HERE; EXAMPLE:
"– EXPERIENCED IN DEVELOPING / SETTING UP COMPUTER SYSTEMS ..."]

2 It is my above experience and skills, in combination with my professional and personal commitment to a career in [NAME OF AREA OF INTEREST], that have me extremely interested in the [NAME OF POSITION] as recently advertised in the [NAME OF PUBLICATION WHERE AD APPEARED].

3 As a professional, I not only have an effective ability to work well with others, but offer a proven track record of success, e.g., [HERE, GIVE AN EXAMPLE, e.g., "I achieved 125% of my sales quota" OR "I was given full responsibility for computer conversion"]; work well as a team member or independently; and -- perhaps most important -- have a personal and long-term commitment to my career.

4 While my resume is enclosed, a personal meeting to discuss my qualifications and your needs would prove mutually beneficial. To expedite this, I will contact your office within the week.

5 Thank you very much.

Sincerely,

[YOUR NAME TYPED HERE, SIGNED ABOVE]

196

COVER LETTER: BOX OFFICE # AD

X

[DATE]

[NAME OF PERSON , IF GIVEN]
[TITLE OR DEPARTMENT, IF GIVEN]
[BOX OFFICE #]
[STREET ADDRESS, IF GIVEN]
[CITY / STATE / ZIP CODE]

Dear [NAME OF PERSON, OR TITLE GIVEN, OR "Sir or Madam"]:

1 [THIS PARAGRAPH WILL BE THE SAME ONE THAT APPEARS AS THREE SEPARATE ITEMS ON COVER LETTER LABELED "COVER LETTER FOR ADVERTISED POSITION," PAGE 196. BEAR IN MIND, HOWEVER, THAT YOU MIGHT WISH TO TAKE SOME OF THE SPECIFIC QUALIFICATIONS ASKED FOR IN THE AD AND CREATE ONE OR MORE LINES OF YOUR OWN. IF YOU DO, SUBSTITUTE THEM FOR ONE OR MORE OF THE THREE LINES THAT NOW APPEAR ON 'COVER LETTER FOR ADVERTISED POSITION' AND MAKE UP PARAGRAPH 1.]

2 In response to your [DATE OF AD] ad in the [NAME OF PUBLICATION] seeking a(n) [NAME OF POSITION], I am very interested in applying for the position.

3 [THIS PARAGRAPH WILL BE THE SAME PARAGRAPH #3 THAT APPEARS ON COVER LETTER LABELED "COVER LETTER FOR ADVERTISED POSITION," PAGE 196.]

4 I have enclosed my resume, and would appreciate the opportunity of personally discussing my qualifications with you. While the nature of your ad makes it impossible for me to call you, I will follow up with a second letter to you shortly. I am very interested in learning more about this career opportunity.

5 Thank you very much, and I look forward to hearing from you soon.

Sincerely,

[YOUR NAME TYPED HERE & SIGNED ABOVE]

___

COVER LETTER: "COLD CALLING" ON A FIRM
(arranging for an interview)

[DATE]

[NAME OF PERSON, IF KNOWN]
[TITLE, IF KNOWN]
[NAME OF COMPANY]
[STREET ADDRESS[
[CITY / STATE / ZIP CODE]

Dear [NAME OF PERSON, OR "Sir or Madam"]:

1 [THIS PARAGRAPH IS THE SAME AS THE FIRST ONE THAT APPEARS ON "ADVERTISED COVER LETTER," PAGE 196.]

2 While I realize that you have not formally advertised a position available, I know that my above skills and abilities [OR "education" OR "experience," WHATEVER RELATES TO THE ITEMS YOU HAVE LISTED] would prove to be a strong asset in your [NAME OF DEPARTMENT, e.g., "Production Department," OR NAME OF DIVISION, e.g., "Creative Division" OR "Mortgage Banking Sector"].

3 I have also researched [NAME OF FIRM OR ORGANIZATION OR SCHOOL, e.g., "Xerox," "CitiBank," "Williamsville Senior High School," ETC.] quite thoroughly, and know that you can offer me the career satisfaction and growth that I seek in employment.

4 [THIS PARAGRAPH IS PARAGRAPH #3 ON "ADVERTISED COVER LETTER," PAGE 196.]

5 A meeting to discuss my qualifications and your employment needs would prove mutually beneficial, I believe. To expedite this, I will contact your office in a few days. [IF FREQUENT USE OF THE PHONE IS AVAILABLE, CALL; IF NOT, WRITE.]

6 Thank you very much.

Sincerely,

[YOUR NAME TYPED HERE AND SIGNED ABOVE]

COVER LETTER: EMPLOYMENT AGENCY
(you have previously spoken with someone at the agency)

[DATE]

[NAME OF PERSON]
[TITLE]
[NAME OF EMPLOYMENT AGENCY]
[STREET ADDRESS]
[CITY / STATE / ZIP CODE]

Dear [NAME OF PERSON]:

1 [THIS PARAGRAPH WILL BE THE SAME PARAGRAPH #1 THAT APPEARS ON "ADVERTISED COVER LETTER", PAGE 196.]

2 As mentioned in my recent [OR SPECIFIC DATE, e.g., "July 24th"] conversation with you, and offering my skills, experience, education, and major accomplishments above [NOTE: IF YOU DO NOT HAVE OR ARE NOT INCLUDING EDUCATION OR ACCOMPLISHMENTS, ETC., LEAVE THAT / THOSE PARTICULAR WORD(S) OUT FROM THIS SENTENCE, AS THEY WILL NOT APPLY], I would appreciate your assistance in securing a professional position in the [NAME OF FIELD OR INDUSTRY], specifically as a(n) [NAME OF POSITION OR JOB TITLE DESCRIPTION].

3 [THIS PARAGRAPH WILL BE THE SAME PARAGRAPH #3 THAT APPEARS ON "ADVERTISED COVER LETTER," PAGE 196.]

4 I have enclosed my resume, and would appreciate the opportunity of personally discussing my qualifications with you. To expedite this, I will contact you shortly to arrange for an appointment.

5 Thank you very much.

Sincerely,

[YOUR NAME TYPED HERE AND SIGNED ABOVE]

COVER LETTER: RETURNING APPLICATION BY MAIL -- #1
(in trying to arrange for an interview)

[DATE]

[NAME OF INDIVIDUAL]
[TITLE]
[NAME OF COMPANY]
[STREET ADDRESS]
[CITY/STATE/ZIP CODE]

Dear [NAME OF PERSON]:

1 In accord with your letter dated [DATE LETTER WAS WRITTEN], I have enclosed the properly filled-out application for employment with [NAME OF COMPANY]. [IF FOR A SPECIFIC POSITION, ADD THE PHRASE "for the position of" {NAME OF POSITION}, THEN END THE SENTENCE WITH A PERIOD.]

2 While I have been as thorough as possible, please don't hesitate to contact me if more information is needed. However, I do feel that this information [IF YOU SEND OR HAVE SENT A RESUME, ADD A PHRASE HERE: ", in combination with my resume,"] will shed the additional information necessary for a positive employment consideration.

3 I do believe that it is only through a personal meeting that my experience and skills can really be demonstrated to you. Whether day, afternoon, evening, or weekend, I can be at your office on short notice after [DATE OF YOUR RELEASE; YOU MAY NEED TO CHANGE WHEN YOU ARE AVAILABLE DEPENDING ON THE TERMS OF YOUR RELEASE / PAROLE] ... and I strongly feel it would be mutually beneficial for us to discuss my qualifications.

4 As you are most likely swamped by resumes and applications, I will assist in the process by contacting you so we might arrange for a meeting. [NOTE ON THIS SENTENCE: IF YOU HAVE ACCESS TO A PHONE, CALL; IF YOU CANNOT USE A PHONE ON A FAIRLY FREQUENT BASIS, THEN WRITE.]

5 Thank you very much, and I look forward to meeting with you.

Very truly yours,

[YOUR NAME TYPED HERE, SIGNED ABOVE]

200

COVER LETTER: RETURNING APPLICATION BY MAIL -- #2
(asking that your resume / application be kept on file)

X

[DATE]

[NAME OF INDIVIDUAL]
[TITLE]
[NAME OF COMPANY]
[STREET ADDRESS]
[CITY/STATE/ZIP CODE]

Dear [NAME OF PERSON]:

1 As requested in your letter dated [DATE LETTER WAS WRITTEN], I have enclosed the properly filled-out application for employment with [NAME OF COMPANY]. [IF FOR A SPECIFIC POSITION, ADD THE PHRASE "for the position of" {NAME OF POSITION}, THEN END THE SENTENCE WITH A PERIOD.]

2 While I have been as thorough as possible, please don't hesitate to contact me if more information is needed. However, I do feel that this information [IF YOU SEND OR HAVE SENT A RESUME, ADD A PHRASE HERE: ", in combination with my resume,"] will shed the additional information necessary for a positive employment consideration.

3 I do believe that it is only through a personal meeting that my experience and skills can really be demonstrated to you. However, as I will not be available for employment until [GIVE SPECIFIC OR APPROXIMATE DATE], please keep my resume and application on file for future employment consideration.

4 Please let me know if I will need to complete another application when I am ready to apply for a position with your organization.

5 Thank you very much.

Very truly yours,

[YOUR NAME TYPED HERE, SIGNED ABOVE]

COVER LETTER: TO FOLLOW UP A POSITIVE CONTACT
(someone at a company / organization may be an "in" for you)

[DATE]

[NAME OF PERSON]
[TITLE]
[NAME OF COMPANY]
[STREET ADDRESS]
[CITY/STATE/ZIP CODE]

Dear [NAME OF PERSON]:

1 In [CHOOSE: "a recent conversation" OR "correspondence"] with [CHOOSE: "an employee of ECS Widgets" OR "Sue Lyons, an employee with ECS Widget" OR "Sue Lyons, Marketing Director with ECS Widgets"], I learned that my auto mechanics experience [OR "middle management experience" OR "tool and die experience" OR WHATEVER YOUR EXPERIENCE IS IN] and specific skills in this area might be of value to [NAME OF FIRM] in your immediate employment needs. I've researched your company, and have no doubt that my accomplishments, abilities, and proven auto mechanics [IF NOT AUTO MECHANICS, SUBSTITUTE YOUR SPECIFIC CAREER SPECIALTY THAT FITS THE JOB IN WHICH YOU ARE INTERESTED] skills can be definite assets in your continued growth.

2 While my resume is enclosed, a brief overview includes:

      [HERE, ADD THREE PHRASES FROM YOUR RESUME -- IN THE FORM PRESENTED
      ON YOUR ADVERTISED COVER LETTER, PAGE 196, PARAGRAPH #1 -- THAT FIT THE
      SPECIFICS OF THE COMPANY OR THE POSITION]

3 Since your firm's growth depends on well-qualified and motivated employees, I'd like the opportunity to personally discuss my background and your anticipated needs. I feel very strongly that a meeting between us would be mutually beneficial. [IF YOU HAVE ACCESS TO A PHONE, INCLUDE THIS NEXT SENTENCE: "To assist in this, I will follow up with a call to your office in a few days."] I look forward to our discussion. [A CALL IS PREFERRED HERE BECAUSE OF YOUR CONTACT IN THE COMPANY.]

Sincerely,

[TYPE YOUR NAME HERE, SIGN ABOVE]

COVER LETTER: READ ABOUT FIRM IN A PUBLICATION
(trying to arrange for an interview)

X

[DATE]

[NAME OF PERSON]
[TITLE]
[NAME OF COMPANY]
[STREET ADDRESS]
[CITY/STATE/ZIP CODE]

Dear [NAME OF PERSON]:

1 I was quite impressed with the ["recent" OR "July 24th, 1998"] article entitled [NAME OF ARTICLE] that appeared in [NAME OF PUBLICATION], and profiled [NAME OF COMPANY OR ORGANIZATION]. My career interests, experience, and education match the direction of your growth, and I am extremely interested in applying for ["the position of ..." OR "a position in your {NAME OF DEPARTMENT} department" OR "a career position with your firm."].

2 While my resume is enclosed, an overview of my qualifications includes:

  – [TAKE ITEM FROM "COVER LETTER FOR ADVERTISED POSITION," PAGE 196]

  – [TAKE ITEM FROM "COVER LETTER FOR ADVERTISED POSITION," PAGE 196]

  – [TAKE ITEM FROM "COVER LETTER FOR ADVERTISED POSITION," PAGE 196]

3 A personal meeting to discuss my abilities and your needs (either present or future) would prove mutually beneficial. To expedite this, I will soon contact your office to arrange for an appointment. [NOTE: IF YOU HAVE FREQUENT USE OF PHONE, CALL; IF NOT, WRITE A FOLLOW-UP LETTER.]

4 Thank you very much.

Sincerely,

[YOUR NAME TYPED HERE, SIGNED ABOVE]

COVER LETTER: INDIVIDUAL WHO IS WEAK ON EDUCATION

X

[DATE]

[NAME OF PERSON]
[POSITION]
[COMPANY]
[STREET ADDRESS]
[CITY / STATE / ZIP CODE]

Dear [NAME OF PERSON OR "Sir or Madam"]:

1 The position recently advertised in [NAME OF PAPER] for [NAME OF POSITION] on [DATE] stresses both experience and education. While I offer the qualifications you seek, my educational background won't fit into the requirements you give.

2 However ...

3 Education, by itself, is not a true measure of an individual's ability to perform on the job, to give quality service and production, to increase sales and bottom line profits, or to handle emergency or problem situations. Taken in combination with my experience, my education becomes not only excellent training -- especially for the position of [NAME OF POSITION] -- but has given me solid background in analyzing, interpreting, developing, and organizing.

4 Look over my enclosed resume thoroughly, and I believe you will find the potential for an excellent job candidate with [NAME OF FIRM OR ORGANIZATION]; give us the opportunity to meet personally, and I know you'll find the employee you've been searching for.

5 To expedite this, I'll follow up to your office in a few days. [NOTE: FIRST WRITE; IF NO RESPONSE -- AND YOU HAVE ACCESS TO A PHONE -- CALL. IF NO PHONE, WRITE AGAIN.]

6 Thank you very much.

Sincerely,

[YOUR NAME TYPED HERE, SIGNED ABOVE]

COVER LETTER: YOU HAVE LIMITED TIMES FOR INTERVIEWING

[DATE]

[NAME OF PERSON]
[TITLE]
[NAME OF COMPANY]
[STREET ADDRESS]
[CITY / STATE / ZIP CODE]

Dear [NAME OF PERSON, OR "Sir or Madam"]:

1 I am extremely interested in your recent advertisement in [DATE / NAME OF PAPER OR MAGAZINE, e.g., "November 6th issue of *The Buffalo News*] for the position of [NAME OF POSITION], and know that I have the right combination of experience, education, and "people skills" this job and your firm demand.

2 However ...

3 I am currently employed [please see enclosed resume] and while this is good in that I can continue to pursue my career search while receiving a salary, it also makes it quite difficult to interview for a new career position, as my "free" hours are limited. But during my lunch hour, prior to or after work during the week, or on weekends I am more than willing to make myself available. [NOTE: THIS LETTER CAN BE USED IF YOU ARE IN PRISON BUT HAVE FURLOUGHS, IN A HALFWAY HOUSE, ETC. SIMPLY CHANGE THE WORDING OF THE LAST SENTENCE OF THIS PARAGRAPH TO FIT THE TIME YOU WOULD BE AVAILABLE.]

4 I think our meeting is not only important, but would prove to be mutually beneficial. To expedite this, I will soon contact your office to arrange for an appointment. [WRITE FIRST; IF NO RESPONSE -- AND YOU HAVE USE OF A PHONE -- CALL. IF NO PHONE, WRITE AGAIN.].

5 Thank you very much.

Sincerely,

[YOUR NAME TYPED HERE, SIGNED ABOVE]

COVER LETTER: MOVING TO A DIFFERENT PART OF COUNTRY

X

[DATE]

[NAME OF PERSON]
[TITLE]
[NAME OF COMPANY]
[STREET ADDRESS]
[CITY / STATE / ZIP CODE]

Dear [NAME OF PERSON]:

1 I am moving to [NAME OF CITY, STATE, OR COUNTY], and am very interested in employment ["as a{n} ..." OR "in the profession of ..."] with [NAME OF FIRM] using my experience and education.

1A [OPTIONAL PARAGRAPH: "{Recently," OR "On July 24th,"} I came across your ad for {NAME OF POSITION} in {NAME OF PUBLICATION}. Your needs and expectations are what I have to offer, and I am keenly interested in applying for this position."]

2 While my resume is enclosed, an overview of my qualifications includes:

   –[TAKE ITEM FROM "COVER LETTER FOR ADVERTISED POSITION," PAGE 196]

   –[TAKE TIME FROM "COVER LETTER FOR ADVERTISED POSITION," PAGE 196]

   –[TAKE TIME FROM "COVER LETTER FOR ADVERTISED POSITION," PAGE 196]

3 I will be in [NAME OF CITY OR STATE OR COUNTY] from [DATE YOU WILL BE INITIALLY VISITING, i.e., "July 25th - August 4th", OR DAY YOU WILL MOVE TO THAT CITY], and would like to personally discuss your needs and further expand on my qualifications. To expedite this meeting, I will soon contact your office to arrange for an appointment [IF USE OF THE PHONE IS AVAILABLE AND YOU CAN MAKE A TOLL CALL, CALL; IF NOT, WRITE].

4 Thank you very much.

Sincerely,

[YOUR NAME TYPED HERE, SIGNED ABOVE]

COVER LETTER: FOLLOW-UP TO COMPANY
(first cover sent / contact made months or years earlier)

[DATE]

[NAME OF PERSON]
[TITLE]
[NAME OF ORGANIZATION]
[STREET ADDRESS]
[CITY / STATE / ZIP CODE]

Dear [NAME OF PERSON]:

1 [NUMBER OF MONTHS OR YEARS THAT IT'S BEEN SINCE YOU SENT YOUR RESUME, FOR EXAMPLE, "4 months ago"] I sent you my resume in pursuit of [HERE, ENTER YOUR PROFESSION, TRADE, OR JOB INTEREST IN ONE OF THE TWO FOLLOWING WAYS: "an Electrician's position." OR "the Electrician's position for which you had advertised."] Today, I am still very interested in similar employment with [NAME OF COMPANY OR ORGANIZATION].

2 While you might have a copy of my resume on file, I have enclosed another for your convenience. An overview of my strengths, education, and accomplishments as they relate to [NAME OF POSITION APPLYING FOR, FOR EXAMPLE, "an Electrician"] include:

3   – [TAKE AN ITEM FROM YOUR RESUME THAT RELATES TO THE POSITION] ...

        – [TAKE AN ITEM FROM YOUR RESUME THAT RELATES TO THE POSITION] ...

        – [TAKE AN ITEM FROM YOUR RESUME THAT RELATES TO THE POSITION] ...

4 You will find that my self-motivated attitude is one that carries over into all aspects of my career. I have no doubt that I would be an excellent team member with [NAME OF ORGANIZATION].

5 Knowing that you are quite busy with daily responsibilities and other resumes, I will contact your office shortly to assist in arranging for an appointment. [NOTE: WRITE FIRST; IF YOU HAVE NO RESPONSE -- AND YOU HAVE USE OF A PHONE -- CALL. IF NO PHONE, WRITE AGAIN.]

Yours truly,

[YOUR NAME TYPED HERE, SIGNED ABOVE]

COVER LETTER: TO BE SENT WHEN YOU DO NOT HAVE A RESUME

[DATE]

[NAME OF PERSON, IF KNOWN]
[TITLE, IF KNOWN]
[NAME OF ORGANIZATION]
[STREET ADDRESS / P.O. BOX #]
[CITY / STATE / ZIP]

Dear [NAME OF PERSON, OR TITLE, OR "Sir or Madam"]:

1 I am extremely interested in [SELECT: "the recently advertised position of {NAME OF POSITION} that appeared in {NAME OF PUBLICATION}" OR "a(n) {NAME OF POSITION OR JOB INTEREST, e.g., "a Line Worker ... "} position with your company {OR "organization"}]. My skills, experience, and education [IF ONE OF THESE DOES NOT FIT THE JOB, LEAVE OUT] [CHOOSE ONE: "match the qualifications you listed." OR "would allow me to become a very productive employee."]

2 While I am in the process of updating my resume (and will forward it to you shortly), a brief overview of my background, as it relates to the position [OR "your industry"] includes:

3   – **[LIST A RELATED POINT FROM YOUR QUALIFICATIONS]** ...

             – **[LIST A RELATED POINT FROM YOUR QUALIFICATIONS]** ...

             – **[LIST A RELATED POINT FROM YOUR QUALIFICATIONS]** ...

4 [IF YOUR RELEASE IS MORE THAN TWO WEEKS AWAY, BEGIN WITH: "I will be available after {DATE OF RELEASE}, and"] I believe a meeting to discuss your needs and my qualifications would prove mutually beneficial. To expedite this, I will shortly contact your office. [WRITE FIRST; IF YOU HAVE NO RESPONSE -- & YOU HAVE USE OF A PHONE -- CALL. IF NOT, WRITE AGAIN.]

5 Thank you very much; I look forward to hearing from you.

Very truly yours,

[YOUR NAME TYPED HERE, SIGNED ABOVE]

208

LETTER SET #2

LETTERS SEEKING EMPLOYMENT / EMPLOYMENT ASSISTANCE
(prison)

COVER LETTER: TELLING SOMEONE YOU ARE IN PRISON -- #1
(asking for employment assistance from someone you don't know)

[DATE]

[NAME OF PERSON]
[TITLE]
[STREET ADDRESS]
[CITY / STATE / ZIP CODE]

Dear [NAME OF PERSON OR TITLE, IF NAME NOT KNOWN]:

1 I have excellent skills, education, and experience [NOTE: LEAVE OUT WHAT YOU DO NOT HAVE; IF YOU DO NOT HAVE THE EXPERIENCE, FOR EXAMPLE, OMIT THAT WORD] in [NAME OF FIELD OR OCCUPATION], but am in a situation where your assistance in my career search would be greatly appreciated.

2 My [WRITE IN NUMBER OF YEARS] years in prison will be over soon, and I will be released on [OR "in"] [GIVE APPROXIMATE DATE OR SPECIFIC DATE, IF KNOWN, FOR EXAMPLE: ""on July 24th of this year." OR "in approximately six months." OR "in 21 days."]. This experience has been a most positive one, including the additional education I've received, and I know that I will be a more capable and productive employee because of what I have learned here.

3 Any information, suggestions, contacts, or support you can offer would help me greatly. I am determined to use my talents in the most productive manner, but as you can imagine, I am a bit more limited in what I can do on my own because of my present situation. However, please understand: I am NOT looking for a handout or someone to do my work, but rather for guidance and information.

4 I have enclosed a copy of my resume for your convenience.

5 Thank you very much; I look forward to hearing from you.

Sincerely,

[YOUR NAME TYPED HERE, SIGNED ABOVE]

COVER LETTER: TELLING SOMEONE YOU ARE IN PRISON -- #2
(asking for employment assistance from someone you do know)

[DATE]

[NAME OF PERSON]
[TITLE]
[STREET ADDRESS]
[CITY / STATE / ZIP CODE]

Dear [NAME OF PERSON]: [NOTE: USE FIRST OR LAST NAME, DEPENDING ON HOW WELL YOU KNOW THE PERSON]

1 As you know [OR, IF MORE APPROPRIATE, "as you may know,"] I will soon be looking for employment. I have excellent skills, education, and experience [NOTE: LEAVE OUT WHAT YOU DO NOT HAVE; IF YOU DO NOT HAVE THE EXPERIENCE, FOR EXAMPLE, OMIT THAT WORD] in [NAME OF FIELD OR OCCUPATION], but would appreciate your assistance.

2 Any information, suggestions, contacts, or support you can offer would help me greatly. I am determined to use my talents in the most productive manner, but as you can imagine, I am a bit more limited in what I can do on my own because of my present situation. However, please understand: I am NOT looking for a handout or someone to do my work, but rather for guidance.

3 [NAME OF PERSON], I have used this time in prison as an opportunity in grow as a person, to improve my education, and to [CHOOSE ONE: "become a better {PUT IN A SPECIFIC JOB OR, IF UNSURE, USE THE WORD, 'worker'}" OR "learn the {"trade" OR "profession," FOR EXAMPLE, "the welding trade."}].

4 I have enclosed a copy of my resume for your convenience.

5 Thank you very much; I look forward to hearing from you.

Sincerely,

[YOUR NAME TYPED HERE, SIGNED ABOVE]

COVER LETTER: ADVERTISED OR NON-ADVERTISED POSITION)
(admitting that you are currently in prison)

[DATE]

[NAME OF PERSON, IF KNOWN] [SKIP A LINE, THEN TITLE, IF KNOWN]
[NAME OF ORGANIZATION] [SKIP A LINE, THEN STREET ADDRESS / P.O. BOX #]
[CITY / STATE / ZIP]

Dear [NAME OF PERSON, OR TITLE, OR "Sir or Madam"]:

1 I'm very interested in [SELECT: "the recently advertised position of {NAME OF POSITION} that appeared in {NAME OF PUBLICATION}" OR "a(n) {NAME OF POSITION OR JOB INTEREST, FOR EXAMPLE, "Line Worker"} position with your company {OR "organization"}]. My skills, experience, and education [IF ONE OF THESE DOES NOT FIT THE JOB, LEAVE OUT] [CHOOSE ONE: "match the qualifications you listed." OR "would allow me to become a very productive employee."]

2 While my resume is enclosed, a brief overview of background, as it relates [CHOOSE ONE: "to the position," OR "to your industry,"] includes:

3 **[LIST A RELATED POINT FROM YOUR RESUME] ...**

[LIST A RELATED POINT FROM YOUR RESUME] ...

[LIST A RELATED POINT FROM YOUR RESUME] [NOTE: IF YOU'LL BE ELIGIBLE FOR ANY GOVT. PROGRAM {SEE Chp. 11, "Miscellaneous," pp. 420-422 }, INSERT HERE] ...

4 I am presently serving the last [CHOOSE ONE: "few weeks" OR "few months"] of a prison sentence, and will be available after [GIVE EXACT DATE OR APPROXIMATE DATE]. I know that a meeting between us would prove mutually beneficial, and you would find me an applicant who is highly enthusiastic, motivated, dedicated, hardworking, and reliable.

5 Due to my current situation, it is impossible for you to contact me by phone. However, I do look forward to hearing from you by mail ... and meeting with you upon my release!

6 Thank you very much.

Sincerely, [SKIP A LINE][YOUR NAME TYPED HERE, SIGNED ABOVE]

LETTER SET #3

MISCELLANEOUS LETTERS

LETTER: ASKING FOR A LETTER OF REFERENCE
(written from prison)

[DATE]

[NAME OF PERSON]
[TITLE]
[NAME OF COMPANY]
[STREET ADDRESS]
[CITY / STATE / ZIP CODE]

Dear [NAME OF PERSON; USE FIRST OR LAST NAME, DEPENDING ON HOW WELL YOU KNOW THE PERSON]:

1 As you know [OR, IF MORE APPROPRIATE, "as you may know,"], I will soon be looking for employment. I have excellent skills, education, and experience [NOTE: LEAVE OUT WHAT YOU DO NOT HAVE; IF YOU DO NOT HAVE THE EXPERIENCE, FOR EXAMPLE, OMIT THAT WORD] in [NAME OF FIELD OR OCCUPATION], and would appreciate being able to use you as a reference.

2 You are familiar with my [SELECT: "work" OR "education'] and what I accomplished, my attitude, and my general work ethic. A letter written by you that touches on these areas would be a big help to me. I am determined to use my talents in the most productive manner, and am now beginning my job search preparation.

3 For your convenience, I have enclosed [SELECT ONE OF THESE: "a copy of my resume and a guideline to assist you in writing my letter of reference" OR "a guideline to assist you in writing my letter of reference. My resume will follow as soon as it is completed."] [NOTE: GUIDELINE FOR WRITING LETTER OF REFERENCE CAN BE FOUND ON PAGE 146.]

4 Thank you very much; I look forward to hearing from you.

Sincerely,

[YOUR NAME TYPED HERE, SIGNED ABOVE]

LETTER: ASKING FOR SPECIAL HELP WHEN RELEASED
(written from prison)

X

[DATE]

[NAME OF PERSON, IF KNOWN]
[TITLE, IF KNOWN]
[ORGANIZATION]
[STREET ADDRESS / P.O. BOX#]
[CITY / STATE / ZIP]

Dear [NAME OF PERSON, OR TITLE, OR "Sir or Madam"]:

1 I will be released from [NAME OF PRISON, INSTITUTION, ETC.; IF LOCATED IN A CITY DIFFERENT FROM YOU WILL BE LIVING, ADD "in {NAME OF CITY; ALSO, NAME OF STATE IF DIFFERENT FROM WHERE YOU WILL BE LIVING}"] on [DATE OF RELEASE; IF ONLY APPROXIMATE DATE IS KNOWN, write "in approximately {GIVE NUMBER OF WEEKS OR MONTHS UNTIL RELEASE}]," and am eager to begin my walk back to a successful and happy life on the outside.

2 However, I need your assistance when I get out ...

3 Prior to my arrest, I was [EXAMPLES: "a heavy gambler" OR "a long term drug user" OR "a chronic drinker" OR WHATEVER IT IS THAT YOU NEED ASSISTANCE IN OVERCOMING]. I'm aware of my addiction, and while I have made definite progress in prison through counseling and much self-analysis, I know that I still have a problem.

4 [ADD WHICHEVER OF THE FOLLOWING TWO SENTENCES IS APPROPRIATE: "I'd appreciate your organization's help." OR "According to the terms of my release, I must obtain professional counseling."] Any information you can send me on the services you provide, meeting days and times, and available staff would be most helpful. While there is much that I can (and must) do on my own, I've also come to realize that recovery is a lifelong process and there is nothing wrong in asking for some back-up guidance along the way.

5 Thank you very much; I look forward to hearing from you.

Very truly yours, [SKIP A LINE]
[YOUR NAME TYPED HERE, SIGNED ABOVE]

COVER LETTER: "COLD CALLING" ON A FIRM
(to learn more about a company or organization)

[DATE]

[NAME OF PERSON, IF KNOWN]
[TITLE, IF KNOWN]
[NAME OF COMPANY]
[STREET ADDRESS[
[CITY / STATE / ZIP CODE]

Dear [NAME OF PERSON, OR "Sir or Madam"]:

1 I am extremely interested in learning more about [NAME OF COMPANY OR ORGANIZATION[, as I feel that I have the skills, experience, and education that could contribute to your [NAME OF DEPARTMENT OR DIVISION {EXAMPLE: "Sales Division"}, UNIT {EXAMPLE: "Nursing Unit"}, OR GENERAL PERSONNEL {EXAMPLE: "staff}"].

2 While I would not be available for employment until [GIVE APPROXIMATE OR SPECIFIC DATE OF RELEASE], any information you could send me about your ["company" OR {IF NOT A COMPANY} "organization"] would be greatly appreciated. Please include corporate annual report, recent articles, and pamphlets, if available.

3 For your files, I have enclosed a copy of my resume.

4 Thank you very much.

Sincerely,

[YOUR NAME TYPED HERE AND SIGNED ABOVE]

LETTER: READ ABOUT FIRM IN A PUBLICATION
(to obtain additional information but not an interview)

X

[DATE]

[NAME OF PERSON]
[TITLE]
[NAME OF COMPANY]
[STREET ADDRESS]
[CITY/STATE/ZIP CODE]

Dear [NAME OF PERSON]:

1 I was quite impressed with the ["recent" OR "July 24th, 1998"] article entitled [NAME OF ARTICLE] that appeared in [NAME OF PUBLICATION], and profiled [NAME OF COMPANY OR ORGANIZATION].   My career interests, experience, and education match the direction of your growth, and I am extremely interested in learning more about your organization.

2 While I would not be available for employment until [GIVE APPROXIMATE OR SPECIFIC DATE OF YOUR RELEASE], I would appreciate you sending me any literature, pamphlets, articles, press releases, or corporate annual reports you have available.

3 For your convenience, I have enclosed a copy of my resume.

4 Thank you very much.

Sincerely,

[YOUR NAME TYPED HERE, SIGNED ABOVE]

LETTER: FOLLOW-UP
(to be sent when you have not had a reply to your resume)

[DATE]

[NAME OF PERSON, IF KNOWN]
[TITLE, IF KNOWN]
[NAME OF ORGANIZATION, IF KNOWN]
[STREET ADDRESS / P.O. BOX #]
[CITY / STATE / ZIP]

Dear [NAME OF PERSON, OR TITLE, OR "Sir or Madam"]:

1 Yes, I'm still quite interested in the position of [NAME OF POSITION; IF THE POSITION WAS ADVERTISED, ADD THE PHRASE "that you advertised in {NAME OF PUBLICATION, IF KNOWN}"], and even though my resume was sent to you several days ago, I continue to be very excited about the prospect of employment with [NAME OF ORGANIZATION].

2 I realize, of course, that you probably received many resumes, and understandably there might be a slight delay in responding to me. However, I know that [NAME OF ORGANIZATION AND/OR DEPARTMENT] would benefit from my skills, experience, and education [IF YOU DO NOT HAVE ONE OF THESE, LEAVE OUT; IF THERE IS ONE YOU WOULD LIKE TO ADD, DO SO]. Likewise, I definitely believe you can give me the career [OR "job"] opportunity and environment for growth that I seek.

3 An additional copy of my resume is enclosed for your convenience.

4 Thank you very much; I look forward to hearing from you soon.

Very truly yours,

[YOUR NAME TYPED HERE, SIGNED ABOVE]

LETTER: TO BE SENT FOLLOWING RECEIPT OF REJECTION LETTER

X

[DATE]

[NAME OF PERSON]
[POSITION]
[NAME OF ORGANIZATION]
[STREET ADDRESS]
[CITY / STATE / ZIP CODE]

Dear [NAME OF PERSON]:

1 I recently [CHOOSE ONE: "applied to" OR "interviewed with"] [NAME OF FIRM] for [CHOOSE ONE: "the position of {NAME OF POSITION}, as advertised in {NAME OF PUBLICATION}, OR "a position as a(n) {NAME OF POSITION}"]. I remain very interested in a career with your firm [OR ORGANIZATION], even though I received a "turn down" letter from you (copy enclosed).

2 I'm very determined in my job search, and have no doubt that I would develop into one of your top [GENERAL NAME OF POSITION, FOR EXAMPLE, "Sales Representatives"]. I realize, of course, that you probably heard from many other applicants for this position, and your decision was based on certain needs and requirements of your firm [IF IT FITS:, "as explained"], and you have a budget to work within.

3 Yet I also believe that, [CHOOSE ONE: "once we meet " OR "if we were to talk again"] you'll find me to be a candidate who would blend well with your company's goals, objectives, and [PICK A MORE SPECIFIC ITEM, FOR EXAMPLE: "continued increase in bottom line profits" OR "customer satisfaction" OR "counseling success" OR "the department's needs for accurate filing"].

4 [SELECT EITHER OF THESE TWO SENTENCES, DEPENDING ON WHAT WAS SAID IN THE REJECTION LETTER ABOUT KEEPING YOUR RESUME: "In case you've filed me away, tossed me in a corner, or scattered me aside, I've enclosed another copy of my resume." OR "While you have indicated my resume is still alive and well in your files, I have enclosed an additional copy for your convenience."] Let's meet so we can see how each might be an asset to the other.

5 Thank you for [CHOOSE: "your initial reply to my cover letter and resume." OR "the interview opportunity."] An eternal optimist, I am, however, looking forward to a more positive response this time!

Sincerely, [SKIP A LINE]
 [YOUR NAME TYPED HERE, SIGNED ABOVE]

LETTER: INTERVIEW THANK YOU -- #1
(to a person you don't know on a personal basis)

[DATE]

[NAME OF PERSON]
[TITLE]
[NAME OF ORGANIZATION]
[STREET ADDRESS]
[CITY / STATE / ZIP CODE]

Dear [NAME OF PERSON]:

1 It was a pleasure meeting with you today [OR, "yesterday" OR WHENEVER, BUT IF MORE THAN TWO DAYS GIVE SPECIFIC DATE], and our conversation gave me an opportunity to fully appreciate the potential [NAME OF ORGANIZATION] offers as a career opportunity.

2 I'd like to re-emphasize my interest in the position of [NAME OF POSITION], and -- based on the points you stressed in our meeting -- again mention my strengths in [NAME THOSE TWO OR THREE ITEMS THAT YOU FEEL BEST MATCH WHAT THE INTERVIEWER SEEMS TO BE LOOKING FOR OR TOLD YOU HE / SHE WAS LOOKING FOR]. I strongly believe that my interest in [NAME YOUR CAREER AREA OF INTEREST OR ANOTHER RELATED AREA], combined with my professional experience, education, and interpersonal skills [IF ONE OF THESE WORDS IS NOT APPROPRIATE, LEAVE IT OUT], would result in a very successful working relationship.

3 Thank you very much for your time, and I look forward to hearing from you soon.

Sincerely,

[YOUR NAME TYPED HERE, SIGNED ABOVE]

LETTER: INTERVIEW THANK YOU -- #2
(to a person you do know on a personal basis)

[DATE]

[NAME OF PERSON]
[TITLE]
[NAME OF ORGANIZATION]
[STREET ADDRESS]
[CITY / STATE / ZIP]

Dear [NAME OF PERSON, AS YOU WOULD USUALLY ADDRESS HIM]:

1 Our recent meeting to discuss my interest in employment as [ADD: "a(n) {NAME OF POSITION OR JOB TITLE, FOR EXAMPLE, "Audit Control Manager"}] was most appreciated, and I have no doubt that I can contribute greatly to [NAME OF ORGANIZATION]'s [ADD PHRASE SUCH AS: "continued growth" OR "expansion plans" OR "regrouping"].

2 After thinking about our discussion, I KNOW that I want the position, and believe that the following points are of special importance:

> **[1 – LIST A POINT THAT YOU FEEL IS IMPORTANT]** –

> **[2 – LIST A POINT THAT YOU FEEL IS IMPORTANT]** –

> **[3 – LIST A POINT THAT YOU FEEL IS IMPORTANT]** –

> **[4 – ETC., IF NECESSARY, BUT NO MORE THAN FOUR]** –

3 [NAME OF PERSON AS YOU NORMALLY ADDRESS HIM], thanks for your time and effort on my behalf. I look forward to speaking with you again soon.

Sincerely,

[YOUR NAME TYPED HERE, SIGNED ABOVE]

LETTER: ACCEPTING INVITATION FOR PLANT / OFFICE VISIT OR INTERVIEW

[DATE]

[NAME OF PERSON]
[TITLE]
[NAME OF ORGANIZATION]
[STREET ADDRESS]
[CITY / STREET / ZIP CODE]

Dear [NAME OF PERSON]:

1 Thank you for your [CHOOSE ONE: "letter of" OR "call on" [DATE] inviting me for a(n) [CHOOSE ONE: "plant visit" OR "office visit" OR "interview""] at [TIME] on [LIST DATE; IF GIVEN CHOICE OF MORE THAN ONE DATE, INCLUDE NEXT PARAGRAPH]:

2 The most convenient date for me would be [DATE]. I will arrive at your office at [TIME]. Please let me know if this is acceptable to you.

3 I have enclosed [CHOOSE ONE: "an additional copy of my resume" OR "a copy of my resume"], [ADD THE FOLLOWING ONLY IF IT APPLIES: " along with the completed application for employment." IF THIS PHRASE DOES NOT APPLY, CHANGE THE COMMA AFTER THE WORD "resume" TO A PERIOD.]

4 [CHOOSE ONE: "The opportunity to visit your {CHOOSE ONE: "plant" OR "office'}" OR "The opportunity to interview with you"] is greatly appreciated. I am very interested and eager to learn more about possible employment opportunities with [NAME OF ORGANIZATION].

5 Thank you very much. I look forward to your reply, and to meeting with you.

Sincerely,

[YOUR NAME TYPED HERE, SIGNED ABOVE]

LETTER: REJECTING A JOB OFFER

[DATE]

[NAME OF PERSON]
[TITLE]
[ORGANIZATION]
[STREET ADDRESS]
[CITY / STATE / ZIP CODE]

Dear [NAME OF PERSON]:

1 After considerable thought, I have decided not to accept your offer of employment as outlined in [CHOOSE ONE: "your letter of {GIVE DATE OF LETTER}" OR "our conversation of {GIVE DATE OF CONVERSATION}"]. This has been a very difficult decision for me. However, I feel I have made the correct one for this point in my career.

2 Thank you for your time, effort, and consideration. Your confidence in me is sincerely appreciated.

Sincerely,

[YOUR NAME TYPED HERE, SIGNED ABOVE]

LETTER: ACCEPTING A JOB OFFER

[DATE]

[NAME OF PERSON]
[TITLE]
[NAME OF ORGANIZATION]
[STREET ADDRESS / P.O. BOX #]
[CITY / STATE / ZIP CODE]

Dear [NAME OF PERSON]:

1 Thank you very much for your job offer for the position of [NAME OF POSITION], as outlined in your [FULL DATE OF LETTER, FOR EXAMPLE: "July 24th, 1998"] letter. I accept and look forward to a long and mutually rewarding relationship with [NAME OF ORGANIZATION].

2 According to the terms of my employment, I will be paid [GIVE SALARY STATED TO YOU]; my employment will begin [GIVE STARTING DATE OF EMPLOYMENT]; and my hours will be [GIVE DAYS AND HOURS {IF APPLICABLE} THAT YOU WILL BE WORKING]. [ADD THIS SENTENCE IF APPROPRIATE: "Also, I will participate in your firm's drug rehabilitation program {OR ANY SPECIAL CONDITIONS THAT THE EMPLOYER HAS LISTED}."]

3 If any of the above information is wrong, please contact me.

4 Again, thank you for this opportunity -- it will be a decision that you will be very happy with.

Sincerely,

[YOUR NAME TYPED HERE, SIGNED ABOVE]

[ADD ONLY IF YOU ARE IN PRISON AND EMPLOYER IS AWARE OF THIS FACT: "P.S. My permanent address, upon release, will be: {GIVE ADDRESS AND PHONE NUMBER}.]

Chapter 6

The Job Interview

"It isn't the mountain that wears you out -- it's the grain of sand in your shoe."

Robert Service, American poet

● INTRODUCTION ●

DON'T FEAR THE INTERVIEW

"We'd like you to come in for an interview."

THE JOY. These words, every day, strike elation and terror into the hearts and minds of job-seekers. There is the joy, of course, at knowing that your initial search campaign did not end in a rejection letter; that you made the first cut; and that the job as yours now seems a stronger possibility.

THE PANIC. But there's also the downside of the interview: what to wear, what to say, what questions to ask, how to control nervousness, where to find out about the company, if your personality matches what the organization seeks, how to ask about salary and benefits ... the list seemingly does not end.

Pogo, that wonderful cartoon character of the 60s and 70s, once remarked, "We have met the enemy and they is us!" Virtually all interviewers will agree: most potential employees are done in by themselves BEFORE the interview begins.

IT DOESN'T HAVE TO BE A BAD EXPERIENCE. Rather than being a terrifying experience with sweaty palms and bouncy legs and twirling thumbs and churning stomachs, it can be the segment of the career or job search that you control and that you know will put the finishing touches on your overall presentation.

IT TAKES WORK TO SUCCEED IN THE INTERVIEW!

But it won't happen overnight: you need to prepare and to practice. LAZINESS is the chief cause of job applicants not getting the job they really want. Once this is cured, all that you hope for in your job search -- including a stunning interview performance -- can be yours.

It's Never Too Late To Start Your Preparation

Much of the preparation you should have begun or have completed during your six months or less left inside, and some of it in the short while that you've been on the outside. Research on the company, purchase of clothes, improvement of your public speaking, going over interview questions -- these and other areas should be well in hand by now. *But if not, don't sweat it – that's what this chapter is all about!*

Keep in mind that it is never too late to begin ... and the possible consequence of not beginning or giving up is going back to prison with more time away from family, friends, and a steady income from a job or career.

> **REMEMBER: Preparing yourself for an interview means always willing to put your best effort into obtaining a job, no matter how much it might interfere with family life, time with friends, and leisure activities. Once you have the job, everything else in your life will be appreciated more.**

THE JOB INTERVIEW IS ESPECIALLY HARD ON EX-INMATES

An ex-inmate is usually especially nervous about interviewing for a job. Why? The primary reason is psychological, that is, he or she thinks that wherever he / she walks there is a large neon sign flashing on-and-off, in very bright letters announcing, "I am an ex-inmate! I am an ex-inmate!"

There Are Some Conditions You Can't Control

Depending on the terms of your release, there may be certain conditions that will remind you, whenever they appear, that you are, in fact, an ex-inmate:

- checking in with your parole or probation office
- not being allowed to vote, to own a firearm, or to visit a foreign country
- having to get permission to travel out of city or out of state
- not being allowed in a bar or out past a certain time
- not being able to join certain government organizations or the military
- not being able to be bonded (see Chapter 8, pages 318 and 324; Chapter 11, pages 420-421)
- and yes, even a tattoo or scar that you "earned" while in prison will give you a quick reminder of the time spent inside

The Key: You Can Control Your Mind

But these are all items over which you have no or little control. However, you DO have control over your mind ... and it is your mind on the outside that will either allow you to make use of your freedom or keep you chained mentally, even though you are physically outside the prison walls.

REMEMBER: If you think of yourself as an ex-inmate, you will act like an ex-inmate: nervous, paranoid, afraid, and insecure; if you think of yourself as a citizen, and begin to put your prison experience behind you, you will feel more "mainstream" and make your re-entry into society much easier.

REMEMBER: Few employers hire ex-inmates who happen to be job applicants, but many employers hire job applicants who happen to be ex-inmates.

---

2 Major Reasons Why Ex-Inmates are Nervous During the Interview

There are two other reasons -- beyond the usual ones that make most people nervous when they interview -- that make ex-inmates nervous immediately prior to and during the interview:

(1) THIS IS PROBABLY THE FIRST TIME IN A LONG WHILE THAT YOU HAD TO "SELL" YOURSELF TO SOMEONE WHO KNOWS LITTLE, IF ANYTHING, ABOUT YOU. While you were in prison, it was fairly comfortable because you knew those around you -- inmates, guards, counselors, administrators, your attorneys, friends and family from the outside. Each accepted you as you, that is, they knew you while you were in prison, so it was no big deal. Even if you had to go before a parole board to "plead your case" so you could get out early, each member knew that you were in prison and was judging you (primarily) on what your behavior was like while INSIDE.

YOU MUST COME ACROSS LIKE ANY OTHER JOB APPLICANT. With a job interview, however, you now must give the impression that you are a "regular person," that you can just as easily handle the personal and professional responsibilities of the job for which you are applying as the next candidate can.

IT'S EASIER TALKING WITH ANOTHER EX-INMATE. To many inmates, having been in prison is a cushion of sorts -- but ONLY when you are talking to someone else who [a] has known you while you were in prison, or [b] meets you once you are out of prison but can identify with you because he or she was in prison or is / has been in some way connected with the corrections industry (examples: parole officer, clergy, psychologist, another ex-inmate).

Like two fraternity brothers or sorority sisters meeting, there is an instant acceptance of one another because of that "secret" common link: prison. Each can identify with the unique problems and obstacles that prison life and brand-new life outside of prison brings. With rare exceptions, this does not exist outside of prison with those who have not been incarcerated, and lack of it is a major contributing factor to being nervous or afraid.

REMEMBER: Being out of prison is important not only for the sake of having your freedom, but because of one of the responsibilities that goes with freedom: standing on your own two feet and simply presenting yourself as a well-qualified applicant looking for a job and **NOT** as an ex-inmate who believes the world is against you and will keep you from getting a job!

(2) DURING YOUR TIME IN PRISON, YOU ARE OFTEN MADE TO THINK OF YOURSELF AS A FAILURE, AS A NEGATIVE CONTRIBUTION TO SOCIETY, AS SOMEONE WHO WILL ALWAYS "SCREW UP." No one wants to fail. Interviewing for a job but not being the candidate selected is viewed by many as a form of failure.

IN THE FREE WORLD, OUTSIDE FORCES STRENGTHEN CONFIDENCE. If you have been existing in a fairly positive environment -- on the outside, with job or educational accomplishments, experience, respect from colleagues and clients, support from family, and knowledge that you have been existing within the acceptable and legal framework of society -- your confidence going into a job interview will be much stronger than if you lived in a negative environment, such as prison.

Once out of prison, you want to always succeed. This is important for your self-image and self-confidence (as it would be for anyone), and with each success will come the word "failure" fading more and more into the background.

DON'T TAKE REJECTION PERSONALLY. Yet it is also a fact of life that we do not get selected for every job we interview; we do get turned down. However, if you have spent those last six months in prison developing yourself -- mentally and physically -- then you will come to realize what most people not selected after a job interview realize:

it is usually not YOU that is being rejected, but rather the "what" of you – skills that may not match, education that's not exactly right, experience that's perhaps too strong in one area or too soft in another.

With each interview, you will learn so you will be better in the next one. The result? THAT one interview where the employer finally says, "Well, when can you start?"

3 NEW TYPES OF INTERVIEWS: BE PREPARED FOR THEM!

(1) THE "SHOW ME YOUR STUFF" INTERVIEW. More employers what to know -- on the spot -- if applicants can really do what their resumes say they can do: would-be cooks are asked to cook, would-be welders are asked to weld, etc. So be sure that whatever you list as experience and skills on your resume is true, because it'll be quite embarrassing if asked to do it during the interview and you can't.

(2) TELEPHONE INTERVIEWS. It saves time and personnel, and many employers believe they can tell as much about an applicant during a spontaneous phone interview than in person. (And more often, for a second interview, the applicant has a set date and time for a phone interview.) This means that your oral communications should be at their best ... and you should always be prepared to be "on."

(3) VIDEO INTERVIEWS. While in use in the general workplace for some years now, video interviews are now gaining favor with employers during job fairs in prisons as well. Most often, video interviews are taped and viewed by the employer at a later time, but sometimes they are live, where you will be talking to an employer located at another site. In either case, your presentation skills become especially important ... and you must remember to both look into the lens and to occasionally smile!

> **REMEMBER: What truly makes people successful is their ability to accept failure as a bumpy lesson of life over which they trip, learn from their fall, and use the experience as positive information and a course correction.**

STRUCTURE OF THIS CHAPTER

The job interview consists of three parts:

- ● **The First Part:** <u>**Prior to the Interview**</u>
- ● **The Second Part:** <u>**During the Job Interview**</u>
- ● **The Third Part:** <u>**After the Interview**</u>

> **REMEMBER: If your learn from a mistake it's no longer a mistake -- it's a lesson.**

● TRACKING YOUR JOB INTERVIEW PROGRESS ●

CAREER SEARCH LOG II -- The Job Interview

In Chapter. 5 (pages 187-189), you were introduced to Career Search Log I, a solid way to keep track of your resumes and cover letters. You also need to track your interviews and the result of each -- this can help you in future interviews. Here's how to best use it:

(1) THERE ARE 7 CATEGORIES ACROSS THE TOP:

"PROSPECTIVE EMPLOYER FOR INTERVIEW": This would be the name of the COMPANY or ORGANIZATION with which you will have the interview.

"CONTACT PERSON": Write in the name of the person who arranged the interview. If there is a phone number that is different from that which appears on Career Search Log I, also write it in this column.

"INTERVIEW DATE / TIME": Write in the date and time of the interview.

"CONFIRMATION LETTER": Write in the date you wrote a letter confirming the date and time of the interview. (See Chapter. 5, page 222, for sample of this letter.)

"THANK YOU": Date you wrote a thank you letter after you went through the interview. (See Chapter. 5, pages 220-221, for two samples of this letter.)

"COMMENTS": Any items you were told to bring to the interview; additional information from the letter / phone call you received (informing you that an interview was being arranged for you) that you feel is important to note.

"REMARKS": Your thoughts (briefly) on high points, low points, etc. of the interview; also, if you did not get the job, the reason why.

(2) THE "REMARKS" SECTION: This section can be very valuable. If you've gone through several interviews and you begin finding that the same low points or the same reasons for not getting the job continue to occur, than this is telling you what you need to work on.

(However, if you find that it is one reason at one company and another somewhere else, this is usually a pretty good indication that you are NOT continually doing one or two things wrong. Rather you are not being hired for lack of budget, someone else had better qualifications, etc. -- something over which you generally have no control.)

(3) KEEP THIS LOG: As with the Career Search Log I (Resumes & Cover Letters), it is important that you keep this Log as well, even after you're hired. It can serve as a good reference tool, including such information as where to re-apply; what your strengths and weaknesses are; and what industries / companies seem to be hiring someone with your qualifications.

(4) NEVER RUN OUT. If you feel you will need more copies of Career Search Log II, either photocopy it or make a handwritten copy.

(5) WRITE! I said this at the end of Career Search Log I, and it's so important that the message is repeated here:

By now, you may feel that you've had it with writing: keeping a journal, perhaps a portfolio; filling out a Self Evaluation Profile and a Resume Development Guide; writing your resume and then your cover letters; keeping a Career Search Log I (for resumes and cover letters), and now Career Search Log II, to keep track of your interview progress.

But getting a job is NOT easy, and as an inmate you've got some major problems to overcome, some major thinking to do. I suggest you do ALL this writing so you can be a job candidate who is exceptionally well-prepared, because if you are not, someone else will come along who is -- and he or she will get the job, not you!

CAREER SEARCH LOG II

Employer for Interview	Contact Person	Interview Date/Time	Confirmation Letter	Thank You	Comments	Remarks

● THE FIRST PART: <u>PRIOR TO THE INTERVIEW</u> ●

THE JOB INTERVIEW TAKES PLANNING

An interview is not something that you simply walk into having given no thought to, say a smiling "Hi, dude!" to the interviewer, and plop down in a chair, believing that the mere fact you were called in for an interview means you have the job. Hardly.

<u>UNDERSTAND ALL ASPECTS OF THE INTERVIEW</u>. You must first have a thorough understanding of the interview process, know how to mentally prepare yourself, and do all the small things that are required. Forget any, and I guarantee someone else will come along who has done his or her homework ... and walk away with the job you want!

WHAT'S THE PURPOSE OF AN INTERVIEW?

A resume and cover letter are nothing more than public relations tools to get you in the door. For the most part, they speak of the "what" (facts), not the "who" (personality). If companies were interested in hiring robots, there probably would be no need for the interview.

<u>REAL IMAGE VS. PAPER IMAGE</u>. However, the individuals doing the hiring want to make sure you can fit in with the type of person already working for them; do your hygiene, dress, and communicative skills present the professional that will positively reflect the company's image; and, in fact, are you the person they have read about on your resume or a paper figment of someone's imagination?

> **REMEMBER: All the Hollywood special effects in the world are not going to help you out in the reality world of the job interview.**

235

WHY DOES THE INTERVIEW MAKE A JOB APPLICANT NERVOUS?

In addition to the two reasons already discussed that relate directly to your prison experience, there are also those same reasons that virtually EVERYONE interviewing goes through that make for nervous times:

You Weren't With Your Resume and Cover Letter

Up until you actually meet the person who will interview you, there has been a very isolated distance between you and the company. When your resume and cover letter went in, it went from Nameless Face One to Nameless Face Two. It was somewhat easy to take much time and think about what you were going to say, perhaps sign your cover letter while wearing jeans or pajamas (or a prison uniform!), or research a company in the library at night, etc.

You Are The Center of Attention at The Interview

Now, however, it's showtime, and you must mentally, physically, and visually dress to impress and go by the time, date, and location of the interviewer. Suddenly, it is only you: everything is noticed about you. Your answers and thoughts must come quickly and intelligently. You must possess that personality that the interviewer believes will click with the company.

Knowing that you must do all this before a person or persons with the power of "who shall live and who shall die" is definitely Nervoustown USA!

HOW CAN YOU OVERCOME YOUR PRE-INTERVIEW NERVOUSNESS? In addition to knowing that you have done your research and are prepared as much as possible for the interview, there are mental and physical exercises that can be done:

3 Mental Exercises To Reduce Your Nervousness

(1) REMEMBER: THE COMPANY NEEDS YOU AS MUCH AS YOU NEED IT. If you did not have something to offer that initially had someone in the company saying (in essence), "This person looks like he/she might have the stuff we need," then you would not be asked to the interview in the first place. While you may be the one looking for a job, they are looking for someone to help their company grow -- it is a two-way street. Keep this in mind; it will put you on a more equal footing with the interviewer.

(2) REMEMBER: YOU ARE CONTINUING THE SAME INTERVIEWING PROCESS THAT THE PERSON INTERVIEWING YOU ONCE WENT THROUGH. Unless he/she married into the company, is politically well connected, or "kept company" with the right person, the person(s) interviewing you also once squirmed, had sweaty palms and a churning stomach, and twirled his/her fingers. Once you are selected for the position, you may eventually be in same position as the interviewer!

(3) REMEMBER: PRIOR TO THE INTERVIEW, DO SOMETHING TOTALLY UNRELATED TO THE INTERVIEW. The more one concentrates on the interview, often the more one gets nervous -- and nervousness certainly doesn't help in the interview. So ... take a walk, read something unrelated to work, watch a TV program, write a friend a letter -- anything that will take your mind off the interview. This will not only help relax you mentally, but will give you a better perspective on the questions you'll be asked.

3 Physical Exercises To Reduce Your Nervousness

The closer you get to the interview, the more tension usually builds up in you.   This reaches its peak the day prior to and the day of the interview. In addition to such tension-relieving activities as sports, walking, and cleaning out the garage (!), try one or both of these -- they both work:

(1) DEEP BREATHING / TAI CHI: An ancient Chinese method of relaxation, this exercise relaxes the mind as well as the body. While there are many aspects to Tai Chi, at its core is deep breathing in a slow, deliberate pace. How it works best:

You can either sit or stand. Close your eyes and begin to picture something quite nice that is relaxing (a quiet summer eve, a walk near a lake, a stroll in a park, etc.) As you do this, begin to breath slowly and deeply, in and out, in and out for 5-15 minutes. As your mind begins to relax from a combination of the slow, deep breathing and the nice image, your body will also begin to relax, sending any nerves to Bye Bye Land. (By the way: you might also want to try this while you are incarcerated. Many inmates do and they find it not only relaxes them but has helped to control their anger and stress, and thus put them in a more mellow state overall -- certainly, something that's always needed on the inside.)

(2) SCREAM! This one is best done when you are by yourself and no one else can hear you, or with people around who really understand you! Called "The Primal Scream," it is simply screaming as loudly as possible until all air is expended. I found that this can be done most effectively when driving to an interview in the privacy of your car. (If taking a bus, you really don't want to try this on the other riders -- do it at home, before you leave!) This not only lets out tension, but also "loosens" your mind and body. (CAUTION: Don't scream too much or your voice might become horse before the interview!)

(3) TIGHTEN & RELAX YOUR MUSCLES. This exercise is extremely effective before and during the interview. It requires no special preparation, can be done with people all around, and is especially good at relaxing the mind as well as the body.

Here's how to do it: While standing, tighten the muscles in your body as much as possible for approximately 5 seconds, then relax; repeat this two more times. If sitting, do the same thing, but squeeze the arms of the chair (if applicable) as hard as possible. What is being done is a "transfer of tension" from your body and mind to the air and/or chair.

> **REMEMBER: No matter how much you prepare and practice for the interview, your biggest enemy can be a case of nerves -- be cool, be very cool and you'll be on your way to owning the interview.**

8 TIPS
TO HELP YOU PREPARE FOR THE INTERVIEW

As with all other aspects of the job search, preparing for the job interview has many parts to it. Forget one and it may be that one item that prevents you from doing a knockout performance at the interview. The interview can be especially perilous because of its three parts: pre-interview, during the interview, and post-interview. Too often, job applicants spend most of their interview preparation time concerned only with the "during the interview" portion, some time on the "pre-interview" portion, and very little time on the "post-interview" portion. You cannot do this. You must -- I repeat, MUST -- put full effort into all components of EACH portion. Read and put into motion ALL tips in this chapter -- they will FULLY prepare you for a highly successful interview experience.

#1
KNOW THE WHO, WHAT, WHERE, & WHY

Make certain you have the correct date, time, and location of the interview. If you are told with whom you will be interviewing, also write that down. Too, be certain that you know how to get to the interview location (especially if you are new to the city) and approximately how long it will take you to arrive. Finally, get specific directions that take you from your arrival at the company's building or plant to the room where the interview will take place.

(If possible, make a run from your house to the interview location at the same time on the same day of the week it will occur; this will give you some idea as to traffic tie-ups, construction problems, detours, bus stops or parking locations, etc.)

#2
BE PUNCTUAL

While the actual "who" of you -- your personality, emotions, oral communicative skills, etc. -- do not come out in mass until the interview, there are several peeks at this the interviewer is given prior to the interview. One of these is through your being on time ... or not. Yes, you can apologize if you're late and the interview will probably still go on ... but what type of initial impression have you made on the interviewer? Might he or she think that you aren't a timely person? That you don't take meeting times seriously? That you can't be depended upon? None of these are a plus, certainly, and any already have you starting in the minus column. So ... be on time! (This is a good reason to do what is suggested in Tip #1: make a dry run before the interview so you know how long it takes to get there.)

REMEMBER: You can never tame time, only make peace with it.

#3
RESEARCH THE ORGANIZATION

While Chapter. 2 discussed researching in general, it's important that you now make a major effort to learn as much as you can about each company you'll be interviewing with. Major cities have business publications that offer weekly, in-depth looks at companies and industries within a profession or industry; corporate reports, summary reports, corporate brochures, etc. can be found in libraries, by contacting the individual companies, on the Internet, and through contact with people who work at the firms; articles on companies appear in the business section of daily and weekly newspapers. (Chapter 9 offers specific information on researching after your release.)

What does all this tell you? That there are tons of sources floating around to offer you much information on just about any company you'll be interviewing with. DON'T use the excuse that you couldn't find anything -- you can, if you put the effort into your search.

#4
BE CONFIDENT OF YOUR APPEARANCE AND HYGIENE

As stressed in Chapter 1, proper appearance and hygiene are essential. You want to make a visual statement that says you are a professional. The following suggestions will help:

Appearance: For Women

- either wear a hint of low-key perfume or none at all
- have your hair done in a manner that is acceptable to the position (example: if you are going for a job in advertising or entertainment where creative hairstyles are more the norm, fine, but don't try these in a banking or purchasing situation) (SEE SPECIAL NOTE ON HAIR, PAGE 243)
- don't wear lipstick or makeup that is too creative or loud
- wear a suit or skirt and blouse combo that doesn't shout out, "Look at my thighs! Look at my breasts!"
- make certain your stockings don't have any runs, keep them skin-toned
- have your shoes shined and/or cleaned
- if you wear glasses, keep them clean ... and no deep-tinted glasses, no sunglasses
- carry a small handbag (in good condition) -- or nothing
- keep fingernails clean and short; use only clear (not colored) nail polish

- keep the jewelry down to a minimal amount (and either cover or eliminate any body piercings!)
- don't try to walk in as if you are trying to outdo a movie star or fashion model; you want to dress fairly conservative (grey, blue, or black with a white or light blue blouse; if you wear a tie or scarf, don't make the style flamboyant [unless it is a flamboyant job such as advertising, music, etc.] but do give yourself a flash of bright color; wear shoes that will match your suit or dress, and stockings that are skin-toned)
- make sure hems aren't too long or too short; make sure sleeves don't hang over wrists
- don't chew gum or bring a backpack to the interview
- if you have any tattoos that might show, try to dress so they will be covered
- weird hair colors / offbeat hair styles: leave them home; you're trying to make a positive impression, not frighten the interviewer away

Appearance: For Men

- don't overplay the handkerchief in the pocket and don't wear a flower in your lapel
- keep your suit or sport coat colors on the conservative side (blues, browns, greys, very muted plaids)
- keep the jewelry down to a minimum (and either cover or eliminate any body piercings; ditch earrings)
- make certain hair is combed in a manner acceptable to the employer (SEE NOTE ON HAIR, PAGE 243)
- have your shoes shined and/or cleaned; keep your fingernails clean and short
- don't have bulging pen packets or other such items in your shirt or jacket pocket
- if you wear glasses, keep them clean ... and no deep-tinted glasses, no sunglasses
- dress to blend in, not to look as if you just stepped off the cover of a men's fashion magazine
- if you have any tattoos that might show, try to dress so they will be covered
- body piercing / weird hair colors / offbeat hair styles: leave them home; you're trying to make a positive Impression, not frighten the interviewer away
- don't chew gum, bring a backpack, wear any cap or hat

REMEMBER: While some of the above items may seem like common sense, it is often the small things that we overlook ... and these same small things trip us up during the interview.

Hygiene: If It's Poor, It Can Quickly Erase Your Positives

Each hygienic negative you present to the interviewer, no matter how big or small, detracts from the positive message you are trying to bring across, takes away concentration from your mind and mouth, and raises questions about you being the right person for the job.

241

Does Poor Hygiene Equal Poor Job Performance?

The interview, although controlled and certainly putting you under much pressure, is -- as was previously mentioned -- the ONLY way in which an interviewer can truly judge your self PRIOR to hiring you. It is a tiny portrait of you professionally, personally, and emotionally. You want to show all positives, no negatives, and much flexibility. Poor hygiene merely offers a potential employer another negative look at the "who" of you, and is certainly not a good indicator of you personally or professionally.

Hygiene Tips for Men and Women

● make certain your teeth are brushed and flossed
● use mouth wash
● have a mouth mint or gum (best: spearmint or wintergreen) prior to the interview
● use underarm deodorant; if you tend to perspire easily, wear a T-shirt or put pads under your arms
    (It is a big turn-off to an interviewer to see [and smell?] perspiration stains.)
● take a shower or bath prior to the interview
● don't drink carbonated liquid just prior to the interview, as it will make you belch
● never take alcohol or drugs prior to the interview
● be certain that you don't have dandruff
● if you have acne, use a good cover medication
● keep your fingernails cleaned, clipped, and attractive
● (for females): make certain you have appropriate feminine hygiene
● if you have sweaty palms, wipe them before you shake hands (suggestion: if you have a serious
    problem with this, use talcum powder before leaving for the interview)
● have a handkerchief available (but out of sight) in the event you need to sneeze or cough
● don't wear any soiled clothes: not only might they be dirty but they will give off a poor odor

REMEMBER: An ugly piece of hygiene outweighs all the nice cologne or perfume you could ever buy.

SOME NOTES ON HAIR: Depending on the institution, you may have been allowed to grow your hair in a fashion or to a length that is not normally acceptable in the business world. Things must change, however, for the interview.

Once you have the job, the chances of you being fired for hair too long are very slim -- but first, you do have to make that initial impression. Hair can always grow back, but a first interview opportunity won't come back.

Specific Hair Suggestions for Men

● cut your hair to a length and style that is fairly conservative (or in a current style that is acceptable in the business world); don't wear a hair net or "setting scarf"; don't have pencils, etc. in your hair
● keep your hair color "soft" and natural -- wear it in its natural or an artificial color that is not harsh
● make certain your hair is clean and combed / brushed; if you use hair spray, use one that is unscented
● if you have a beard and / or mustache make certain it / they are neatly trimmed, or, if you think the circumstances warrant it, shaved off
● make certain that the hairs in your nose and ears (and eyebrows, if applicable) are clipped
● if you nick yourself while shaving, be certain that blood has not gotten onto your shirt, that the bleeding has stopped, and that you wiped it clean from your neck and face
● don't shave with an electric razor after you've gotten dressed: "hair dust" may litter your shirt and coat, and the shirt makes it more difficult to shave your neck cleanly
● if you wear a wig or toupee, make sure it looks good ... not one that makes it look like you've got a "rug"!

Specific Hair Suggestions for Women

● cut your hair to a length and style that is fairly conservative (or in a current style that is acceptable in the business world)
● keep your hair color "soft" and natural -- wear it in its natural or an artificial color that is not harsh
● make certain your hair is clean and combed / brushed;   if you use hair spray, use one that is unscented
● if you grew a beard or other body hair that is not usually associated with a female, get rid of it
● don't wear a hair net, hair curlers or rollers, or bobby pins that show; don't stick pencils, etc. in your hair

---

REMEMBER: Nothing can so quickly destroy an image of professionalism than stringy, outlandish, dirty, smelly, too cute, overdone, wild, multicolored, spiked, teased, grotesque, ratty-looking, bug infested, or roots-leaking hair.

#5
AVOID THE MISTAKE MADE BY 99% OF APPLICANTS

Must not be terribly important, you think, if just about everybody makes this mistake. Remember what I previously said: it's the little things that most often do someone in during the interview, not the big things. And when you are coming from prison, you have more than your share of little things to watch out for.

What is this one thing? Think about the following scenario -- something that just about everyone does prior to leaving for the interview -- and find the ONE thing wrong with it:

THE MIRROR. You stand in front of a full length mirror checking yourself out: you are all dressed; hygiene is fine; hair is combed; socks or stockings are on straight and not wrinkled; shoes are shined; tie or scarf is on straight. Satisfied, you walk away, confident that you look good. But is there one thing the job applicant didn't do?

THE ANSWER. The one thing wrong? When was the last time you interviewed for a job -- standing up!? When you are preparing yourself for an interview, you want to get as close to the "real thing" as possible. By sitting down when you look yourself over, you will be looking at yourself as the interviewer would, and thus have a more realistic approach to your interview.

YOU THOROUGHLY LOOK YOURSELF OVER BUT ONCE. After you pass VISUAL judgment on yourself (that is, the way you look), you basically are saying, "Okay, I look fine -- no need to check me over so thoroughly again." And you don't. If you think about it for a moment, it's usually only the following items that you re-check once you arrive at the building where the interview is to take place: your hair ... your shoes ... your scarf or tie (to make certain it's tied correctly and / or lying flat) ... (for a woman) make-up. Yet there is so much more that you can overlook -- and can detract from you getting your message across during the interview -- if you don't take the time to check yourself out in a mirror by sitting down.

Just what can go wrong if you don't check yourself out while sitting down? Consider the following:

244

The Once-over-Look-in-the-Mirror Problems for Men

● you may not realize that, when you sit down, your pants ride up and expose bare leg because you are wearing ankle-length socks shirt, thus giving you a bunched-up, messy look
● if you wait until you sit down to unbutton your suitcoat, it may not fall neatly to your sides
● you may not have a feel as to how best to sit in a chair; this practice session gives you the opportunity so you can appear relaxed during the interview

The Once-over-Look-in-the-Mirror Problems for Women

● you may not notice, until you sit down, that your blouse and / or skirt or dress do(es) not fit correctly and / or that there is an unsightly gap or pull in the fabric
● if your makeup is on too heavy or too low on your neck, it may get on the collar of your blouse
● you may have stockings with a run that can't be seen until you sit down
● you may not have a feel as to how to best sit in a chair; this practice session gives you the opportunity so you can appear relaxed during the interview

#6
KNOW WHAT TO BRING TO THE INTERVIEW

What you don't want to do is to come to the interview without:

● extra copies of your resume (yours may have been lost or misplaced, more than one person may interview you, and/or an additional interviewer may unexpectedly come into the room)
● a copy of your cover letter (for you to read in the car or bus). It may have been several weeks since you sent it in and it's possible that something in it caught the eye of the initial reader; make certain you are familiar with it
● notes on the company (again, to refresh your memory on who and what they are)
● references (don't give unless asked for)
● supporting information you think might be of help to you (e.g., portfolio, writing samples, articles about you; samples or pictures or video of your work, etc.)

245

● pad, pencil, and pen (to take notes and/or to possibly fill out a form [such as an employment application] or to take a test)
● copy of your release papers / any other legal papers associated with your time in prison that may be needed
● any information you have on special programs available to employers as incentives to hire ex-inmates (see Chapter 11, pages 420-422, for details on this)
● a "palm card": this is an index-size card on which you would write information that you would not have on your resume but might be asked for on an employment application, e.g., name of past or present supervisors, their telephone numbers, street addresses of former and current employers, and your social security number

What all this shows is one major point: you are thinking ahead, you are a planner.

#7
DON'T FORGET THE "JOB INTERVIEW EMERGENCY KIT"

No matter how prepared you are for the interview, there are those little things that can go wrong or that you hadn't planned: scuffed shoes ... a run in your stockings ... the unexpected need to make a phone call (examples: for a reference check; for emergency automobile assistance; or for clarification on directions) ... change for a parking meter ... a brush or comb ... an extra pen or pencil ... shoelaces for the one that breaks ... a back-up tie ... umbrella and / or shoe totes ... tissues ... extra tampon.

There are certainly others you may think of, but bring those along you think could come in handy. It is much better to be prepared and not have to use the extras, than to gamble that the extras won't be necessary ... and find out, when it's too late, that they are!

REMEMBER: "Be Prepared!" is the motto of the Boy Scouts ... and the job applicant.

#8
PREPARE QUESTIONS FOR THE INTERVIEW

Most job applicants are concerned with the questions the interviewer asks of them. Certainly, the interview does revolve around this. But it's also important that you have questions -- intelligent, focused questions -- to ask of the interviewer. Since these will be asked by you during the interview, specifics on how to prepare these, what types of questions to ask (and not to ask!), and other related items are discussed in the next section of this chapter -- "During the Interview" -- beginning on the next page.

IN SUMMARY:
EVERYTHING COUNTS, NO MATTER HOW SMALL!

No matter how small or insignificant an item may be, you don't know whether or not an interviewer will notice it. And very often the interviewer will not CONSCIOUSLY notice it, but it will subtly influence him or her.

(Did you ever find yourself saying, "There's something about him/her I don't like, but I just can't put my finger on it"? This is the same thing that sometimes happens with interviewers -- it's called a SUBLIMINAL effect. What you want the interviewer to say, before the interview begins, is: "There's something about this person I like already -- I can't put my finger in it, but he/she sure makes a good impression!")

REMEMBER: You only have one chance to make a first impression -- make sure it's not a depression.

● THE SECOND PART: <u>DURING THE INTERVIEW</u> ●

TIME TO PRESENT YOURSELF

You are now fully prepared to "go on stage." As I suggested, you will feel much more relaxed and confident about going into the interview once you have done your pre-interview preparation. You will feel even stronger during the interview if you know how to make the interview work for you.

Some of the mental and physical preparation for the interview has already been covered in "The First Part: Prior To the Interview." However, once you fully understand the nature of the interview, your intellectual, physical, and emotional sharpness can be at their fullest ... allowing you to be the very best during the interview.

WHEN DOES THE INTERVIEW BEGIN?

This may seem like a very foolish question with a very obvious answer, but of course it isn't. Most job seekers, when asked this question, answer by saying "when the interviewer begins asking questions."

Just the opposite -- the interview begins the moment you step foot onto that organization's property, whether it be an office building, a plant, a job site, a suite of offices, or one room.

REMEMBER: If you keep in mind that you are an actor, the company's property is your stage, each employee is a member of the audience, and the interviewer is the casting director, you will never go wrong.

---

12 TIPS
TO HELP YOU MAKE IT THROUGH THE INTERVIEW

Beyond the questions you will be asked (covered in the next two chapters), there are other aspects of the job interview that are also quite important. Remember: this is the "who" portion of your quest to get hired, and thus everything you do and say will be taken into account in deciding whether you would make a good addition to the company.

Each of the following items offers suggestions, insights, and information into the interview process. Take these seriously: you've made it to the interview, and with so much effort on your part expended to get this far, it would be a shame to "blow it" because you overlooked one or two relatively simple items.

#1
<u>BE OBSERVANT</u>

LOOK AROUND. In addition to all your research, there is much you can learn from being observant: Does the company have an art collection? How are the employees dressed? Are there any awards or commendations on the wall? What do you notice about the company's operation? Is there any literature available to you that you did not know about? Any of this can be valuable information to you during the interview.

#2
<u>BE WISE WHILE WAITING TO BE INTERVIEWED</u>

THE RECEPTIONIST. Each employee you encounter on the day of your interview should be viewed as a possible interviewer ... and none more so than the secretary / receptionist who has invited you to "have a seat" until the interviewer calls you in.

The Receptionist Is Important

A MEMBER OF THE INTERVIEWING TEAM? Why is the secretary / receptionist so important? Very often he/she is called upon (whether as an informal or formal member of the interviewing team) to give his/her views on you as a potential employee. Yet most interviewees will not turn themselves "on" until they actually meet with the primary interviewer.

The possible result? Your "real" self comes out in conversations with (and/or actions in front of) the secretary / receptionist, and when compared with what you say and do while being interviewed, may show two different yous, and thus inconsistencies or -- even worse -- a perception of you as a liar.

5 Guidelines to Follow While Waiting to Be Interviewed

(1) BE CONSISTENT IN YOUR ANSWERS. If asked questions by the secretary / receptionist, give the same answers that you would give if you were being formally interviewed.

Example

You are asked by the Secretary / Receptionist why you want to work for the company; you tell him/her, "because I heard the benefits are great and I really do need a job." Yet when asked the SAME question by the interviewer, you tell him/her, "because I believe my skills, experience, and education match your firm's needs, and your company can give me the career growth I seek." Sounds impressive, yes – but when compared with your first answer, your second answer begins to sound less than sincere.

(2) WHILE WAITING TO BE CALLED IN, USE YOUR TIME PRODUCTIVELY: Don't waste your time by reading copies of _People Magazine, TV Guide_, or the like. You are in a business environment, and ALL your actions should be geared toward that environment ... and the job you seek.

Many have been the times when an interviewer has asked an applicant a question that relates to one or more of the examples below ... only to see how observant he/she is.

Examples

[A] The organization may have literature laying around that talks more about the company (annual report, sales brochures, etc.); look at them.

[B] In case there is no such reading material, always bring a copy of a business publication or some type of textbook with you so your LOOK will be total business.

[C] Glance around the room in which you are waiting: note any certificates or awards on the walls; the name of the secretary / receptionist if he/she has a name plate on his/her desk; the color(s) of the wall, the carpeting; if there are plants around; what other employees are wearing.

[D] Listen for any information you can pick up on the firm through employees speaking with one another or something the secretary / receptionist says to someone on the phone.

(3) DON'T BE AFRAID TO MAKE SOME CONVERSATION WITH THE SECRETARY / RECEPTIONIST: Remember, you are going to be judged on your personality (the "who," as I stated earlier). There have been many instances when an applicant -- displaying some sign of friendliness, cheerfulness, or being outgoing to the secretary / receptionist -- has given himself / herself the edge over other candidates who were also waiting to be interviewed.

Just don't overdo it. You might make "peas and carrots" conversation about the weather or mention how nice the office is; you might ask a few innocent questions about the company or his / her job. (But NOT questions that you should have already known the answers to, for example, "What does your company sell?" or "When was your organization founded?")

(4) DO NOT FLIRT WITH THE SECRETARY / RECEPTIONIST!! If you do mix business and pleasure, this is certainly not the time to do it. For someone in prison who has been away from the opposite sex for a long period of time, this becomes more difficult than it would be for the non-prison applicant. Again: you are ALL business on this day of the interview!

(5) THIS IS NOT THE TIME TO GET DRESSED! Don't start getting dressed or re-combing your hair or checking your makeup or other such things during this wait. It's almost showtime, and that means these items should have been done PRIOR to waiting in the reception area. Visit a rest room first, and give yourself a final look over and touch-up.

> **REMEMBER: Once on the organization's property, you must assume that you are always being interviewed by someone and act accordingly.**

> **REMEMBER: No matter how good you are in the interview, one mistake is like a black dot on the white wall: the wall is no longer seen, only the dot.**

#3
<u>KNOW THE 2 INTERVIEW LEVELS</u>

When you interview, you are always judged on two levels:

LEVEL #1: THE SURFACE LEVEL

Here, the interviewer reacts to what is immediately seen and heard. As an example, if the interviewer sees that you have some specks of dandruff on your suit coat or dress, his or her eyes and mind will be drawn to this. This dandruff has been noticed, pure and simple, just as you would on someone else.

<u>*POSITIVE REACTIONS*</u>. There are also positive reactions on this level. If you are dressed nicely and your hair is combed, the interviewer will take notice of it, just as you would on someone else.

<u>*THE "WHAT" OF YOU*</u>. At this level, the interviewer reacts more to the "whats" of you: your dress, your hygiene, facts that may be wrong, ability to communicate, answering your questions. More than anything else, this level of interviewing does nothing more than confirm or deny what is stated in your resume and cover letter.

LEVEL #2: THE BENEATH-THE-SURFACE LEVEL

It is here where the interviewer will eventually make the decision on whether or not to hire you.

THE "WHO" OF YOU. Now the interviewer is getting to know the "who" of you: personality, listening ability, confidence and self-motivation, whether or not you are a quick thinker, your honesty, and other such traits that are you but are not readily seen through a resume or cover letter.

At Level #2, What Type of Questions Are Asked?

On this level, the interviewer transforms surface information (Level #1) into questions that many interviewers can't wait to ask -- and answer, such as:

- Are you confident?
- Can you think quickly?
- Can you make immediate decisions?
- What values do you hold?
- Are you a leader?
- Do you easily intimidate?
- Do you stay calm or get easily rattled?

Example

Using the earlier example of some specks of dandruff on your suit coat or dress, the interviewer may equate this with the following: not attentive to detail; does things in a hurry; not particular about appearance; does not make the special effort necessary to succeed.

The interviewer will take these negatives and then "drop" them onto the job to which you are applying ... and suddenly there are several reasons why you SHOULD NOT be hired. And all this from some tiny specks of dandruff. (A good example, also, of how those little things I talked about earlier can make such a difference in the interview.)

Do You Fit in With Their Employees' Personality?

At Level #2, the interviewer(s) is (are) getting to know you as a person. The chemistry that exists between you and the interviewer, and the personality you offer compared to that of the general personality makeup of the company's employees, go a long way in determining if you will fit within the COMPANY'S personality.

In getting to know the "who" of you, interviews tend more to be psychological probes and less a simple "let's find out more about your experience and education." Two areas -- the personal you and your common sense -- tend to be concentrated upon, and because people very seldom hold conversations with themselves, applicants often do poorly in interviews.

REMEMBER: An interview is the ultimate magician: it makes the importance of your resume and cover letter vanish then instantly brings you on stage as the main act!

REMEMBER: You have to learn how to play the game of the interviewer; you have to learn how to bob and weave.

#4
CONTINUE TO CONTROL YOUR NERVOUSNESS!

If you think too much about the interview, it will increase your nervousness. If you go into the interview thinking "I've got to get this job," "I'm not going to be nervous," or something similar, you probably will be very nervous ... you probably won't get the job.

On pages 236-238 of this chapter, specific suggestions are offered for controlling your nervousness. Once again, however, let me repeat: the night before your interview, do something that has no relation to the interview; I previously suggested sports, walking, or cleaning the garage as examples, but you might also try a movie, a book, some TV, dancing, or a play.

On the day of the interview review some of your notes, but walk into the interview with a casual business attitude, not one that is "up tight."

#5
<u>A GRAB-BAG OF "DON'TS"</u>

There are several items -- most common sense -- that you shouldn't do during the interview. These are:

- Don't chew gum, smoke, or make nervous throat noises / nervous coughing.
- As with the receptionist, don't get personal with the interviewer. This is a business relationship only; calling the interviewer by his / her first name (unless told to), becoming too friendly, touching things on his / her desk, telling jokes: none of these are professional.
- Don't ever knock former or current employers. Not only is this a negative you are offering, but the interviewer might think, "If he/she is doing this to others, will he / she do it to me?"
- Don't beg for a job! You may want and, in fact, need the job desperately, but begging will only backfire -- your confidence, strengths, and skills you've already offered will be quickly forgotten.
- While I have strongly suggested that you have intelligent questions to ask (SEE PAGES 266 FOR DETAILS), don't begin with questions about salary, benefits, coffee breaks, vacation, etc. If you do, you are telling the interviewer, "I'm only here for the money and benefits; I care little about the job or the company."   While this may be true, the interviewer is certainly not going to be impressed.
- Don't offer up opinions and information that may be controversial, may offend, or may not be in sync with the company's / interviewer's beliefs. These areas include religion, politics, unions, drug usage, etc.

REMEMBER: To do one "don't" during the interview can undo your chance to get hired.

#6
GET A BUSINESS CARD FROM EACH INTERVIEWER

If not offered one, ask for a business card of each person interviewing you so you can have the correct spelling of his/her name and proper title for your "thank you" letter (more about this at the end of this chapter, page 270). If a business card is not available, ask for the name(s) / title(s) from the secretary / receptionist.

#7
UNDERSTAND WHAT INTERVIEWERS FIRST NOTICE

There are four things, more than anything else, that interviewers notice about the applicant. While not all four may be taken into consideration, it is a sure bet that at least one will be.

The 4 Most Noticed Items By The Interviewer

(1) THE WAY YOU ARE DRESSED: To the point, you want to be dressed so the interviewer does not really notice the way you are dressed. What do I mean? When you interview, you want EVERYTHING to be either positive or neutral, nothing that will show up as a negative. (See pages 240-241, 245 for details on dressing for the interview.)

Dress poorly or have something amiss with your clothes and the interviewer will notice; dress flamboyantly or too expensively, and the interviewer will also notice, but not as a positive.

You simply want the interviewer to think, "hmmm ... dresses like a smart business professional ... blends in nicely ... okay, nothing wrong here." You've heard it said that the first couple of minutes of the interview are the most important. Not so important, perhaps, as to what you will say later during the interview, but certainly important because it is the first time the interviewer sees you.

And if you begin with a couple of negatives against you -- no matter how small -- it is much more difficult to erase these than to begin with positives or neutrals.

A Special Note For Those Who Won't Usually Wear a Suit / Sports Jacket and Tie on The Job

Positions such as cook, laborer, artist, many industry jobs, construction worker, telephone repair person, dock worker, and jobs where a uniform of some sort is worn (hospital orderly, auto technician / mechanic, etc.) do not call for you to be "dressed up" when on duty.

The reasons include: a job that is easier to perform in more comfortable clothes; the nature of the job might mean that your clothes will get dirty; or it might be dangerous to be in a suit and tie / scarf (example: tie getting caught in a piece of machinery).

However, when you interview -- unless told otherwise -- you go to the interview presenting yourself as a professional.

REMEMBER: Getting dressed translates into taking pride in yourself and wanting to make a positive impression, as well as putting you in a more businesslike mood for the interview.

---

(2) THE HANDSHAKE: Is there anything really important about the handshake? In a word, yes! As I stated previously, it is the small things that so often will do in the positives ... and here is a good example of a gesture thought about very little, yet one that can have a profound effect.

specifics

● **The "dead fish" or "Hercules" handshake**: Think about the times you shook hands with someone and you remembered his/her handshake. Chances are the reason that handshake stuck in your mind was because it was too weak ("he shakes hands like a dead fish") or too strong ("who does she think she is, a professional wrestler?").

● **A poor handshake can give a negative impression**: This memory translates into a NEGATIVE, and you know that is definitely something you do not want to give the interviewer.

● **Let the interviewer make the first move**: Remember what I said earlier: you only have one chance to make a first impression. When you shake hands with the person interviewing you, don't be the first one to squeeze; rather, let the interviewer establish the amount of pressure his or her handshake holds, then you match. (If the interviewer has a "dead fish" handshake, return it with one that has just slight pressure.)

Why? The thoughts you may have had about someone else with a too weak or too strong handshake now apply to you ... and are IMMEDIATELY registered on that so very important second level of the interview -- the "WHO" -- that was earlier discussed.

● **What a weak handshake could indicate about you**: If you have a weak handshake and the interviewer's is strong, he or she may think you are an intellectual weakling, someone who is not a "take charge" person, someone who is not outgoing enough.

● **What an overly strong handshake might indicate about you**: Conversely, if your handshake is very strong and the interviewer's weak, he or she may perceive you as being too aggressive, too gung ho, too quick to make a decision.

● **What a proper handshake will indicate about you**: In either instance, you have started the interview with one of those negatives mentioned earlier. However, if you give back the same amount of pressure given you in the handshake, the result will be the same type of thought that went through the interviewer's mind when he or she noticed that you were properly and neatly dressed: the right thing to do as a part of business etiquette.

(3) YOUR SHOES: I already mentioned that your shoes are merely one of the items that go into making you visually appealing as a job candidate. Yet there are many instances when shoes are the one determining factor in deciding whether or not someone gets a job.

Some employers judge job applicants only by their shoes. Indeed, there are those employers who IMMEDIATELY make up their mind about potential candidates based on whether or not their shoes are presentable. It's no excuse that you were in prison: your shoes should be in keeping with the rest of your neat appearance.

6 Tips to Make Sure Your Shoes are Acceptable

1] Shine your shoes: The most obvious: be sure they are shined! And when you shine them, don't forget the tip of the shoe -- this is the part of the shoe that most people forget to shine, yet the first part of the shoe that stares into the face of the interviewer.

2] Have two pairs of shoes: If you can, wear a different pair of shoes when you drive, walk, or take a bus; this will prevent you from scraping or scratching your shoes. (If you can't afford two pair of shoes, see #3 and #4, below.)

3] Reshine your shoes: Make sure you stop in a rest room in the organization's building prior to your interview to give your shoes a quick once-over. Even if you carried your interview shoes in a bag, a bit of dust will somehow attach to your shoes and dull their shine. Wipe the dull away!

4] A great little investment: One of the best small investments I ever made was less than a dollar for a little sponge that contains some oil and lemon scent. (Something similar also comes in little packets in the form of a folded tissue.) When buffed over your shoes, it gives them a nice, quick shine.

5] Shine only your shoes: Be careful when you shine your shoes that you don't get polish on your socks, your stockings, or your pants.

6] Wear shoes that look professional: If possible, try to wear shoes that don't look as if they are made of plastic, and certainly never wear sandals or sneakers. Also, don't wear patent leather -- that very bright shine focuses attention TO your shoes, and usually in a negative way.

(4) YOUR HAIR. Interviewers quickly notice an applicant's hair. While you should, of course, re-check it just prior to going in for the interview, there are several things you can do and shouldn't do relating to you hair. See page 243 of this chapter for specifics.

... and don't forget

Remove your hat, cap, or head scarf! No matter how stylish you may think it is, wearing a hat (or the like) distracts from your message ... and can come across as being rude.

REMEMBER: You want the interviewer to focus on your mind and your mouth, nothing else!

#8
<u>KNOW THE WHERE & HOW OF INTERVIEW SITTING</u>

This can most definitely make a big difference during the interview! Body language (non-verbal communication) plays a very important part in the interview. It can tell the interviewer how confident you feel, whether or not you are intimidated by the interviewer, or if you are bored.

<u>*The 3 Most Common Types of Interview Chair Setups*</u>

(1) "THE PEACE PIPE" ARRANGEMENT.   Here, there are two chairs facing each other, perhaps with a small table or a circular table between them. This is very comfortable and makes it easy for you to be on a 1:1 basis with the interviewer.

(2) "THE I-AM-THE-BIG-CHEESE" ARRANGEMENT. Here, the interviewer distances himself / herself from you via a desk, and you not only have his / her authority as interviewer, but the added authority and burden of this massive barrier.

(3) "THE SIDECAR" ARRANGEMENT. The worst of the three, with a chair right next to the desk, and the interviewer behind the desk.

<u>*TURN YOUR CHAIR TO FACE THE INTERVIEWER*</u>. In each scenario, the first thing you want to do is establish a presence of confidence for yourself. How do you do this? Simple -- just take your chair and turn it towards the interviewer. By doing this, you show that you are not afraid, that you have confidence in yourself, and that your attention is focused on the interviewer.

(Exception: If you are sitting in a chair that is quite heavy, and thus very difficult for you to move, simply move your entire body around in the chair so it faces the interviewer.)

When You First Sit: 6 Suggestions

(1) DON'T CROSS YOUR LEGS.   Do not cross your legs when you sit down, as it shows you to be too relaxed. The best posture? Sit somewhat at the edge of your chair, leaning slightly forward (it gives the impression of your focused attention); either cross your legs at the ankles or not at all.

(2) DON'T CROSS YOUR ARMS.   Don't cross your arms in front of you, as it is perceived as a sign that you are bored or closed off to suggestions.

(3) DON'T TOUCH THE INTERVIEWER'S DESK.   Never, unless invited to do so, touch the desk of the interviewer (or anything on his / her desk). It is an extension of him or her, and touching it is the same as touching some very personal part of the interviewer or invading his or her personal space.

(4) TAKE A QUICK LOOK AROUND THE ROOM.   When you first enter the interview room, take a quick scan around. There may be some items that you can bring into conversation later (to help establish a personal rapport).

(5) DON'T ACCEPT A DRINK.   If offered something to drink, refuse: better not to encumber yourself or risk the possibility of spilling. (If, however, you want something to wet a dry throat or feel it would be best because EVERYONE else is sipping on something, opt for water or juice, not a hot liquid or a liquid with carbonation in it, and certainly not alcohol.)

(6) IF OFFERED A SMOKE, ALWAYS REFUSE. With smoking very much on the wane, and many companies with policies that don't allow smoking on their premises, the chances of you being offered a cigarette or cigar are becoming quite small. However, if it does happen, refuse -- it presents a negative image (and some companies won't hire smokers because of increased health insurance costs for smokers).

REMEMBER: Control your chair, control the room; if not, they can quickly control you.

#9
BE SMART IN ANSWERING THE INTERVIEW QUESTIONS

As I indicated earlier, chapters 7 and 8 cover specific interview questions. Beyond the answers you give, however, is how you answer the questions. The following suggestions, if followed, will help you immensely:

The 15 "Hows" of Answering Job Interview Questions

(1) ONLY ANSWER WHAT IS ASKED OF YOU. Pretend that you are in court and the interviewer is a lawyer. By giving away too much, you may hurt yourself. Long answers can hurt you, shorter ones can help.

(A trick the interviewer sometimes uses is to say nothing after you've given an answer, thus having you believe that more is wanted. In actuality, he / she wants to see if he / she can intimidate you into giving additional, unneeded information. If you are satisfied with your answer, then wait for the next question.)

(2) LISTEN VERY CAREFULLY TO THE QUESTION ASKED. It may determine if your answer is acceptable to the interviewer. (Example: if someone asks for ONE thought about the job, give just one thought.)

(3) LOOK THE INTERVIEWER IN THE EYE WHEN YOU ARE TALKING AND WHEN YOU ARE BEING SPOKEN TO. This shows confidence. (If more than one interviewer, don't give ALL your eye contact to the one who asked the question. Rather, give approximately 2/3 of your eye contact to him / her, 1/3 to the others.)

(4) DON'T FIDGET OR KEEP SHIFTING AROUND. It gives the impression you are not focused on the interview, that you are nervous, or both.

(5) BE YOURSELF. Rather than worry about giving the interviewer what you think he wants, be yourself.

(6) COMMUNICATE CLEARLY. Beware of the five deadly speech cousins: uh, um, right, you know, okay, and like. Don't mumble, don't speak too fast, pronounce your words clearly. (For detailed information on this, refer to the Index, under "Communications.")

(7) THINK YOUR ANSWER THROUGH BEFORE GIVING IT. Don't be so quick to give an answer, but take a few seconds to be sure. When you are thinking, rather than have your head bounce around like one of those dogs that sits on the car's back seat ledge, simply turn your head aside, get the thought, and come on back to the interviewer. Don't begin talking until you are looking at the interviewer, for the chances are strong that the answer you give won't be the one you had intended to give.

(8) USE THE RIGHT TONE OF VOICE. If your voice rises while giving an answer, it leads one to believe that you are unsure or afraid; if your voice drops in tone as you speak, it indicates that you are sure of yourself and you stand pat on your answer -- a good indicator of self-confidence!

(9) KEEP YOUR COOL. Even if a question is off the wall or you don't know the answer, don't give the outward appearance of same. Your reaction to the interviewer should be, "hey, no problem -- I was expecting that" ... even if you are sweating bullets inside! And if a question is asked that upsets you -- it could be one about your conviction, for example -- stay calm, remain positive. You always want to give the impression of being in control.

(10) DON'T REPEAT THE QUESTION. When asked a question, don't repeat the question (unless you genuinely did not hear it); it only indicates to the interviewer that you are stalling for time or are not paying attention.

(11) USE THE INTERVIEWER'S NAME. During the interview, it's good form to occasionally use the interviewer's name when addressing him / her. For example: "Mr. Glickman, I do have a question to ask." ... "Ms. Franklin, I'm really interested in this job." ... "Dr. Tomiski, my goals for the next five years are ..." Using the interviewer's name (last, not first!) Gives the impression that you are really interested in what's being said and that you are focused on the interview.

(12) BE ENTHUSIASTIC ... AND SMILE! No matter how prepared you are, and no matter how qualified you are, if you don't show enthusiasm and smile once-in-awhile you are not going to get the job. Period. Interviewers want to hire someone who is really excited about the job opportunity, who really wants to work, who shows a nice and enjoyable personality through a smile. Just sit there answering questions with no expression (or, worse, a sour expression) on your face and you've just wasted your and the interviewer's time.

(13) STAY FOCUSED ON WHAT YOU CAN DO FOR THE EMPLOYER, RATHER THAN THE OPPOSITE. While the employer certainly can do many things for you -- including giving you an income -- the interview is about what you can contribute to the interviewer's company. When you begin to stray from this, you are telling the interviewer that you are only interested in what you can get out of the deal -- a very bad move.

(14) ANTICIPATE GETTING NEGATIVE QUESTIONS. It's easy to answer positive questions (such as, "How do you think you can help us?") but much more difficult -- and at times unpleasant -- to answer the negative ones (such as, (Were you ever fired and why?"). Always expect to get negative as well as positive questions -- this way, you won't be surprised when they come. (The next two chapters contain examples of several negative questions and suggestions on how to respond.)

(15) ALWAYS BE HONEST IN YOUR ANSWERS. If not, your lie will come back to eventually bite you in the rear end ... and most certainly ruin your credibility. You'll be respected for your honesty.

REMEMBER: It's much easier to live within honesty than to sleep under dishonesty.

#10
KNOW HOW TO TURN YOUR NEGATIVES INTO POSITIVES

While it is always important to stress your strong points during the interview, it is also an excellent opportunity to show the employer how what may be seen as your weaknesses may actually be strengths. The examples below are of common liabilities and suggestions as to how you can turn them into positives -- as your assets. Think about other negatives which you may have and how to present them as strengths. (Of course, ALWAYS work to turn these weaknesses around!)

● **YOU ARE NOT A LEADER.** Most jobs require people who are able to accept guidance and carry out assignments. The fact that you are a capable follower is a strength.

● **YOU ARE INEXPERIENCED.** Newcomers have an open mind, are flexible, and don't need to "unlearn" habits formed on another job. You are also eager to learn.

● **YOU ARE APPLYING FOR YOUR FIRST FULL-TIME JOB.** You have no pre-conceived ideas about your work role, are prepared to learn what to do, to work within the employer's guidelines, and to put in whatever hours are necessary.

● **YOU WERE FIRED FROM YOUR LAST JOB.** Never blame your former employer in the interview. If the subject should come up, emphasize what you learned from the experience and how it has made you a better person for it.

● **YOU ARE HANDICAPPED.** A job is especially important to you. You are determined to do well at it -- both for your sake and the sake of your employers. And you can always be depended upon to be at work on time and to get the job done.

● **YOU ARE SHY.** People who are shy tend to listen carefully and perform well because they can follow directions better than most. You do not get easily sidetracked, and focus intently on the work before you.

● **YOU DIDN'T HAVE VERY GOOD GRADES.** Perhaps school was only a part of your life and much of your learning took place in prison, during extracurricular activities, on paid and volunteer jobs, and through community involvement. Often, achievements in prison and the other activities may be a better predictor of success on the job than grades.

● **YOU ARE YOUNG.** Many careers begin with young people. Tell the interviewer you have the important energy and enthusiasm that go with youth.

● **YOU HAVE CHILDREN & MAY HAVE TO LEAVE WORK RIGHT ON TIME.** There are few jobs as complex as raising children, and you have had to learn to handle many different kinds of things efficiently. You know how to (for example) work hard, establish priorities, be patient, and meet deadlines.

> **REMEMBER: Negatives are caterpillars waiting to become moths -- squish them before they eat holes in your life.**

#11
WHAT KINDS OF QUESTIONS SHOULD BE ASKED OF THE INTERVIEWER?

There will be times for you to ask questions during the interview, but it is especially important that you ask questions about the company and the position at the end of the interview.

2 Reasons Why Questions Should Be Asked By You

(1) IT WILL SHOW INTERVIEWERS THAT YOU ARE INTERESTED IN THEIR ORGANIZATION. An applicant who answers the questions of the interviewer but asks none of his own is seen to be passive, not curious, and apparently not very interested in the job or the organization.

(2) THE ANSWERS TO YOUR QUESTIONS MAY GIVE YOU SOME ADDITIONAL INSIGHT INTO THE JOB AND ORGANIZATION: This could prove extremely helpful in your decision to pursue the position, or to accept or reject the job if offered it.

Examples of Questions You Should Ask
That Show Your Interest in the Job and Company

- What type of company training is available?
- What added responsibilities could I expect?
- Will my territory be expanded if my sales increase?
- Is my creative input welcome?
- Why is this position available?
- How much travel is normally expected?
- Do employees normally work many hours of overtime?
- Can I progress at my own pace or is it structured?
- What is the average age of your first level supervisors?
- How much contact & exposure to management is there?
- How much freedom is given and discipline required of new people?
- How often are performance reviews given?
- Have any new product lines been added recently?
- Is your policy to promote from within or are many senior jobs filled by experienced people from the outside?

Ask Questions That Relate To The Job

These sample questions, and others you may think of, should be asked based on those questions applicable to the job for which you are interviewing. (Example: You would not ask about sales territory if you are applying for a job as an electrician.)

Asking Questions About Salary and Benefits

Only after you have shown interest in the company and the position by asking these questions can you then explore the "I" questions, that is, those that focus on your needs, such as salary, benefits, etc. (See Chapter 10, pp. 376-378, where salary and benefits negotiation are discussed in more detail.)

#12
BE PREPARED FOR THE END OF THE INTERVIEW

Just because the interview is drawing to a close does not mean that you can let up, that you can now breathe a sigh of relief -- you still have work to do. First, consider the various ways in which an interview may end:

When the Interview is Over: 6 Possible Endings

(1) WANTS YOU TO COME BACK. The interviewer tells you that he / she would like you back for a second interview.

(2) MIGHT WANT YOU TO COME BACK. The interviewer tells you there may be a second interview and you will be contacted if the company wants to see you again.

(3) JOB WILL BE DECIDED THROUGH THIS INTERVIEW. The interviewer tells you this is the interview upon which the job will be decided, and you will be notified.

(4) THE JOB IS OFFERED TO YOU. You are offered the job after the first interview.

(5) YOU ARE NOT RIGHT FOR THE JOB. The interviewer tells you that he / she does not think you would work out in the position (for whatever reason given).

(6) YOU DON'T WANT THE JOB. You decide, after the interview has been completed, that the job is not right for you, and you decline to go any further.

Now, based on which of the endings you experience, you need to be certain that your reaction is professional ... and takes YOU into account:

6 Suggestions on How You Should React When The Interview is Over

(1) <u>ALWAYS</u> BE POLITE.   No matter how much you may dislike the person or the job, there's no need to "burn any bridges." Also: some employers are eager for an opportunity to badmouth an ex-inmate to a business colleague, perhaps someone in a company to which you are going to apply.

(2) TAKE A DAY OR SO TO THINK ABOUT ANY JOB OFFER. If offered the position, unless you are positive you want the job, ask if you could have a day (or more, depending on the responsibilities and salary involved) to think it over.

More reasonable decisions can be made away from the emotion of the interview. And don't forget: there may be some aspect(s) of your parole that may interfere with the hours you would be expected to work, possible travel, etc. It's best to check this out first to be certain you would not be in violation of the conditions of your release.

(3) DON'T BE AFRAID TO SPEAK UP. If the interviewer says something like, "Thank you very much for your interest -- we'll be in touch," don't leave it like that: he / she hasn't given you a focused direction of his/her interest in you. Don't be afraid to ask, "Where do we go from here?" Remember: You are JUST as important as the interviewer!

(4) ASK FOR A BUSINESS CARD.   Mentioned earlier, but it's important.   Possible help to you: [1] allows you to be correct in his/her name, title, and address when you write him/her [thank you letter, follow up letter, etc.]; [2] gives you tangible proof that you have been looking for a job [often required by city, state, or federal agencies if they are giving you some type of assistance monies or support, or are helping you find employment]; [3] the person can become a future networking contact in the event this job opportunity does not work out. [Also: if it appears that this job may not work out for you, don't hesitate to ask for other names the interviewer might recommend as possible job opportunities.]

(5) SHAKE HANDS AND SAY "THANK YOU."   Correct business etiquette dictates that you shake hands with those who interviewed you. Also, be sure to say something like, "I want to thank you for this opportunity; thanks for meeting with me." OR "Thank you very much for this opportunity -- I'm more enthusiastic than ever about this job possibility!"

(6) TAKE EVERYTHING YOU BROUGHT WITH YOU.   Forgetting an item may give the interviewer some negative thought about your thoroughness or being nervous.

Okay, it's almost time to move on to your activities after the interview. But before we leave this section, I thought you'd like to know ...

THE MOST COMMON COMPLAINTS BY INTERVIEWERS ABOUT APPLICANTS
(in order of most frequent to least frequent)

1) Is caught lying
2) Shows lack of interest in the interview; merely shopping around
3) Has a hostile attitude; is rude or impolite
4) Unable to express himself clearly; weak communicative skills
5) Lacks sincerity
6) Is evasive concerning information about himself / herself
7) Is concerned only about salary
8) Is unable to concentrate
9) Displays a lack of initiative
10) Is indecisive
11) Has an arrogant attitude
12) Has a persecuted attitude ("They were out to get me.")
13) Tries to use pull to get a job
14) Has dirty hands or face
15) Is cynical
16) Is intolerant and has strong prejudices
17) Is late for the interview
18) Has a limp-fish handshake
19) Shows lack of planning for career
20) Has not done research into history and products of the company
21) Wants to start in an executive position
22) Lacks maturity
23) Has low moral standards
24) Presents extreme appearance
25) Oversells case

● THE THIRD PART: <u>AFTER THE INTERVIEW</u> ●

Of the three parts in the interview process, this one is probably most ignored. Communication must be maintained to show that you are indeed interested in the position. Often, it is what is or is not done following the interview that determines the final choice for the job.

3 TIPS
TO HELP YOU AFTER THE INTERVIEW

#1
<u>THE FIRST THING TO DO: SEND A "THANK YOU" LETTER</u>

Thank you letters -- their importance cannot be stated enough! Yet too often job applicants forget about this crucial piece of correspondence ... a piece of correspondence that can actually make the difference between you getting or not getting the position for which you interviewed. So read and follow closely these suggestions:

<u>6 Reasons to Send a "Thank You" Letter the Same Day</u>

(1) SHOWS YOUR APPRECIATION. It lets the interviewer know that you appreciated his or her time and effort.

(2) INDICATES YOUR INTEREST. It tells the interviewer that you are sincerely interested in the position (if this is so).

(3) DEMONSTRATES EXTRA EFFORT. It indicates that you don't mind putting in the extra effort needed to get the job.

(4) MAINTAINS GOOD RELATIONSHIP. It allows you to maintain good terms: even if you do not want the job, still write the letter. It is better to keep good relations with someone who may be of help at another time, than forget about the person.

If you personally did not care for the interviewer, don't let that color your opinion of the organization: 90% of the time you do not end up being supervised by the person who first interviewed you.

(5) SERVES AS A MINI-INTERVIEW. Your "thank you" letter can become a mini-interview that you fully control: This is an opportunity for you to resell your qualifications that most directly relate to what you believe the company needs from a successful applicant (based on what was said in the interview).

(6) EXPANDS THE INTERVIEW. You can more fully explore a topic: there may have been a topic that you did not fully get to explore in the interview, but would have liked to; a topic that was not covered or brought up, but you wanted to explore; or an area that you disagreed on with the interviewer(s).

[For example: the interviewer believing that you don't have enough sales experience, you feeling that you do, but you did not want to bog down the interview by arguing your point.]

In the "thank you" letter, you can "make your case" with no interruptions, as well as have more time to compose your thoughts than you would during an interview situation.

#2
IF YOU DON'T HEAR FROM AN ORGANIZATION FOLLOWING THE INTERVIEW

This point was mentioned in the previous chapter, but it bears repeating here:

5 Reasons Why An Organization May Not Respond

(1) The company is simply slow in getting back.
(2) They are having a difficult time in deciding.
(3) Someone else was hired: they chose another candidate and felt they could take their time in telling you.
(4) The position fell though.
(5) The organization does not send replies: it maintains a policy of not sending notice to those individuals interviewed but who were not selected for the position.

It's Up To You To Find Out What's Happening

No matter what the reason, I've always believed that the company or organization should, out of courtesy (certainly not because of legal reasons), inform you of your status. However, the real world very often dictates otherwise.

So ... unless the company tells you it will be 10 days or so, after 7-10 days write and find out what is happening. (And if they HAVE given you a certain amount of days, but these pass and you hear nothing: call. Also: if, after sending out a letter asking what the status of your resume is, you still have not heard from the company, call.)

(NOTE: Refer to Chapter 5, page 218, for a sample cover letter to be used when you do not receive a reply to your resume.)

#3
2 THINGS TO DO IF YOU DON'T GET THE JOB

Unfortunately, this is not a perfect world, and this imperfection extends to job interviews as well: not every one is going to end with you getting the job. It goes with the territory; it's not something to yell and scream about. Rather, the interview should be used as a learning experience ... and you continue to go forward, looking for other interviews. The following will help when you've been interviewed but not selected:

(1) ASK WHY YOU DID NOT GET THE JOB. Each piece of information you receive will perhaps help you to better understand yourself, to correct an error you made, or to learn more about the nature of the hiring process.

(2) SEND ANOTHER LETTER. Thank them for their time and tell them you are still interested in working for the company (if this is true). Just because you didn't get the job this time doesn't mean you won't have a shot another time. [SEE PAGE 219 FOR A SAMPLE LETTER FOR THIS PURPOSE.]

REMEMBER: Each interview you go through will give you valuable information about yourself and the world of business that will make you a better interviewee, a better employee, and a better person.

REMEMBER: Where a job does not exist today, there is always the possibility of it existing tomorrow. Each day, people are fired, quit, or laid off; companies land new accounts, receive grants, obtain additional orders. Persistence will eventually pay off for you!!

● A FINAL NOTE ON BEING AN EX-INMATE INTERVIEWING FOR A JOB ●

When you go to interview for a job -- even if the employer already knows that you are an ex-inmate -- you interview with confidence as a professional who is just as qualified as the next person.

Constantly thinking about having been in prison will do nothing except make you more nervous than any interview would normally do ... and probably assure you of NOT getting the job.

THERE ARE EMPLOYERS WHO WILL WELCOME YOU!

Employers, generally, are not stupid. When money can be saved and an excellent employee can be gained -- at the same time -- this is a combination difficult to turn down. In addition to this chapter's suggestions (and those in chapters 7 and 8), don't forget to make employers aware of any federal salary / tax incentive programs for which you may be eligible (Chapter 11, pages 420-422, contain a detailed look at these), as well as other state, city, or local ones.

IF YOU HAVE ADDITIONAL QUESTIONS

Certainly, there are many other questions about the job interview that will come up -- no matter how much is covered, more will be left unanswered. But by following the suggestions in this chapter, and the other related chapters in this book, you are assured of having the very best possible interview ... and giving yourself the best possible shot at landing the job you really want!

And remember: you can always drop me a letter (our address is listed in the front of this book and in the introduction) with any questions. I can't promise you a response within a few days but you hear from me -- I promise.

REMEMBER: You will be stepping on eggshells when you are released from prison and looking for employment, while other job seekers are merely stepping on pavement.

Chapter 7

The Most Commonly Asked Interview Questions

"Speaking without thinking
is shooting
without taking aim."

Spanish proverb

● INTRODUCTION ●

THE PERSON BEHIND THE RESUME

Once you are in the interview, forget that your resume and cover letter ever existed. They got you in for the interview, now it's your turn to get you out ... with a job.

As we discussed in the previous chapter, the interview is an opportunity for the employer to get to know the "who" of you. Beyond your dress, look, body language, and general demeanor, the questions that the interviewer(s) ask are meant to test you in several ways:

What Interviewers Learn from Their Questions

There are thousands of questions that interviewers can choose from, and a good picture of you can develop from your answers. The examples that follow -- and similar questions -- were discussed in general in the previous chapter:

● Do you know what you are talking about, or just winging it as you go along?
● Does your personality blend in with what the company seeks in its employees?
● Are you quick on your feet?
● Do you have a sense of humor?
● Are you creative?
● Are you willing to take a stand or are you a "yes man"?
● Are you easily intimidated?
● Are you confident?
● Are you a good listener? A good communicator?

> **REMEMBER:** The keys to answering the interviewer's questions are listening to the question, taking the time to think about your answer before speaking, not talking too much, having a sense of humor, and -- perhaps most important -- giving the impression that you genuinely want the job.

SOME NOTES ABOUT THIS CHAPTER

Remember, These are Sample Questions

The sample questions in this chapter are intended to provide examples of some of the kinds of things you may be asked to discuss in employment interviews. Obviously, not all of these questions will be asked.

Additionally, the chances are pretty good that you will be asked questions that are not amongst these samples. (It always happens: I could give you 500 questions, and it would be the 501st that you are asked!).

Your Education and Experience are Not Included in These Samples

These questions are a good cross-section that cover a wide variety of areas. You will note that questions covering your experience and education are not included, as these amount to little more than simply giving the interviewer FACTS; they do not require you to THINK, per se.

Ask Someone to Help You Practice

You may find it helpful to ask a cellmate, teacher, friend, family member, or other person you are close with (and can spend time with!) to participate with you in a practice session in which you take turns as employer and candidate in raising and answering these questions.

By assuming both roles, you gain some experience in representing yourself and get a feel for the employer's perspective.

REMEMBER: **Reaching out for another's help with the interview questions is smart -- it puts you into the world of warts, potholes, and cracked sidewalks that exist in the reality of the job interview.**

Regarding Interview Questions That Ask About Prison, Etc.

None of the questions in this chapter directly mention, ask about, or hint of any prison, arrest, conviction, etc., experience. Chapter 8 -- "Were You Ever in Prison? and Other Related Questions" -- deals with these subjects exclusively.

The questions found in this chapter are a variety that could be asked of ANY job applicant.

(**NOTE ON QUESTIONS** 1, 13, 15, 25, 29, 35, 36, 37, 38, 41, 43, 45, 46, & 48: Some of the hints contain possible answers from you based on the interviewer having knowledge that you are an ex-inmate. Other suggestions demonstrate how your replies can give an opportunity to capitalize on something you accomplished while in prison or contain information relating to various prison-related activities.)

REMEMBER: To answer interview questions in the best fashion: always think objectively. That is, think from the view of what you would want as an answer if you were asking the interview question just asked of you.

The Questions

#1

"What are your long range and short range career goals and objectives, when and why did you establish these goals, and how are you preparing yourself to achieve them?"

HINT: **TELLS THEM IF YOU THINK BEYOND DAY-TO-DAY.** They want to know if you are a planner, if you have thought about your future, and what you are CONTINUALLY doing to improve yourself so that you can achieve your goals.

THIS IS ESPECIALLY IMPORTANT FOR THE EX-INMATE. It gives you a chance to show that you have used your time inside wisely, and that your plans include never going back to prison!

#2

"I've read your resume and noticed your experience and education, but why should we hire you?"

HINT: **YOU NEED TO TALK ABOUT YOURSELF.** One of the most difficult questions to answer, because it necessitates you talking about yourself, a very uncomfortable situation for most people.

HINT: **DON'T TALK ABOUT YOUR EDUCATION OR EXPERIENCE.** A big trap that many job candidates fall into: they answer this question by giving a recap of their experience and education. Remember that the interviewer has, at the very least, glanced over your resume and is familiar with your qualifications.

TALK ABOUT WHAT THE INTERVIEWER DOESN'T KNOW. In this instance, the interviewer wants you to talk about what he/she doesn't know much about: YOU! So, relate those qualities that you would bring to the organization. Examples: your confidence, your ability to work well with others, your punctuality and dedication, your ability to handle several tasks at once, your ability to work well in an individual or team setting, your communicative skills.

<u>**HINT:**</u> **MAKE YOUR ANSWER INTERESTING.** People get bored very quickly when someone starts rattling off a list. The key to truly making this question effective is to weave your answers into the fabric of the company, while also revealing something of your past (a nice way to toss in an accomplishment of yours without being asked to give it!).

An Example of How to Answer This Question

"Well, in addition to my experience and education that you've read on my resume, I also communicate very well with all ages. I know that this position would put me in contact with many youngsters and senior citizens, and I communicate easily with them.

"Also, I am very punctual. You'll find me at my work station approximately 15 minutes before 8:00 a.m. and not ready to leave until my work has been completed and my work station cleaned.

"I work nicely in a team situation. In my previous position, I was team leader and credited with motivating the others in my group to a higher degree of quality and production.

"I'm also very resourceful. The many questions from clients that would come my way in this position will often require research. Rather that throw up my hands and take an easy way out by asking a supervisor, I'll always take the initiative to track down the information."

Explanation of the Answer

This answer takes the form of a story, and it is more apt to hold the interviewer's attention than if you simply said, "I communicate well, am very punctual, work well in a team situation, know how to research, and have much initiative." This one sounds boring, and gives the impression that you merely memorized a list you found in a book.

#3

"What specific goals, other than those related to your occupation, have you established for yourself for the next 10 years?"

HINT: TALKS ABOUT YOUR LIFE OUTSIDE OF WORK. This question differs from #1 because the interviewer wants to know about your life OUTSIDE of work.

Included may be plans to continue your education and obtain two degrees (if so, tell the interviewer this will be in your spare time, and won't affect your job), a decision to pursue and become expert at a specific hobby or two, an organization you've decided to join and gain a leadership position in, or perhaps to get married and have children.

HINT: THE KEY ITEM IN THIS QUESTION IS THE 10 YEARS. If you tell someone that you are going to join an organization, get involved in a hobby, or continue your education -- and nothing more -- you give the impression that you are a person who will level off after a certain period of time, rather than continuing to strive for more, better, or improvement.

In the first HINT, I mentioned "obtaining two degrees," becoming an "expert," gaining a "leadership position," and perhaps getting "married and having children." Not only do each of these show that you have specific goals set, but each takes more than a few months to accomplish, and usually end up involving several years.

#4

"What do you see yourself doing 5 years from now?"

HINT: DON'T CHALLENGE THE INTERVIEWERS. This is a question that has hurt many interviewees because they are so quick to say, "I want your job!" Such an answer does nothing except to set up a confrontational -- and perhaps threatening -- situation. And if interviewers perceive you as a threat to their job, do you think they're going to hire you or recommend you for hiring? Highly unlikely.

2 Examples of How to Answer This Question

Here are two possibilities for answers, neither of which threaten. (The job you are applying for is a sales position; the person interviewing you is vice president of sales, the second highest sales position in the company):

(1) *"Through a combination of my efforts and others in the sales department, I know that the need will be there for a second vice president of sales – and I know that I will have proven myself capable and deserving of that promotion within five years."*

(2) *"Knowing that the company will have expanded through my sales accomplishments, as well as the others in the division, I'm certain that you will become Senior Vice President of Sales. I'd like to fill the empty Vice President of Sales slot you left behind."*

#5

"What do you really want to do in life?"

<u>**HINT**</u>: **DON'T BE AFRAID TO SPEAK UP.** Possibly another tricky question, and one that could keep you from getting the job if you don't answer it correctly. If you really want to stay with this company and truly enjoy the type work for which you are applying, fine -- say it.

DON'T TELL THE INTERVIEWER YOU WANT THE JOB JUST FOR THE MONEY. However, as often is the case when someone is first released from prison, you may be interested in this job just to have a job and bring in some money. Of course, if you tell this to the interviewer, chances are that you won't get the job. After all, an employer does not want to invest training time, money, and scheduling into an employee who is there just for the short haul.

DON'T LIE; ESTABLISH CREDIBILITY. So, what do you do? Before I give you a suggestion, I must ask you to keep in mind one very important item: you need a job and income as soon as you are released. You also want to establish credibility and be accepted as someone who is sincere.

Although the temptation is very great to lie ("I want a lifelong career in the grocery business" even though you know you will leave as soon as something better comes along), DON'T!! Rather, use the flexibility of the English language to your advantage:

2 Examples of How to Answer This Question

(1) *"Most important to me is a company that can offer the career growth and personal challenge that I need, while allowing me the opportunity to contribute and to improve the company. I'm certainly hopeful that this will be that career move for me."*

(2) *"I'd be less than honest with you if I said I wanted to remain a cleaning lady. Yes, I'm a hard worker, dedicated to my job, and will always give 100%. However, I believe that after I've proven my work other opportunities with your firm will be available to me."*

#6

"What is your long-range career objective?"

HINT: **YOU NEED TO LISTEN.** The answer to this can be found in question #1, above. Why include this, then? Note that this question asks for ONE specific item, while question #1 asks for a few. Be careful that you LISTEN to the question so that you give only what is asked, nothing more, nothing less.

#7

"How do you plan to achieve your career goals?"

HINT: **DESCRIBE THE EFFORTS YOU ARE TAKING.** This is a variation of question #1 in that it focuses on your future. However, rather than expect you to talk about what you want to do, the interviewer wants to know what you are going to do to achieve your goals.

EXAMPLES OF ITEMS TO BE INCLUDED: Additional education, involvement in professional organizations (to learn more about your field), participation in company programs, working whatever time is necessary to accomplish your tasks, and community / volunteer membership.

#8

"What are the most important rewards you expect in your career?"

HINT: **COMBINE TANGIBLE WITH INTANGIBLE REWARDS.** Too many people immediately answer this question by mentioning ONLY such things as "knowing I've done a good job," "increasing the company's bottom line," "motivating my staff to improve their productivity," and the like.

While items such as these are important, you must also think of the TOTAL picture, that is, what's in it for YOU. Such things as financial security, expertise in your field, recognition by your employer, company car, the bonus trip to Hawaii, and other such rewards / compensation should be blended in with the other items.

#9

"What do you expect to be earning in five years?"

HINT: **COMBINES WHAT YOU NEED AND WHAT YOU DESERVE TO EARN.** First, this answer depends on whether your career / job offers a salary or a salary plus commission (or bonus).

Secondly, the question really asks you to combine two items: (a) what do you think you DESERVE to be earning in five years (based on your experience, accomplishments, etc.); and (b) what do you think you will NEED to be earning in five years (based on mortgage and car payments, food and housing expenses, etc.).

HINT: **FIND OUT WHAT THE POSITION GENERALLY PAYS.** Get a feel BEFORE the interview as to what the job you are applying for pays on a national average AND the job you hope to have in five years pays, again on a national average.

How to Figure Your Earnings After 5 Years

Take the present inflation rate (let's say 4%), multiply it by the average weekly salary, then take 4% of that number, etc. (three more times, for a total of four times), and you'll have the MINIMUM you should be earning in five years.

284

Add to this minimum a figure that you believe you will have earned through experience, accomplishments, etc., and, finally, add to this a percentage of the amount you think you'll need to live on in five years -- this final figure will give you an approximate figure of what you might expect to be earning.

An Example of Calculating Earnings After 5 Years

Your initial salary would be $200 per week. 4% of $200 is $8.00, so the second year would be $208 per week; 4% of $208 would be $8.32, so the third year would be $216.32; 4% of $216.32 would be $8.65, so the weekly total for year four would be $224.97; 4% of $224.97 would be $8.99, so your weekly salary after five years -- just to keep up with inflation -- would equal $233.96.

Next, add on an amount that you feel you would be justified in receiving due to experience, accomplishments, etc. after five years. Let's say that figure is $50; add this to your five year inflation figure of $233.96 and you are now up to $283.96 per week.

Finally, add to this a percentage or weekly figure increase after five years of what you need to live on -- let's say $100 -- and you wind up with $383.96 weekly, or an annual salary of $19,965.92 after five years (versus your starting salary of $10,400).

HINT: YOU ARE SHOWING THE INTERVIEWER THAT YOU DO YOUR HOMEWORK.
While this math may seem rather complicated, it does show the interviewer TWO very important points (beyond a justifiable figure as an answer): [a] you can back up your figure with specific facts; [b] you are a thorough planner.

HINT: DON'T FORGET COMMISSIONS AND INCENTIVES. If you are also going to receive a commission and / or incentives, these too must be factored in.

#10

"Sum up your professional strengths in one word."

HINT: THE ANSWER GOES BEYOND THE OBVIOUS. Somewhat of a trick question, because it is IMPOSSIBLE to sum up your strengths in one word -- professional, personal, or otherwise.

The Interviewer is Looking for Three Things

(1) Listening skills: Did you give your answer in only one word or more than one word?

(2) How well do you know yourself? Pick a strength that would give a good picture of what you think you are.

(3) How much self-confidence do you have? Did you look the interviewer in the eye when you gave your answer? Was your voice strong, going from high to low in tone, rather than being weak and going from low to high?

#11

"Why did you choose the career for which you are preparing?"

HINT: **DON'T CONCENTRATE ON ONLY MONEY AND NEED.** Don't tell the interviewer that you simply need a job and just want to make some money. (Exception: If you are taking a laborer-type job and are, in fact, just in it to get a job. This also often happens with temporary employment agencies.)

WHAT REALLY INTERESTED YOU. Rather, talk about those areas that TRULY interested you enough to get you to apply for this job or go into the industry.

EXAMPLES: Reasons can be as diverse as a sister who was developmentally disabled (occupation examples: special education teacher or social worker); a summer job you took just for the money and it turned out you liked the profession (virtually any occupation); a book you happened to read or a movie you saw, etc.

Most important: give your answer sincerely.

REMEMBER: You may have been the coolest thing alive in prison, but in the job interview you're just another applicant ... until you set yourself apart through enthusiasm, confidence, and well thought-out answers.

#12

"Which is more important to you, the money or the type of job?"

HINT: **LOOK TOWARD THE FUTURE.** While it may be true that the money is most important to you in the short run, in the long run happiness with what you are doing should be more important to you.

An old piece of wisdom says that if you truly enjoy your work, then you will be good at it; if you are truly good at your work, then financial success will follow.

(Obviously, there are those professions where an individual KNOWS that he / she will never become monetarily rich through his or her job, but still is most happy doing that type of work. Some examples are: social worker, cashier, teacher, mill worker, secretary. Ultimately, what's important is that you are satisfied with work that also meets your financial needs.)

MAKE CERTAIN THE INTERVIEWER KNOWS YOU HOLD JOB CONTENTMENT VERY HIGH. Tell him or her that, while money is certainly important because you cannot buy the things needed to live without it, happiness and contentment at what you do is even more (or just as) important.

Sadly, there are many people who make good money but when asked about their job, always come back with an answer such as, "I can't wait until 5:00 comes" or "I can't wait until the weekend."

Remember the wonderful feeling you had when you learned the date of your release, what you felt on the day of your release, or some other joyous occasion? Well, getting up in the morning and going to work at a job you really like will come close to giving you that same feeling!

#13

"What do you consider to be your greatest strengths and weaknesses?"

HINT: **RE-READ CHAPTER 2.** A good way to be certain of your answer to this is to go over the exercises you did in Chapter 2 on personal strengths and weaknesses.

HINT: EVERYBODY HAS FAULTS. Strengths are always easy to give an interviewer; it is our weaknesses that are difficult. Why? Hard enough as it is to admit to a friend or family member that you have faults, it is even more difficult to tell a potential employer, as conventional wisdom says that faults are negatives, and negatives don't help applicants land jobs.

In this case, however, the employer wants to see how well you know yourself, as well as how REAL you are. NOBODY is perfect, and if you tell an employer that you can't think of any faults, he / she will jump all over you. (Example: "I've got 20 years more work experience than you and I still can find things about me that I'd like to improve -- why are you so perfect?")

HINT: "POSITIVE NEGATIVES." The negatives that the employers are looking for are what I call "positive negatives," that is, items that can be improved upon but won't really affect your job performance.

EXAMPLES: Not the best public speaker; too much of a perfectionist; tend to get so involved in all aspects of the job that I take too much work home with me; need to improve time management; don't always delegate as I should.

In each of these examples, make certain you tell the employer that you are working on improving that particular area of weakness.

HINT: DON'T START TALKING ABOUT WHAT GOT YOU INTO PRISON. DO NOT -- I repeat, DO NOT -- start talking about those things that got you into prison (unless the employer directly asks you about them). You don't want to use your prison experience as a crutch, and you certainly don't want to draw attention to yourself as an ex-inmate.

Remember: You are trying to impress the interviewer as a job applicant, not as an ex-inmate.

HINT: REFER TO TIP. In Chapter 6, pages 264-265, Tip #10 discusses turning your negatives into positives. Several items are listed that an interviewer may at first perceive as a weakness; this section shows you how to turn these into positive selling points.

#14

"How would you describe yourself?"

HINT: DESCRIBE YOURSELF IN TERMS OF THE "WHO" AND THE "WHAT" OF YOU.
This question is very similar to #2 (this chapter), but is more open-ended because you don't have to relate your strengths to the job for which you applied.

Focus on those personal items that make up your "who," but also bring in some other "what" items (facts) such as family, organization, and hobbies. Again, keep in mind that the interviewer has very likely read or glanced over your resume, but knows little about how you see yourself. So make certain your answer is a mix of 2/3 "whos" and 1/3 "whats!"

Also: Don't give statistics, such as, "I'm 5' tall, weigh 112#, and wear a size 9 hat." These are somewhat obvious to the interviewer, are boring, and don't contribute very much to filling in the outline of you the interviewer already has.   And besides: give an answer like this and the interviewer will think you are trying to be cute. You're not, and it will probably cost you any opportunity you had for the job.

#15

"How do you think a friend or professor who knows you well would describe you?"

HINT: TWO PIECES OF INFORMATION ARE NEEDED:

(1) A description of the "who" of you.

(2) An indication as to whether or not others see you the same way you see yourself. Have some people in mind before the interview -- your mother or father, a close friend, teacher from prison, parole officer, counselor, friend, or past employer, perhaps.

#16

"Let's play 'pretend' for a moment. You've now been working for us for 5 years -- why should we promote you?"

HINT: **PERFORMING YOUR REGULAR DUTIES IS NOT ENOUGH.** This question has many pitfalls in it, and if you're not careful, you'll definitely get snared. First, keep in mind that merely doing your work as initially outlined when hired (or promoted) to your present position does not qualify you for a raise.

However, most job candidates, when asked this question, immediately reply something like, "Well, I've done a good job for five years, have always been on time, and completed all assigned tasks." The problem with this answer? This is what you are expected to do, and, if anything, you are telling the employer why he or she should keep you in your present job!

TELL WHAT YOU'VE DONE BEYOND YOUR JOB DESCRIPTION. To successfully answer this question, keep in mind that a promotion usually comes about because you have demonstrated an ability to take on additional responsibilities; have saved the company time and money; have increased sales; have taken the initiative when someone else "dropped the ball;" have obtained a degree (or an advanced degree); and other such items.

HINT: **IF THE INTERVIEWER IS PLAYING PRETEND, SO CAN YOU.** Remember question #2, where I suggested you put your list of personal selling points in story form because it makes it more interesting? Well, the same goes here.

Start your answer by pretending that you ARE in the position for which you are being hired. Then relate various successes, accomplishments, etc., within this position. This will not only make your answer more interesting, but show that you can be creative, as well.

#17

"What motivates you to put forth your greatest effort?"

HINT: **MENTION YOUR ENJOYMENT OF THE WORK AND SALARY.** A reward of some kind -- money, bonus, etc. -- is what usually motivates us in a career position (versus a volunteer involvement).

However, you don't want to give the impression to employers that your first concern is money. They will probably think, "Hey, this applicant would probably leave my company if offered 10 cents more an hour by another firm -- why should I invest my company's time and train him / her if he's / she's only going to leave?"

Instead, mention your enjoyment of the particular type of work, perhaps knowing that your efforts will help improve others' lives, the feeling of a job well done, etc.

After you've mentioned a few of these, THEN say something about money. (Example: "... and, of course, I also enjoy receiving a nice paycheck so that I afford to keep on coming to work each day!" -- a little bit of humor never hurt anyone.)

HINT: ALWAYS LOOK TO FUTURE POSSIBILITIES, EVEN IN A LABORER JOB. You may be taking a temporary (or full time job) where little more than a strong back or being able to put 1000 screws and nuts together each day is required. In these work situations, there is seldom much self-fulfillment, other than the pay & benefits. Still, let the interviewer know how you like to feel you've done a good job -- other employment opportunities may be available that the employer could mention to you.

#18

"How has your college experience prepared you for a career?"

HINT: COMBINE ACADEMICS WITH NON-ACADEMICS. If you do have a college education -- no matter how little -- stress two items: [a] the academics, that is, what you learned in the classroom, and [b] the non-academic "people" experience you picked up.

Examples of non-academic college-type level experience: leadership experience (perhaps through involvement in clubs, fraternities, sororities, etc.); can take on responsibility, a good problem-solver, and interact well with a wide variety of people (jobs held while in school, volunteer work); and other personal or technical skills that you felt were developed or enhanced by some outside activities.

HINT: IF YOU DON'T HAVE A COLLEGE EDUCATION, YOU CAN STILL SELL YOURSELF. If you don't have a college education, chances are this question will not be asked because you did not list it on your resume. However, if somehow this gets by the interviewer and he / she still asks you about college experience, don't say, "I don't have one."

Example: Any question asked is an opportunity for you to sell yourself. Simply say something like, "My college education amounts to a Ph.D. from Street University (or: "My college education was not the usual route"): I've learned how to deal with people, how to make decisions, how to think on my feet, how to work well in a team situation, how to devise a budget, and how to become a leader through part time jobs, and helping to raise five brothers and two sisters."

(**Regarding membership in a gang**: it can offer you plenty of areas to talk about regarding education. Leadership, and life skills. What were your responsibilities? Did you learn any transferable skills or crafts? Did you have a leadership role? Remember -- turn what others perceive as negatives into positives!)

#19

"What qualifications do you have that make you think you will be successful in your chosen field?"

HINT: INCLUDE THE FACTS. This is a variation of question # 2, but here the interviewer DOES want to know about your experience, education, and other FACTS, in addition to the personal qualities you can contribute.

ANSWER OBJECTIVELY. Remember when I suggested you answer the questions OBJECTIVELY, that is, from the viewpoint of the interviewer? Well, this question is an excellent example.

ALMOST EVERYTHING COUNTS. Simply put, you are trying to think of EVERYTHING that makes you qualified for the job. (However, keep in mind that because your father thinks you'd do a good job, a fortune cookie stated that you would succeed in this field, or you think it would be "neat" are NOT good reasons to mention!)

#20

"How do you determine or evaluate success?"

HINT: DON'T ONLY TALK OF MONEY. This is a cousin of question #17. The interviewer wants to know what qualities are most important for you to determine someone -- or something -- else being successful. If you start your answer by talking about a fancy car, nice clothes, and a big salary -- and only talk about those items -- then the interviewer will probably think you are very shallow.

Certainly, these niceties are ONE measure of success, but don't forget to include those other areas I suggested in question #17.

#21

"What do you think it takes to be successful in an organization like ours?"

HINT: TWO THINGS ARE LOOKED FOR IN THIS ANSWER:

(1) Your familiarity with the organization

(2) Your qualities. The qualities you offer that match what you feel is needed to succeed in the job with this employer.

#22

"In what ways do you think you can make a contribution to our organization?"

HINT: INCLUDE YOUR INVOLVEMENT IN THE ORGANIZATION. Very closely related to question #21, with one difference: not only do you need to talk about those skills you bring that would allow you to be successful in the job for which you are applying, but also relate other skills you can contribute to various organizations, clubs, etc. that exist within the company.

3 Examples of How to Answer This Question

(1) You have past experience in editing a company, prison, or school newspaper, and the company you are interviewing with has an employee newsletter.

(2) You are a good softball player, and this company belongs to a softball league.

(3) You enjoy babysitting and can offer your services -- in your SPARE time -- to those employees looking for a babysitter.

AN EXCELLENT OPPORTUNITY TO SHOW YOUR VALUE. A question like this can do much to make you appear to be valuable to the company in several areas and on different levels!

#23

"What qualities should a successful manager possess?"

HINT: **THIS QUESTION ASKS FOR TWO ITEMS:**

(1) Personal makeup. Those general, personal strengths that have been asked for in some of the previous questions [for example, question #2].

(2) Management skills. Those skills that are specific for a manager.

Examples of management skills: Good ability to delegate; someone who listens and can communicate well; good ability to organize; a decision-maker; someone who is sincerely interested in the well-being of his staff; a good time manager but someone who is not a clock watcher; someone always looking to improve his / her skills through formal training and self-study; a person with a friendly personality but also someone who knows where to draw the line and assert his/her authority.

#24

"Describe the relationship that should exist between a supervisor and those reporting to him / her."

HINT: **DEMANDS AND COMMANDS RESPECT.** This is perhaps best answered by the last item listed in the examples for question #23: friendly, but knows when to become the boss. How is this accomplished?

294

EXAMPLES: Mention such things as demand respect by position but command (earn) respect by being a nice person; not afraid to admit a mistake; willing to take the time and teach employees how to improve their skills; keeps an open office door policy (during set hours); a relationship where the supervisor is not isolated from the staff, and shows that he/she is right in there, working hard.

Based on the type of job and position, other such items can be included.

#25

"What two or three accomplishments have given you the most satisfaction? Why?"

<u>HINT</u>: **AN OPPORTUNITY TO BRAG.** An enjoyable question, because it gives you the opportunity to do something each of us enjoys doing at one time or another, whether openly or to ourselves: brag!

DON'T OVERDO IT. Of course, you don't want to say things like "I'm the greatest!" or "No one can come close to me in my field." Rather, talk about those items you did that made you feel good and their importance to you and to the organization.

<u>HINT</u>: **IF THE INTERVIEWER KNOWS YOU SPENT TIME IN PRISON.** This is an excellent opportunity to talk about something you accomplished while inside. It could be a sporting event, getting your high school or college degree, learning to read, becoming a leader in some group or club -- anything that shows you using your time wisely and helping you grow. (See Question #1; see Chapter 8.)

#26

"Describe your most rewarding college / high school experience."

<u>HINT</u>: **IT SHOULD HELP YOU IMPROVE.** Be honest, but make certain it is something that has somehow contributed to your growth as a person. Interviewers use questions like this to find out what is important to you, how much depth there is to your makeup, and how you are able to look beneath the surface. (By the way: don't forget any GED classes you may have taken in prison.)

EXAMPLE. You won a billiard championship in school. On the surface, this doesn't seem to compare to getting an "A" in physics or being elected student body president. But beneath the surface, this may have helped you become more of a leader; improved your ability to concentrate and practice; assisted your competitive nature; let you get to know people better; improved your communicative skills; and helped you understand the importance of preparation and presentation to achieve success.

> **REMEMBER: Beyond the fun and laughter and good times of a great experience, always seek out what you also learned from it -- this will double its value immediately.**

#27

"If you were hiring someone for this position, what qualities would you look for?"

HINT: **THINK OBJECTIVELY.** If you do, you'll score much higher in this question. A good idea is to play a little game of pretend before the interview, and write down those qualities you'd expect in a person if you were hiring that person for the job for which you are applying.

You'll find that when you WRITE out the answer to a question, rather than merely think it out (or, sometimes, even talk it out), you put more effort into your answer. Why? Simple -- it takes longer to write!

HINT: **USE THE INTERVIEW PROCESS AS A GUIDE.** Start with those items that an employer might first notice about you SO THAT THE INTERVIEWER GETS TO KNOW YOU THROUGH AN INTERVIEW: first, the resume (what experience, education, etc. do you have?); next, the visual contact (are you dressed nicely; do you have a generally nice appearance?); then, communicative skills; lastly, those personal qualities that have been covered in several questions above.

(See Chapter 6, page 269, for the most common complaints interviewers have about job applicants ... then develop responses that are the opposite of these complaints; they'll make excellent answers for this question as well!)

#28

"Why did you select your college or university?"

HINT: **TELL THE TRUTH.** If you went to college or attended a university, tell the truth as to why you initially chose your school: it could be the academics; it might be the athletics; or it could be its affordability and / or proximity to home; and several other reasons.

ADD ITEMS FROM YOUR SCHOOL EXPERIENCE. Virtually every student finds out there are additional academics to be learned or other non-academic aspects that end up attracting him or her to the school beyond his or her initial reason for attending. Make certain you mention these.

#29

"What led you to choose your field of major study?"

HINT: **SELECT FROM YOUR MOST RECENT LEVEL OF SCHOOLING, WHETHER IT BE HIGH SCHOOL OR COLLEGE.** If you did not graduate from high school, tell the employer what most interested you in high school ... and assure him / her that you are going to get your GED.

HINT: **DON'T WORRY IF YOUR WORK INTEREST AND PAST FIELD(S) OF STUDY DON'T MATCH.** This could relate to question #11, if your major field(s) of study led into your most recent profession or interest in a profession.

However, there are many people who major in one area yet a particular life event causes them to go in a seemingly different direction.

EXAMPLES: My brothers are good examples. One majored and graduated with a degree in forestry, and is now a worldwide recognized expert in a particular style of art. The other tried four colleges, left each one with no set major to speak of, and today is founder and president of an extremely successful medical services support company.

HINT: **IF YOU DON'T MIND TALKING ABOUT YOUR PRISON EXPERIENCE.** There are many ex-inmates who first got turned on to learning and a specific field of study while in prison. Don't be afraid to mention it. (As you will see in Chapter 8, questions and information that surround your prison experience can, at times, prove very beneficial if handled the right way.)

#30

"What college and / or high school subjects did you like BEST? Why?"

HINT: **BE TRUTHFUL.** Don't give the interviewer the answer you think he/she WANTS to hear, but rather the truth. The answer to this may also tie in to question #29.

#31

"What college and / or high school subjects did you like LEAST? Why?"

HINT: **AN OPPORTUNITY TO SHOW YOU ARE NOT BETTER THAN ANYONE ELSE.**
Questions like this are very important (see question #13), as it shows the interviewer you are real, that is, that you can dislike things, not do well at certain things, and, in general, be as human as the rest of the human race. In addition, it gives added material to the interviewer as he / she continues to build his / her profile of your "who."

#32

"If you could do so, how would you plan your academic studies differently? Why?"

HINT: **YOU ACCEPT WHAT ALWAYS COMES YOUR WAY OR YOU CAN MAKE A CHANGE WHEN YOU FEEL IT'S NECESSARY.** This question, asked another way, wants to know why you aren't happy with what you've studied / are studying, and why you haven't done anything about it.

AT TIMES, THERE IS NO CHOICE. Sometimes, of course, there are subjects in school that are taken because the school says you must. Other times, courses of studies are pursued because that's all that was left; your parents thought it would be in "your best interests" to study a particular field; or you take classes just to take classes, not having any real goal or plan except to get out.

WHAT THE INTERVIEWER LEARNS. This answer focuses more on your determination and confidence in knowing what you want, as well as an understanding of the various forces around you and how you can be / have been affected by them.

#33

"How do you go about making important decisions?"

HINT: **SHOW THAT YOU ARE A PLANNER WITH GUMPTION.** This question combines your abilities to plan, to have patience, to weigh a variety of possibilities, and to not be afraid to make a decision.

DON'T FORGET ABOUT IMMEDIATE DECISIONS. Remember: sometimes decisions have to be made immediately, on-the-spot; when this happens, there is more reliance on your past experience, familiarity with the situation, and "gut feeling." At most other times, however, decision makers rely on those traits I mentioned at the beginning of this HINT. Your answer should include both types of decisions.

#34

"What would you like to do when you retire?"

HINT: **THE INTERVIEWER WANTS TO KNOW IF YOU:**

(a) are just going to be marking time until you can leave and do what you REALLY want to do (thus thinking that perhaps you may just go through the motions at the job, if hired)

OR

(b) intend on pursuing (either full time or expanded time) a hobby, do volunteer work, continue in some way that connects with the type work you are now seeking, or a combination of these items.

WILL YOU BE WITH THE COMPANY FOR A LONG TIME? In addition, the interviewer may be trying to see if you are planning on working for his company for "the long haul," that is, until you retire.

(**NOTE**: The nature of employment has changed in many ways over the past several years, and one of these is in the length of time many employees stay with their employer. While an employer hopes that he / she can count on your services for a very long time [as long as you are productive!], the reality is that employees too often do not stay with one employer beyond a few years or so. However, even if the employer is aware of this, it is still your role to convince the employer that you'd like to retire from his / her firm IF this looks like a job or career you'd like to pursue for a long time. Certainly, this would not hold true if you were interviewing for a temporary job, or an obvious entry-level job just to make some money until something better comes along.)

#35

"Do you think that your grades are a good indication of your academic achievement?"

<u>**HINT**</u>: **GRADES DO NOT AN EDUCATION MAKE.** Very often, ex-inmates have not had an outstanding academic career, or they have done well ONLY in those courses where they have an interest ... yet they have learned much more than those grades show.

EXPLAIN FULLY. If you fall into one of these descriptions, tell the interviewer WHY you did not do well and what you feel that you learned that is not shown in the grade you received. There are also times when a student will absorb and learn the information that is taught in class, but -- for any number of reasons -- did not do well on the tests.

<u>**HINT**</u>: **WHAT ELSE DID YOU LEARN IN CLASS?** No matter how good you did on your grades, remember that you can always find additional items that you learned in class that are not reflected in your grades.

EXAMPLE: You may have received an "A" in English, for example, but what was not reflected in that "A" grade was that you learned how to study, you learned how to organize, or you learned the importance of communication. Each of these is a contributing factor to your high grade, but none of these are usually the main factor in determining your grade.

#36

"What have you learned from participation in extra-curricular activities?"

HINT: **NON-ACADEMIC SKILLS.** This is an excellent opportunity for you to talk about those skills you've gained while obtaining that Ph.D. from Street University that was mentioned earlier (see question #18). And don't rely ONLY on those activities with which you were involved while in school, although DO start your answer with these.

IF THE EMPLOYER KNOWS YOU'VE BEEN IN PRISON. After you've given some items from school, move on to other outside activities -- including those from prison IF the employer knows about your prison experience at this point in the interview.

#37

"In what kind of work environment are you most comfortable?"

HINT: **YOUR ANSWER DESCRIBES YOU.** A question that exposes much about you, as it tells the interviewer whether or not you work well with others / in a team environment, enjoy people, are bothered by noise (and other distractions), can handle people interrupting you, understand that you need to work your way up to that corner office, and blend in and work around the environment that's given you (if hired).

BE FLEXIBLE. Don't make out like someone who will work only if your office decor, etc., needs are met. An employer much more readily appreciates someone who will work (and work to his / her best ability) no matter what the work environment.

HINT: **MOST EMPLOYERS ARE LOOKING FOR "TEAM PLAYERS."** Prison life turns many an inmate into a loner, a person who tends to stay away from others ... a trait that is not usually desirable in the business world.

As you know, this loner trait often grows out of an unwritten piece of prison / inmate advice that says you keep your mouth shut, you don't seek out trouble, and you don't look to be a troublemaker. Often, this is reinforced by the guards, prison rules, and your fear of not making parole / getting out when scheduled. In Chapter 9, I discuss readjustment to the free world, and leaving the negatives of prison behind.

#38

"How do you work under pressure?"

HINT: STRESS IS NOT AN EXCUSE FOR A POOR JOB OR PERSONAL PERFORMANCE. An extremely important question, as it focuses on how you react under stress and when your work environment is not as you would like it to be. You certainly don't want the interviewer to get the impression that you "fly off the handle," do sloppy work, get into fights, become careless, or physically suffer when pressure comes tapping you on the shoulder.

HOW TO ANSWER THE QUESTION. At first, tell the interviewer that you function fine under pressure. This answer, by itself, however, needs some explanation.

So ... go on to tell the interviewer how you don't let stress bother you (for example: you exercise); you realize that the stress of the moment will eventually pass; you understand that if you give in to stress you are letting yourself down, as well as those around you; and / or you always take a few minutes now-and-then for a short "self-break" (a cup of coffee, a brief walk outside, a snack, a look at the newspaper, etc.) to get your mind away from the present work situation and relax just a bit.

WHAT THIS ANSWER TELLS THE INTERVIEWER. This answer not only shows the employer that you know how pressure can be harmful, but that you know what to do to best handle it.

HINT: IF YOU CAN'T HANDLE STRESS. Don't lie to employers and tell them you can. Eventually, your inability to handle pressure will show up. Instead, you should focus on a type of employment where stress is low. Get to know the work environment and the duties of the job so you'll have an idea as to whether or not the stress is too much for you.

HINT: THE STRESS INTERVIEW. There are interviews or interview questions that are meant to do one thing: see how well you handle pressure and stress. This may consist of questions that seem to be shouted at you, constant disagreement from the interviewer, long silent pauses from the interviewer, or constant interruptions during the interview. DON'T LET ANY OF THESE GET TO YOU!

INDICATE THAT YOU ARE USED TO WORKING UNDER STRESS. The key to doing well in the stress interview is to act as if that type of interview / stress situation is something you are quite used to, so it doesn't faze you. The interview won't go on forever, but your actions and reactions will leave a lasting effect on the interviewer.

<u>**HINT**</u>: **IF THE INTERVIEWER KNOWS THAT YOU WERE IN PRISON.** This question becomes even more potentially harmful if your prison record is known. Why? The perception of MANY business people (who have not been behind bars) is that the typical inmate is very unstable, cannot handle pressure, and will snap if under too much stress.

OUTSIDE PERCEPTION OF FEDERAL VS. STATE & COUNTY INSTITUTIONS. More often, it is the inmates in state or county prisons who get this "can't function under stress" tag. Federal inmates are often perceived as being able to function well under pressure. This is usually because of the seemingly complex crime that got them into prison, not to mention the sometimes very large amounts of money or goods involved. The thinking here is that the person involved must be able to handle stress with such a complex crime involved.

Additionally, it is no secret that federal inmates, on the average, have a higher level of completed educational studies than those in state or local institutions; many people hold that the more educated a person, the better he / she is able to handle stress. This, of course, is not true, yet the belief persists amongst many.

TAKE ANY PRESCRIBED "ANTI-STRESS" MEDICATION. If you are taking any medication to help calm you down, by all means, take it -- and take it as prescribed!

You are in a situation where you not only have to prove yourself the best candidate for the job, but also prove that whatever you did that landed you in prison (and any other negatives the interviewer thinks you might have done while inside) is COMPLETELY over, and that person no longer exists.

(**NOTE**: Stress reduction is discussed in Chapter 2, pages 42-44, and Chapter 11, Pages 387-388.)

#39

"Why have you changed jobs so frequently?"

<u>**HINT**</u>: **WHAT WAS THEN IS NOW DIFFERENT.** While this situation fits millions of people, there is a higher concentration of job-jumping among those individuals who have spent time in prison. (Chapter 4, "Writing and Using Resumes," explains how to downplay this in constructing your resume.)

Rather than tell the interviewer that you didn't like the people, they didn't understand you, the hours weren't right, they were prejudiced / racist, or the like (all reasons that show you to be a person who might make trouble on the job and / or a person who has a tendency to blame others for your mistakes), let the interviewer know the UNDERLYING truth.

4 Examples of How to Answer This Question

(1) *"I really didn't have any direction or know what I wanted to do."*

(2) *"Well, I was a bit wilder in those days and didn't think too much about the consequences of my actions."*

(3) *"It took me a while to realize it wasn't everyone else that was wrong and me that was right; I had to do some learning and growing up."*

(4) *"There are some bad luck clouds that don't show up on my resume: company going bankrupt, another firm being bought out and then laying off the newest hires, my last company where the steel industry took a nosedive and they closed down, and that second job where the company moved its location where there wasn't any bus transportation, so I had to quit."*

WHAT YOUR ANSWER TELLS THE INTERVIEWER. The key here is to focus on your awareness that the world was not out to get you, and that you are a different person now from the one who went through all those jobs.

QUESTIONS THAT DEAL WITH GAPS IN YOUR JOB HISTORY. A question that relates to this one is, "Why were you out of work so long?" or, "Please explain the long gaps between jobs." Again, give reasons that show you have grown since those experiences.

Possible Answers to These Questions

"I really didn't know how to look for a job" ... "I was in a difficult market, and it took me much longer to find a position similar to the one I left" ... "My mother was ill and I had to take care of her" ... "I was in an auto accident and could not work for a year."

DON'T TALK ABOUT NEGATIVE HEALTH CONDITIONS. Unless it is medically imperative that you do so, DON'T raise the question of you being in less than 100% excellent medical condition.

REMEMBER: Difficult situations are merely opportunities for you to push your mind further and succeed at a higher level.

#40

"What kinds of people appeal most / least to you as work associates?"

<u>HINT</u>: **MATCHING YOUR PERSONALITY TO THOSE IN THE ORGANIZATION.** Your potential employer wants to know how accepting you are of others, with what types of people you tend to work better, and what kind of personality you have.

A WINNING EXAMPLE. If you are an auto technician, for example, and prefer work associates who tend to stay to themselves, are not afraid to give information or ask for assistance, and are dedicated to doing their job, then you would seem to fit in with the personality traits of most other auto technicians.

A LOSING EXAMPLE. However, if you tell the employer that you like to work with people who enjoy having a good time, like their work but are not consumed by it, and don't mind going out for a drink after work, you've just blown the interview. Why? Employers don't want to gamble on someone they think may keep others from doing their work, perhaps is not as dedicated to his / her field as he / she would like the interviewer to believe, and possibly has a drinking problem.

PERCEPTION OFTEN OVERSHADOWS REALITY. Even though there is nothing wrong in having a good time, not being consumed by work, and going out for a drink, it is the PERCEPTION of those items that overshadows the reality.

CARE ABOUT THE CUSTOMER AND THE COMPANY. You do better if you describe individuals who are serious in their attitude toward work, care about the customer, want the whole department to get ahead, have a good sense of humor, are open to suggestions and will help out when needed, and other such items.

#41

"What books have you read in the past three months?"

<u>HINT</u>: **ADDS TO A DESCRIPTION OF YOU.** This tells the interviewer what types of outside interests you are pulled toward, if you have a curious mind, if you can get away from your job and relax your mind, and how TRULY interested you are in your profession.

POSITIVE EXAMPLE: If you worked as a retail sales clerk and have recently read some science fiction, that's nice. It shows a mind that can go beyond the boundaries of that particular job -- a mind that appreciates creativity.

NEGATIVE EXAMPLE: If you were a computer operator, however, and ALL your reading has to do with computers, the interviewer may think you have nothing else on your mind but computers, and thus believe it's a bad thing because you don't have an outlet to relax (even though that is not necessarily true).

DON'T LIE. Don't, however, mention a book that you didn't read, thinking you will impress the interviewer: how embarrassing if he or she has read it, asks you about a particular character, and you are caught in a lie!

<u>**HINT:**</u> **DON'T TALK ABOUT SEX BOOKS.** In prison, westerns, romances, thrillers, horror stories, science fiction, and sex books are the top subjects of many an inmate's reading. Each of these subjects is okay to mention, WITH THE EXCEPTION OF THE LAST ONE: SEX.

Again, while most of society thinks about, reads about, sees, and / or participates in sex in some form, it is still something that most people are not comfortable having discussed in public ... and this is especially true in a business interview. Also, today's society companies are especially guarded against any possible employee who may show the potential for practicing sexual harassment ... don't let that be you!

IF THE INTERVIEWER KNOWS YOU WERE IN PRISON. To make matters worse, there is that old perception of the prison inmate that I keep mentioning. Those individuals who have not been in prison see an ex-inmate who, among other things, has a less than honorable or society-acceptable respect for sex, and thus these ex-inmates are more apt to sexually harass (or worse) fellow employees. So, leave the sex books OUT of the discussion if asked a question like this!

#42

"Why are manhole covers round?"

<u>**HINT:**</u> **TELLS THE INTERVIEWER HOW YOU HANDLE UNEXPECTED SITUATIONS.**
Whoa!, you say -- where did this come from, why did they ask it, and what do they want?! First, you must understand why a question like this would be asked.

All 41 interview questions prior to this one (and ten that follow) tend to be the type of questions you might expect in an interview: relating, in a serious way, to the job you seek. This question is equally important, and its only difference is that it is somewhat of a humorous question, probably guaranteed to put at least a smile on your face.

DAYS DON'T ALWAYS GO AS PLANNED. Interviewers know, however, that if you are hired, your typical day (everyone falls into a routine on a job, no matter how much they want to deny it) does have its share of unexpected crises and events: a fire breaks out ... a sale is about to be lost ... there is a holdup in the store ... an accident occurs ... your computer won't boot up or crashes. These, and other such non-typical parts of the day, will cause you to react -- but how?

By asking you this question that appears to "come out of left field" and does not seem related to your work, the interviewer can get a sense of your reaction when something unexpected happens.

REFER TO CHAPTER 6. As was discussed in Chapter 6, #9, page 263, give the outward impression that you were expecting this question, and let your sweating and confusion remain on the inside!

HINT: A "PRETEND ANSWER" IS OKAY. How do you answer this question? In Question #16, I suggested that if the interviewer wants to play pretend, then you can also play pretend. Don't take too long to think of an answer to this question (shows you, perhaps, as a person who can't make a quick decision or is slow on his/her feet), but rather give the first answer that comes to mind. A client once asked me this question, and I answered by saying, "So round pizzas can fit through them, of course!"

REMEMBER: The weird, the happenstance, the fluke, the "oops," and the "uh, oh" -- just another typical day at work, so learn to expect it.

#43

"Why did you decide to seek a position with this company?"

HINT: THEY WANT YOU TO FIT INTO THEIR MAKEUP. The interviewer is not asking you how you learned about the job opening, but why you want to work for them. Questions #21 & #22 touched on this question. It is hoped that in your answer something will be included showing you've researched the company and are drawn to that firm because of a match of your qualifications and their services, product, attitude, etc.

HINT: **BE HONEST.** Again, if you are interviewing with a company for a position such as a laborer, janitor, piecemeal worker, seasonal worker, etc. -- only to have employment (perhaps to satisfy one of the conditions of your parole) and to bring in some money until a better position comes along -- be honest about it.

SELL YOUR POSITIVES. Present your positives to the employer: good work skills, dedication, a non-drinker and non-smoker, punctuality, always giving 100% effort, and other such items.

#44

"What do you know about our company?"

HINT: **REFER TO CHAPTER 2.** In Chapter 2, I discussed in detail how you can research an organization while in prison (and continue doing the research once released, although with greater access to phones, books, and buildings).

TELLS THE INTERVIEWER MANY THINGS ABOUT YOU. Employers want to know that you are willing to put in the time and effort necessary to learn about their company. Not only does this give the impression that you are sincerely interested in the company, but also says something about your researching skills and your ability to stick with something until you get what you are after.

HINT: **THERE IS ALWAYS MORE TO LEARN.** As was mentioned in Chapter 6, learning about the company does not end on the day you leave for the interview. On and in that company's property, be observant for anything that might also give you information about the firm: an award on the wall, the manner in which employees are dressed, some corporate material that is available for reading, etc. Be ever alert; you never know when it will pay off!

#45

"What have you learned from your mistakes?"

HINT: **UNLESS DIRECTLY ASKED, DON'T INCLUDE PRISON-RELATED ITEMS.** First, you want to answer this as if you were not in prison (this aspect of the question will be discussed in Chp. 8).

SHOW THE POSITIVES THAT YOU'VE GAINED. The interviewer is not only looking to see what mistakes you've made, but if you have the capability of turning negatives into positives, that is, learning how to improve yourself (and certainly how not to make the same mistakes). If you can show this, then you are showing the interviewer that you look at every opportunity to improve yourself, your work, and your education.

EXAMPLES. Conclude your answer by giving examples of improvements you've made over past mistakes (the same or similar to these: obtained a better sense of time management ... have to slow down and not rush just to get it over with ... make certain to read the directions (or manual) before I go ahead ... double check dates ... check for spelling errors ... don't be so quick to judge ... to remember that everyone makes mistakes ... to not stay out so late the night before work ... to keep my opinions of others in the company to myself.

#46

"Can you take instructions without feeling bothered by it?"

HINT: CAN YOU FOLLOW DIRECTIONS? No one in prison really enjoys taking orders all the time, yet that is the nature of almost every prison (some more than others). In the business world, when working for someone else, you must follow orders and take directions on a regular basis. Accept this as one of those things that is okay with you, and you won't have any trouble with this question.

There are those people who do not enjoy being told what to do. (Often, this factor contributes to why someone loses a job and / or ends up in prison.) Yet everybody has to answer to someone else, even if you own your business.

IT SHOWS THAT YOU DON'T "BUCK THE SYSTEM." Employers tend to prefer those employees who "color inside the lines," rather than outside the lines (that is, an employee who is likely to continually go off on his or her own, not follow directions, and "upset the apple cart").

(This is not to say that creativity nor initiative are not appreciated; virtually all companies do. First, however, you need to understand and demonstrate your ability to work within the structure of the company and description of your job.)

#47

"Who are the three most important people in your life, living or dead, and not related to you?"

HINT: **TELLS THE EMPLOYER QUALITIES YOU ADMIRE AND IDENTIFY WITH.** Questions like this (that focus on those people who have had an influence on your life or whom you admire) are asked to get a better idea as to what types of qualities you tend to admire in others, how these people might have influenced you, and if there are people you identify with who have somewhat negative qualities.

MY ANSWER. When I was once asked this question, I came up with Walt Disney, Lord Baden-Powell (founder of the Boy Scouts), and Larry Bird (former star basketball player for the Boston Celtics). Each of these people have personal qualities and have accomplished things that I tremendously admire, and each of these three has had a very positive influence on my life.

HINT: **HAVE AN ANSWER PREPARED.** This is a question that requires some thought, unless you have thought it out prior to the interview. There are literally millions of people in history -- both alive and dead -- from whom you can pick three. As was suggested in Chapter 6, take a few seconds out when this question is asked, turn your head to the side, think out your answer carefully, and then look the interviewer in the eyes and give him / her your answer.

HINT: **LISTEN TO THE QUESTION.** In this version, you cannot select any family member (a natural choice of an important person in your life).

Also, be careful that you do give the name of a NON-PERSON in your answer. For example, while "Jesus Christ" or "Mohammed" would be acceptable, "God" would not be; likewise, Walt Disney or Bill Cosby would be fine, but Donald Duck or Bart Simpson would not. The question asks for "people," and while God, Donald Duck, or Bart Simpson may be important in your life, they are not real people!

Finally, there are THREE people asked for in this question, so give three people.

REMEMBER: As the flowers are influenced by rain and the beaches by the waves, likewise are we influenced by those who have come into our lives: by acknowledging them, you admit that your growth as a person becomes that much better through the deeds and thoughts of others. How nice to be so open to learning!

#48

"If the following situation occurred, what would you do?" (Interviewer then gives you a hypothetical work situation, and wants to see how you'd handle it.)

HINT: ASKS FOR COMMON SENSE AND YOUR KNOWLEDGE OF A PARTICULAR SUBJECT OR ITEM. Examples for questions that are NOT controversial or ethically questionable: how you would close a particular sale ... how you would motivate a group ... how you would sell an item ... what you would do if someone claims you gave him / her the wrong change and you know you did not ... how to handle someone asking you to work late when you have previous plans outside of work.

PLACE YOURSELF IN THE SITUATION. Take a few moments to put yourself in that situation, call on your past experience and common sense, then answer.

IF THE SCENARIO DEALS WITH AN ILLEGAL OR UNETHICAL SITUATION. There are those scenarios, however, than CAN be controversial or ethically questionable: What would you do if you saw an employee taking cocaine on the job or stealing? ... Would you cross a picket line? ... What if your supervisor told you to do something even though you knew he / she was wrong? ... What if you knew someone in the company was having an affair with your supervisor's spouse?

YOU NEED TO BE HONEST, KNOW THE COMPANY, & USE COMMON SENSE. These questions need three additional items from you: honesty, as much information as possible about the organization, and good use of common sense. Sometimes the event is none of your concern, other times you need to make it your concern, and occasionally the item directly concerns you! Chances are 50-50 of you giving the answer the interviewer wants.

3 Points to Remember for this Question

(1) HONESTY. You are being honest with yourself, something that is extremely important if you are going to succeed out of prison (and stay out).

(2) ONE "WRONG" ANSWER WILL SELDOM RUIN AN INTERVIEW. Very seldom is someone NOT hired for a position because one answer (out of the entire interview) is not exactly on the mark. (Unless, of course, you go overboard and tell the employer that you will rob him / her blind, always be late for work, and not pay attention to detail!)

(3) THE INTERVIEWER USUALLY EXPLAINS HIS / HER VIEW. If you have interviewed pretty well and one of your answers is a bit off the mark, the interviewer will usually discuss your answer. This will give you a better understanding of what the company is expecting & how you might see another perspective that perhaps will change your answer. (NOTE: Do not "sell yourself out"; the lie isn't worth it.)

#49

"Are world (or national) events important to you? Why?" (or, "Why not?")

HINT: HOW "GLOBAL" ARE YOU? The interviewer wants to see how curious you are about other aspects of life, and what interests you have beyond work. (This question has some overlap to questions #36 and #41.)

Too, your answer will give an indication as to how worldly you are, if you concern yourself about others beyond your city, and (perhaps) what some of your pet causes are.

HINT: BE AWARE OF THE ORGANIZATION'S NATIONAL / INTERNATIONAL ACTIVITIES AND / OR OFFICES. Make certain that you have some idea as to what is happening with the company on a national / international basis (if applicable), and what problems or opportunities may be confronting them now because of their geographic location. Not only does this show that you are knowledgeable in general, but that you have taken the time to really learn about the company.

#50

"Do you plan on furthering your education?"

HINT: ANSWER "YES." If you have college studies or a college degree, you have already shown the employer that education is important to you. If you are in the process of finishing your GED, of course tell the interviewer this. If you have graduated from high school and do plan to attend college, again, tell the interviewer. If you have not completed high school or grammar school, and are not now currently doing so, tell the interviewer you plan on finishing (and if grammar school, continuing on to at least get a GED). And don't forget: there are other methods of furthering education, even if you are not interested in continuing with college. ALWAYS ANSWER "YES" TO THIS QUESTION!

YOU NEED TO STAY ON TOP OF NEW TECHNOLOGY. We live in a world where information is becoming outdated at a much faster pace than just a few years ago, and you need to continually educate yourself so that you can stay on top of your field.

YOU BECOME A BETTER ASSET TO THE ORGANIZATION. There will be ample opportunity for you to take seminars, workshops, and courses that focus on technical and interpersonal matters, each of which will not only help you improve your skills, but also make you a better candidate for raises and promotions. Also: NEVER forget about mentioning your plans for self-study!!

<u>**HINT**</u>: **YOUR JOB COMES FIRST, EDUCATION SECOND.** In all instances, tell your employer that you will be furthering your education in your spare time (see question #3); you don't want him or her to get the impression that you will squeeze your job around your study schedule. Work must come first to the employer, so let him or her know that.

#51

"You are responsible for all your company's computer programs, and one night you're working late, cataloging them. The only other people in your building are a man in a wheelchair, a woman, the company president, and a child. Suddenly, a fire breaks out and you're in charge. Tell me the order of the people to go out of the building first, second, third, etc. -- and why."

<u>**HINT**</u>: **THE ANSWER LOOKS TO SEE HOW CONCERNED YOU ARE FOR OTHERS, HOW YOU VALUE OTHERS, AND HOW THOROUGH YOU THINK THROUGH UNEXPECTED SITUATIONS.** Somewhat similar to #42 in that this questions deals with an unusual situation, it also is a good way for the interviewer to get a better understanding of how you see yourself in comparison to others. While you are expected to by loyal to the company and its survival, it's also important that you show a concern for and sensitivity toward others.

ALL HAVE LEGITIMATE CLAIMS. Each of the individuals -- including you -- can make a legitimate claim to being the first out of the building. The wheelchair-bound man, because of his obvious difficulty in getting out by himself; the woman, because she IS a woman and our society is strong on "women and children first"; the company president, because he IS the president; the child, because not only is the country strong on "women and children first" but the child has the greatest number of life years to lose; and you, because you are the one person who can reprogram the computer files if they are lost in the fire.

TAKE A LOOK AT YOUR ANSWER OBJECTIVELY. While you are the only one who can reprogram the computer programs lost in the fire, it would also look very selfish on your part to go first, not to mention your indifference to the others. Also, imagine the public relations nightmare if you went first -- it would definitely hurt your firm's image. The same holds true if the company president went before the other three -- too "me" oriented, and, again, a terrible PR problem for the company.

YOU GO LAST. As for the woman, there is no indication that she would need any extra assistance in exiting the building. The company president also appears, from the initial description of the interviewer, to be fit. This leaves the handicapped man and the baby -- choose the baby first, the handicapped man second. Why? The baby is most vulnerable to smoke inhalation and very dependent on adults to help it through the early years of its life ... and, it IS a baby! The wheelchair-bound man, while certainly in need of assistance, is an adult and can at least help himself somewhat in surviving. The rest? The woman, the company president, then you -- if you do perish, you've saved four others, including two who probably would not have made it without your help ... and as much as you might like to think you are indispensable to the company, others CAN do the reprogramming. As for the company president going first, well, he not only is the company president but you were left in charge -- you must be there to oversee the TOTAL rescue of the others.

#52

"If you were told that you could only take one possession with you to heaven (assuming there is a heaven), what would it be and why?"

<u>HINT</u>: **YOUR CHOICE HELPS DEFINE THE "WHO" OF YOU.** Which object you pick will tell the interviewer much about what you REALLY cherish in your life, so choose wisely. The best answer will be that which is irreplaceable and / or has had a major impact on you -- letters from your now-deceased father, your wedding ring, a childhood memento, parole papers (if the interviewer knows you were incarcerated and if you consider the experience a major turning point in your life), etc. For those who choose money, titles, and the like they have quickly indicated that they view life and what is most valuable in a very superficial manner -- not the type of candidate most companies would be proud to have. And remember: the question uses the word "possession," so any answer that includes "my wife," "my husband," "my girlfriend," "my boyfriend," etc. is wrong -- people are NOT possessions!

REMEMBER: Each interview question adds to the portrait the interviewer is painting of you; each answer you give adds the color, tone, and quality of the portrait. Your goal is to have that portrait become so valuable that it's something the employer must have!

Chapter 8

"Were you ever in prison?" and Other Related Questions

"Do not be too timid and squeamish about your actions. All life is an experiment."

Ralph Waldo Emerson, American author & essayist

● TO REVEAL OR NOT REVEAL ●

They are almost always found on job applications and sometimes asked during the job interview: those questions that want to know whether you ever were arrested, spent time in prison, and several others that relate to your prison experience.

WHY THESE QUESTIONS ARE SO DIFFICULT TO ANSWER

Fear That You'll Lose the Job

Understandably, these are the most difficult for most ex-inmates to answer, because there tends to be a belief that if you answer the question honestly, you will automatically be turned down for the job. While this certainly happens, it does not happen as often as you might think ... and it can happen much less IF you know how to properly answer the "prison question."

Fear of Follow-Up Questions

In addition, if an ex-inmate does answer the question honestly, he or she knows that it will leave him / her open to a host of follow up questions: What were you in prison for? How can I be certain that you won't do this again? Can you assure me that this won't hinder your job performance? What do you feel you've learned from your prison experience?

These, and similar questions, make the ex-inmate feel as if he's / she's on trial again. Too often, because the ex-inmate does not know how to handle these questions, that individual does poorly in his or her answers, and loses the job.

IS IT LEGAL TO ASK SOMEONE IS HE / SHE HAS EVER BEEN ARRESTED OR CONVICTED OF A CRIME?

It Depends!

Asking job applicants if they have been arrested or convicted of a crime may be legal or illegal, depending on the state in which you plan to work. In my state (New York), for example, it is illegal to ask applicants if they have ever been arrested, but legal to ask if they ever have been convicted.

To be certain, you should contact your state's Department of Labor. Usually, it will have a Division of Human Rights or Division of Affirmative Action Programs or something similar that can supply you with the rulings on these questions.

If you are unable to obtain the address of your state's Department of Labor closest to you, write the U.S. Department of Labor for that information. Their address: U.S. Department of Labor, Employment & Training Administration, 200 Constitution Avenue, NW, Washington, DC 20210.

When It's Illegal To Ask About Being Arrested

If it is illegal, it's usually based on the following two reasons:

(1) Because blacks are arrested more than whites, a federal court has held, such a question could be discriminatory against blacks.

(2) The Equal Employment Opportunity Commission has held that such a question violates Title VII. It reasons that the mere request may discourage applicants or induce an individual to give false information, thus opening the employer or interviewer to possible penalties.

REMEMBER: Don't ever tell an interviewer it's illegal to ask a question about your prison background, for while you may win the battle you'll most assuredly lose the war.

EMPLOYERS DON'T ALWAYS FOLLOW THE RULES

However, what is not supposed to be asked and what is actually asked are often the same thing.

When the Employer Doesn't Know You've Been in Prison

What prompts employers to suspect you've been in prison? They may notice something unusual in the dates you put down on your resume (see Chapter 4), there may be something you said in the interview to arouse their suspicion, you may fit a pre-conceived image the interviewers have of someone they think sounds like or looks like he / she has spent time in prison, or it may simply be a routine question they ask of all applicants.

WHY MANY EMPLOYERS WILL NOT HIRE EX-INMATES

Many employers will justify not hiring a convicted felon as a business necessity for such reasons as:

● **BONDING.** Not being able to bond the person (see Chapter 11, pages 420-421).

● **RISK FACTOR.** Believing that the type of crime you committed will cause you to be a risk in the job for which you are applying. (Example: if you were convicted for use or distribution of cocaine and you apply for a job working in a hospital pharmacy, the employer might think it will be too tempting to have you near the medications.)

◔ **HOSTILITY.** Detecting hostility or anger in your attitude about your prison experience (see Chapter 2 and Chapter 3) that the employer thinks may carry over to your job performance or ability to get along with co-workers.

● **MORAL CHARACTER.** Believing that you are of "poor moral character" and thus not a good example as a representative for his / her company or organization, or that you will have a negative influence on others in the company (if they know you are an ex-inmate).

IF AN EMPLOYER DOESN'T WANT TO HIRE YOU BECAUSE OF YOUR PRISON RECORD

If an employer DOES believe that something regarding your conviction (or prison sentence, etc.) will cause a problem, he/she usually will not come right out and tell you. Why? With so many legal decisions happening daily, and more employers open to possible suits against them for discrimination (due, again, to new court rulings), the employer is less likely to be candid with you.

It's Easy for the Employer to Cover the Real Reason

Instead, you would probably receive a rejection letter or phone call from the employer that says, in essence, "I'm sorry, but your qualifications do not match our needs. Best of luck." This is very safe, and it is almost always possible to somehow prove that you just don't have the background that the employer is looking for. (Remember: if the nature of your conviction is at odds with the company's product or service, the employer may be within his / her rights to turn down an ex-inmate.)

It's Your Word vs. The Employer's Word

If an interviewer DOES tell you that you won't get the job because you were arrested, for your conviction, etc., he / she can always later deny saying it ... and whom do you think most people will believe? What goes on in that room during your interview only the two of you will know.

IF YOU THINK IT'S ILLEGAL. Somehow, save the application (or other employment form) you had to fill out. Take it to your state's Department of Labor (Division of Human Rights, Affirmative Action, etc.), prove you had qualifications at least equal to other applicants, and you possibly can take legal action against the employer. But: it will be on you to prove the burden of guilt, very difficult to do without much documentation and proof.

TELLING THE TRUTH ABOUT YOUR PRISON BACKGROUND

Lying About Your Prison History Seems Safer

OTHERS HAVE TOLD YOU TO LIE. Many, many inmates and newly released ex-inmates are told by others (including family, friends, career counseling agencies, other employers ... and ESPECIALLY other inmates!) to LIE about having been in prison. If you deny it, the reasoning goes, chances are between slim and next-to-none that the employer will double check to see if you were telling the truth.

YOU MAY HAVE LIED ABOUT IT IN THE PAST. If you've been in prison prior to this experience, you may have lied in the past when applying for a job, and had nothing happen. Or you may believe that by giving a strong non-prison image and having nothing on your resume about prison, the employer will never suspect that you were incarcerated if you lie about it.

5 Reasons to Tell the Truth About Being in Prison

(1) MORE COMPANIES ARE CHECKING OUT APPLICANTS' BACKGROUNDS. With crime always a concern in this country (with more sophisticated crimes seemingly taking place every day, including larger number of crimes taking place over the Internet), and a constant stream of news in the papers and on TV & radio about crime, an increasing number of companies are going through more exhaustive measures when hiring to find possible problems with potential employees.

Personality tests, a meeting with a company psychologist, background checks through firms hired to research the credentials of your resume, and -- depending on the nature of the job -- fingerprint or social security scans with law enforcement agencies are used. Sometimes you know these are being included as part of your interview process, sometimes not.

(2) YOU WILL PROBABLY EVENTUALLY LET IT SLIP THAT YOU SPENT TIME IN PRISON. More often than not, it is not so much in the interview where an ex-inmate raises questions about himself / herself, but when he / she has the job. Understand that the interview is something you prepare for, it is showtime, you have rehearsed and gone over your answers to possible questions, have practiced your body language and speaking, and studied just about everything that you think can come up.

But like the exam you study hard for, and then forget most of the information you've memorized after you take the test, once you have the job you tend to let your guard down. You are more casual, you don't have to feel that each moment of each day has to be as perfect as it had to be for interview.

It could be an offhand comment, your reaction to something said or done, or during a casual conversation with a fellow employee after work: you let it slip that you were or may have been in prison. Suddenly, there is a contradiction in what you told the employer when you were hired. Just cause has now been given the employer to fire you, and -- at the very least -- certainly to question your honesty about other things.

(3) AN UNEXPECTED VISIT FROM A PAROLE OFFICER OR A FORMER PRISON "BUDDY."
It has happened more times than you think that a parole officer has called at your new job or come around to see you, just to make certain you are working. Or perhaps an old "buddy" from your prison days (or someone else who knew you were in prison) stops by and accidentally mentions that you were in prison. In either case, you have again shown the employer that you were not up front and honest when asked about having been arrested, in prison, etc.

(4) A PROMOTION OR ADDED RESPONSIBILITIES MAY RESULT IN A BACKGROUND CHECK. Very few people -- ex-inmate or not -- think about this yet it happens every day: the unexpected background check. This may be the result of a promotion that includes a company car, and thus a company policy check of your Department of Motor Vehicles record ... it could be added responsibilities that means you must now be bonded, and thus the bonding company has to do its standard check of your background ... perhaps your doing electrical repair work on the premises of a pharmaceutical firm, and its policy is that anybody working on company property must be checked for prior controlled substance abuse problems or convictions related to drugs. The list goes on. But in each instance, your background IS checked (and you won't always know about it) and if you denied having been incarcerated during the interview, the company will now find out that you lied. Care to guess at your job security?

(5) SOME PEOPLE JUST WANT TO MAKE TROUBLE FOR YOU. Unfortunately, there are those people who want to make trouble for you after your release, who want to make certain that people find out you spent time in prison ... especially those people you'd prefer didn't know.

Examples: Who are these people? Ex-lovers, wives, and husbands; past friends whom you have decided not to hang around with because they could be bad influences; the person(s) upon whom you committed your crime; reporters (either claiming that they are doing a public service or merely looking to increase their ratings / newspaper circulation); inmate buddies of yours still in prison who, for whatever reason, have it in for you -- all of these have been guilty of purposely letting an employer know that you were in prison.

Again, the end result is that you did not tell the employer the truth about your "item" when asked during the interview. At the most, this is just cause to fire you. At the least, it creates doubts about your credibility. *It's much better that your employer first hears about your past incarceration from you, not someone else!*

> **REMEMBER:** The lie denying you've been in prison might give you a brief smile, but the truth that admits your incarceration can bring long-term happiness.

> **REMEMBER:** Credibility is earned over a period of time, not something that you can pick up on demand at a drive-through window.

VOLUNTEERING YOUR PRISON RECORD IF IT'S NOT REQUESTED

If the subject of having been arrested or spending time in prison never comes up in the interview, and was not addressed in any manner on the employment application, should you mention it?

If Certain Factors Do or Probably Will Exist, the Answer is YES

(1) TO SPARE A LIE OR A MISPERCEPTION. The answer would be yes, of course, if you can pretty well count on one of the previous 5 items (detailed on pp. 320-321) coming up. You may have heard the saying, "the best defense is a good offense," and here it would be a wise thing to do. As stated earlier, the perception many business professionals have of the ex-inmate is not the most flattering, so your honesty can go a long way in turning a skeptical employer around. And, again, you don't want to be caught in a lie.

(2) EMPLOYERS MAY "REWARD" YOUR HONESTY. There are occasions when an employer will give you a plus point for revealing something about yourself that you didn't have to reveal. Telling the interviewer you were in prison makes the interviewer believe that you feel you have nothing to hide, and that you are honest and self-confident enough to reveal this aspect of your past ... and thus can probably be counted on to be an honest and dependable employee.

(3) WHEN THE EMPLOYER IS MORE ACCEPTING OF EX-INMATE EMPLOYEES. You will, of course, run into employers and interviewers who are very accepting and open to not only your honesty but to you wanting to start over. As I told you in the Introduction, there are more ex-inmates than ever in the work force (many in positions to hire), as well as many companies with ex-inmates working for them who have proved to be excellent employees. Thus, telling the truth about your prison record is not, quite frankly, as big a deal as it would have been just a few years ago.

If Certain Factors Do or Probably Will Exist, the Answer is NO

(1) IF YOU HAVE AN EMPLOYMENT TRACK RECORD, THE CHANCES OF YOUR PRISON RECORD BEING EXPLORED ARE SLIGHT. Employers tend to be more concerned about your most recent history. If you've been out of prison for some time and have established a good job history, something that happened a year or so ago will not draw the same attention of something that happened only a few weeks ago. There are exceptions: some professions, especially government jobs, the computer industry, and other "sensitive" professions (as well as situations mentioned on page 321, #4) do a routine background check of most applications.

[**NOTE**: There are many ex-inmates who have been out of prison for some time, and successfully lie about their prison background when asked if they've been arrested, convicted, etc. Most are off parole and almost always have established a good record of employment, community involvement, etc., with no indication of something that might give them away as an ex-convict. Obviously, this is a choice you have -- but it's a gamble. Again, there are always the possibilities that I have listed on pages 320-321.]

(2) WHEN COMPANIES ARE HIRING ENTRY-LEVEL POSITIONS AND ONLY NEED THE BAREST OF REQUIREMENTS. There are many hiring scenarios when companies are in need of people who have minimal skills, are primarily concerned with getting a body into a work situation, and / or pay a minimum or slightly-above minimum wage. In situations like this, there is a high rate of turnover, and it would cost the companies an extensive amount of money and hours to do a background check on each person. Thus, you would probably not need to reveal your prison background.

REMEMBER: When you lose an interview or a job because you were honest about your background as an ex-inmate, two more will take its place.

THE PROFESSIONS THAT ARE HARDEST / EASIEST ON EX-INMATES REGARDING THE QUESTION OF INCARCERATION

HARDEST. Those professions that are extremely concerned about their image -- banks, insurance companies, hospitals, for example -- tend to be hardest. Also, those professions where high security, government regulated products, and exceptional concern for customers or clients are involved are also strong in background checks. These would include day care centers, pharmaceutical companies, liquor stores and distributors, virtually all avenues of the computer industry, high-tech manufacturers, and schools.

EASIEST. Those professions that have high turnover of employees -- restaurants, car dealerships, sales organizations, telemarketing, call service centers, construction, general labor are examples -- are usually not as thorough in their follow-up check of information supplied by the applicant on his or her resume and during the interview.

Often, these need to fill jobs in less time than a background check would take. Of course, this does not guarantee that a background check of some sort won't occur.

● TRICKS OF THE INTERVIEWER ●

As stated at the beginning of this chapter, it is possible your state has made it illegal to ask ANY of the sample questions (and variations of these) found later in this chapter. (This might also include questions on employment applications and any other questions asked during the interview, again depending on your state laws.) However, there are ways in which an employer can still learn about your arrest, prison, etc., record while staying within the law. These include:

(1) BONDING. The employer will ask you if you've ever been bonded; if you answer "yes," he / she will then ask you, "With whom were you bonded?" If you've previously been bonded as an ex-inmate just out of prison, it was through the Federal Bonding Program (see pages 420-421); when you reveal this, you've opened the door to a line of questioning about your current status. Of course, the employer could also ask if you've ever had trouble getting bonded, another question that -- through your subsequent answer -- may lead to the interviewer learning of your current status as an ex-inmate.

(2) YOUR RESUME. Unexplained large gaps of time or questionable job descriptions may tip an interviewer to you being an ex-inmate. (See Chapter 4, "Writing and Using Resumes.")

(3) ASSISTANCE PROGRAMS. Employers may ask you if you are eligible for Job Training Partnership Act (JTPA) or Work Tax Credit (WTC) programs. If you answer "yes," they may ask why you are eligible. (See Chapter 11, pages 420-422.)

(4) "FLEXIBILITY" QUESTIONS. Interviewers may need to ask if you are free to travel out of the state or country, if you have a valid driver's license, if you can work the "graveyard" shift, or if you mind calling on bar and tavern accounts. Such questions may interfere with the terms of your parole, causing you to possibly reveal your prison background.

(5) NICKNAMES. Almost everyone in prison has one or more nicknames (mine were "Doc," "Hamster," and "Scrounge"!). If you include this on your resume or tell the interviewer that you prefer being called "XXXX," he / she may ask you how or where you got the nickname ... and you just may tell its prison history!

● THE JOB APPLICATION ●

WHEN THE APPLICATION ASKS "THE QUESTION"

One of the more hotly debated questions amongst inmates and ex-inmates -- not to mention correctional educators and counselors -- is how ex-inmates should answer the question on an application that deals with one having been arrested or convicted of a felony. First, remember what I said earlier: the legality of this question depends on the individual states' rulings. However, when it does appear, it's important that you approach the question and your subsequent response in the same thorough, thought-out manner that you've done all other aspects of your job search. Make the wrong decision in answering this question and you stand a good chance of NOT being interviewed for the job.

First, let's take a look at the most common forms this question takes:

The 3 Most Common Forms of "The Question" That Appears on Employment Applications

(1) *"Were you ever arrested or convicted of a crime? If you answer yes, give details below."*

(2) *"Were you ever convicted of a crime other than a misdemeanor? If you answer yes, give details below."* *(Alternate: "Have you ever been convicted of a crime in the past seven years, excluding misdemeanors and summary offenses, that have not been annulled, expunged, or sealed by a court?")*

[IMPORTANT NOTE: More and more job applications are asking the question in a form such as, *"Have you been convicted of a felony during the past seven years?"* This is done due to the Statute of Limitations -- 7 years -- and certain lawsuits that have been filed under this. Please do NOT let this question trick you: if you had been in prison for more than seven years, you probably were not CONVICTED of the crime in the past seven years. Likewise, if you've been out of prison and crime-free for several years, it may have been more than seven years since you were convicted of the crime. If either of these situations holds true, you may HONESTLY answer "no" to the question.]

(3) *"Did you ever spend time in prison as an inmate? If you answer yes, in the space below give the nature of your crime and how long you were in prison."*

Unlike an Interview, You Don't Have Your Mouth Available

In the interview you have your mouth to speak for you, and it can add, subtract, highlight, explain, and downplay the information on your application and resume. (See Chapter 6.)

But an application does not allow for this, and while you can give additional information on your resume, most applications are cut-and-dry, wanting only direct answers to the questions.

6 Tips For Handling "The Question" on a Job Application

(1) DON'T LIE! Just as the chances of getting caught lying to a similar question in the job interview are great, so are they with a job application. It's not worth it ... and when you do lie and get away with it, you constantly have to create more lies to protect the first lie and be on your guard against slipping up and revealing your lie.

(2) DON'T MERELY WRITE "YES" AND EXPLAIN THE NATURE OF YOUR CRIME. Chances are very high that you will not get in for the interview if you handle the question this way. Why? You are offering the interviewer a reason NOT to interview you -- without meeting you, without listening to you, he or she who reads the application only knows that you were in prison and you committed a crime. Any fear that person may have had previously has just been increased a bit by you. You want your mind and mouth and live presence to interact with the interviewer, not merely a piece of paper.

(3) DON'T LEAVE THE QUESTION BLANK. This only draws attention to it, and often leaves the reader wondering if you have been arrested, convicted, etc. By not filling it in, you are being, in essence, semi-dishonest, giving the impression of saying, "Oh, I hope the interviewer won't notice, I hope the interviewer won't notice." Hey, get real -- the interviewer will notice!

(4) LET YOUR "STATUS" AS AN EX-INMATE WORK FOR YOU! How many employers have met and talked with a "real, live ex-inmate"? Not many, and there is still this *National Enquirer*-like draw to anyone who has spent time in prison. So, instead of answering "yes" with the details, write in "yes; will discuss in interview" OR "yes; please see attached explanation" (the interview answer hints, pages 337-338, suggest what to include in this written explanation, a most POSITIVE approach to your time inside) OR "yes; please see attached resume" (refer to Chp. 4 for information on writing a "prison" resume).

When an interviewer sees this answer, you are offering bait to go in and speak with him or her, with what it seems like is a promise to reveal the sordid details of your past once in the interview. Once in, of course, you then DO have the one-on-one meeting where your mind and mouth can take over and show yourself to be the well-prepared, professional candidate you are.

(5) THINK AHEAD. Something that has worked out well for many inmates has to do with an item that was mentioned in Chapters 1 & 2: THINKING AHEAD. This involves having prepared, on only one page, the positives that you gained from your prison experience (or a note that has been included in your resume doing the same thing). In addition to using the pluses suggested for writing the "prison" resumes (Chp. 4), you'll also find several suggestions of what to include in this note from the various sample interview questions that appear later in this chapter.

(6) IF YOU ARE A JUVENILE OR YOU WERE CONVICTED OF A MISDEMEANOR. If the job application merely asks, "Have you ever been convicted of a crime?", this would obviously include both felonies and misdemeanors. Your answer, then, would be the same as suggested in #4, above. If it only asks for felony convictions, then you can honestly answer, "no."

However, if you are a convicted juvenile you can answer "no" to this question, because you ARE of juvenile status . *It is important, though, to check with your state for the specific guidelines, as these vary on a state-by-state basis.*

Some General Tips on Filling Out the Job Application

(1) THOROUGHLY READ THE APPLICATION, INCLUDING FINE PRINT. The application may ask for some specific information that you don't have; also, some questions may not pertain to you.

(2) HAVE A FACT SHEET READY TO FILL IN THE ITEMS THAT WOULD NOT USUALLY APPEAR ON YOUR RESUME. Name of supervisors, company street addresses and phone numbers, your salaries (starting and ending), reason for leaving, specific dates of employment, military information (if applicable), and names / addresses / phone numbers of references are the most common information usually needed on a job application that would not be included on a resume.

(3) FILL IN ALL ITEMS THAT PERTAIN TO YOU. Not only does an application list facts about you, it also gives the employer an indication of your attention to detail and thoroughness. Remember: if it's not filled out properly, you may not be considered for employment!

(4) NEATNESS & SPELLING DO COUNT. As you've no doubt noticed, I've stressed the importance of taking your time when doing any part of the job search. This also holds true for the job application. In addition to being certain that your information is accurate and all pertinent questions are answered, don't forget to check for spelling errors (if you are a weak speller, take along a pocket dictionary) and don't get coffee stains or the like on the application. These small things tell the interviewer much about you -- and as was discussed in Chapter 7 under dressing correctly for the interview, you want to be certain that you begin on all positive or neutral notes -- nothing negative!

(5) ALWAYS COME PREPARED. This means having YOUR own pen, YOUR own pad or blank sheets of paper (in case you need to take down information), and -- if possible -- a small stapler so that you can attach the job application to your resume. Again, these are relatively small items but they all help paint a picture of you as being prepared ... and this leaves a nice impression on the interviewer.

(6) DON'T FORGET YOUR MANNERS! "May I please have an employment application?" ... "Excuse me, ma'am, could you please tell me where I could find the employment office?" ... "Thank you very much for the application; here it is, all filled out." ... "I'd appreciate it if you could answer a question for me." -- all of these are examples of simply using good manners. They may have nothing to do with your skills and abilities, but boy do they go a long way in making a positive impression!

(7) AVOID THE MOST COMMON MISTAKES: Not signing the application ... using a pencil (it can smudge; bring an erasable pen) ... for any "Comments" section, sell yourself, rather than simply saying, "I'd really like a job" or something else that is not only obvious but does nothing to impress the interviewer.

REMEMBER: Honesty is like a balloon: once a tiny hole appears, it will never again be viewed as whole.

The Questions

"So ... what's this prison thing all about?"

PREPARE YOURSELF FOR INTERVIEW QUESTIONS ABOUT PRISON

<u>*My Story*</u>

A story about what happened to me within the first few weeks of my release is appropriate here. Like most newly released ex-inmates, I needed employment. I wasn't sure if I wanted to return to the work I did prior to my arrest -- career counseling, writing, and corporate training -- or something else.

One day I was reading the want ads and noticed that a just-launched newspaper was looking for a Managing Editor. I applied, and was hired. (No, the question of my having been arrested or in prison never came up, there was no application ... and I never brought it up.)

Two weeks into my job, I received a call from a local TV reporter who told me he had heard about our efforts to publish this newspaper, and asked if he could interview me. Well, to say that I was excited would be an understatement.

Here, I thought, was my opportunity to show those people who knew I had been in prison that I was just as good as anyone else. I also felt this was a badge of sorts for me: I finally had put my prison life behind me and returned to a "normal" life, as if my years in prison had not happened.

The day of the interview, I was dressed in my best suit; I was happy; I was looking forward to this session with the reporter. A knock on my office door, and a reporter entered, microphone in hand, with a cameraman whirring away behind him. Then came the question: "Excuse me, Mr. Sull, is it true you spent several years in a state prison?"

Well, I was surprised and stunned by his question. Not in my wildest imagination did I think such a question would turn up. In the moment I had to think -- it seemed like forever -- I knew I had three choices: to deny I was in prison (which would only cause him to press harder or do more research); to say "no comment," which is the same as admitting that I had been in prison except indicating that I was trying to hide it; or simply admitting that, yes, I had been in prison.

I looked right into the camera, and told the truth.

The newspapers, as well as two other TV stations and one radio station, also picked up the story. That evening and through the next day, more than a million-and-a-half residents of my hometown area knew that I had been in prison.

The Two Lessons Learned From My TV Episode

There are two very important lessons to be learned from what happened to me:

(1) EXPECT TO BE ASKED, AND BE PREPARED TO ANSWER, ANY QUESTIONS THAT COME UP REGARDING YOUR TIME AS AN INMATE.

YOU CAN BE ASKED AT ANY TIME. The suggestions I'm about to give you are, of course, especially important for the interview, but as you can see from what happened to me, you can be asked about having been in prison at any time.

And it could happen almost anywhere: it could be at a family gathering or out with friends; it could be in conversation with some fellow employees at work or with a new mate; it might be in a situation such as mine, where you are constantly in the public eye and always open to questions.

4 Guidelines to Help You Respond to Interview Questions About Prison

(1) ASSUME THAT A QUESTION ABOUT YOUR PRISON TIME WILL BE ASKED IN AN INTERVIEW. Always have in mind that anyone can ask you a question or questions about being in prison. When you walk in for that interview, if the employer does not know you have been in prison, you must play "worst case scenario," that is, you assume that sometime during the interview THE question will be asked. If it isn't asked, that's fine (but always follow the guidelines outlined on pp. 322-323 when the question is not asked).

If it is asked, however, you won't be caught off guard (like I was); you'll be prepared and answer it as if you were expecting it all along. (For some related information on answering any question as if you expected it, see Chapter 7.)

(2) HAVE ANSWERS TO PRISON-RELATED QUESTIONS PREPARED. Know how you are going to answer questions that deal with your time in prison: it's one thing to expect a question or questions about being in prison, it's another thing to answer them smoothly. The sample questions and hints for answering them at the end of this chapter should help you.

(And it can be a big help if you **have someone role play a job interview with you** prior to your real interview, asking you, amongst other questions, prison-related ones. This way you'll feel more confident of your answers when asked the same or similar questions in the real job interview.)

(3) DON'T LOSE YOUR TEMPER. Don't ever let a question about being in prison get you angry or upset. In Chapter 3, I talked about "DONT'S" ... and I mentioned that anger, hostility, etc., do nothing except put you in the stereotype mold that many businesspeople in the free world already hold of an ex-inmate. This becomes especially true in an interview session, where you are trying to impress the interviewer as a well-qualified job applicant.

Accept the fact that your time behind bars or fence is going to follow you around once in a while. Rather than fight it, take the question in stride, and answer it / discuss it in as calm, cool, and self-assured a voice as you would if someone asked you for your name.

REMEMBER: You can't be as good as any other job applicant, you can't be better than any other job applicant -- you have to be the best job applicant.

---

(4)   NEVER TELL INTERVIEWERS YOU DON'T KNOW WHY YOU COMMITTED THE CRIME. To say "I don't know why I did it" or "Just for the fun, I guess" or similar answers tell the interviewers you haven't given much thought to why you committed the crime -- and they probably will not give much thought to hiring you.

(2) THINK OUT WHAT YOUR REACTIONS AND ACTIONS WILL BE IF THERE ARE ANY NEGATIVE CONSEQUENCES TO YOU AS A RESULT OF YOU TELLING THE TRUTH ABOUT HAVING BEEN INCARCERATED.

Negative Actions & Feedback Can Happen Anytime

In the episode I told about myself, I obviously was not prepared. While I was concerned about the effect the TV story would have on my integrity with others, I was more concerned about how it would affect my family and the newspaper. But I hadn't thought through what I would do in a situation like mine.

For nearly a year after my story hit the TV, radio, and newspaper, I received at least two anonymous messages daily on my answering machine telling me to get out of town, calling me names, or threatening me ... all because I was an "ex-con."

Because of the nature of my job, I was highly exposed to the public, and thus there was a much greater risk factor involved in more people knowing about my time in prison. Unless you have a job similar to this one, or you were incarcerated for an extremely heinous crime. the chances of something this major happening to you are slight.

HOWEVER ... there are very cruel people in this world, as you might find out after your release (or may have learned in a prior release). While you may want to put your prison experience behind you, you ALWAYS will be an ex-inmate, and thus a possible target of name-calling, dislike, and / or mistrust for others. The wise ex-inmate, however, learns the right way to respond, as the next section shows.

How to Handle Negative Reactions When Others Learn You're an Ex-Inmate

(1) DON'T DWELL ON ANY NEGATIVE REACTION TO YOU AS AN EX-INMATE. If you lose out on getting an interview, lose out on a job during the interview, lose your job, or have people call you names / say nasty things about you because you told the truth about being in prison or they found out from someone else, FORGET ABOUT IT!

No "prison mentality!" Yes, you will be angry, frustrated, disappointed, and hurt, but it is much better for you to show that you do not have a "prison mentality." People will have greater respect for you. If you yell, fight, or snap back, however, you are simply proving what many already believe: that you ARE lower than most other people!

[**NOTE #1:** It not only helps you but helps better the image of all ex-inmates if, when someone directly says something negative to you about being an ex-inmate, you respond with, *"Yes, that's EX-inmate ... **being in prison was the best thing that ever happened to me,** because I really turned my life around."* This is something that won't be expected by the other person ... especially if you say it in a very nice, matter-of-fact, and friendly manner!]

[**NOTE #2:** If the interviewer tells you that **you can't be considered because of the type crime for which you went to prison,** or simply says that the company has a policy against hiring any ex-felons, DON'T GET ANGRY OR UPSET! Any chances of you changing his / her mind or re-applying at a later time will be blown if you "lose your cool!" Rather, continue to try and sell yourself through your many positives, don't hesitate to ask for other names the interviewer might be able to give you as potential job leads, and indicate that you'd like to keep in touch as you are very interested in the position. By doing these three things alone you are helping to show the interviewer -- and the company -- that an ex-inmate can be a professional, serious worker who can make a good contribution to his / her company.]

333

[**NOTE# 3:** Yes, you can protest or fight what you consider to be **discrimination.** Many times, you will be right. Just keep in mind the time, possible cost, and effort on your part this will take.]

> **REMEMBER: Don't ever forget that you are just as good as anyone else, no matter if you were in prison.**

(2) **CONSIDER THE SOURCE.** You must also consider the source of the person who denies you a job or says something negative because you were in prison. That individual is ill-informed, possibly afraid (most likely from the many sensational stories about inmates he / she has read in the papers, heard on the news, or seen in movies), and certainly is not looking at you BENEATH THE SURFACE, as a human being. It is his or her loss, ultimately, not yours; it is he or she who is being the fool, not you.

(See Chapter 5 for guidelines on writing cover letters / letters of application for various ways of discussing your prison experience.)

> **REMEMBER: Do not give someone the benefit of being able to say, "See I told you: once an inmate, always an inmate."**

SAMPLE QUESTIONS RELATING TO YOUR PRISON EXPERIENCE

Learn from these Questions

Like the general questions that were explained in Chapter 7, the prison-related questions in this chapter are not the only ones that can be asked. While they are the most common, it is always possible to get questions not listed here. However, you can learn enough from how the questions listed here are answered so you can easily answer any other prison-related question.

The Questions

#1

"Were you ever arrested?"

HINT: DON'T BE A JERK! As discussed earlier in this chapter, this question may or may not be legal. Many ex-inmates, however, don't know this. Don't answer by saying something such as, "Excuse me, but isn't it illegal to ask me that question?" You do nothing more than give the interviewer an excuse for not hiring you.

He or she might think of you as being uncooperative, trying to hide something, a troublemaker, someone who might cause trouble in his organization. Instead, accept the question and answer it truthfully.

HINT: EMPHASIZE THE POSITIVES. I mentioned earlier about the best defense being a good offense. When a question such as this is asked, it gives you an opportunity to do two things: to show a positive and to throw the interviewer off.

As an example, you might say, "It was one of the best things that ever happened to me." The interviewer will not be expecting this type of answer, and will certainly be curious as to what you mean. When he or she asks you to explain your answer, talk about a few of the positives that were discussed in Chapter 2. (Whether talking about only arrest or arrest and conviction, there are positives from each experience.)

HINT: DON'T FORGET THE WORD "BUT..." Many, many inmates answer this question (as well as the next one, #2) by telling what they were arrested or convicted for, then throw in the word "but," followed by such things as "I've changed my life around" or "I earned a GED while in prison" or "Prison was a really positive experience" or something similar. **Don't bother with this approach!** You've started out with a negative, and chances are slim that what comes after the "but" is going to be heard or carry much weight. When you start off with a positive, however, you are not only throwing the interviewer off but you are accentuating what you should: your POSITIVES! (See Question #2, the hint at the bottom pf 336.)

HINT: IF NOT CONVICTED. As was discussed at the beginning of this chapter, being arrested does not necessarily mean being convicted -- the major reason why many states have made this question illegal to ask. If you were arrested but never convicted, there may or may not be a record of your arrest (depending on federal, state, or local policies) -- I mention this because employers still can check someone's rap sheet to see if you are lying.

If you have been arrested, however, and you feel that not admitting it might get you into some credibility problem, tell the truth but in a smart way. How? Something like this:

"Yes, I was arrested once for selling drugs, but never convicted. But that was a few years ago when I not only was younger but really didn't have a solid grip on what was important and what was stupid in life. The person who was arrested back there is not the person sitting here today, but I'll tell you: my arrest helped make me this excellent job candidate. How? Because it scared me pretty bad – sitting in that cell, getting fingerprinted, embarrassing my family; it all made me realize what really was important in life."

How Would You Answer This Question?

Now it's your turn. In the spaces below, write out the answer you would give if you were asked during an interview, "Were you ever arrested?"

_____

_____

_____

_____

_____

#2

"Were you ever in prison?" (Variations: [1] "So ... what's this prison thing all about?" [2] "Were you ever convicted of a crime?")

HINT: A QUESTION THAT CAN REALLY HELP YOU. The first three hints I gave in Question #1 apply here. However, this question already assumes that you were arrested, and goes right to heart of the matter: conviction and a subsequent prison sentence. (This question is usually the result of you being honest on the job application or the person knowing you were in prison some other way.) I truly enjoy this question being asked, because it is an opportunity to show others:

● I'm not trying to hide my prison experience
● I gained much from the time I spent locked-up
● I don't regard it as any big deal
● As a result of the experiences I had in prison, I am a much better qualified career counselor, speaker, trainer, and writer

336

A Key Point to Answering This Question

A key point to this question (and others like it) is that you must look at your prison experience not as time in prison, but rather X number of years of additional education at a specialized university ... a sabbatical that you were granted to do research ... a retreat from the world so you could pursue spiritual and intellectual studies.

Give positives. These type of approaches will let you have a more positive mental attitude, and begin to focus on the pluses that you gained from prison. Again, this is not what the interviewer will expect, and you will find that what could have been a negative has begun turning into a positive.

HINT: **THE FIRST FEW WORDS OF YOUR ANSWER ARE MOST IMPORTANT.** When you answer this question, and questions similar to it, keep in mind that interviewers hear most loudly the first few words of your answer. Thus, if you begin to answer this question by saying "Yes," the interviewer will usually not hear the pluses that follow your "yes" as clearly as he heard you admit that you spent time in prison. (And don't forget what was said about the word "but" under Question #1, page 335.)

Suggestions On How You Might Answer This Question

(1) *"One of the best periods of my life was the four years I spent in prison. As you know, many business people take various seminars and workshops to improve their skills. Well, my time in prison was the equivalent of several courses in interpersonal communications, time management, stress management, organization, sales techniques, and confidence building. In addition, my overall attitude changed from somewhat negative to very positive."*

(2) *"I consider my time in prison to be the most valuable education I had, and one of the major reasons why I am so qualified for this position. For two years I worked in all aspects of auto mechanics, and have the proven skills to work on cars, trucks, vans, and construction equipment."*

(3) *"I'm going to be the best cashier you have because of my time in prison. I really turned my attitude back to a positive one and learned how to handle negative situations, to talk with a variety of age backgrounds, to be patient, to listen, to use a computer, and to be more outgoing."*

(4) *"I never knew how valuable a prison education could be until I looked at the skills and experience I gained. For example, I was Treasurer of a Jaycees chapter, led tours inside the institution, helped out on visitor's day, and was elected cell unit representative for our block.*

"These leadership involvements, in addition to my experience as a typist aide in the Assistant Warden's office, have given me skills that many college students don't have when they graduate."

(5) "*I spent five-and-a-half years digging ditches, picking potatoes, and cleaning floors in prison. You are looking for a dependable, punctual, hardworking employee who doesn't drink and is not on drugs. I'm your person, and probably have better experience than most and as equally outstanding a work record as anyone else applying for this position.*"

(6) "*Oh, I'm quite happy that I had the time in prison because it gave me an opportunity to not only get an education, but to fully understand what I want to do: work in the health care field.*

"*I was a Dental Hygienist Aide for one-and-a-half years, and have excellent references from the dentist and dental hygienist. In addition, I also learned how to work extremely well with people.*"

2 Additional Items To Consider In Your Answer

There are many more types of scenarios that could be given, but I think you get an idea of the various ways you can approach this question. In each of these examples, there are two items that each answer contains, and must be considered in answering this question correctly:

(1) DON'T GIVE A "CUT-AND-DRY" ANSWER.   As I mentioned above, none of the answers begin with the word "yes," and, in fact, none of the examples answer the question AT ANY POINT with a "yes." Why? Words paint pictures for people, and some words are more picturesque and can either soften or harden an image based on the word(s) chosen. "Yes" is cut-and-dry, and too often will cut off other information included in your answer.

Keep the interviewer's attention. However, by choosing words that say the same thing (that is, admitting to having been in prison) but that are more picturesque and tell a story, the listener will be more inclined to listen to all of your answer. What this amounts to is the psychological use of the English language.

2) LEAVE NEGATIVES OUT OF YOUR ANSWER.   None of the above answer examples (page 337) to this question contains ANY negatives in them. It is very tempting to complain about the work you did, to tell someone that you would have liked to have done the work out of prison, to tell someone that you really had it rough, etc.

The interviewer wants positives. But the interviewer is not looking for your tale(s) of woe and grief. Rather, he / she simply wants positives from you or, at the very least, neutrals. Having admitted that you were in prison is, as was already discussed, a negative in the minds of most employers. It makes no sense to throw in additional negatives by complaining.

The two levels of interviewing. Also, keep in mind what was said in Chapter 6 about the two levels of interviewing ("who" versus "what"). If your answer contains complaints about various aspects of prison life, the interviewer may see this as a negative attitude on your part; someone with a chip on his / her shoulder; a person who does not TRULY know how to find the positives; an individual who will "air his / her dirty laundry" (and later, air the mistakes the company may make?) to those who should not hear about it. The result? You probably won't be hired.

How Would You Answer This Question?

Your turn, once more. In the spaces below, write out the answer you would give if asked, "So ... what's this prison thing all about?"

_____
_____
_____
_____
_____
_____

#3

"Do you feel you've been rehabilitated?" (variation: "Do you feel you've been habilitated?" In the English language, both words have come to mean pretty much the same thing: returning one to a useful life through education and / or therapy.)

<u>HINT</u>: Questions like this ask if you believe that you've:

● mended your ways
● learned right from wrong
● changed to the point that what landed you in prison cannot again happen
● "learned your lesson"

<u>HINT</u>: **MANY IN SOCIETY DO NOT BELIEVE THAT REHABILITATION IS POSSIBLE.**
It is important for you to understand why this question is being asked and the possible beliefs of the person asking this question when you give a "yes" type of answer.

Many people who have worked IN or visited IN a prison, as well as a vast majority of those who have never experienced a single day behind bars, believe that inmates cannot be rehabilitated, that prison only makes them more bitter, and that prison is nothing more than a school for thieves.

Most Ex-Inmates Want a Clean, Straight Life on the Outside

While it is certainly true that seasoned cons teach others the tricks of many trades (I sat in on quite a few of these when I was inside!), it is not true that all inmates leave prison feeling more bitter and having not learned much. In fact, just the opposite is true: the vast majority of those men and women who have spent time behind bars want only one thing: to make a straight and productive life for themselves on the outside.

Focus on the Positives

This includes using what you learned in prison -- even if this means learning how NOT to get into a fight, how NOT to let your temper explode, or how NOT to believe that everybody is out to get you.

As you've seen in questions #1 and #2 in this chapter, you have many positives that you can offer in almost any question about being arrested, being in prison, etc. Don't forget to include these in your answer to this question. And make sure you answer immediately: any delay will seem as if you're not sure!

HINT: BEGIN YOUR ANSWER WITH "YES." Whether or not the person asking the question believes in a prison's effectiveness at what is usually referred to as rehabilitation, it is a question that begs for a positive answer. Unlike question #2, where "yes" admitted to something negative, in THIS question it is advisable to begin with "yes."

MAKE IT ENTHUSIASTIC AND BELIEVABLE. Just a laid-back "yes" or a "yes" with an attitude (like a smirk or edge of bitterness in your voice) won't do you any good and, in fact, will probably hurt you. Rather, you need to get across the idea that you are certain of the positive effects incarceration has had on your life. Indeed, when the question is asked of you, saying a very enthusiastic "Yes!" or "Definitely!" or "Without a doubt!" can go a long way in beginning to erase any doubts the interviewer may have about you.

Don't Forget To Make Your Answer Into a Story

You still want to make your answer into a bit of a story (as explained in the previous two questions), but you first want to put the interviewer's mind at rest.

In your answer, what you are REALLY saying to him or her is, "Yes, I've learned never to do my evil deed again. Now, let me tell you some things I learned while in prison that not only guarantees I'm not the same person who committed the crime, but that what I've learned and how I am make me a qualified candidate for this job."

HINT: **INTERVIEWERS SOMETIMES ASK YOU QUESTIONS ABOUT YOUR PRISON EXPERIENCE OUT OF PERSONAL CURIOSITY.** If you don't know yet, you will quickly find out upon your release: the general public is fascinated with what goes on behind prison walls. So don't be surprised if you begin to get the feeling that the interviewer is asking you questions about your time in prison not only as a potential employer but also as a curious person.

I have found friends, colleagues, business associates, clients, and even family members fascinated by what I experienced when locked up ... and perhaps even more fascinated by what they THINK went on. Just accept this attitude as one that is common and part of human nature. (After all, aren't we all just a bit guilty of wanting to read, hear, and watch something that we would never want to do, but are glad that somebody else did so we can learn about it?)

(See page 327, #4, for additional comments on this subject.)

HINT: **THIS QUESTION OFTEN LEAVES THE DOOR OPEN FOR SIMILAR FOLLOW-UP QUESTIONS.** Questions such as this one often lead to opening up other questions about your prison life. Don't be surprised. Most times these additional questions, in fact, are asked to make certain you really ARE a changed person and would make a good employee, but other times the interviewer will also be asking just out of plain old curiosity (as mentioned at the beginning of this chapter and in the previous Hint) . As always, be courteous and polite.

HINT: **NEVER DISCUSS ANY ILLEGAL OR NEGATIVE PRISON ACTIVITIES IN WHICH YOU WERE INVOLVED.** *NEVER – and I mean NEVER – talk to a potential employer, or anyone in the slightest way connected to the company, about negatives you may have observed, been familiar with, or participated in while INSIDE prison!*

You know as well as I do that there are murders, rapes, fights, stabbings, stealing, drug dealing, prostitution, scams, and other such things that go on in many prisons. But knowing about them on the inside -- for whatever reason -- and talking about them on the outside are two different things.

It Doesn't Impress

Many ex-inmates think that it impresses someone in the free world when they brag about or mention something they did in prison that involves hurt, pain, greed, intimidation, etc. -- their "war stories." Well, it may impress some from a tabloid factor but in terms of helping you land (and keep) employment it will hurt you -- big time.

Prison Groupies Do Exist -- Stay Away from Them!

There are some people who do find it thrilling to know someone who did something very wrong that society does not accept. There are even women -- known as Prison Groupies -- who are extremely attracted to men who have been in prison. But not only do these people make up a very small minority of the free world population, they also are admiring ex-inmates for those same things that landed them / can land them in prison. This is NOT what you want to be respected or admired for!

Sure, it's very possible that you'll feel quite lonely on the outside -- not only will you not have your other prison buddies around (unless you happen to be in a halfway house, when others who can identify with what you're going through can be a big help!) but any status you may have held on the inside is gone the moment of your release.

It could be a real kick -- and perhaps make you feel like you've got a bit of status again -- if you find people on the outside who are attracted to you because you're an ex-inmate. But is this REALLY what you want people attracted to? I doubt it. Rather, let others grow to admire you and respect you as a good person and as a well-qualified, productive, and dependable employee. That's respect spelled R-E-S-P-E-C-T!

If You Need to Talk About The Negatives from Prison, Choose the Right Person

Let people come to know you because of the positives you offer. If you feel a need to talk about these prison negatives (for a reason other than because you think "it's cool" or because you want to scare someone), speak with a counselor, psychologist, social worker, clergy member, psychiatrist, family physician, or a trusted family member. Meanwhile, leave them out of the job interview!

How Would You Answer This Question?

In the spaces below, write out your answer for a question such as, "Do you feel you have been rehabilitated?"

_____

_____

_____

_____

_____

_____

_____

> **REMEMBER: Do you wish to make the jump from former inmate to present warthog? Let others cling onto the ugliness of your past and you will have joined company with this singular creature.**

#4

"What crime did you commit?" (variation: "Why were you in prison?"):

<u>**HINT**</u>: **ANSWER HONESTLY, BUT SOFTEN IT BY PUTTING YOUR ANSWER IN STORY FORM.** While this question cannot be danced around, the way you give your answer can soften the blow of the act you reveal that landed you in prison.

2 Examples: Which One Would You Choose?

Let me give you two examples as to how this question could be answered, and then you select the one which seems to have the more positive effect:

(a) *"I killed a man."*

(b) *"I was going through some pretty rough times at home. My husband left me, one of my children was on drugs, and I lost my job. One night my husband came home drunk, and started cursing me and beating me pretty bad. I couldn't stand it anymore, so I grabbed a gun and shot him."*

The Correct Answer Explained

In the second answer, (b), the ex-inmate is giving a background that led up to the one act for which she was convicted. Not only does it, perhaps, make the killing sound a bit more understandable, but by "hiding" the fact that she killed someone [dropping this fact inside the sentence, in example (b)], the act does not stand out ["*...and shot him*" doesn't sound as jarring as "*I killed a man*"], and thus its impact on the listener is not as harsh.

2 More Examples: Again, Which Would You Choose?

Again, choose the better of the two answers:

(a) *"For distributing cocaine."*

(b) *"I was working as a clerk in a jewelry store, not making too much money, when a friend of mine told me I could make a lot of money distributing cocaine. Well, I made a lot of money, all right, but it certainly wasn't worth the constant looking over my shoulder, wondering if I was going to get arrested or killed, and certainly not the time in prison.*

"I've come to realize it's better to earn less money and be able to enjoy life without breaking the law, worrying about getting hurt, or making up stories."

The Correct Answer Explained

For the same reasons listed in the first set of examples, here (b) is also correct. In addition, note that the correct answer also ends with a brief explanation of what the ex-inmate has learned from his/her prison experience and why he/she is certain that he'll/she'll never again distribute cocaine or return to prison. The story holds the interviewer's attention ... and gives assurances as to why this type of behavior will never be repeated, a most positive end to a negative question!

How Would You Answer This Question?

Now, it's your turn. In the spaces below, write out the answer you would give if asked a question such as, "What did you do to end up in prison?"

_____

_____

_____

_____

_____

_____

#5

"How can I be certain that you won't commit this crime again?"

HINT: **THE EMPLOYER IS LOOKING FOR ASSURANCE AND INTELLIGENCE.** If employers have reached the point of asking this question, they usually have already gotten over any surprise that you were in prison, have begun to see you as a well-qualified applicant, and are more than a little interested in hiring you for the position.

The Interviewer Needs 2 Things in Your Answer

(1) VALIDATION FROM YOU THAT YOUR DAYS OF BEING A CRIMINAL ARE OVER, that YOU will guarantee them they won't have to worry about you getting into trouble. The interviewers have already drawn positive conclusions based on the answers you have thus far given and the overall manner in which you have so far presented yourself.

What the employers do not yet have is YOUR assurance, either because one of their previous "prison questions" did not ask for such a validation, or you have not yet included it in one of your previous "prison answers." Once you give them an answer, you can almost hear them thinking, "well, that's what we thought, but we just needed to hear it from you."

(2) AN INTELLIGENT, SINCERE, WELL THOUGHT-OUT ANSWER SHOWING YOU TRULY UNDERSTAND WHY YOU DID THAT WHICH LANDED YOU IN PRISON, and what now leads you to be so positive it won't happen again. More than mere assurance from you, the employer wants to be certain you have spent time thinking about all the events and situations leading up to you being sent to prison, as well as what steps you have taken to make certain nothing similar will reoccur.

When an ex-inmate can sit down with another person and OBJECTIVELY, CALMLY, SINCERELY, and COOLLY discuss the reasons behind his / her going to prison and why he / she knows a repeat of a trip to prison is impossible, that ex-inmate will gain respect, admiration, and acceptance.

HINT: **GIVE AN IMMEDIATE POSITIVE RESPONSE.** Like the question that focused on rehabilitation, this question also needs an immediate, up front positive answer. Any delay in answering this question will give the impression that you're NOT sure it won't happen again ... and offer the interviewer what he / she needs not to hire you.

3 Examples of Possible Answers

(1) *"You won't ever have to worry about that; the person who committed that crime seven years ago is not the same person sitting here now. I was immature back then, and thought it was cool to break the law and take shortcuts to get what I wanted.*

"Being in prison was an excellent opportunity for me to grow up, to realize how much can be accomplished through honest work, and how nice it feels just to ride with everyone else in society, rather than against them. And I'll tell you: I truly feel sorry for the hurt I inflicted in those days."

(2) *"Because I give you my word, and while that may not have meant much two years ago, it means everything to me now. I learned a lot from my time locked up – including how to be the best metalworker your company will hire in a long time! I know those things I didn't care about too much before mean a great deal to me now.*

"I also know I got into trouble because I didn't really know how to study and felt I could never get a good paying job. All that's changed now. I respect people, I respect the law, and I really like the idea of being a regular person."

(3) *"Because I don't ever want to go back to prison again or hurt my family like I did. While there's much I learned in prison that has made me a better person, I also learned it's no fun being penned up and not being able to go to the store when you want or not being able to hold down a regular job. Also, my family means the whole world to me, and I'll never do anything to hurt them again.*

"I've worked through why I robbed the store, and besides knowing it's not the way to get along in the free world, it's just not worth the aggravation, hurt, loss of time, and loss of self-respect."

3 Similarities These Examples Share With Other Answers You've Given to Prison-Related Questions

You'll note in each of these examples there are similarities with some of the other prison questions:

(1) YOU WON'T BE GOING BACK TO PRISON. Up front, an immediate assurance to the interviewer that you won't be going back to prison.

(2) POSITIVES & AN UNDERSTANDING OF SELF. An expansion of your answer in the form of a story so you can show the interviewer WHY you know you won't be going back to prison, as well as adding a few of the pluses you gained from your prison experience.

(3) NO PRISON HORROR STORIES. No negatives or stories about the bad things that happened to you or that you saw while inside. (Example [3] of possible answers to this question, this page, talks about the general negative of being in prison, but immediately gives the interviewer a feeling of a positive answer by stressing the pluses the ex-inmate has missed: family, time, and freedom.)

How Would You Answer This Question?

Okay, time for you to take a turn at it. In the spaces below, write the answer you would give if asked a question similar to, "How can I be certain you won't commit this crime again?"

_____

_____

_____

_____

_____

_____

_____

_____

REMEMBER: Before you convince anyone else you won't again commit a crime you must first convince yourself.

#6

"What do you feel you've learned from your prison experience?"

HINT: PREVIOUS SAMPLE QUESTIONS IN THIS CHAPTER GIVE YOU SEVERAL SUGGESTIONS. By now, you should have a good idea of how to answer this question. Chapter 1 and Chapter 2 talked about this in general; this chapter's introduction and previous questions discuss this question in detail.

<u>**HINT**</u>: **AN EXCELLENT OPPORTUNITY TO SELL YOURSELF.** Probably the easiest of the prison questions to answer, as it gives you exactly what you want: an opportunity to sell all the positives that you gained from your prison experience. It is best to combine some education and/or job experience you gained with those interpersonal skills (time management, communication, etc.) that were discussed earlier, as well as mentioning how your attitude has changed for the better.

a neat thing to do. Be smart -- look at the specific job for which you're interviewing, then pick out those positives from your prison experience that fit it. What you're doing is offering the positives AND continuing to sell yourself SPECIFICALLY for the job!

<u>**HINT**</u>: **DON'T MAKE YOUR ANSWER TOO BRIEF.** You should not give an answer that is so short it really doesn't answer the question. "I learned how to sew" or "I learned to read" may be true, but answers like this are not giving the interviewer what he or she wants to hear.

Remember our friends "what" and "who" that were discussed in Chapter 6 on interviewing? Well, telling the interviewer that all you gained from your time in prison was learning how to sew or read is telling him or her nothing more than the "what" -- and interviews, you may remember, are searching for the "who" of you. Don't forget to add those personal improvements you gained from your time in prison.

<u>**HINT**</u>: **BE ENTHUSIASTIC IN YOUR ANSWER!** As in Question #3, it is important that you show the interviewer your excitement and true pleasure in what you've learned and how you've grown! Anything less will sound as if you are not sincere, and probably just giving the interviewer what you think he / she wants to hear. The interviewer is not stupid and will see through this immediately.

3 Examples of Possible Answers

(1) ANSWER WHEN YOU INTERVIEW FOR NO SPECIFIC JOB: *"I'm now very skilled at using the computer, including the most current software. In addition, I have my GED and this not only gave me valuable information but I learned to really appreciate the value and importance of learning. And having to interact everyday with a wide variety of people with various ethnic and religious backgrounds gave me an increased ability to work effectively with just about everybody!"*

(2) ANSWER WHEN INTERVIEWING FOR A SPECIFIC JOB (store clerk): *"I earned my GED while inside and through this I gained good math, problem-solving, writing, and reading skills. Also, I used to be shy but being in prison I had to learn to be more outgoing, I gained a good ability to get along well with others, and I certainly became focused in my studies. While these positives all have helped me in general they also are very important for the position of Store Clerk, where all these skills are used."*

(3) ANSWER WHEN INTERVIEWING FOR A SPECIFIC JOB (restaurant worker): *"My prison assignment was cook, and through the almost four years I did this I not only learned how to cook fairly well I also learned just about every other job it takes to work in a kitchen: washing dishes, ordering goods, checking inventory, cleaning. I also learned about the importance of safety and OSHA, was sometimes given responsibility for supervising newer cooks, and often worked on the line, serving. This last item gave me good skills in dealing with the public. Oh, yeah – I even came up with a few of my own recipes, a few that the kitchen supervisor used!"*

How Would You Answer This Question?

Once more, it's your turn. Write out your answer to the question, "What did you learn from your prison experience?," in the spaces below:

_____

_____

_____

_____

_____

_____

_____

_____

REMEMBER: Prison University offers some of the best personal development courses in the world -- take as many as you can, for they will be investments that appreciate greatly in value and pay huge dividends to you on a daily basis.

REMEMBER: Practice these questions once and you will have borrowed them; practice them many times and you'll own them.

#7

"Can I trust you?" (alternate: "Are you honest?")

<u>**HINT**</u>: **WANTS YOU TO CONFIRM WHAT THE INTERVIEWER IS BEGINNING TO BELIEVE – THAT YOU'LL BE OKAY..** This question is almost always asked by the interviewer of an ex-inmate job applicant when [a] the interviewer knows that he / she is an ex-inmate; [b] the interviewer is beginning to feel quite positive about you as a person and you as a potential employee. It's up to you not to blow it!

Start your answer out by giving examples. As was said in some of the previous questions in this chapter, the more you can paint a positive picture, the better. This means no brief answers, such as "Yes" or "You bet." What the interviewer is looking for is some details from you that show his or her initial judgment, i.e., "You know, I think I'm going to be able to trust this person," is right on the money. What will help you best is to give examples of trustworthiness you have demonstrated while in prison and since your release, as well as any one outstanding example that may come to mind prior to your incarceration (if not longer than three years ago).

2 Examples of How to Answer This Question

(1) *"The best way to answer you question is by giving you an example. When I was in prison, there was a Jaycees chapter, and I was the Treasurer. There really wasn't a lot of money – I think the most we ever had in our treasury was $455. But I was in charge of it, I could write checks. And every month, that checkbook balanced. So, yes, you sure can trust me – that you can, and you don't ever have to worry about me abusing that trust.*

(2) "Yes, you can trust me because I'm honest. I'll give you a little example. There was also a store I ran in prison, you know, something like a black market – a way for me to make some extra money inside. I'd buy and sell things like snack cakes, toothpaste, cigarettes, Coke – and the guys, they knew they could trust me. If I told them a certain price, they know I would not charge them different. Or if I didn't have change, my promise to give that guy his change at a certain time could always be counted on. And while I've only been out of prison three months, my parole officer knows that she can trust me to come in when I'm supposed to and to show up at any job interview on time and when I'm supposed to. Starting over again is important to me, and I know it all begins with trust."

REMEMBER: One speck of dirt on honesty is more difficult to clean than a carpet full of mud.

Chapter 9

The Job Search After Your Release

"You never really lose until you quit trying."

Mike Ditka, professional football coach

● INTRODUCTION ●

YOUR FIRST FEW DAYS OF FREEDOM

FINALLY, FREEDOM. No matter if you'd been a trustee with furlough privileges or spent a great deal of time in solitary confinement (the hole) with no time spent outside; if you've been an ideal prisoner who did a 10 year bid or one who got into a bit of trouble in the two years you were inside: your first few days of freedom have one thing in common -- waking on the outside, with the opportunity to never again see the inside of a prison!

A FRESH LOOK. In addition, things that you took for granted before being locked up take on new importance: going to the refrigerator when you desire ... choosing the TV program YOU want to watch ... being able to talk on the phone for as long as you like whenever you like ... making new friends ... going to a beach or park or to a mall or for an aimless drive ... spending the afternoon with your family and friends. These and similar items will certainly occupy some of your time.

GIVE YOURSELF TIME TO UNWIND. While obtaining employment and continuing your education are both very important, you must allow yourself time to absorb some of what you've missed when in prison. Much anticipation of freedom will have been building up in you as your release day approaches. The first few days of your release should be set aside to satisfy this anticipation -- it's important to your mind and body.

HONOR COMMITMENTS. If you have a job or education commitment, if you need to meet with your parole officer or attend an AA (or similar) meeting, certainly honor it -- you cannot use the excuse that your first few days out of prison are a holiday. If you made an agreement to begin a new job or school studies within the first day or so of your freedom, you must honor that agreement. However, do take some time to smell the roses that you couldn't even see while inside.

REMEMBER: The most important thing to do for yourself upon release is ... nothing. Take time to get to know the world again and for it to get to know you -- your mind and body will both be the better for it.

Reporting to Your Parole Office

DON'T FORGET IT. If you are released on parole, the conditions of your release include reporting to your parole office within the first few days after you are out. DO IT!   This is one agreement that, if broken, can send you back to prison.

A WORD OF CAUTION. Don't forget that there are certain terms to be followed as part of your parole. Remember: this period of reporting will eventually end. More importantly, you now can begin to re-establish a positive life on the OUTSIDE. Living by the rules of your parole is a small price to pay for that.

Continuing What You Started Inside

Your career search has some time behind it now, as you began exploring employment opportunities while inside. (If you did not or were not able to begin your career search while in prison, be certain to read Chapter 2. The suggestions found in that chapter, as well as this one, still apply to you. It is NEVER too late to look for a job!)

Networking, responding to job advertisements, cold calling on organizations that have not advertised, and researching will still continue. **Additionally, three job search tools are now available to you that previously were not:**

(1) EXPANDED TELEPHONE TIME. While you may have had limited phone time on the inside, now you can call whenever you'd like. This allows for quicker follow-up on job opportunities, and information. You also will usually have a phone number where you can be reached.

(2) TRAVEL FLEXIBILITY. Car, bus, taxi, train, plane, by foot: all are now options, and allow you to attend interviews, visit libraries for research, and meet networking contacts.

(3) HIRING YOURSELF FULL TIME, UP FROM PART TIME. In prison you could not job hunt full time: job assignments, counseling sessions, education classes, and institution limits on when you could and not could not work on your job search made this effort part time. Now, however, aside from time devoted to your family, you have all your waking hours to focus on getting employed. So be a full time employee of your own company, Getting Me Hired, Inc., and become successful!

● YOUR JOB SEARCH AFTER PRISON: THE SPECIFICS ●

While you were able to do a great deal on the inside, you can do so much more on the outside because of the telephone availability and flexibility I just described. Yet there's also nitty-gritty work that has to be with your resumes, cover letters, and other tools of your job search. This time right after your release is a CRUCIAL time in your job search, and you cannot let it lapse.

Be certain to take into account the following tips; they will greatly help you improve your job search efforts after prison:

10 TIPS
TO HELP YOU WITH YOUR JOB SEARCH AFTER PRISON

#1
REFRESH YOUR RESUMES & COVER LETTERS

3 Items to Check Once You are Released

(1) UPGRADE YOUR RESUMES & LETTERS. If you did not have the paper and envelope stock you preferred inside, purchase it. Have your resumes reprinted on this new stock; also, use it for your cover letters (and other job-related letters).

Money is often tight with a newly released ex-inmate, however, so purchasing new paper and envelopes may not be possible. If you must stick with a paper and envelope stock that is not ideal, don't worry about it. As I told you in chapters 4 & 5, most important is the quality of the information in your resumes and cover letters, and making certain that the paper and envelopes are neat and clean.

(2) UPGRADE YOUR WRITING TOOL. Ideally, resumes should be composed on a desktop publishing program to give it the ultimate professional look. Likewise, letters should be done on a wordprocessor or typewriter (see Tip #7, page 364). If you must handwrite your resumes and cover letters, what I said above is true here: the quality of the information (as well as neatness and cleanliness) is more important than the writing tool used.

(3) MAKE ADDITIONAL COPIES OF YOUR RESUME. Make certain you have enough copies of your resume handy so you can send them out as necessary. Also, don't forget to have an equal amount of matching envelopes and blank cover letter stationery.

#2
RE-ORGANIZE YOUR MATERIALS

You organized your career search materials and responses as best as you could while incarcerated. Now, if possible, stake out a space on a table, a desk, or on a cupboard where you can better keep track of all aspects of your job hunt. If available, make use of file cabinets, computers, and copiers.

Additional office items that can help you organize include: index cards, stapler, bulletin board, file folders, briefcase, appointment book, address book, ruled pads, and marking pens.

Get your resumes, cover letters, networking contacts, and other job search tools neatly organized. If you like, continue using the Networking Worksheet (page 95) and Networking Index File Cards (page 96 I discussed in Chapter 2. The more organized you are, the better you'll be able to handle your job search.

(And there's a bonus to all this organization: you'll have an up-close look at what it's like to work! And you thought this organization business was only for the job search -- ha!)

> **REMEMBER:** What a nice helper is Organization -- it makes life easier to navigate, time seems to be house-broken, and frustration actually sleeps more.

#3
UNDERSTAND WHAT CAREER COUNSELING AGENCIES
& RESUME WRITING SERVICES ARE ALL ABOUT

You may find it helpful to visit with one of these firms to obtain personal, one-on-one guidance and assistance in your career search (listed in the phone book and the classifieds). Depending on the company, their services can include resume and cover letter composition and production; interview role playing; computer database (listing) of organizations; and general career counseling.

10 Check Points on Career Counseling Agencies

Before you commit your time and money, check:

(1) SEVERAL AGENCIES. Unless you have heard rave reviews about an agency from someone you trust, call or visit a few. Not only will this give you the opportunity to compare costs, services, and qualifications, but it is also important that you feel comfortable with the person who will be working with you.

(2) COST. With few exceptions (see page 364), these firms charge a fee for their services. If an agency is reluctant to give you a cost over the phone, be wary: some agencies wait to find out what work you do or how you are dressed, then give you a fee based on what they think you can afford. This is illegal.

More than one fee. Some firms will give you more than one fee, based on the type of service you want from them. For example, for writing only a resume you may be given a figure that is on the low end of their fee structure, while a "full blown" career search (resumes, cover letters, several counseling sessions, etc.) may be at the high end.

"Bait-and-switch." Unfortunately, a small percentage of the agencies will try a "bait-and-switch" tactic on you: giving you a low ball figure so you will come in, then telling you that you also need other services (at an extra cost) if your career search is to be successful. Ask the individuals to FULLY explain all services their various fees include.

(3) DON'T GET SUCKERED. Ex-inmates can be easy prey for anyone who gives the hint of helping an ex-inmate obtain employment. After all, employment is a key factor in keeping you from returning to prison. If someone offers to toss you what seems like a lifesaver, there is a heavy temptation to accept it. Before you do, weigh carefully ALL the information you are given and that you gather on the agency.

356

(4) SERVICES NEEDED. By shopping around, you will find those services that YOU need. You don't need to buy services for which you have no use. On the other side, some agencies will not supply enough of the services that you need: you don't want a snack when what you need is a full course dinner.

Some examples to watch for: Be certain that an agency does not tell you they will sell or give you ONE cover letter; as you can see from Chapter 5 in this book, there is no such thing as a universal cover letter ... if a company "promises " or "guarantees" you a job, or promises to give you a list of companies that are "definitely" hiring, be wary: seldom can a resume writing firm or career counseling agency come through with these promises ... if you talk with one person, are told that a second will write your resume, and perhaps meet with a third for counseling, you would be better off not to work with this assembly line approach: it is especially important to have one person work with you through all steps, so he / she can better and more thoroughly assess you and job opportunities for you.

(5) QUALIFICATIONS. Ideally, career counselors / resume writers should have a combination of proven skills in writing, speaking, and career counseling. A person may have a Ph.D. in English, for example, but not know very much about the career counseling field. Also, be careful of those individuals who tell you something like, "I was in Personnel for 15 years and saw many resumes -- I know what works and what doesn't." Perhaps the individual does know this for his / her company or industry, but what experience does he / she have with other fields? Has the counselor worked with job seekers in such areas as interviewing, target marketing, and interpersonal skills development?

Outside involvements. In addition, well-qualified counselors will have involvement in other aspects of their profession. Examples include: writing for publications; appearing as a guest on radio or TV discussing career counseling; a member of a professional organization that somehow relates to resume writing / career counseling; teaching or lecturing on a career or career-related specialty; writing books.

(6) FREEBIES. Some agencies promise you "free" services such as lifetime updating, first counseling session, and printing. While there is nothing wrong with this, be certain to ask for a full explanation of the free service to assure there are no hidden costs. Ask if the firm is willing to put any offer of free services in writing; if not, you need be suspicious.

(7) RECEIPT. Be certain that you are given a receipt of any deposit you leave with the company, as well as a final receipt indicating the total you paid and that your bill was paid in full. It should also detail the services provided for you.

Tax deductible. Often, various services provided by a career counseling agency or resume writing firm are tax deductible. Depending on your financial situation during the first year out of prison, you may be able to claim these deductions, but you will need a copy / copies of these receipt(s). Check with a tax accountant or the Internal Revenue Service for additional information.

(8) SAMPLES OF WORK. Ask the counselors or writers you meet if they can show you samples of their work. If the work is not professional or they balk at this request, this may be an indication that you need to search elsewhere.

(9) BETTER BUSINESS BUREAU / ATTORNEY GENERAL'S OFFICE. If you are unsure of the ethics of an agency or want to see if they have had any past complaints that have not been resolved, contact your local office of the Better Business Bureau and / or Attorney General's Office.

(10) DON'T BE AFRAID TO TELL THE COUNSELOR YOU ARE A RECENTLY RELEASED EX-INMATE. Sometimes, your needs are going to be special and a bit different from those of his / her usual clients. Ask if he / she would have any problem in assisting you, if the counselor has previously worked with ex-inmates, and how the counselor thinks he / she can help you.

> **REMEMBER: You are asking someone to help you with your professional life. This is not to be taken lightly, and you should ask, listen, and observe very carefully: a mistake on your part could be a mistake for a very long time.**

> **REMEMBER: Be careful when you grab a life preserver -- some are made of wood and float, while others are made of concrete and sink.**

#4
UNDERSTAND EMPLOYMENT AGENCIES & SEARCH FIRMS
(Permanent)

These companies specialize NOT in career counseling or resume writing, but in matching job applicants with PERMANENT (rather than temporary) job openings. As with career counseling and resume writing firms, they can prove very helpful to you in your job search.

The vast majority of these companies are legitimate, are sincerely interested in helping you find employment, and may even assist you with other aspects of your career search (resume, interviewing, etc.).

358

10 POINTS TO KEEP IN MIND

(1) COMPARE. Many of the items listed in the previous section apply to these firms as well. Don't be afraid to ask questions.

(2) CHECK SPECIALTIES. Some agencies specialize in sales, while others may deal in computers; you will find some firms primarily involved in entry-level positions, while others will concentrate on middle and upper-level management. Ask the representatives if they work in your career area and at your level.

(3) KNOW THE DIFFERENCE. In general, an employment agency depends on job applicants coming to them, either through ads for jobs they placed or from applicants calling for appointments. Search firms -- commonly known as "headhunters" -- primarily work on a contractual basis for companies, and seek out job applicants for their positions.

In addition, search firms will usually (but certainly not always) deal in salaries and job titles that are much higher and have greater responsibilities than those offered by employment agencies.

(4) WHERE TO FIND THEM. In addition to listings in newspapers (ads and under separate listings), they also can be found in the business portion of telephone directories.

(5) FEES. Generally, these companies divide fees into two categories: AFP (applicant fee paid, where you pay any fee) and EFP (employer fee paid, where the employer pays any fee). Search firms rarely will have positions that are APF, while employment agencies can have AFP, EFP, or a combination of both.

Additional fee structures. Additional fee structures also exist, including a "split fee" (where you pay half and the employer pays half) and a "six month reimbursed fee" (you initially pay the fee, but the employer will pay it back to you if you work with the organization for at least six months). Others exist as well.

When fees are to be paid. The above-described fees are paid only AFTER you have been offered and have accepted employment with a company represented by the agency. Details and structures of fee payments vary by state and by agency / firms. (Any information regarding laws governing employment agencies and search firms can usually be obtained through your state's Department of Labor.)

Registration fee. Also, some agencies and firms will charge a small registration fee, this paid to the agency before it begins working with you. Check with your state's Department of Labor or Attorney General's office to see if this is legal and, if so, the maximum that can be charged.

(6) BONDED. Some states have laws that make it mandatory for employment agencies and / or search firms to be bonded (carry a special type of insurance). You might want to check the law in your state: if yours are required to be bonded, don't be afraid to ask the agency's representative.

(7) CALL FIRST. While some agencies don't mind you walking in without an appointment, most prefer that you call first. This saves time, as the agency can quickly determine if it can be of assistance to you; also, you can ask some initial fact-finding questions of them. (EXCEPTION: An ad placed by an agency may instruct you to send in your resume and cover letter to it.)

(8) WHAT TO BRING. In addition to a FEW copies of your resume and samples of your work (through photos or actual pieces), also bring any references you have. The agency acts as a screen for the employer, so dress as you would if going for THE interview: you need to make a solid impression at this first meeting, as well as in later interviews.

(9) WHAT TO LOOK FOR AT THE AGENCY. Once you arrive at the employment agency or search firm, there are some signs you should look for as indications of its ability to give you quality service:

● **What's going on in the office**. Be leery if you see receptionists reading novels or buffing their nails, if it looks as if things are very disorganized, or it appears as if nothing is being done. A good agency does not have time for its people to sit around; they should be busy.

● **During the interview**.   If the interviewer does not ask you questions related to your job search, does not want to know about your references, is not inviting questions from you, or shows a general lack of interest, chances are that agency is not right for you.

You need a representative who is interested in helping you, and will take the time to learn about your strengths, your interests, and your long-range career plans.

● **License on the wall**.   Most states require agencies and search firms to be licensed, and to have their license "prominently displayed" on the wall. Look for it; if you don't see it, ask about it.

(10) FOLLOW UP. After you have sent your resume to the agency or interviewed with them, don't be afraid to call them to check on their progress. While it is possible they may not have anything for you at present, they should not be forgetting about you and letting your resume gather dust in a file cabinet.

Most agencies are sincerely interested in helping you find employment. Some, however, wholesale resumes (they'll take as many resumes they can get in all fields). While they might make money this way, it does little to help you land a job.

REMEMBER: While employment agencies and search firms account for only 15% - 30% of all available jobs, you cannot afford to ignore this legitimate assistance -- the competition for employment demands that you use all job search resources.

#5
UNDERSTAND EMPLOYMENT AGENCIES & SEARCH FIRMS
(Temporary)

For a great number of ex-inmates seeking employment, TEMPORARY employment agencies may be the answer to your job search. Millions of people work as temporaries; the demand is increasing, and it will continue to grow.

4 Reasons to Work as a Temporary Employee

(1) YOUR PRISON RECORD. Sometimes, your prison record may be a roadblock to landing a permanent position. Temporary work -- depending on the industry or profession -- is often more forgiving because their clients' needs are immediate and usually don't have the luxury of long, slow applicant searches.

(2) A CHANCE TO GET PAID WHILE INVESTIGATING PERMANENT JOB POSSIBILITIES, OBTAINING ADDED OR NEW WORK EXPERIENCE, BRUSHING UP ON DUSTY SKILLS, & MEETING NEW PEOPLE. Many newly released ex-inmates have little money and can't afford the longer amount of time usually involved in a career search. In addition, you can add to your previous work experience, gain new work experience, or refresh skills you haven't used in a while -- extremely valuable when the time comes to apply for a permanent position. Lastly, it's an excellent opportunity to meet new people (and perhaps make new friends), so important in re-entering the free world, especially if you are in a new city.

361

(3) FILLING A TIME GAP. You may have secured employment prior to your release or soon after your release, but won't start working at your new job for several weeks or months. Or, if you've elected to go to school full time after you get out, there may be vacation time when you want or need to work. Also, if you are working at a permanent job, you may decide that you'd like to moonlight for some extra money. Working as a temporary would be an excellent solution in each of these cases.

(4) FINDING PERMANENT EMPLOYMENT THROUGH A TEMPORARY ASSIGNMENT. "Getting your foot in the door" often means you have first crack at new openings in your specialty. One note of caution: Permanent jobs found through temporary help companies are not necessarily the same ones performed on assignment.

5 Points to Note About Temporary Job Assignments

(1) YOU WORK FOR THE TEMPORARY AGENCY, NOT THE ORGANIZATION WHERE YOU ARE ASSIGNED. Your salary, benefits, next assignment, when you work, etc., are determined by the temporary agency.

(2) TEMPORARY COMPANIES CANNOT GUARANTEE YOUR WORK SCHEDULE. However, a good temp agency can give you a realistic assessment of what you can expect.

(3) YOUR WORK ENVIRONMENT IS OFTEN CHANGING. Unless you have a long term assignment, you usually don't have time to get acquainted, to talk over a problem with a peer, or to run a personal errand. This also means being expected to catch on quickly to unfamiliar material.

(4) POSSIBLE LACK OF LONG TIME JOB HISTORY. If all of your assignments are short, that long term history of a job with one or two firms that some companies seek may elude you. However, if you work in the same field (for example, clerical) for a long time but with a variety of short-term assignments, then you can offer extended experience to potential employers in your career choice.

(5) YOU MAY NOT HAVE BENEFITS. Since you are most often working on short term jobs, most agencies give a salary but no benefits. (Two notes: [a] With specialty or long-term assignments, temp agencies may provide paid lunch hours, group medical insurance, seniority, and referral bonuses; [b] No benefits often means a wage that is higher than if you had the same position on a permanent basis.)

3 Reasons Why Organizations Use Temporaries

(1) TO FILL IN FOR SUDDEN VACANCIES, EMPLOYEES "OUT SICK," OR VACATIONING PERSONNEL. These situations can hit any company in any profession, another good reason to hit the temporary agencies.

(2) FOR WORK OVERLOADS, SPECIAL JOBS, SEASONAL NEEDS, & JOBS WITH HIGH TURNOVERS OF STAFF. For several years now, and with no end in sight, the labor market has seen downsizing of companies, either as a result of mergers or lack of business. Often, however, employees who are laid off are recalled on a temporary basis -- it's less expensive for the companies but it does provide employment.

(3) TO TEST OUT POTENTIAL PERMANENT EMPLOYEES BEFORE HIRING THEM. It gives them a chance to see the "real" you (and also reduces their unemployment insurance and other costs).

Finding a Temp Agency and Registering With It

(1) LOOK IN THE PHONE BOOK & NEWSPAPER. They're in the Yellow Pages under "Employment Contractors (or Agencies) -- Temporary Help," as well as under specific technical service listings (such as "Nursing" or "Writers"). Also look in the classified section of newspapers.

(2) PRIOR TO YOUR RELEASE. Get the addresses of temp agencies through telephone books and newspapers (if they're not available, ask someone on the outside to send or bring them to you). Use your networking letter or letter for an employment agency (see Chapter 5).

(3) AFTER YOUR RELEASE. Just register with one or several of the temporaries in your area, fill out an application, take any qualifying tests (such as keyboarding / typing, spelling, word usage), and be interviewed (and, if necessary, trained). You are then ready to be sent out on assignments.

(4) PAY CLOSE ATTENTION TO WHAT IS ADVERTISED. Is stress placed on years of service or is the emphasis on salary and benefits? Some services recruit special audiences (senior citizens, electricians, typists, etc.).

Scheduling Appointments / Questions to Ask

(1) SCHEDULE APPOINTMENTS WITH YOUR TOP THREE CHOICES. You don't want to schedule with many, as it does not allow you the time to concentrate your efforts and often employment agencies may contact one another -- if one sees that you are taking a "shotgun approach" it may not be as interested in helping you.

(2) PAY ATTENTION TO HOW YOU ARE TREATED. Do you and the counselor "click" on a personal level? Are you being treated with dignity or are you being brushed off? Do the proposed matches between you and your assignments seem right?

(3) QUESTIONS TO ASK.   Does the company offer paid vacations? Is there a medical and hospitalization plan? What are the benefits? Does the company have "seniority" bonuses for their "permanent"-basis employees? Do you get paid for referring other workers? Are you paid locally or out of another city? What are your chances of being kept busy? What's the length of a typical assignment? What is the company's policy on permanent job opportunities? What about turnover of the agency's staff?

#6
DON'T FORGET ABOUT STATE, COUNTY, & CITY CAREER AGENCIES

In addition to the private (for a fee) career counseling, resume writing, employment, and search firms previously discussed, all states have some type of job service assistance available. They are usually a part of the Unemployment Division, Department of Labor. (If you do not know how to get in contact with the office closest to where you will be living, check the Index under "Labor, Department of.") There is seldom any fee involved.

Cities and counties also frequently administer their own employment assistance programs. If you do not know of one in your area and cannot find a listing in the phone book, ask your parole officer or call your city or county hall. Again, there is seldom any cost to use these. Finally: don't forget about career development centers at a school you may be attending.

#7
USE THE LIBRARY

In case you haven't been to one lately, your local city or county library has tons of great resources to help you find employment. The best resource most libraries now offer is free -- read that word again: FREE! -- use of computers and use of the Internet. Often, job availabilities, company and profession / industry profiles, and interesting career search-related web sites can be found simply by you spending a few hours in front of a computer at the library. *Do not forget about this excellent post-release resource!*

#8
FIND A JOB SEARCH SUPPORT GROUP

Many cities have formal and informal job search support groups. These can be found in several ways:

- the phone book (usually listed under "Employment Support")
- through your parole officer
- the Department of Labor (state)
- through local, state, or national employment newspapers / newsletters (usually available in grocery stores and book stores)
- through postings in churches and temples, local newspapers, and on bulletin boards at community centers
- universities, colleges, libraries, and certain non-profit specialty organizations may offer a support group

These support groups can help you in several ways: by giving you additional support to problems you are encountering in your job search (both emotional and logistical); by sharing leads with you of companies that may be hiring in your field or hiring that seems to meet your overall needs; and by meeting new people and thus making new friends (always good to have when going through a difficult time, as a job search can be).

#9
DON'T FORGET TO USE YOUR STATE'S
DEPARTMENT OF LABOR RESOURCES FOR JOB LEADS

This is a resource that is so often overlooked by newly-released ex-inmates yet can offer you great resources as well as potential job leads. First, you'll find many job postings, and often they have a nice mixture: entry-level jobs that pay minimum wage or a bit more to higher-end jobs that offer good starting salaries. What's nice about this is that there usually is a nice supply of "starter jobs," so often the first job that fresh ex-inmates need because of the conditions of their parole, perhaps a lack of job skills and / or education, and not having much time -- at first -- to job search.

In addition, you'll find computers and various programs that can help you find more information related to your career search, allow you to update and print out your resume, and counselors who can help you as well -- all at no cost to you! As I said at the end of Tip # 7: *do not forget about this excellent post-release resource!*

#10
DO NOT LET YOUR CAREER SEARCH OVERWHELM YOU!

It can be somewhat frightening once you are on the outside ... and perhaps nothing so much frightening as looking for a job. Inside, you always knew that you had, at least, a place you could always count on, meals and clothing and medical services that were always available, and counselors, teachers, and other inmates who would always understand you and be there to talk to.

Now, however, you are working toward independence ... and in the job search, this sometimes means rejection, sometimes means frustration and disappointment, sometimes means finding it difficult to motivate yourself for one more day of job searching. <u>BUT DON'T GIVE IN & DON'T EVER GIVE UP -- EVER!</u> It takes guts and fortitude and drive and ambition and determination to make the transition from inmate to employed ex-inmate. You CAN do it ... and there are many people -- including me -- who believe you can do it. Yet ultimately, you must do it for yourself: you will be the ultimate victor of the effort you put in to landing a job, but the ultimate loser if you decide to give up.

REMEMBER: **Being released from prison amounts to no victory, no reward, no accomplishment; rather, it is how you greet and embrace your new-found freedom that will determine your place in the history of humankind.**

Chapter 10
Now That You Have a Job, Keep It!

"Without work all life goes rotten."

Albert Camus, French author

● KEEPING YOUR JOB ●

Too many ex-inmates think that their worries are over once they land employment. This could not be further from the truth. In fact, approximately 60% of all ex-inmates lose their first job within the first month of their employment! To understand why this figure is so high, you need understand the situations and environment you face when hired right out of prison.

Your first few days, weeks, and months on the job will be a combination of learning, awkwardness, introductions, uncertainty ... and perhaps some mistakes. To help you better make it through this time, and to assist you in growing into a solid and producing member of the company that employs you, keep in mind the suggestions that follow:

6 Tips to Help You Get Off to a Good Start

(1) DON'T EXPECT EXCITEMENT. Minor details -- where you work, how to do certain tasks, where to find things you need, how to use the telephone system, etc. -- will come your way. Also, you will probably have to fill out employment, health, liability, and other forms. And you may be given an employee or other handbook to read (ask if you can take any reading materials home to read at night). Concentrate on all these items; it will make your job much easier.

(2) YOU'LL HAVE MANY QUESTIONS. Don't be afraid to ask them. Use a small notebook to write down the answers (as well as additional questions that you may think of when you're not at work).

(3) EXPECT TO BE SOMEWHAT CONFUSED. There will be new names, new faces, new rules, and new responsibilities. Make a point to remember the people you meet and how they fit into the organization. Jot down names and functions as you meet people.

(4) DON'T BE A PEST. Limit the number of times you interrupt the people working around you.

(5) ACCEPT A STUDENT ROLE. There are many ways you can be trained: formal orientation or training program, on-the-job instruction, and / or learning on your own. Take it all seriously, as if you are striving for an "A" in a school course. Remember one of the most important unwritten rules of prison life when you first started serving your time: keep your mouth shut and your ears open. On the job, it's not quite as harsh as this, but do listen & don't start your new job by running your mouth -- you'll quickly turn people off.

(6) LEARN THE RULES. There will be many, from working hours to breaks to getting new supplies. Follow the rules, get to know what can and cannot be done. When in doubt about something, ask someone.

15 Tips to Help You Maintain Productive, Long-Term Employment

(1) GET TO KNOW THE "UNWRITTEN RULES."   Once on the job, you should ask colleagues about additional information -- the "unwritten rules" -- that they feel you ought to know (information such as office politics, personalities of supervisors, etc.). This knowledge can make it much easier to work within the company, department, and specific position ... the same as it does in prison!

(2) GET TO KNOW THE FLOW [i.e., dress, habits, hangouts, etc.] OF YOUR COMPANY AND COLLEAGUES. While it's important for ex-inmate employees to always retain their individuality, it's also important -- and makes work much easier and more enjoyable -- if they make an attempt to fit in with the others. Examples include: having lunch or stopping for some after-work socialization at a favorite restaurant or hangout of colleagues ... becoming involved in a sports team, social / work improvement committee, or volunteer/community activity ... attending a workers' party that the ex-inmate employee may be invited to attend.   (If you're on parole, always be certain that NONE of these activities violate any conditions of parole!)

In addition, pay attention to the "personality props" of the office: how others are dressed, what pictures and personal items they keep in their desk or work area, when they go for coffee / snack breaks, the TV shows and movies they discuss, the news items they debate. Certainly, you -- as an ex-inmate employee -- need not (and should not) try to parrot all of these. But becoming familiar with a few and perhaps adopting some will help them in being considered as one of the team.

REMEMBER: Cats, not employees, have nine lives.

---

(3) UNDERSTAND YOUR PERSONALITY NEGATIVES / WEAKNESSES AND WORK HARD TO OVERCOME THEM.   Remember reading about these negatives in Chapter 1 and 2? Well, you need to continue working at getting rid of or getting control of your negatives and weaknesses if you plan on staying employed.   While everyone has these -- impatience, short temper, sloppiness, lack of self-motivation, too much of a loner are some examples (as well as various addictions) -- ex-inmates tend to have these in more abundant supply. Why? Most ex-inmates, of course, have educational, home, work, and environmental backgrounds that are not the most positive. While these are often accepted by others in prison because everyone is, in fact, an inmate (or trained to work with inmates), in the workplace these negatives are not acceptable.

While I've certainly impressed upon you (as have your teachers in prison) the need to overcome these negatives, it is especially important to do so once you are out of prison and on the job. It may take some time (you cannot expect them to disappear in only a day or two, no matter how confident you might be!). And it may even be necessary for you to initially to speak with a professional counselor about these items. But if you intend on staying employed (and, in fact, wish to progress on the job), you need put in whatever effort is necessary in taming any negative personality forces that continue to linger.

(4) MUST UNDERSTAND THAT DIRECTIONS, ORDERS, TASKS, AND ASSIGNMENTS ARE PART OF A JOB AND LEARN TO ACCEPT THEM. The very nature of incarceration means being given orders, directions, tasks, and assignments ... and no one has yet met an inmate who enjoys this. But in the daily life of the work world, being told what, when, where, how, and why to do is very much the norm ... and it's important that as an employee you both understand and accept this.

NOTE: Most of the time, if an employee is told to do something but does not understand why, feels there is no purpose in it, or needs a clarification, he / she can certainly ask for more information. However, you should also understand that there will be times when you are expected to do something -- no questions asked. This is the nature of just about any job, and only through experience will you learn when you've run into one of these directives. And the positives to be gained are many: an employee who follows directions, who gets along with others, who is loyal to the company / supervisor all help in cementing that employee's place in the company, as well as preparing him / her for promotions, raises, etc.

(5) IT'S IMPORTANT TO ADOPT PUNCTUALITY, FOLLOW-UP AND FOLLOW-THROUGH, EFFECTIVE COMMUNICATIONS, AND SELF-MOTIVATION AS A LIFESTYLE. These are grouped together because they are often overlooked aspects of one's makeup that can help or hinder employment. Let's take a closer look at each:

● **Punctuality.** This is rather obvious, but unfortunately it is also an area in which many ex-inmates trip. To the point: you must be on time for everything, whether it be when you are supposed to be at work or when you are supposed to leave (never early, unless for an emergency); for a coffee break or for a scheduled meeting; for an after work get-together or a training session. You want to develop a reputation as someone who can always be depended upon to be on time (as well as for all other aspects of the job); nothing less is acceptable. (And if you do find that being late is unavoidable, whenever possible call ahead and let your supervisor know.)

● **Follow-up and follow-through**. Being given an assignment and following through on it or following up on work that has yet to be completed -- WITHOUT being reminded or asked to do so -- are qualities that employers greatly admire in an employee. Examples can include: seeing a project through to completion, returning a client's phone call or calling a customer with information he/she wanted, double-checking work done to make sure it's up to the standards needed or expected, obtaining the research data someone in the company requested, completing all assigned work without having to be prompted.   There are many other such scenarios but they all translate the same: the employee can be trusted to get the job done, and doesn't have to be reminded to do so.

● **<u>Must have good communications</u>**. Already mentioned several times in this book (and again, in detail, in Chp. 11), the importance of good communications can never be stressed enough. And on the job, an ex-inmate employee's ability to speak, to write, to listen, and to remember, as well as how and when to use so-called "body language," are often the foundations upon which all their work is based.

● **<u>Self-motivation</u>**. Another rather obvious one, but still an item with which many ex-inmates find themselves struggling. While incarcerated, the need for self-motivation is somewhat diminished because there is almost always someone around telling you what to do and reminding you if you haven't yet done it. But in the workplace, employees are depended upon to motivate themselves -- to get to work on time, to do their assignments and projects, to check their quality, to further their education, etc. It is only those individuals with a great deal of self-motivation who stay on the job and who are promoted.

Yes, at times it may be difficult for you to motivate yourself, but everyone goes through this one time or another. What's important is that this down time not last too long: if it does, someone else who has self-motivation will be applying for your job!

(6) NEVER MERELY DO YOUR JOB! Many are the employees who simply put in their hours, do their assigned or outlined job, obey company policies, and go home.   And while these individuals certainly contribute to the company's product development and sales, these are NOT the workers who generally get pay raises, promotions, or long job tenure.   Ex-inmate employees need to go "beyond the call of duty," i.e., you can't be hesitant to work late, to offer new ideas or suggestions, to fill in when another can't come to work or do his / her job, to volunteer when it's not required, to assist (a customer or colleague) beyond the scope of your assigned responsibilities.

This "beyond the call of duty" is also closely related to you displaying enthusiasm for your work, something employers greatly appreciate. Whether it be hammering in a nail, washing a glass, inputting at a computer, talking with clients, holding a meeting, or selling a product, if done with gusto and pride -- even if the job is of the most basic or menial kind -- it tells others that you will take pride in any position held, that you can find enjoyment in any job for which you've been hired or assigned. When employers and supervisors see this, they know you care and will usually treat you accordingly (including keeping you employed, giving bonuses, raises, etc.). Customers, co-workers, and vendors will return your enthusiastic efforts by having a more favorable impression of the employer's company, of the employee (you!), and / or of the firm's products / services.

NOTE: It would be nice to think that all employers reward or even expect such "beyond the call of duty" efforts by their employees. Sadly, this is not always the case. And some jobs -- especially those that are very repetitious and monotonous -- make it very difficult to want to do more than is required. However, if it is not for the employer, the working conditions, the pay, or the services / products produced, you should still "go the extra mile" for yourself: not only will you feel better, but it will become a habit that will serve you well in other aspects of life and / or other employment situations.

(7) KEEP IN MIND THAT A GOOD-NATURED AND FRIENDLY PERSONALITY IS A BIG ASSET. It's an old expression: "nobody likes a sourpuss." You'll find that colleagues, clients, staff, etc. will react to you in a much more positive way if you display a good-natured, friendly personality with a smile tossed in now-and-then. In addition, you'll find that it will help with your attitude towards work ... and it doesn't cost any extra to do!

Once you start giving off some easy-to-get-along-with vibes, you'll find that you'll most often get the same in return ... and what a nice difference that will make for you on the job (specifically) and in life (generally).

(8) YOU MUST LEARN TO ORGANIZE YOUR WAY TO SUCCESS. Mentioned a few times earlier, this is also especially true on the job. Once employed, you must understand the importance of and put into practice good organizational skills.

These could be as simple as: planning what to wear to work the next day ... knowing what time to catch the bus on the way to and from work ... scheduling all daily appointments and activities so you won't forget any, know where and when you're supposed to be, and can allow yourself enough time for each. A big help for you will be a schedule book, whether it be one purchased or one you make. The more organized you become at work, the more you'll get done ... and the less frustrated and stressed out you'll become!

> **REMEMBER: An ex-inmate's first job may be as refreshing as a popsicle or as repugnant as sludge -- but it is still something, always much better than nothing.**

372

(9) KEEP THE PRISON TALES AND STORIES OUT OF THE WORKPLACE! All ex-inmates do it eventually: tell someone an item from the days inside. It makes no difference how much they wish to put the experience behind them, how much they want to forget it: a stay in prison -- no matter how long or short -- makes a profound impact on one's life and eventually finds its way from mind to mouth. (On the other side, there are those ex-inmates who actually brag about their experiences or wallow in pity about how bad things were "in the joint." DON'T engage in this! Not only can it re-enforce someone's negative image of you as an ex-inmate, but it also can keep you from going forward with your life.) Also: as quickly as possible, don't forget to lose any prison lingo from your vocabulary, especially at work.

And when it is important for you to talk about your prison experiences in an attempt to learn from it and / or put it in the past, do so NOT on the job or with employees: you want people to think of you ONLY as a good employee and good person. Letting work colleagues know or reminding them of the days spent as an inmate can only work against you.

NOTE: There is an exception to not talking about the prison experience on the job. If someone at work knows that you are an ex-inmate and asks a "non-tabloid" question about your incarceration experience, be polite, answer the question in a general sense (e.g.: "Yes, I was in prison" ... "Yes, it helped turn my life around and gave me the skills that allowed me to get this job" ... etc.), and conclude with something like, "That's a portion of my life that's behind me -- let's get to know me as an employee of X company (OR: "-- let's get to know me as John Smith or Debbi Juarez."). However, when the question is very personal or really none of the asker's business, simply avoid answering the question directly; rather, answer with the "That's a portion of my life ..." answer given above.

(10) STRIVE TO EDUCATE, IMPROVE, AND DEVELOP YOURSELF -- CONTINUALLY. Mentioned in the previous chapter and again here, because education is SO important to your continued success after prison. The technology of yesterday often becomes outdated by tomorrow (how prepared are you for the so-called information highway? will you be versed in word processing software, in spreadsheets, in desktop publishing, in the Internet?) ... new management techniques and ideas help businesses each year (are you aware of such business languages, theories, developments, and practices as TQM, eCommerce, and JITM?) ... improved methods of construction, materials, and tools are introduced at a frenetic pace ... with new legislations, greater ability to communicate, and faster available transportation, global marketing with more foreign countries increases ... thousands of new products and services are invented, created, and discovered every year.

It is especially important for you to stay abreast of these changes. Why? The days of being able to make a living with only a strong back are diminishing, for technology and more sophisticated business approaches are being felt in virtually all jobs and professions today. If you, as an employee, do not continue your education, soon you'll will be seen as outdated ... and someone else will come along who DOES have the necessary education to handle your job!

And never forget: continuing your education is another of those key factors that is often considered in raises, promotions, and bonuses.

(11) DISPLAY DECISIVENESS AND CONFIDENCE. One of the most important qualities that an employer looks for is confidence. Being hired indicates that you have displayed some confidence or at least the potential for confidence. However, if you don't keep up your confidence, very soon you'll find yourself looking for another job.

Along with confidence is the ability and willingness to make decisions, rather than "sit on the fence" or pass that decision along to someone else. (Often, an employer would rather have someone who makes a decision that turns out to be wrong instead of someone who is constantly afraid of making a decision.) This confidence and ability to make decisions almost always translate into those employees who are viewed as extremely valuable to the company; they are usually the employees selected for management / supervisory positions. You be that employee!

REMEMBER: Being hired is the first open acknowledgment by another that you have at least a few sparks of self-confidence; it will now be your responsibility to fan these into inextinguishable flames.

(12) IT WOULD BE WISE TO ALWAYS TAKE NOTES AND KEEP A JOURNAL. Ah, the journal again -- but this time, for you to keep on the outside. Smart businesspeople keep journals and take notes: of a meeting or a speaker, from a class or for a sudden idea, to jot down something heard on a radio or TV show, during a discussion with colleagues or clients -- the list goes on.

It must be remembered that the people who have photographic memories are rare. The result is that many people overlook, forget, misquote, and err; most -- if not all -- of these oversights could have been avoided if notes were taken.

For you as an ex-inmate employee, notes and / or a journal can be especially helpful on the job (as well as in school). Company policies and procedures, a suggestion or direction, criticism or praise, a new idea or reworking of an old one -- these and many other such on-the-job items can make your life as an employee much smoother if they are jotted down in a notebook or journal.   Why?   Reasons include: to keep current on the organization's policies, rules, etc. ... as a reference so an error is not repeated ... to help in making a job-related decision ... to help keep yourself focused and motivated.

One final note on the journal. In looking over entries from several weeks, months, or years, you can also see where and how you've grown as a person. This becomes an important motivating tool (as well as simply being a fun thing to do).

(13) DON'T EVER SETTLE FOR THE STATUS QUO BUT RATHER KEEP STRIVING FOR BETTER. This point does not necessarily translate into meaning a higher position. Indeed, there are many people who simply don't want to leave the position they currently hold. This is fine, but no matter what type of person you are -- one who continually strives for a higher position (with the same or another company) or one who prefers to stay in the same job -- you should not fall into a habit of staying at the same level of productivity, of quality, of responsibilities (if desired). You should always look to better yourself; not only will you feel better about yourself but your employer will recognize you as an employee truly worth having.

One aspect of this point that can go a long way in helping you better cement your place in the company is through the development of networking links with customers and clients. No matter what form this may take -- from a satisfied customer to an additional vendor source to a resource person -- the more of these links that you have established, the better help to the company through positive image, better efficiency and productivity, and / or increased sales. These types of accomplishments -- no matter what position you hold -- always impress supervisors and employers.

(14) DON'T BE A SHOWOFF OR BRAGGART. We've all known at least one: the person who brags about his or her accomplishments (sometimes imagined ones), the person who likes to show off (muscles? clothes? car? money?). Certainly, having confidence is wonderful and being proud of what one has accomplished is fine ... but when an ex-inmate starts forcing these at and throwing them upon others, they've crossed the line of what is acceptable at the workplace (or any place, for that matter). Rather, you should understand that it's much better to let people be impressed by you for simply being yourself, NOT for what you wish to impress on others. Showoffs and braggarts, even if good at their jobs, seldom have good relationships with customers, colleagues, and management.

(15) ALWAYS KEEP A HEALTHY PERSPECTIVE. There will be days at work that do not go well, days when you'll feel like quitting, days when you'll feel like telling off your employer. These go with the territory of work; everyone experiences such feelings at times. Most often, they are momentary, the result of one or two items of short duration. Before you decide to act on these negative feelings -- and perhaps find yourself out of a job -- keep a perspective of what life was like in prison ... and what having a job has allowed you to do that, prior to release, was impossible or depended on others doing.

As time passes, you will find yourself thinking less about what was -- i.e., life as an inmate -- and more about what is and what can be. This is obviously good. However, you should never lose perspective as to how fortunate you are in working, in being able to earn money legally, in having so much control over the direction of the rest of your life. Many would like to have your job ... and many in prison would consider you "lucky" to be in such a position.

NOTE: Certainly, there are justifiable problems that occur on the job. Racism, gender bias, sexual harassment, and a host of personality problems or disagreement over approach to various business situations are common. But it's important to know the difference between these (and the importance of discussing these with your supervisor or a lawyer) and the relatively minor eruptions that can occur daily.

These guidelines -- if followed -- will go a long way in helping keep the job for which you've been hired. You will notice that many of these are the same type of suggestions that any person -- whether having been in prison or not -- would benefit from. Yet ex-inmates often have a more difficult time keeping employment because they've mastered the flip side of one or more of these suggestions ... now it's time for you to turn over many a new leaf and be a successful employee!

"Yes -- I got the raise!!"

REMEMBER: Everybody has a first day -- you are no different from anyone else and you are just as good as anyone else.

● NEGOTIATING SALARY & BENEFITS ●

I've decided to include this important section in this chapter, rather than a previous one, as salary and benefits negotiation -- for the ex-inmate employee -- will usually come into play after your first or second job. The reason for this, of course, is that being in prison with no income (or a minor one at best) and then going to being hired usually has the mind set of, "Just give me the job so I can work and make some money -- we'll talk about negotiations for higher salary and some benefits later!" And there's also the fear that, fresh out of prison, if you start asking about more money during the interview you might be seen as a troublemaker, and the job will go to someone else.

There will be times, of course, when it will be in your best interests to negotiate salary and benefits in your first job offer after prison. Situations that would warrant this include ex-inmates with extensive education; those who are highly skilled in various trades areas; or those who are applying for a position where they have at least some experience, and employees -- for that type of job -- are somewhat difficult to come by. So, no matter if you need to negotiate salary and benefits in your first job after prison or another further along, you'll find this section quite helpful.

Don't Be Weak in Your Negotiations

Usually, salary is discussed at the end of a first or second interview. Unfortunately, if you come across as weak and unsure of yourself on this subject, it may reflect on the entire interview.

When an interviewer asks you for a salary figure, don't be afraid to look him / her in the eye and give your answer. If you've reached a point during the interview where wages are being discussed, the employer is not going to throw you out of the room because you e salary figure is higher than he / she expected.

6 Keys Points to Remember

(1) HAVE A GENERAL IDEA OF A FAIR WAGE. If the job pays $10 - $15 an hour, based on experience, don't ask for $30 an hour; it shows you don't know the field and are only guessing at a figure.

(2) DON'T SELL YOURSELF SHORT. Many applicants are afraid to ask for the salary and wages they believe they deserve. If you know the types of monies being paid in your field and can back up your requests with a foundation of proven experience, education, and / or accomplishments, go for it!

(3) DON'T USE WORDS SUCH AS "DEMAND," "COULD USE," "IT WOULD BE NICE IF," ETC. Salary & benefits negotiation is not a time to be demanding nor is it a time to appear "wishy-washy." Use phrases such as "I need" or "I am worth" or "My salary request is."

(4) DIFFERENT JOBS, DIFFERENT APPROACHES. Sometimes, there is a "take-it-or-leave-it" figure given, especially if someone knows you've spent time in prison. This could be okay if the employer has a fair opportunity for you to advance. Other positions, however, may require you to give one figure ($6.50 an hour, for example) or a range (example: $15,000 - $18,000).

NOTE: See pages 184-185 for a clearer understanding of how to present salary figure that is more in line with your abilities and the industry norm.

(5) IN MOST CASES, BEGIN WITH A FIGURE THAT IS HIGHER THAN YOU WOULD ACTUALLY ACCEPT. You can never negotiate up, only down.

(6) UNDERSTAND THAT IN MOST MINIMUM WAGE JOBS, THERE IS LITTLE ROOM FOR SALARY NEGOTIATION. In entry-level (so-called "low end") jobs, employers often have many applicants from which to choose. Unless you can offer solid evidence that shows you are worth more that the pay being offered (such as past experience in the field and/ or better education that one might normally hold for the position), the hourly or weekly rate will probably be non-negotiable. However, be quick to ask about opportunities for wage increases: this not only gives you a better idea as to what kind of pay you can make with this company but it's your first indication to the employer that you are ambitious and looking to increase your salary based on hard efforts.

> **REMEMBER:** Just because you're good-looking, know how to dress well, and show up on time doesn't mean you're worth more money; rather, it's the worth of your past history in terms of future productivity to the employer that will add smiles to your wallet and hugs to your bank account.

Chapter 11

Miscellaneous

"All things are to be examined and called into question. There are no limits set to thought."

Edith Hamilton, American classical scholar and author

Just when I thought I had all the information and points I wanted to cover for this book, along came something else I had forgotten about. These began to add up, and pretty soon I had enough to fill another chapter -- this one. They represent items that, for the most part, did not fit comfortably in any one chapter or could have been included in more than one chapter. There also are items that I feel are very important for you to know about even though they may not be directly related to your career search.

The items in this chapter focus both on life inside prison and after your release. Read each section carefully: just because each item does not have its own chapter does not mean it's not important. Remember what little David did to Goliath?

CONTINUING YOUR EDUCATION

MANY SOURCES ARE AVAILABLE. Many inmates continue their education while in prison; it's equally important to do so after your release. This can take various forms: some complete their high school education and receive a GED (General Equivalency Diploma); others begin college courses, perhaps completing one or more degrees; various prison activities offer non-formal learning sessions, seminars, workshops, videos, and movies; and a large number of inmates do self-study through reading of some sort.

To best take advantage of educational opportunities, both while in prison and afterwards, keep in mind:

● **EDUCATION CAN HELP YOU WITH EMPLOYMENT.** You will find that the vast majority of employers look very favorably on those job applicants / employees who have a solid education or are in the process of improving their education.

Often, education determines who gets hired, is assigned the "plum" jobs, receives the promotion, or gets the larger raise. And, with the exception of some laborer positions, employers almost always insist on at least a high school education. (Although in today's society, the A.A.S. degree -- Associates of Applied Sciences, a two-year college degree -- is becoming the barest minimum that some jobs require. Thus, some jobs that used to accept a minimum of a GED degree now accept, at a minimum, an A.A.S. degree -- all the more incentive for you to continue your education.)

● **SOMETIMES YOU HAVE NO CHOICE.** There are times when inmates will take a course or educational program because they want to make the time pass faster or because they must. (This latter instance is based, perhaps, on test scores, a judge's order, a parole board's decision, a prison official's determination, or a potential employer's condition of hiring a newly released ex-inmate.) While you may not like it, this form of "continuing education" will serve you well beyond the specific reason for your doing it, so accept it and look to see where you can build upon it.

● **STAYING ON TOP OF YOUR JOB.** Continued education also allows you to stay on top of the latest developments in your field, and gives you greater flexibility (and leverage) when looking for your next job. And with technology so rapidly changing, it becomes crucial for you to constantly update your education ... if you want to hold onto your current job!

● **START INVESTIGATING WHILE IN PRISON.** The time to begin exploring your educational opportunities and options is while you are inside. Talk to the prison's Educational Director, a teacher, a counselor, or clergy member for guidance and suggestions; discuss your educational plans with family and friends. Equally important: write to different schools and training programs for information on their courses, degrees, tuition assistance, beginning and ending dates, and their requirements for admission. (For information on financial aid from the U.S. government for college, send for a free guide, *The Student Guide – Financial Aid from the U.S. Government*, Federal Student Aid Information Center, Box 84, Washington DC 20044. You can also call: 800-433-3243.)

● **CORRESPONDENCE SCHOOLS & COURSES.** In addition to the educational opportunities that are available for most inmates through programs sponsored / sanctioned by the prison (or state or federal corrections departments), there are also many technical, retail, business, and other schools and courses available through the mail.

BE CAREFUL OF RIP-OFFS. While the vast majority of these are legitimate, there are some that exist only to make money and will not provide the quality service you were promised in their brochures. Many inmates, eager to improve their minds and bodies, have lost money with little chance of recovering it from these pseudo-schools.

INVESTIGATE. Before you authorize any payment to a correspondence school, ask a counselor (or some other staff member) for his / her opinion. Find out if there have been any complaints lodged against the school with the Better Business Bureau or the Attorney General's office. Make certain you receive, in writing, what the school promises it will and will not do for you; if credits earned are transferrable; what you have to accomplish; and what their policy is on tuition and refunds.

● **DON'T DELAY UPON RELEASE.** I realize, of course, that your first order of business when you are released will probably be (and should be) to find employment and spend some time with your family. But don't put off your educational studies for too long: as time goes on, the only one to really suffer from your lack of additional education will be you.

> **REMEMBER:** The years you served in prison finally unlocked the bars and doors to the outside world; only you can unlock your mind ... and education is the best set of picks you'll ever find.

GETTING THE RIGHT CLOTHES

If money is not going to be a problem for you, then purchase the most appropriate clothing you need for the job search, interview, and employment. However, if funds are limited, you must be more resourceful to do the best with what you have.

3 Tips for Looking Your Best When on a Tight Budget

(1) CLOTHES GIVEN UPON RELEASE. There are many prisons that still give inmates a suit of clothes on the day of release. While these suits are usually not made of the finest worsted wools, they are clean. Don't be ashamed at starting at the bottom -- it's better than having no bottom at all.

(*A TRUE STORY*: When I was finally released, I was given a pair of brown, plastic [!] shoes and a green, polyester suit. Sure, I was embarrassed, but I wore them to a few interviews, always keeping the suit clean and pressed and the shoes polished. And what I was amazed at was how many times other candidates would be waiting to be interviewed in clothes that were obviously much more expensive and of better quality than mine, but didn't look as good because they were NOT kept clean, pressed, and polished!)

(2) USE YOUR MONEY WISELY. There are many discount stores (such as K-Mart) where you can buy a nice outfit at a fairly inexpensive price. Also, don't forget about such thrift shops as the Salvation Army and local community outlets.

(3) CLEAN & NEAT ARE MOST IMPORTANT. No matter where you receive your clothes, always keep them looking nice. An inexpensive dress or suit that is pressed will give a far better impression than one that cost $1000 but is wrinkled. And don't get spots on your tie, runs in your stockings, scuffs and dirt on your shoes, and stains on your clothes. (See Chapter 6, pages 240-241, for complete details.)

ADDITIONAL PAPERWORK & CARDS TO SECURE

Depending on your situation, it might be in your best interest to secure:

● **BIRTH CERTIFICATE.** An important document if you need to establish proof of your age; is also used as acceptable I.D. in some instances, and is needed for passport applications. Contact Bureau of Vital Statistics, listed in the government guide of your local city or town's listing in the phone book.

● **MILITARY DISCHARGE PAPERS.** Valuable as they not only offer proof of your military service but can give you titles and positions of jobs you held in the military, important for your resume. If you've misplaced yours, a copy can be had by contacting: Military Personnel Records Center, 9700 Page Boulevard, St. Louis MO 63132 / 314-263-3901.

(By the way, as long as we're on the topic of the military, if you are a U.S. service veteran who served between the years 1959-1975, the Veterans Incarcerated Committee of Vietnam Veterans of America has two free publications they will send you: [1] *From Felon to Freedom* -- to assist veterans soon to be released to the community; [2] *The Liaison Manual* -- to assist in the active development of rehabilitational programs prior to and during community release. To obtain copies, contact them at: 1224 M Street, NW, Washington DC 20005 / 202-628-2700.)

● **ALIEN REGISTRATION CARD.** If you are not a U.S. citizen and have misplaced your green card -- needed to work legally in this country -- contact the U.S. Dept. of Immigration and Naturalization, found in the government listing in the phone book. There is also a national phone number that will connect you to INS headquarters in Washington DC: 202-514-2000.

● **TRANSCRIPTS OF GRADES / PROOF OF GRADUATION.** If your grades are good, they can be of help to you in both applying for jobs and if you decide to go onto college (or to further your college education); if they are not good, they still will be needed for applications to college and to verify that you have completed X course. Proof of graduation -- especially if you've only recently completed your GED or high school degree -- can be needed for various assistance programs eligibility, for employment, and for application to college / enrollment in additional education programs. Contact your school (including the Education Department in prison) where you took courses and / or received your degree(s) for copies (there sometimes is a small fee for this).

● **RAP SHEET.** A rap sheet, of course, is an official listing of any arrest, fingerprinting, and conviction you had. This can be checked by: criminal and law enforcement agencies; some public and private employers (especially if fingerprinting employees is a standard part of their hiring process); occupational licensing agencies (often, the agency issuing the license requires that the applicants possess "good moral character" before licenses are granted; there are also some occupational licensing agencies that either bar or put on probation ex-inmates, thus the need to check the rap sheet); bonding agencies (explained in detail later in this chapter, under "Federal Bonding Program"); and you.

Why should you get a copy of your rap sheet? Three reasons: [1] you can check for mistakes; [2] you may not remember everything (you may answer an interviewer's question about what you remember of your criminal history, only to honestly leave out a conviction that you had forgotten or the exact name of the crime for which you were convicted; if the interviewer checks, he or she may think you were lying); and [3] seeing your rap sheet can better help you prepare to answer any questions the interviewer may have about the nature of your convictions.

Rap sheets may be obtained two ways: [1] Each state has its own agency that is responsible for maintaining rap sheets, usually under a heading similar to "Department of Criminal Justice Services." Write or call for more information. [2] No matter which state you are in, you can contact the Federal Bureau of Investigation (FBI) to obtain a copy of your rap sheet; contact them at: FBI, C.J.I.S., ATTN: SCU-MOD-D2, 1000 Cluster Hollow Road, Clarksburg, W.V. 26306.

● **PROFESSIONAL / OCCUPATIONAL LICENSING REQUIREMENTS.** As I mentioned under Rap Sheet, above, various professions and occupations require licensing (such as barber, real estate broker, social workers, certified public accountant, nurse, and taxi driver). While many have no problem with someone being an ex-inmate, others bar ex-inmates from obtaining licenses, have certain limitations for them, or issue the licence but on a conditional or probationary status. To learn more about specific professions and occupations, contact your state's Division of Professional Licensing.

● **SOCIAL SECURITY CARD.** Upon your release from incarceration, you may be required to furnish your social security number to obtain some services or get a job. Many times you will be asked to show your Social Security Card as evidence of the number assigned to you. Often, inmates will have but two forms of I.D. available to them when first outside: parole papers (or other release papers) and a Social Security card. Driver's license, credit cards, library card, voter registration card, etc., usually must wait until you establish employment, a permanent residence, a good credit history, and / or you go through the required application process.

How to Obtain a Social Security Card

If you are age 18 or older and have never had a Social Security number: You will need to apply for one in person at any Social Security office.

If you have a Social Security number but not your card or are under 18 and have never had a number: You can apply for a card prior to your release by writing any Social Security office and requesting an Application Form SS-5. Complete the application and mail it back to the Social Security office with the required evidence. (The application explains what documents are required, depending on whether you are applying for an original or a replacement card.)

For more information. If you do not have the address of the office nearest you, write to: Office of Public Inquiry, Social Security Administration, Department of Health and Human Services, 6401 Security Boulevard, Baltimore, MD 20235 / (301) 965-7700.

> **REMEMBER: As an ex-inmate, the more proof of your existence the better; but without proof of a Social Security number, you're invisible ... especially to employers.**

● **CHECKING / SAVINGS ACCOUNTS.** It may have been some time since you had one or both of these, or perhaps you never did. Life can be much easier through having these, but keep in mind: (1) You need a picture I.D., such as a Driver's License, and usually a Social Security # and a permanent address to open these; (2) If you've had a bad history with credit and / or a record of bounced checks, this may still be on record and could be checked by the bank prior to giving you an account; (3) If you open either of these accounts, and you later a judgment is entered against you, your accounts may be seized for payment.

● **LIBRARY CARD / DRIVER'S LICENSE / CREDIT CARDS.** Depending on your job, lifestyle, and interests prior to prison, chances are you had a library card, driver's license, and / or credit cards. Prior to your release, find out what you need to do to re-obtain / reopen these items. This will not only save you time when you are released, but also can make your career search easier for you. However, do keep the following in mind:

Depending on your conviction, individual state laws, federal laws, city and county laws, and specific requirements of the agency or organization to which you are re-applying or must go through, you will have either an easy, moderate, or hard time getting back that which you had to give up or was taken from you.

Driver's license. A driver's license can be a very important item for you to obtain, even if you won't have a car to drive right away. Not only does it allow you to drive, but there are certain jobs that require a valid driver's license; also, a driver's license is often required as PHOTO identification.

Sheriff's Card, County Card, etc. There are many communities where an alternative to a driver's license is issued. These go by many names, almost always have your photo and birth date included on them, are usually accepted as a substitute for a driver's license, and there usually is no fee to get one. Check with your Parole Officer or County Sheriff's Office if you'd like more information. (By the way: if you cannot get a driver's license and a sheriff's card or the like is not available in your community, you'll need to get a copy of your Birth Certificate -- very seldom are Social Security cards accepted as I.D.)

Library card. It may have been some time since you had one of these, or perhaps you've never had one. No matter. A library card can prove to be one of the most important "keys" you can get -- at not cost! -- when out of prison. Several times in this book I've referred to use of a computer, after release, at the library ... continuing your education, after release, at the library ... obtaining job and career information, after your release, at the library. This one little card can make it all possible.

(_NOTE_: You may have forgotten about them while inside, but the library's tracking system usually doesn't: overdue books or outstanding fines credited to you! You can't get a library card until these are taken care of, so contact your hometown library PRIOR to your release to check on your status.)

Credit cards. Credit cards should be something you stay away from, at least for awhile. First, your credit history may not be that great, so chances may be strong that you'll be turned down. But if you do get one -- even a so-called "secured" credit card where you have to deposit a certain amount of money, as collateral, before you can be issued one -- use it very carefully. More people go into bankruptcy because they got into credit debt they couldn't repay ... and with ex-inmates, the temptation is great to get some items they haven't had for some time and not have to pay for those items immediately. So be VERY careful with credit cards.) (See pages 413-415, "The Ex-Inmate as Victim: Scams and Sucker Bets.")

● **CREDIT HISTORY REPORT.** You may not be aware of it but there's a very good chance that you are listed with a credit reporting agency somewhere in the United States. How you are listed -- that is, if you have a good or bad credit rating -- is very important to you. Not only do credit card companies use these agencies in making a decision as to whether to issue you a credit card, but banks, retail stores, mortgage brokers, auto dealers, and many other types of businesses use credit reporting agencies. Depending on what type of credit rating you have, it could affect any effort on your part to open a checking account, secure a home mortgage, rent an apartment, rent furniture or appliances (or any other item that can be rented), purchase an automobile. While this may not seem important to you right out of prison, having a good credit rating will prove more and more useful as you become more a part of mainstream society.

What You Can Learn by Reading Your Credit History

Gives you a listing of any outstanding debts or judgments that you incurred. Often, inmates will have forgotten -- and in some cases not even know -- about past bills that were not paid to firms or judgments that were entered against the inmate (these often are entered against the inmate when he or she is in prison, and thus not aware of it). Your credit report will have these listed. As you begin to get financially stable , it would be in your best interest to contact the firms and courts listed on your credit report and let them know of your intention to repay the debt. No little how much you can pay each week, it will be one step closer to rebuilding your credit history.

Indicates what companies have you listed as being a good credit risk. f you have paid some or all of your past bills on time, some firms will have this listed on your credit report. These would be good companies to pick up where you left off: re-establishing the good credit record you have with them, something you can then use to help you establish better credit at other establishments.

Gives you information of credit reports that are wrong or no longer valid. As an example, bankruptcies appear on your credit record for seven years, but after seven years they are supposed to be taken off. If you had filed for bankruptcy at one time, but it was more than seven years ago yet the information still appears on your credit report, other firms checking your credit will use this outdated information against you. So check all the information on your credit report thoroughly; if you don't think something's right, write the credit agency and let it know.

How to Check Out Your Credit History

There are many credit reporting agencies in this country, and when you contact any for a copy of your report you must have your Social Security # available. There are two good ways that you can secure a copy of your credit report:

(1) Apply for a credit card. If you've had a spotty job history or a poor credit history, you will be turned down for the card. This does NOT affect your credit in any way but it does allow you to write to the credit reporting agency and receive a FREE copy of your credit report. (When you write you must include a copy of the turndown letter you received.) (Most credit agencies also include a brochure on how to read your report; if not, ask your counselor or teacher to help you with it.) Applications for credit cards can be found in magazines; you'll hear toll free application numbers on the radio and TV; you can ask friends or relatives to send you an application; or you can ask a teacher to turn it into a classroom exercise.

(2) Write to a credit reporting agency. Listed under "Credit Reporting Agencies" in the Yellow Pages, these firms will supply you with one copy of your credit report for a small fee (usually $3-$5) if you write them.

Don't Be Afraid to Seek Out Credit Counseling

If you find that you do have a load of unpaid past bills and find yourself stumped as to how to repay them, don't hesitate to contact a debt or credit counseling agency. Most are free and they help people with large debts everyday. No, they won't give you money; rather, they look at your current pay, decide how much you can realistically pay each firm, then will contact these companies and let them know of your intentions. For more information, look in the Yellow Pages, under "Credit & Debt Counseling Services." But remember: you've got to be serious about doing this!

● **CERTIFICATE OF GOOD CONDUCT / CERTIFICATE OF RELIEF FROM DISABILITY.**
These certificates exist in most states and may or may not prove helpful to an ex-inmate, depending on the requirements of the job he / she is seeking and /or the laws in your state regarding various civil rights.

The Specifics

Certificate of Relief from Disability. If you have only one felony conviction and finish parole without another conviction, you may be eligible for a Certificate of Relief from Disability.

Certificate of Good Conduct. If you have more than one felony conviction, but nothing else for X amount of time, you may be Eligible for a Certificate of Good Conduct.

What these certificates can do. These are both mechanisms to restore rights that may have been taken from you when you were convicted, such as the right to vote, professional licenses, and the right to own firearms.

Who issues them. The certificates are issued by a state's Division of Parole (or Parole & Probation) or the governor of that state. (Do keep in mind that your state's rules for issuing such a certificate may vary from other states.) To find out if your state issues these or similar certificates (and who issues them), contact The United States Office of Pardon Attorney, U.S. Dept. Of Justice, 5550 Friendship Boulevard, Chevy Chase MD 20015 / 301-492-5910.

● **WORKING PAPERS.** If you are between the ages of 14-17, you usually need to obtain these so you can apply for a job. For the specifics -- including where to obtain an application form -- contact your local Board of Education or Department of Labor.

REMEMBER: If you can't be punctual, dedicated, energetic, trainable, goal-oriented, honest, friendly, well-spoken, organized, flexible, optimistic, focused, dependable, self-disciplined, team-oriented, highly motivated, timely, open to new ideas, good at problem-solving, and closed to crime then you might as well find employment as a mushroom.

THE RIGHTS OF EX-INMATES

A GOOD BOOK TO GET. Probably the most comprehensive discussion of the rights of ex-offenders -- such as the right to vote, to hold public office, or to retain citizenship -- is found in a paperback titled *The Rights of Ex-Offenders* (David Rudenstine; an American Civil Liberties Handbook). This book is out-of-print, but if you can obtain one, read it. Many prison libraries, long-timers, and bookstores that specialize in used paperbacks have a copy. It offers good insight regarding what can and cannot be done.

CHECK THOROUGHLY. Of course, it is best to ask your counselor, clergy representative, attorney, or family member to get more specific information for you. Also, contact your state Attorney's General office (and a little tip: ask for their Law Library; I've found it extremely helpful in getting the specifics on rights and laws relating to ex-inmates), your state's Department of Labor, and your state's Equal Employment Opportunity Commission. Sometimes these rights may have a direct effect on you being hired, other times they won't. Don't assume anything. (See also: pp. 387-388, Certificate of Good Conduct, et al.)

GOING INTO BUSINESS FOR YOURSELF

I cannot begin to tell you how many inmates make up their mind to go into their own business ... and then fail. Certainly, being one's own boss is the dream of many (including those people who have never spent a day in prison), and for an inmate, it often seems like the answer to not getting into trouble, to making much money legally, and to not having to answer to anyone but yourself.

THE COURSE I TOOK. When I was inside, the administration hired an outside consultant to give an 8-week course (one day per week, 2&1/2 hours each session) on going into business for yourself. Having owned my own business, I knew that many of the statements said by the consultant were inflated, misleading, or simply not true.

After one evening's class on economics, for example, he told us that "you can talk economics on the level of any college economist." Upon completion of the course, he assured us that "you now can walk into any Small Business Administration office and, just because you took this course, be given an SBA loan." Unfortunately, most of the class believed these two statements ... and neither was true.

Let me give it to you straight: you cannot learn all you need to know about going into business for yourself from one person over eight meetings. You must have the basics: a solid business plan, a product or service that will sell (legitimately, I might add!), a telephone, and other related items. And perhaps, most important, you need to have capital -- money or credit -- to carry you for at least six and preferably 12 months until your business starts producing enough income to pay for itself ... including a salary to you!

IT'S TOUGHER FOR AN EX-INMATE. Depending on the type of business and geographic location, 60% - 80% of new businesses fail within their first year; over the course of five years, according to the U.S. Department of Labor, the average rate is 75% -- 75% of new businesses fail within the first five years! And for ex-inmates the figure is even higher: the only study on this done is still on-going, but for the two years worth of ex-inmates studied who went into business for themselves, 91% -- 91%!!! -- failed. Obviously, if you decide to become your own boss, as an ex-inmate you will likely have more difficulties than a person who has never been in prison.

YOU VS. THE FREE WORLD BUSINESSPEOPLE. Their credit is probably good, they have maintained a steady history with their bank, they have business contacts and clients, and they have had the opportunity to study their market and talk with many people before making business decisions. You, however, have little (if any) of these in your corner.

I'M NOT SAYING DON'T DO IT. Rather, I am advising you to be very careful and plan out all aspects of going into your own business. Sadly, many ex-inmates who have failed in their own business panic and do something that puts them back in prison. You're just about out or newly out ... and I know you don't want to go back.

Two Good Resources to Help You

Both of these have free pamphlets and brochures available for individuals interested in going into business for themselves. I STRONGLY suggest you send for and read these before making any move into self-employment.

● **S.C.O.R.E. (SERVICE CORPS OF RETIRED EXECUTIVES ASSOCIATION).** 409 3rd Street, SW, Washington DC 20024 / 800-634-0245

● **SBA (The U.S. Small Business Administration).** 200 N. College Street, Suite A-2015, Charlotte NC / 800-827-5722.

OVERCOMING DEPRESSION & FRUSTRATION

There will be those times when depression and frustration may set in. You know that there are many possible situations when this could occur: rejection from a job, lack of money, problems with a relationship, having the fact that you are an ex-inmate tossed in your face, and generally starting your life over, on the outside.

REMEMBER TO FOCUS ON THE POSITIVES. First of all, it's okay to have these negative feelings once-in-a-while. I did when I first got out, and thousands of ex-inmates go through these every day. The key to overcoming them is to keep focusing on the positives, keep believing in yourself, and -- above all -- maintain a philosophy of achieving the goals you set for yourself while still in prison. (And don't forget to look at your journal, if you brought it with you -- it's a good reminder of your accomplishments, pluses, etc.)

IT MAY HURT DEEPLY SOMETIMES. There are many possibilities, including: When someone implies or tells you that he / she can't hire you because you're an ex-inmate ... when someone you care for very deeply breaks the news that he or she has left you for someone else because you spent time in prison and he/she couldn't wait ... when you don't have enough money to buy some of the basics you need or some other items you'd like.

DON'T GIVE UP. Don't allow yourself to get so far down that you finally toss in the towel and say, "Ah, what the hell, I might as well go back to what got me in prison; at least I'll make some money." It's just not worth it, especially when there are so many options available for you.

HELP IS AVAILABLE. There are many professionals on the outside who will help you, at little or no cost. In every city and town and hamlet you will find a crisis hotline, rehabilitation programs, social workers, clergy, psychologists / psychiatrists, or parole / probation officers who will gladly counsel you. If they can't, they will refer you to someone who can.

REMEMBER: Accept the fact that some negatives may come your way after prison and simply write them off as the dues you have to pay to achieve your positives.

LEARN TO MANAGE STRESS

IT'S EVERYWHERE. Stress is a natural part of everyday life. Deadlines, arguments, bounced checks, traffic jams, sports competition, crowds, the copier breaking down when you need to use it, getting new clothes dirty, breakups of relationships, a pen running out of ink, death: these all bring about stress of one level or another.

INMATES TEND TO HAVE INCREASED STRESS. This is due to several factors, including: living in a small, confined area; being told what to do and not to do; embarrassment of being in prison; fear of what has been lost / will be lost from your life on the outside; prison violence; illness; not getting along with your cellmate(s) or other inmates.

PRISON-RELATED STRESS CAN SPILL OVER TO THE OUTSIDE. If you let these "get under your skin," the resulting stress keeps you from thinking objectively or remaining level-headed, and (very often) carries over to the outside when you are released. The only good that can come from this is no good. What to do?

Fighting Stress: Some Guidelines

● **ASKING A QUESTION.** First, step back from the situation causing you stress, and ask yourself: "How really important is this to the overall blueprint of my life?" Almost every time you ask this question, you'll find the answer is the same: it's not very important. When you understand this, you can look at the situation from a stronger position. If you begin to conquer the stressful situation, and not let it conquer you, you will greatly reduce its bad effect.

● **SOMETIMES, YOU JUST NEED TO LET IT ALL OUT.** In addition, there are many avenues available to help take your mind and body off the items that may cause stress. Examples, while certainly more plentiful on the outside, still exist inside and include: reading a book; physical exercise; movies or TV programs; eating a snack; writing (poetry, a short story, etc.); participating in a club or group sponsored by the prison; taking a walk; playing chess, cards, or board games; having an enjoyable conversation with someone; and sleeping. A release of physical or mental tension will relax you.

● **MEDITATION -- IT'S NOT GOOFY!** Spending some quiet time by yourself, just thinking nice thoughts, gazing at the sky, looking at a flower or tree, enjoying some pictures on a wall or in a magazine or book, listening to music -- these and similar solo activities will help you to relax, to refresh. It's the most inexpensive high you can obtain anywhere! (See page 237 for information on Tai Chi.)

● **ONCE A SITUATION BECOMES HISTORY, FORGET IT!** You can't bring back time or events; you can only go forward and perhaps have learned something from the experience. Tell yourself: "It's done, finito, over -- I had a momentary human burst of negative emotion at the time, but life does go on."

● **CUT DOWN ON CAFFEINE, NICOTINE, & RELATED ITEMS.** Caffeine is known as a stimulant that directly increases stress. Coffee, chocolate, tea, and many soft drinks contain caffeine. Additives in processed foods often have an adverse effect on emotional control and well-being. In addition, the nicotine in cigarettes is another stress-inducing ingredient. And most illegal drugs and alcohol (especially "prison hooch"!) also contribute to raised stress levels. You have little control over the food you are served, but you can make healthier choices about what you drink, and certainly make serious steps toward cutting out any alcohol, cigarettes, or drugs you may be taking.

● **WHEN ALL ELSE FAILS.** There may be times when you feel that you need something stronger than what I've suggested. When this happens, DON'T turn to drugs, alcohol, etc. As I mentioned under "Overcoming Depression & Frustration" (page 391)), there are professionals who are trained to help you cope with your stress. Call on them -- the other side is to let stress eat you alive. No sense in letting that happen, is there?

REMEMBER: "should've," "would've," "could've," "if only," "might've been," and "why didn't I?" are only good for dictionaries ... and stress!

GOAL SETTING

In Chapter 2, I talked about what you should be doing when you've only got six months left. One of the items I referred to was goal setting. This is especially important, for goals give you levels, items, accomplishments, and "things" to strive for.

Many inmates, when asked about their lives BEFORE prison, admit that they had few or no goals in life, and that they did not know how to properly achieve those they had.

CHOOSING YOUR GOALS

At first, this sounds easy: pick what you want to achieve and go after it. In theory, this is right. However, you must be careful not to select goals that are beyond your reach or for which you don't allow enough time. Likewise, setting goals that are too easy to achieve can also cause you problems. Let's take a closer look at both of these:

Goals That Are Out of Reach

If a goal is beyond your ability to achieve (at least at the time you attempt it) or you have not allowed yourself enough time to achieve it, then the goal is out of reach. Examples are many, but would include: buying a new car on your release day when you have little money or credit; sending out 1000 resumes over the course of four weeks; having every company you applied to for a job respond to you within 10 days; losing 50 pounds in two weeks.

● **DON'T FRUSTRATE YOURSELF.** Goals such as these bring frustration, disappointment, and depression ... and very often a feeling of little self-worth. (Each of the examples listed above, by the way, is attainable; they simply need the right amount of time attached to them.)

> **REMEMBER: When you have no control over an achievement, you're considered lucky; when you're responsible for the achievement, you're recognized as brilliant.**

Goals That Are Too Easy to Reach

If I set as my goals to brush my teeth, walk 50 feet, read five pages of a book, write one letter, and watch one TV program -- all in one day -- you'd probably say that I really wasn't accomplishing very much. You'd be right. All of what I mentioned I would normally do anyway, so what real goals have I set?

● **DON'T FOOL YOURSELF.** Every day, people set goals that are extremely easy to achieve, and they do it for one reason: to delude themselves into thinking they are accomplishing something. The real result is going nowhere very fast.

Realistic Goals

● **START OUT SMALL.** One of the best ways of achieving your goals -- and giving you a continual feeling of accomplishment along the way -- is to start with small, rather easy goals. Examples could include: finishing all school assignments on time for the week; getting all spelling words correct in the next test; writing at least one letter to a family member and one letter to a friend within a week; sending out at least one resume and cover letter each week for three weeks. These "easy-doin'" goals will also give you a taste at to what's involved in achieving your goals, so as your goals become more involved with a longer time frame, you'll better know how to achieve them.

An important note: as you begin to achieve small goals, there might be a tendency on your part to stay at that level -- don't! You need to constantly expand your goals so you can carry your life both forward and to greater heights!

● **NOW IT'S YOUR TURN.** In the blank spaces on the next page, write down those goals you want to achieve; include the time period you are giving yourself to achieve these goals. Periodically, go back to this list and mark in your progress, any setbacks you've experienced, and any changes you've had to make in your efforts to achieve these goals.

● **BEFORE YOU WRITE, THINK.** Before you write anything, think through the goal you want to reach. More often, it is not the goal that is unrealistic, but the time allotted to achieve that goal. Be realistic; challenge yourself; and once you begin to strive toward your goals, don't stop until you succeed!

GOAL PLANNING WORKLIST

1) GOAL / DATE BEGUN: _____
   TIME TO ACHIEVE: _____
   NOTES: _____
   _____
   _____

2) GOAL / DATE BEGUN: _____
   TIME TO ACHIEVE: _____
   NOTES:_____
   _____
   _____

3) GOAL / DATE BEGUN: _____
   TIME TO ACHIEVE: _____
   NOTES: _____
   _____
   _____

4) GOAL / DATE BEGUN:_____
   TIME TO ACHIEVE: _____
   NOTES: _____
   _____
   _____

5) GOAL / DATE BEGUN: _____
   TIME TO ACHIEVE: _____
   NOTES: _____
   _____
   _____

6) GOAL / DATE BEGUN: _____
   TIME TO ACHIEVE: _____
   NOTES:_____
   _____
   _____

If You Fail to Achieve One or More of Your Goals

● **YOU'RE NOT A FAILURE**. Because you have set a goal for yourself and, for whatever reason, failed to achieve that goal, you should not toss your hands up in the air and declare yourself a failure.

● **TRY, TRY AGAIN**. Each day, hundreds of thousands of sales professionals fail to close sales they had set their sights on, and had planned on making commissions from. If sales professionals are good, however, they look at this missed sale NOT as a failure, but merely the end of Phase One. They rethink their approach, analyze why the sales were not theirs, and try once again -- what I call Phase Two. Eventually, their persistence will pay off.

● **YOU CAN ACHIEVE YOUR GOALS**. If you don't reach your goal by the day or time you had planned, there is no cliff you are going to be pushed over, no shards of glass you are going to be made to walk upon, no stone wall you will run into, no burning pyre upon which you'll be thrown. No, you can still achieve your goal.

● **PARTIAL SUCCESS IS BETTER THAN NO SUCCESS**. Also, while you may have missed your self-imposed deadline for meeting your goal, you HAVE reached part of your goal ... and that is much more than you had before you began pursuing your goal.

> **REMEMBER: Goals are set for the purpose of improving, bettering, overcoming, discovering, reducing, enhancing, measuring, increasing, decreasing, building, or repairing -- so that your life can be happy, fulfilling, and enjoyable.**

EFFECTIVE COMMUNICATIONS

There is probably no one skill you will use more or be of greater overall importance than your ability to communicate effectively. In fact, the higher up you go in just about any organization, the less you will use the skills for which you were initially hired and the more you will have to communicate. (It is for this reason that I have so often mentioned communicative skills throughout this book!)

In addition, inmates and ex-inmates often are very poor communicators. Why? Much of this, of course, goes back to a rather weak education and growing up and running with others who may not have had solid communicative abilities. There also is the environment of the prison, which re-enforces communications that are effective within the prison but too often are not at the level that is acceptable in the business world.

THE THREE MAJOR COMPONENTS OF COMMUNICATIONS

The three major components of communications are: writing, speaking, and listening. If you can do a good job at raising your abilities in each of these, you'll vastly improve your image, for a person who can communicate effectively is automatically given such labels as "leader," "educated," and "confident."

LEAVING THE INMATE IMAGE BEHIND. In the chapter on interviewing, I talked about the interviewers' image of the ex-inmate. Many, of course, hold this picture in their heads: that the ex-inmate has only a couple of teeth, a "Death Before Dishonor" tattoo, and communicates at the level of grunts and groans. Too many Hollywood late night movies, of course, but the bit about the grunts and groans is not too far off very often. Yet if you walk into an interview and can speak effectively, if you can write a decent letter on the job, and if you come across to all as a good listener, any prior image others may have held of you as being ignorant simply because you are an ex-inmate will vanish like dust on the wind.

> **REMEMBER:** Hard biceps and harsh words may have been your communications tools on the inside, but they won't get you far in the business world ... except "we'll call you if we need you," "no promotion," and "you're fired."

#1 -- Effective Writing

It is impossible, of course, to teach you how to become a good writer in a portion of this book or, for that matter, the whole of another book. For good writing comes about through practice and more practice ... and a determination on the student's part to put in the effort necessary. It's not easy and, quite frankly, it's often not fun. Yet the end result will be worth all the trouble, for you will be able to write business letters, memos, reports, E-mail, summaries, and cover letters (and any personal writing you do) on a level that tells others you really DO know how to communicate effectively in writing.

Let me give you a quick list of some of the more common writing problems found amongst inmates and ex-inmates. If some of these fit you, work to erase them from your writing. (And for a quick evaluation of your writing skill, ask one of your teachers or a counselor.) And always remember: everybody can stand at least some improvement or fine tuning in their writing.

<u>The most common writing problems</u>:

- incomplete sentences (also called sentence fragment)
- sentence, paragraph, or entire paper does not flow smoothly
- punctuation problems (biggest ones: use of the semi-colon [;], too many commas)
- fused sentences (also known as run-on sentences)
- comma splices (joining two independent clauses with a comma)
- spelling errors (don't ever be afraid to use a dictionary!)
- capitalization (either capitalizing words that should not be capitalized or vice versa)
- mixing singular and plural (e.g., "They is going to the beach" should be "They <u>are</u> going to the beach")
- poor sentence structure (e.g., "He be going to the movies" should be "He <u>is</u> going to the movies")
- beginning two consecutive sentences with the same word (makes your writing sound childish)
- poor proofreading

<u>NOTE</u>: The last one listed -- poor proofreading -- is by far the most common problem, yet there is no need for it. This has nothing to do with knowing how to write, but rather with checking over your words and sentences for typos, misspellings, punctuation left out, etc. The more you proofread, the better your writing will be.

> **REMEMBER: Your ultimate signature is your writing ability, for it tells another so much about you as leader, thinker, and communicator.**

#2 -- Effective Speaking

Although you need to send in your resume and cover letter, I have given you some good guidelines to follow so that when these are received by the company you will have gotten off on the right foot with the initial writing portion of your communications. However, I can't be with you on the telephone, I won't be with you in the interview, and I will not be walking with you on a daily basis. This means that you have to speak fully on your own, and how you speak will leave a lasting impression with those who listen to you.

Again, I can't offer you a course in public speaking, and while there are books on the topic, once more it's going to take practice on your part. In some ways, your ability to speak well may be, at least initially, more important than your ability to write well. Why? Simple: nearly 100% of the job interview is done ORALLY, that is, through speaking, and thus the impression you make in the interview depends a great deal on how you present yourself through your ability to speak.

Let me offer you the following suggestions, beginning with the most common amongst inmates and ex-inmates. What follows will be an additional listing of speaking problems.

SPEECH DEMONS

In Chapter 2, I discussed the importance of using correct grammar when you speak. Just as important is getting rid of six speech demons that can kill the message you are trying to get across.

How many of these do you say or have you heard:

- "uh"
- "um"
- "you know"
- "right"
- "okay"
- "like"

In sentence form, you've said them or heard them similar to the following:

- "I, uh, don't have any stamps."
- "Um, is there any mail for me?"
- "I was playing, you know, basketball that day."
- "I went to the mess hall to grab some chow, right?"
- "So I went into the store the next day, okay?"
- "It's, like, three Little Debbies, like, okay man?"

WHY THESE MISTAKES ARE MADE. Do you know why people speak like this? It's because of an interesting fact: our mouth is ready to speak much faster than our brain usually thinks, and the result is some "down time" for our mouth.

The listener won't lose interest. That would be okay if we didn't say anything for those few brief moments when we're trying to put together our next thoughts. But the problem is that when it's our turn to speak, we know others are watching us and listening to us; there is a fear that, if we don't have SOMETHING coming out of our mouth, the listener will lose interest. This is not true.

Pauses aren't noticed. What you may think is a long space of time between thoughts -- because you are closest to your voice -- is barely noticed by the person(s) to whom you are speaking.

Words that don't fit are noticed. They DO, however, notice those words or non-words that seem to be dropped right in the middle of the sentence with no legitimate reason for being there. In an interview, this is especially harmful as the interviewer is focusing all of his or her attention on you, and wants to see and hear what you do right and do wrong. Many job candidates have lost out because a speech demon or two got in the way.

3 Tips to Erase Your Speech Demons

If you follow these, I guarantee that your speech demons will eventually become a memory:

(1) SLOW DOWN. Most people have a tendency to speak too fast. This "uses up" all the words your brain has given you for a certain period of time, and puts you in a position of having a mouth that thinks it needs to talk but has nothing to say.

If you do speak too fast, practice slowing down. This will allow you more time to think of your next thoughts, and result in less "down time" for your mouth.

(2) TAKE THE TIME TO THINK. When you find yourself with nothing to say for a moment or so while you are piecing together your next thoughts, don't say anything. Take that time to turn your head to the side, and when you know what you next want to say, look back at your audience and speak.

You'll find the listener(s) will have more respect for you, as you not only have greatly cut down on your stumbling, but have demonstrated (by what you DIDN'T say!) that you have enough confidence in yourself to stop for a brief moment and think. You did not need to use a speech demon for a crutch to get you from one thought to the next.

(3) NOTICE WHEN YOU DO MAKE A MISTAKE. As you practice paying more attention to what you are saying, you will catch yourself using speech demons. This will make you more aware of it, and they will begin to disappear as your determination grows to improve your speech.

ADDITIONAL SUGGESTIONS FOR IMPROVING YOUR PUBLIC SPEAKING

● **LOOK THE AUDIENCE IN THE EYES..** No matter if your audience is one or many, it's important that you look them in the eyes when speaking. This not only shows the audience your interest in and enthusiasm for them, but also gives you high marks in self-confidence.

● **PROJECT YOUR VOICE.** A wimpy-sounding voice gives a very poor impression of you and your self-confidence, and will result in the audience not hearing everything you say.

● **BE CAREFUL OF YOUR "BODY LANGUAGE."** How you stand, if you move or don't move your arms, the amount of time you spend moving back-and-forth, whether you slouch when sitting, if you fold your hands across your chest [don't!] -- all of these give off signs as to who you are. Additionally, when your body language is too much, it causes the audience to be distracted from your mind and your mouth.

● **BE SURE TO VARY YOUR VOICE TONE.** You want your voice to rise up and down, somewhat like a roller coaster, to give emphasis to certain thoughts and words and to downplay others. Good voice tone also holds the audience's attention better -- a flat tone is called a monotone, and it will quickly turn off the audience's listening.

● **SMILE.** Nothing warms up an audience more than when you smile occasionally -- it lets them know that you're relaxed, that you're one of them, and that you're a nice person.

● **REMEMBER THAT GOOD GRAMMAR & ORGANIZATION COUNT.** Just because you're speaking rather than writing doesn't mean that you can let your grammar and overall organization slip. Use your best English grammar -- or whatever native language you would use when speaking -- and don't forget to organize your speech so that it flows in an orderly, progressive fashion.

● **PRONOUNCE THE WORDS CORRECTLY & PRECISELY.** This is called "enunciation," and many people don't do it! And if you don't, to the listener it sounds as if you have marbles in your mouth and the impression you leave can be a very bad one. So: learn the correct pronunciation of others' names ... don't pronounce the word "ask" as "axe" (as in, "I want to axe you a question.") or "library" as "library" or other such common mispronunciations ... don't "swallow" the word as you say it but rather pronounce it completely. Follow these suggestions and the listener will be most appreciative!

● **DRESS APPROPRIATELY.** Remember that you are trying to make a POSITIVE impression on your audience, so dress neatly, dress professionally -- as much as you are able. Jeans just don't cut it when you're interviewing for an inside job but perhaps might be appropriate if you are interviewing on the outside, for a construction or bricklayer's job, for example. (Check out pages 240-241 for specifics.)

● **WATCH THE JOKES, WATCH THE FOUL LANGUAGE.** Certainly leave the foul language out. (See pages 52-53 for comments on leaving prison lingo behind.) As for jokes, I'd suggest leaving them out too: few speakers can tell jokes effectively, and jokes are NEVER told simply for the sake of laughter but rather to make a point about something in your speech or presentation or answer.

REMEMBER: You want your spoken message to come across smoothly, not like a mouthful of chunky peanut butter.

#3 -- Effective Listening

For many people, effective listening is the "forgotten" communicative skill. When we write, we are actively concentrating on our writing because we are producing something -- words, sentences, paragraphs; when we speak, we also actively concentrate on it because we are, again, producing something -- words, sentences, and paragraphs.

PASSIVE LISTENING. Yet when we listen, well, it's done rather passively -- we can do many other things while we are listening ... at least, so we think. Unfortunately, most people are poor listeners. (In fact, research has shown that the average listener forgets about ½ of what was said immediately after someone has spoken; after two months, the average listener remembers only 1/4 of what was said.) And it is because of poor listening that billions of dollars are lost every year in this country: people mishear directions, orders, delivery dates, instructions, inventory amounts, requests ... the list goes on.

INMATES NEED AN EXTRA EFFORT. As an inmate or newly-released ex-inmate, you must put special emphasis on your listening. The reason for this is because in prison your listening often does not get the kind of workout it will on the outside. And, in fact, very often inmates make it a point of turning their listening "off," at least to certain people and sounds.

While there can be several specific areas where an inmate must have good listening skills -- hearing orders from a correctional officer, questions and information from a teacher, and certain important situations between inmates -- there just are not the number and complexity of listening scenarios inside as there are out. (Examples: questions asked in interviews, orders given at work, information given on TV or the radio, suggestions offered in meetings, inventory figures mentioned at the plant.) In addition, one of the major reasons behind poor listening -- distractions -- abounds in prison.

The following suggestions will help you improve your listening ability; start practicing them now and you'll be amazed at how much better a listener you are.

TO IMPROVE YOUR LISTENING

● **CONCENTRATE ON THE SPEAKER.** There will always be outside distractions, but when someone is speaking to you that person should become your whole world. Listen to what's being said, how it's being said, and why it's being said ... you'll leave with a better understanding of the message.

● **IF YOU DON'T UNDERSTAND SOMETHING, SPEAK UP & ASK.** Too many people are either afraid or too lazy to ask a speaker to explain a certain word or a particular concept. When this happens, it can throw the entire meaning of the speaker's message off ... and perhaps tune you out in the process. Yet asking for clarity can keep the speaker's message on track ... and keep your listening tuned in.

● **SHOW INTEREST IN THE SPEAKER'S MESSAGE.** Most people are, unfortunately, poor presenters. It's up to you, as a good listener, to convey the message, "I'm interested; tell me more." By showing interest in the message it not only helps you to focus but indicates an interest on your part, something that will certainly be appreciated by the speaker.

● **IMPROVE YOUR MEMORY.** A good memory can be of immense help when listening to someone else. It will allow you to come away with more of the message, it forces you to concentrate more on the listener, and is a big help in being more accurate when recalling the specifics of what the speaker said.

● **DON'T BE QUICK TO INTERRUPT.**   One of the biggest problems that listeners have is to jump in and not give the speaker a chance to finish. Not only is this rude on the listener's part but often the listener does not get the full or correct message, responds to what he / she thinks was heard, and ends up looking like a fool. Rather, let the speaker finish a thought; then, if you want to respond, do so. This shows class and politeness on your part.

● **LISTEN WITH YOUR WHOLE BODY.**   Use facial expressions and body movements to tell the speaker that you ARE listening and that you DO understand his / her message. Sit forward in your chair. Nod when you agree. Raise your eyebrows when you are confused or startled. Smile when you are pleased. Not only will these movements tell the speaker you are listening, but by being a whole listener you will find it easier to absorb the message and primary thoughts of the speaker.

REMEMBER: Always listen to another as if your ears were homing pigeons to the message.

EQUAL EMPLOYMENT OPPORTUNITY COMMISSION

The Equal Employment Opportunity Commission can be of assistance to you if you feel you are being discriminated against while you are looking for a job or once you are hired. This federal organization enforces a law called Title VII of the Civil Rights Act of 1964. (You may remember that Title VII was mentioned at the beginning of Chapter 8, page 317.)

Under Title VII, it is unlawful for an employer to discriminate with regard to:

● job advertisements
● recruitment
● testing
● hiring and firing
● compensation, assignment, or classification of workers
● transfer, promotion, layoff, or recall
● use of company facilities
● training and apprenticeship programs
● fringe benefits (such as life and health insurance)
● pay, retirement plans, and disability leave
● causing or attempting to cause a union to discriminate
● other terms and conditions of employment

For More Information

Either visit or call your local office of the EEOC. If this is not possible, they may be reached with a toll free call at: 800-449-EEOC. (Two other numbers, which are specifically for the hearing impaired, are NOT toll free: 202-663-4387 and 202-663-4394.) You can write to the EEOC at: The U.S. Equal Employment Opportunity Commission, 1801 L Street, N.W., Washington, DC 20507.

REMEMBER: You may be an ex-inmate but you're a human first who happens to be just as equal as anyone else -- don't ever forget that.

TIME MANAGEMENT

Being able to wisely and most productively use the time you have -- whether in or out of prison -- is very important. Not only will you be able to accomplish more, but you'll find that it's easier to organize your life, complete tasks on schedule, and end up with more free hours for leisure activities.

BALANCING YOUR TIME IN PRISON

Wise use of your time becomes especially important when looking for a job. In prison, you usually have more available time to conduct your career search than if you were doing it on the outside. (There are exceptions: certain work camps and military-style boot camps where "free time" is extremely limited.) However, this can often be more of a hindrance than a help if you fill your time with sleep, sports, non-employment reading, and other such activities. In moderation, these are fine, but you must start allotting a certain amount of time each day for your job search.

BALANCING YOUR TIME OUT OF PRISON

Once on the outside, you will find many more opportunities for interruptions of your time. With major items being priorities in your life -- most certainly employment, perhaps education, possibly a family -- you need to carefully weigh what you are going to do for how long and at what time. Organizing your time will have a positive effect on the professional and personal sides of your self. You will feel more in control of what happens to you. Problems and crises will be at a minimum. And your life will experience more contentment and relaxation. (See Chapter 2, pages 38-40, for additional information on Time Management.)

"TIME BANDITS"

Each day, you are robbed of valuable time by interruptions, unplanned events, and needless errands -- these are your time bandits.

In Prison: Examples of Time Bandits

- spending all free time / study time on "fun" things
- waiting in line: at the PX / camp store, during visitors' day, during room checks and frisks, to get a haircut
- being interrupted by others when studying, reading, in the middle of a meeting
- having time checks and set prison schedules prevent you from completing activities
- relying more on the mail for various materials than you would if on the outside, thus causing work delays
- poor work organization
- limited access to telephone (causing delays)
- the "unexpecteds": lockdowns, disturbances, construction repairs, overcrowded conditions
- lack of proper materials, thus extra time involved in obtaining information, materials you need
- allowing yourself to wallow in misery, loneliness, etc. brought on by being incarcerated
- having schedules or rules changed by new administrator, teacher, or counselor

Not all of these will fit your institution or you, and I'm certain there are others you can identify.

Out of Prison: Examples of Time Bandits

● telephone calls (both receiving and returning)
● meeting interruptions
● business or family crisis (large or small)
● bogged down with paper work
● not delegating responsibilities (when you can)
● taking too many breaks when you should be working
● indecision
● unnecessary conversation / communication
● not using machines, devices, etc., that can save time (example: collating by hand when a copier or printer could do it for you; not using a fax or E-mail but rather relying on regular postal delivery)
● junk mail
● not training staff correctly, thus spending too much time disciplining, correcting, and retraining
● lack of proper and thorough follow-up
● waiting for connection to the Internet, being put on hold, going through electronic phone message options

There are many more than I've listed here. Also, some of these will not apply to you.

IMPROVING YOUR TIME MANAGEMENT

Some Things You Cannot Control

INSIDE PRISON. First, accept the fact that there are some time bandits over which you have no control. In prison, for example, time checks, delays because of limited phone time, heavy reliance on mail, and frisks are part of prison life. While you may not like these, you have to work around them.

OUTSIDE PRISON. Likewise outside of prison: crises, interruptions, and unplanned events (flat tire, copier breakdown, computer crash, the flu, etc.) can't be foretold and so must be dealt with, thus "robbing" some of our time.

Set Priorities / Become More Efficient

PRIORITIES. Make a list of which tasks, responsibilities, etc. are MOST important, which are MODERATELY important, and which are LEAST important. Use this as a guide so that you can get the greatest amount completed in the most efficient manner.

EFFICIENCY. Learn to work in a manner that will make the best use of your time.

Examples:

● In addition to relying on mail, contact friends and family to see if they will do some of the leg work; this is called delegating work to others who can capably handle it.
● Do your work before you decide to play.
● Don't be afraid to put a "do not disturb" sign on your door when you don't want to be interrupted.
● (On the outside): Not taking phone calls as they come in, but rather returning them later in the day (with the exception of those that DO demand immediate attention).

Plan Ahead

Rather than adjust or plan as things happen, plan ahead as much as you can. This will allow you to make the best use of your time, as well as productively use unexpected "dead time" (waiting, electricity going off, a rainy day, a strike, etc.).

Some examples on planning ahead:

● planning your free time agenda for the next day
● setting mini one-day goals
● bringing along a book or other reading material in case you must wait (in line, at a doctor's office, etc.)
● having projects ready to start in case of unexpected free time
● laying out your next day's clothes the night before
● mentally preparing a speech, presentation, or debate the night prior to showtime
● paying bills, getting the garden ready, keeping your car in shape, working on your career search before you HAVE to or before it's too late

---

REMEMBER: Time was not sentenced to prison, you were.

EX-INMATES WITH CHILDREN

When you search for employment, it is important that you make any necessary arrangements for babysitters, school, etc., so that you can conduct your job search, go on interviews, and work without having to worry about your child.

ON-SITE SERVICES. Fortunately, a growing number of employers are helping working moms and dads meet their parenting needs through on-site day care centers and other related services. Ask the employer if such programs are available.

RESEARCH. In addition, ask your counselor (or others who may be helping you prepare for your release) about resource organizations that have programs to assist with parenting needs.

A WORD OF CAUTION. Do not use the excuse of having children to care for as a reason why you can't work certain hours, can't work on certain days, etc. Employers don't want to hear excuses; this is YOUR situation and you must learn to work around it. However, also know that very important item of COMMUNICATIONS can help you in this area. Find out what work options -- if any -- are available regarding shifts, times, etc., then work around that which is best suited to your schedule at home.

A RESOURCE. The most comprehensive list I've seen of resources for parenting needs is in the Prisoners Assistance Directory. (Published by The National Prison Project, 1875 Connecticut Avenue, NW, Suite 410, Washington, DC 20009 / 202-234-4830; the cost is $30.00.)

IF YOU SMOKE

Many inmates smoke cigarettes (some also smoke cigars and pipes or chew tobacco). The reasons include: it's a habit carried over from the outside; it helps relieve the boredom or tension; it's often one of the few things that you can do inside that can give you a "taste" of the outside.

A WORD OF CAUTION. Smoking laws have become very restrictive, with fewer and fewer workplaces allowing smoking on their sites (and many not allowing smoking simply because they've been mandated by state or local laws). Also, an increasing number of companies will not hire applicants if they admit -- either on an application or in an interview -- that they smoke (for health insurance cost reasons). Smoking is getting to be a habit you might have to quit if you want a job (aside from the fact that it's just not good for your health), so it would be wise on your part to start quitting now!

PREPARING A BUDGET

Oh my, oh my, oh my -- freedom from prison means, perhaps, leaving with some money, and landing employment means more money. And here's where many ex-inmates crash and burn: they don't know how to budget their money. Look: there are going to be some regular, fixed costs that you need pay; items such as rent, clothing, utilities (perhaps), bus fare or gas for a car, food -- these and others must be paid, on time. And while it may seem that a few pennies here and some dollars over there for non-necessities (a movie, magazines, snack foods, etc.) aren't really much, they do add up. These expenses can cut into monies that MUST be paid for the basics of your everyday life ... and if you don't have it, what are you going to do? (Don't even think about committing a crime!)

So ... before you even leave prison, begin preparing a budget; continue to keep it well after you leave.

Tips on Developing and Maintaining a Workable Budget:

● **LIST YOUR NECESSITIES.** Make a list of all the necessities (food, clothing, etc.) that you'll have to pay for after prison; next to each item, write down its individual cost and, next to it, the TOTAL cost you'll need spend on that item for a month.

● **START NOW.** To give you a good sense of how helpful your budget can be on the outside, try maintaining a real budget on the inside, no matter how small an amount you have to work with. This will give you a start in the area of fiscal management and discipline!

● **PRIORITIZE.** When listing the basics, do so in order of priority (most important, first; that which is important but you could cut back on or -- in a pinch -- live without, toward the middle; etc.).

● **FIGURE YOUR INCOME.** Next, write down the amount of income (approximate if you don't know the exact amount) you'll be receiving each week, and, next to it, the total for the month.

● **MATCH BASICS WITH INCOME.** Look over your basics: break them down according to your income; if you find that your income will not cover all of your basics, look over your list in terms of priorities: you may have to limit or cut out some of the items farther down the list so that you don't overspend.

● **CONTINUALLY TRACK YOUR BUDGET.** Each week or each month -- depending when your bills need be paid -- check over your budget to be certain you are not overspending; when a bill is paid in full for the week or month, check it off. Not only will this give you a constant updated record of your budget but it's a nice feel-good look at the progress you're making in staying on top of your bills.

Some Fine Points on Keeping Your Budget

● **SAVE LEFTOVER FUNDS.** If you have a small amount left over at the end of a month, don't blow it simply because it's there. Rather, put it in a "fund" of sorts: in your checking account (if you have one), in your drawer, in a jar -- someplace out of the way where it can be used in case of a shortfall another month.

● **REWARD YOURSELF.** When your budget is quite tight with little or nothing left over at the end of a month, it's still nice to reward yourself with a "treat" now-and-then. Here's how: take a look at your basics -- food is a good one -- to see where you might cut back (buying a cheaper brand, for example). Do this upon occasion, and with the extra money buy yourself something that you normally wouldn't purchase (on your present budget). Call it a reward for doing a good job on your budget ... and it's also a nice motivator to help you over the bare times of a bare bones budget.

● **READ A HOW-TO BOOK.** Check out a book on preparing and keeping a budget if you are having a hard time. Chances are pretty good that you were given instructions on how to keep a budget by one of your teachers in prison. But if you still have a few problems -- either inside or out -- head for the library; you'll find a variety of books offering instruction on keeping a budget.

● **A BUDGET CAN HELP IN YOUR JOB INTERVIEW.** It's not going to do you much good if you take a job at a certain pay, only to find out that it's not going to meet payment of your basic needs. By figuring out how much you need to make prior to an interview it can help you in landing a salary that will pay you what you need to get by. The key, of course, in how you sell this figure to the interviewer (see Chapter 10, pages 376-378), but having a solid budget in hand can be a help to you in securing a realistic pay.

● **KEEP ACCURATE RECORDS FOR TAX PURPOSES.** We might as well get this out of the way now, as distasteful as the subject may be. Once you are employed, you'll be responsible for paying income taxes by April 15 of each year. Your budget can help if you have an envelope attached to it where you can put any important documents you might need for tax preparation, such as an employer's W-2 form (tells how much you made in a year and what taxes and other monies were taken out), health bills, and prescription receipts. This is a good way to expand the usefulness of your budget.

● **STICK TO THE SPECIFICS OF YOUR BUDGET.** Don't have a tendency to borrow from one category to pay another! The key word here is "tendency": there may be times when you are a bit short for rent one month, and so you decide to cut back on another allowance so you can pay your rent. Nothing wrong with that, as long as you don't make a habit out of it. A budget is to keep you on track to pay X items with X amount of money: if you can't do this, you need consider a second job (which many people -- non-ex-inmates and ex-inmates alike -- do), getting another job that pays more, or re-adjusting your budget.

> **REMEMBER: Buy anything you want ... as long as your budget says you can afford it.**

THE EX-INMATE AS VICTIM: SCAMS & SUCKER BETS

Ex-inmates are ripe for scams and what I call "sucker bets": items that look like a sure or easy thing, only to learn later that it's not. And just because you've spent time in prison, don't cop a macho attitude (male or female, it doesn't matter) and say, "Hey, that could never happen to me!" Well, not only could it happen but it does happen ... every day. So before you venture out into the free world, be aware of:

● **RESUME SERVICES & EMPLOYMENT AGENCIES THAT CHARGE A FEE BUT SHOULDN'T.** Sometimes, when resume services and employment agencies that aren't fully honest know that someone is desperate for a job -- such as an ex-inmate -- they will charge an up-front fee when it's illegal to do so. Read over Chp. 9, pp. 356-364, so you understand how to tell the difference between honest and dishonest ones.

● **CONVENIENCE STORES LOCATED RIGHT OFF PRISON PROPERTY.** There are convenience store owners who know that inmates in certain prisons leave with money in their pockets ... and these store owners want to take full advantage of it. While not dishonest, the store does hit an obvious weak spot of the very newly released ex-inmate: offer him or her items for purchase that the ex-inmate has not had in a long time, sometimes years. Again and again I've heard stories from ex-inmates and inmates back in again: they had enough money for a bus ticket home, but spent their money on junk food, cans of soda or beer, and other such items; suddenly, they find themselves with not enough money to buy their bus ticket. Be smart; use self-discipline when confronted with such a situation. Your basics are MOST important at first; they'll be plenty of time (and certainly more money) to indulge yourself later.

● **SECURED CREDIT CARDS.** Ah, how many times have I heard from ex-inmates who have fallen into this trip! The ads are on TV, on the radio, and arrive in the mail: send in X amount of dollars and you'll immediately be issued your own credit card with a credit limit to match your deposit (called "collateral"). What's wrong with this? First, chances are VERY high that the ex-inmate who sends in the $200 or $300 or $500 or whatever can't afford it; he or she really needs that money for basics. Second, no sooner does the card arrive than the ex-inmate spends at the limit of the card.

It's too easy to let it slide. Then the bill arrives for the card purchases and all too often the ex-inmate can't pay. Okay, no big deal; I'll just let them take my deposit, so thinks the ex-inmate. That's fine, except for two things: #1 -- not paying the card and letting the company take your deposit will be reported to a credit agency, and you've started off a new life with a major negative on your credit history; #2 -- you are not being fiscally responsible, and thus establishing a pattern for yourself that could lead you back to committing a crime (to pay for merchandise). My advice? Wait until you build up your credit and have established a pattern of budgetary responsibility for yourself, then start applying for real credit cards. You'll be in a much better position mentally and financially to handle the bills.

(See pages 386-387, this chapter, for information on your credit history.)

● **TELEMARKETING & MAIL PROMISES OF "FREE" GIFTS & "GUARANTEED WINNER."**
Remember the saying that if anything sounds too good to be true it probably is? Well, it certainly holds true here. Yet ex-inmates continue to fall victim to these promises, thinking that it's an easy way to quick money, free vacations, and the like. Read the fine print; ask if any purchase is required; NEVER give out your social security number or a "yes" over the phone (in some states, a verbal "yes" is equal to you signing a contract). And if it sounds like an offer that's legitimate and you are interested, call your local Better Business Bureau or Attorney General's office first to check the company out.

● **LOTTERY TICKETS.** Everyone's big chance to win a gazillion dollars, right? Well, a chance, yes -- but your odds of winning are, well, very, very small. Yet many ex-inmates see lottery-type contests as their big ticket, the chance to finally be financially independent ... and day after day, week after week spend X amount of dollars in search of this elusive dream. Until you have extra money (meaning that ALL basic and important bills can be paid by you in full and on time), leave the lottery chances alone. It can become addictive, and you don't want to find that when bills are due all you have to pay them with are a bunch of non-winning lottery tickets.

You'll run into other similar situations, of course, and you are going to have to use your common sense to decide what's real and what's not, what's worth it and what's not. But do think each scenario through; you've come too far to have something set you back financially when it didn't have to happen.

REMEMBER: Make your life decisions as a traffic light directs daily travel: caution, go, and stop.

SAFE SEX / HIV & AIDS

Okay, no lecture here; you're men and women who have at least some idea as to the what and how of safe sex, and what can happen if you don't take precautions. But because inmates and ex-inmates are in such a high-risk group -- primarily because of shared needles and prostitution -- it needs to be mentioned. Beyond the importance of using condoms when you have sex and not using shared needles, it's also important that you seek out assistance -- both medical and counseling -- if you are HIV positive / have AIDS or feel that you want more information. Just about every city has some type of AIDS service / agency that can offer you information and counseling; they're listed in the Yellow Pages, under "AIDS Information & Testing." There is also a national HIV/AIDS # that can provide you with a wide range of information: 800-342-2437 (Spanish: 800-344-7432; hearing impaired: 800-243-7889)

APPRENTICESHIPS

Known to just about all who work in skilled trades (carpenters, plumbers, and welders, for example), apprenticeships offer a combination of on-the-job training and classroom instruction. While most apprenticeship programs last 3 years and entail (approximately) 144 hours in the classroom, they are well worth it as you will be trained in a skilled trade -- with certification -- that will allow you to command a higher salary and fairly constant

415

employment. Many prisons, in fact, offer courses of training that closely parallel the apprenticeship training in professions on the outside; be sure to ask your counselor or teacher about this.

For more information on apprenticeships, contact one of the following:

● (your state) Department of Labor
Division of Apprenticeship
(street address)
(city / state / zip code)

● U.S. Department of Labor
Apprenticeships
200 Constitution Avenue, N.W.
Washington DC 20210
202-219-5921

IF YOU HAVE A HANDICAP

Whether your handicap be one that is physical, emotional, or mental there are certainly job opportunities for you, as well as counseling agencies on the outside to assist you. If you haven't already done so, ask your counselor or a teacher for information on social service agencies available outside of prison; in the phone book, they are listed in the Yellow Pages under "Social & Human Service Organizations."

MARKET YOUR STRENGTHS. If you go into a job interview with the attitude of, "I'm handicapped but I'm a good worker" it's the same as saying, "I was convicted of a crime but I've turned my life around": you are starting with a NEGATIVE, and the employer is not going to hear much past the "but." What's most important is that you approach an interview with the mind set of, "I'm a great worker who just happens to be handicapped." Here, you are mentally starting off with a POSITIVE, and then you sell yourself to the interviewer as ANY job applicant would: with your education, your experience, your personal assets. There is not one handicap in this country that someone has not overcome to become a contributing and successful employee ... and there is no reason why you can't be another.

416

LEGISLATIVE ASSISTANCE. This could be a great help to you:

● **THE AMERICANS WITH DISABILITIES ACT (ADA).** Signed into law in 1992 (and administered by the federal government), ADA, in its simplest form, has three parts: [1] Employers cannot discriminate in hiring because an applicant has a disability; [2] An employer's place of work must be made physically accessible for the disabled; [3] The disabled must be able to occupy public facilities (e.g., bathrooms) at the employer's place of business. In addition, one cannot charge a disabled person more for the same service offered a non-disabled person, even if extra services, personnel, or efforts are needed to give these same services.

For further information, contact: Office on the Americans with Disabilities Act, Civil Rights Division, U.S. Department of Justice, P.O. Box 66118, Washington DC 20035-6118 / (202) 514-0301.

YOUR FAMILY AS A SUPPORT GROUP

There are many support groups that have been discussed in this book, but none that can be quite as powerful and encompassing as your family. Depending on the relationship you had or have with your family, you may find that coming back to them after prison can be both terrifying and exhilarating, anxious and calming, enjoyable and tense. Yet working on establishing closer family ties (both while in prison and out) can bring you many benefits, including -- and perhaps most important -- love.

Some Guidelines to Help You Re-establish or Strengthen Family Ties

● **OPEN & HONEST COMMUNICATIONS IS THE MOST IMPORTANT KEY TO A CLOSER RELATIONSHIP WITH YOUR FAMILY.** No matter how much you may be loved, the label of "inmate" and "ex-inmate" may cast a shadow over that love. Be honest in all that you say and do, and make it a point to continually communicate with your family ... especially about those feelings of frustration, depression, guilt, and loneliness you will have upon occasion. They want you to be open with them, not closed off.

● **A CLOSER FAMILY RELATIONSHIP WILL NOT HAPPEN IN ONE DAY OR ONE WORD, BUT RATHER TAKES TIME.** Depending on the nature of your crime, time away, and prior relationship with your family, it's going to take longer than you may think for them to fully welcome you back into the fold. Don't lose patience. They need the time to get to know you again, as do you need to know them again. (And by the way: it's also important that your family understand YOU also need more than a day or a word for change and adjustment to take place.)

● **KEEP ANY ANGER & FRUSTRATION WITH YOUR FAMILY IN CHECK.** Often through concern, family members will ask questions of you and sometimes appear to be overly protective. While this may not be what you want -- especially because this is somewhat similar to the treatment your received in prison -- don't let your anger or stress get the better part of you. Rather, talk out your feelings with your family, let them help ... and take out any of your anger and frustration on a jog, a punching bag, or a bicycle. (See discussion on "Anger Management," pages 42-44 and page 419.)

● **LET YOUR FAMILY KNOW ALL THE CONDITIONS OF YOUR RELEASE.** You should first let your family see your release papers that outline the conditions of your release and under what circumstances you could have you parole revoked. (If you are returning home to live with your family, this can be helpful in another way: certain aspects of the neighborhood may have changed, and what may not have been a parole violation X years ago may now be.)

● **HAVE YOUR FAMILY TELL OTHERS THEY SUPPORT YOU.** It could be advantageous for your family to get in touch with those individuals who had something to do with your arrest, conviction, and release, specifically the judge, lawyer, parole or probation officer; any professional social service worker active with you (in substance abuse programs, etc.,); and other similar professionals. This would be done for two reasons: [a] the family member has a contact directly involved in your life in case something needs be discussed; [b] it is always helpful when those who have worked / are working for (or against) you know that there is at least one person who truly cares about you and will be there as a support person.

● **LET YOUR FAMILY KNOW ABOUT THE RESOURCES & SUPPORT GROUPS ASSISTING YOU.** These include career counseling firms, state labor departments, social service agencies, educational institutions, special programs (JTPA, for example), addiction counseling groups (Alcoholics Anonymous, Gamblers Anonymous, etc.), and others -- the more a family member becomes aware of these, the better the transition safety net you'll have.

● **EVEN IF ALL IS GOING WELL BETWEEN YOU & YOUR FAMILY, MAKE AN EFFORT FOR YOU & AT LEAST ONE FAMILY MEMBER TO MEET WITH A PROFESSIONAL COUNSELOR.** The experience of prison versus the normal life at home can be at odds with one another; obviously, both you and your family want the transition to be as smooth as possible. Suggestions can be had from books, articles, and well-intended friends and acquaintances, and family members can rely heavily on their own experiences, but there are areas where a counselor will know better than all ... and maybe be able to assist better than any. He or she can offer insights and guidance based on experience with, perhaps, others who have been in similar situations. Be open to these meetings, for any assistance that can help make for a closer family relationship is well worth the time spent.

REMEMBER: When you feel that all the world's slings and arrows are aimed at you, it's not bad to have a family member or two around to help with bandages, kind words, and a hug.

ANGER MANAGEMENT

Anger is one of those emotions that inmates and ex-inmates can quickly fall victim to because of the often frustrating and stressful nature of prison and getting settled once out of prison. Entire books are devoted to anger management, and certainly you are encouraged to refer to these for detailed information on the subject; also, don't hesitate to speak with a professional counselor if your anger presents a constant problem. But for a quick "course" in anger management, the information that follows will help. (And also refer to pages 42-44 and 392-393 for information on Stress Management.)

Suggestions for Anger Management

● **TAKE DEEP BREATHS AND A MIND TRIP.** The deeper you breath and the more you visualize some nice scenes, the more relaxed you'll feel. This not only has a physiological calming effect on the entire body but it also allows your mind time to mellow out. (Also: refer to page 237 for information on Tai Chi.)

● **GIVE YOURSELF SOME TIME OUT.** Beyond the momentary effect of some deep breaths and a mind trip, you may need to get away -- for several minutes or a few hours -- from the situation that brought on your anger. And while away, engage in activities that can counter your anger -- `entertainment, physical activity, positive talk, writing a letter, reading a book (that has nothing to do with the anger source).

● **ADMIT THAT YOU'RE ANGRY.** The more you suppress the thought, the more frustrated -- and angrier -- you'll become. Once you've accepted the fact that you're into a negative emotional state, it becomes easier to "come down." Also helpful: physical exercise to vent your anger (e.g., running, weights).

● **UNDERSTAND WHAT MADE YOU ANGRY AND WHY.** The more you can pinpoint the source, the better you'll be able to understand why it made you angry -- and this closer scrutiny of the anger source may result in you believing that the event or item or situation was not quite as bad as you first thought.

● **TALK OUT YOUR ANGER WITH ANOTHER.** The need to "get it off my chest" is a real one. Talking with a close friend, teacher or counselor, family member, clergy member, or parole officer may give you some insight on the problem that you previously did not have. And talking it out will also allow the anger to be released slowly, saving you from possible embarrassment and helping you to calm down.

● **CONFRONT THE SITUATION WITH POSITIVE SELF-TALK.** This puts you more in control of the situation and allows you to confront the anger source, and thus guides you through your anger in a more manageable manner. Telling yourself such things as "I'm okay," "I can handle this," "It's no big deal," "It's not worth the aggravation," and "I've got to keep my mouth shut and my hands to myself" will go a long way in minimizing your own anger and keeping in check what could have been a bad situation for you.

FEDERAL GOVERNMENT ASSISTANCE PROGRAMS

There are many programs throughout the United States and elsewhere (private; and public, i.e., county, city or town, state or province, and Federal) that are either specific for ex-inmates or that ex-inmates qualify for. While it is impossible to list these -- and I urge you to check these out on your own -- there are five programs that the U.S. government has available, all of which offer assistance of some sort and all of which ex-inmates MAY qualify for.

***IMPORTANT:** Since these programs are subject to the whims of the political process, it is impossible to say if they will exist in their present form a few weeks, months, or years from now ... or if they will exist at all. So I very strongly suggest you do two things: (1) Always check first with the contact address or phone number listed at the end of each program description for updated information; (2) Always look to fall back -- first and foremost -- on yourself, rather than outside assistance. For if you become too dependent on programs such as these you not only lose your independence but will panic greatly when you learn, one day, that a program is no longer around to help you.*

Vocational Rehabilitation

The Federal government has money put aside to help with individuals suffering from various disabilities. These include: blindness & other visual impairment, deafness & other hearing impairment, skeletal and joint disease, learning disabilities, brain trauma, epilepsy, heart disease, drug addiction, spinal injury, neurological disease, muscular disease, speech impairment, amputation, mental retardation, mental illness, and alcoholism. Services provided can include counseling and guidance, job-seeking skills training, occupational licenses, tools, equipment, and supplies, transportation, and others. Find your Vocational Rehabilitation office in the Yellow Pages, under "Social Agencies," "Vocational Rehabilitation," or "Rehabilitation." A complete listing, with addresses and phone #s, can also be found on the Internet: at: http://trfn.clpgh.org/scrac/state-vr.html

Federal Bonding Program (FBP)

● **FIDELITY BOND.** Many employers carry what is called a fidelity bond. This is a guarantee, provided through a bonding company, that provides insurance against any loss by a dishonest employee (theft or embezzlement, for example). Obviously, these fidelity bonding companies wish to keep their losses at a minimum, so they establish certain hiring policies that employers must follow if they want to obtain a fidelity bond.

● **WHY A BOND MAY NOT BE ISSUED.** Many of the commercial insurance carriers providing the fidelity bonding insurance often refuse to cover individuals because of:

✓ **record of arrest, conviction, or imprisonment**
✓ **track record of poor credit rating**
✓ **history of drug or alcohol abuse**
✓ **lack of employment history**
✓ **dishonorable military discharge**
✓ **other special situations requiring fidelity bonding**

● **WHY THE FEDERAL BONDING PROGRAM.** The Federal Bonding Program was established to provide individual fidelity bonds for applicants who are (or may be) denied coverage by commercial bonding carriers. To qualify, you MUST meet two groups of criteria:

(A): The applicant must: be qualified for the employment in question; have a firm job offer; not otherwise be commercially bondable; and not have previously defaulted under the FBP

(B): The job must offer: full time, steady work; reasonable expectation of permanence; adequate working conditions and wages; and not be self-employment

● **AMOUNT OF BOND.** The maximum bond given under the Federal Bonding Program is $10,000.

● **TO APPLY.** Either you as the job applicant or the prospective employer (on behalf of an applicant or employee) can apply for fidelity bonding insurance through this program. The individual applying MUST APPEAR IN PERSON at a local office of your state's employment / job service network. The procedure is fast and quite simple: an application is filled out and job service personnel will certify the information you provide. Normally, the process takes only a day or two. Bonding coverage becomes effective immediately when the information is certified and you have begun working.

● **ADDITIONAL INFORMATION.** If you'd like additional information about this program, and do not have the address of your state's employment / job service network, write to: The Federal Bonding Program, c/o The McLaughlin Company, 2000L Street, NW, Suite 803, Washington, DC 20036

Work Opportunity Tax Credit (WOTC)

● **SERVES AS AN INCENTIVE TO HIRE YOU.** The employer directly benefits from this, so the WOTC acts as an incentive to hire you, the ex-inmate. (You will be given a voucher indicating you are eligible under WOTC; show this to the employer and leave it with him / her ONLY if you're hired.) It is specifically set up to encourage employers to hire persons who have special difficulties in finding work.

● **AMOUNT.** The WOTC program gives employers 25% of up to $6000 in wages for a maximum of $1500 in federal tax credits for one year for a new hire and that person works for at least 120 hours but fewer than 400 hours. If the employee works for at least 400 hours WOTC increases the tax savings to the employer up to 40% of a $6000 cap in wages, or $2400.

● **ELIGIBILITY.** To qualify, the ex-inmate must: (1) be certified as being eligible for the program by either a state labor agency or a one-stop skills center [not available in all states but expanding to eventually include each one]; (2) the hiring date can be no more than one year from the ex-inmate's release; (3) the ex-inmate must have been a member of a family for at least six months prior to his / her incarceration AND that family must have had an income at 70% or less of the then "official" poverty level income. [NOTE: Being eligible for and taking advantage of the JTPA program does NOT prevent you from making use of the WOTC program; also, if you are not eligible for JTPA you may still be eligible for WOTC.]

● **ADDITIONAL INFORMATION.** If you'd like additional information about this program, and do not have the address of your state's employment I job service network or a one-stop skills center in your state, write to: Work Opportunity Tax Credit, U.S. Department of Labor, Employment & Training Administration 200 Constitution Avenue, Washington, DC 2021 0 / 202-219-5257.

Welfare-to-Work Tax Credit

● **WHAT IT DOES.** Provides that the Welfare-to-Work Tax Credit is 35% of qualified wages for the first year of employment, if employed at least 180 days or 400 hours, and 50% for the second year. The cap of qualified wages to the employer is $10,000 per year, for a maximum tax savings of $8500 per new hire.

● **ELIGIBILITY.** For long-term family assistance recipients (someone who received Aid to Families with Dependent Children or Temporary Assistance to Needy Families, for at least 18 months before date of hire OR whose AFDC or TANF eligibility expired under federal or state law after August 5, 1997 OR that received AFDC for a total of at least 18 months beginning after August 5, 1997).

● **ADDITIONAL INFORMATION.** If you'd like additional information about this program, and do not have the address of your state's employment / job service network or a one-stop skills center in your state, write to: Welfare-to-Work Tax Credit, U.S. Department of Labor, Employment & Training Administration, 200 Constitution Avenue, Washington, DC 20210/ 202-219-5257.

Job Training Partnership Act (JTPA)

● **WHAT IT DID.** This program assisted ex-inmates in job training and finding employment. As of July 1, 2000, this program expired; portions of the program have been taken over by the Workforce Investment Act (WIA). For additional information contact Job Training Partnership Act, U.S. Department of Labor, Employment & Training Administration, 200 Constitution Avenue, Washington, DC 20210/ 202-219-6825.

Workforce Investment Act (WIA)

● **WHAT IT DOES.** Signed into law August 7th, 1998, WIA takes much of the national efforts of the JTPA and puts this into State and local jurisdiction. Its two primary components are Workforce Labor Boards (comprised of elected local officials and professionals in the employment sector) and One Stops, virtual one-stop shopping centers. The One-Stops include (for ex-inmates): job listings; information about local, state, and national job markets; job and career resource room; testing and assessment; job search skills; and other related services. WIA is helpful for both adult ex-inmates and previous youthful offenders. For detailed information contact:: Office of Career Transition Assistance, Employment & Training Administration, 200 Constitution Avenue, NW, Room S4231, Washington DC 20210. 202-219-7831 ... 202-219-8506 [fax] ... wia98tf@doleta.gov (E-mail) ... http://www.usworkforce.org/asp/team.asp (Web)

Social Security / Supplemental Security Income

● **SOCIAL SECURITY.** Social Security exists as a benefit package of protection for you and your family upon retirement, disability, or survivorship.

● **SUPPLEMENTAL SECURITY INCOME (SSI).** Supplemental Security Income (SSI) is an income maintenance program for poor people who are elderly (age 65 and older), blind, or disabled. If you are single, you cannot have more than $2000 total in savings and checking accounts in order to receive this; for couples, this figure is $3000.

● **STRICT ELIGIBILITY REQUIREMENTS.** While NEITHER of these programs is designed to target offenders / ex-offenders, they are available to all citizens of the United States (as well as legally admitted refugees and sponsored aliens) ... but ONLY if they qualify under very strict eligibility requirements.

● **FOR ADDITIONAL INFORMATION.** To learn more about either of these programs, contact your local Social Security Administration office in person or on the phone (listed under "Federal Government" or "United States Government" in your telephone directory). If this is not possible, write or call (toll free) their main office: Social Security Administration, Department of Health and Human Services, 300 N. Green Street, Baltimore, MD 21201 / 800-772-1213 [7 am-7pm, EST].

● **TO FIND OUT HOW MUCH YOU CURRENTLY HAVE IN SOCIAL SECURITY BENEFITS.** It makes no difference that you've been in prison: if you ever worked where Social Security benefits were taken out of your paycheck, that money is still tagged by the Federal government as available for you once you retire. If you'd like to find out how much is thus far in your Social Security pot, write to the address above (under "For Additional Information") and request a "Benefits Estimate Statement." (You must know your Social Security number.) Fill it out, return it, and the Federal government will give you the figure it has for your current Social Security benefits.

MOTIVATION

What better way to end this book than a few words on motivation! I've sprinkled suggestions, tips, and thoughts on motivation throughout the chapters because keeping yourself motivated IS so important. The difficulties you encounter, the complications that arise will require, at times, major self-motivation on your part, but if you want to make it after prison -- if you REALLY want to make it -- you'll keep going forward. With this thought, I leave you the following suggestions ... and wish you the *BEST*!!

● **SURROUND YOURSELF WITH TRIUMPHS & SUCCESSES.** No matter how small, they help.
● **WHEN WORRIED, DEJECTED, OR FRUSTRATED, TELL SOMEONE CLOSE.** It helps!
● **BREAK YOUR MOLD NOW-&-THEN.** When in a rut, do something different; it washes the mind.
● **BAD DAYS & MOMENTS DO EVENTUALLY END.** Sunshine and success WILL triumph!
● **I MADE IT, OTHERS MADE IT.** If we can do it, so can you; join us as another successful ex-inmate!

REMEMBER: The odds against an ex-inmate becoming successful remain high ... but then who would have thought that a man would walk on the moon?

Index

A

B

C

Index

Index

Index

Index

Notes

Notes

Notes

"When you can snatch the pebble from my hand, it will be time for you to go ..."

Master Khan to Grasshopper (Kwai Chang Caine) in "Kung Fu," 1970s TV drama (as Kwai Chang Caine enters the Shaolin temple to begin his studies)

"Time for you to go."

Master Khan to Grasshopper (after he has snatched the pebble from Master Khan's hand for the first time, upon completion of Kwai Chang Caine's studies)